ReFocus: The Films of Claire Denis

ReFocus: The International Directors Series

Series Editors: Robert Singer, Gary D. Rhodes and Stefanie Van de Peer

Board of advisors:
Lizelle Bisschoff (Glasgow University)
Stephanie Hemelryck Donald (University of Lincoln)
Anna Misiak (Falmouth University)
Des O'Rawe (Queen's University Belfast)

ReFocus is a series of contemporary methodological and theoretical approaches to the interdisciplinary analyses and interpretations of international film directors, from the celebrated to the ignored, in direct relationship to their respective culture – its myths, values and historical precepts – and the broader parameters of international film history and theory.

Titles in the series include:

ReFocus: The Films of Susanne Bier Edited by Missy Molloy, Mimi Nielsen, and Meryl Shriver-Rice

ReFocus: The Films of Francis Veber Keith Corson

ReFocus: The Films of Xavier Dolan Edited by Andrée Lafontaine

ReFocus: The Films of Pedro Costa: Producing and Consuming Contemporary Art Cinema Nuno Barradas Jorge

ReFocus: The Films of Sohrab Shahid Saless: Exile, Displacement and the Stateless Moving Image Edited by Azadeh Fatehrad

ReFocus: The Films of Pablo Larraín Edited by Laura Hatry

ReFocus: The Films of Michel Gondry Edited by Marcelline Block and Jennifer Kirby

ReFocus: The Films of Rachid Bouchareb Edited by Michael Gott and Leslie Kealhofer-Kemp

ReFocus: The Films of Andrei Tarkovsky Edited by Sergey Toymentsev

ReFocus: The Films of Paul Leni Edited by Erica Tortolani and Martin F. Norden

ReFocus: The Films of Rakhshan Banietemad Edited by Maryam Ghorbankarimi

ReFocus: The Films of Jocelyn Saab: Films, Artworks and Cultural Events for the Arab World Edited by Mathilde Rouxel and Stefanie Van de Peer

ReFocus: The Films of François Ozon Edited by Loïc Bourdeau

ReFocus: The Films of Teuvo Tulio Henry Bacon, Kimmo Laine and Jaakko Seppälä

ReFocus: The Films of João Pedro Rodrigues and João Rui Guerra da Mata Edited by José Duarte and Filipa Rosário

ReFocus: The Films of Lucrecia Martel Edited by Natalia Christofoletti Barrenha, Julia Kratje and Paul Merchant

ReFocus: The Films of Shyam Benegal Edited by Sneha Kar Chaudhuri and Ramit Samaddar

ReFocus: The Films of Denis Villeneuve Edited by Jeri English and Marie Pascal

ReFocus: The Films of Antoinetta Angelidi Edited by Penny Bouska and Sotiris Petridis

ReFocus: The Films of Ken Russell Edited by Matthew Melia

ReFocus: The Films of Kim Ki-young Edited by Chung-kang Kim

ReFocus: The Films of Jane Campion Edited by Alexia L. Bowler and Adele Jones

ReFocus: The Films of Alejandro Jodorowsky Edited by Michael Newell Witte

ReFocus: The Films of Nuri Bilge Ceylan Edited by Gönül Dönmez-Colin

ReFocus: The Films of Claire Denis Edited by Peter Sloane

edinburghuniversitypress.com/series/refocint

ReFocus:
The Films of Claire Denis

Peter Sloane

EDINBURGH
University Press

Edinburgh University Press is one of the leading university presses in the UK. We publish academic books and journals in our selected subject areas across the humanities and social sciences, combining cutting-edge scholarship with high editorial and production values to produce academic works of lasting importance. For more information visit our website: edinburghuniversitypress.com

© editorial matter and organisation Peter Sloane, 2023
© the chapters their several authors 2023

Grateful acknowledgement is made to the sources listed in the List of Illustrations for permission to reproduce material previously published elsewhere. Every effort has been made to trace the copyright holders, but if any have been inadvertently overlooked, the publisher will be pleased to make the necessary arrangements at the first opportunity.

Edinburgh University Press Ltd
The Tun – Holyrood Road
12(2f) Jackson's Entry
Edinburgh EH8 8PJ

Typeset in 11/13 Ehrhardt MT by
IDSUK (DataConnection) Ltd, and
printed and bound in Great Britain

A CIP record for this book is available from the British Library

ISBN 978 1 3995 1120 9 (hardback)
ISBN 978 1 3995 1122 3 (webready PDF)
ISBN 978 1 3995 1123 0 (epub)

The right of Peter Sloane to be identified as the editor of this work has been asserted in accordance with the Copyright, Designs and Patents Act 1988, and the Copyright and Related Rights Regulations 2003 (SI No. 2498).

Contents

Figures   vii
List of Contributors   ix

    Introduction: Ambiguous Transgressions   1
    Peter Sloane
1   L'eau Life: The Hydrous and Haptic Cinema of Claire Denis   15
    Rowena Santos Aquino
2   Good Work or Exploitation? *Beau travail* and *35 rhums* and
    the Fear of Individualism   32
    Kyle Barrett
3   A Thing on a Friday Night: Objects and Desire in *Vendredi soir*   50
    Helena Gurfinkel
4   'A lover's hand? A breath, An abyss': Aloneness in Claire Denis   65
    Peter Sloane
5   Claire Denis, Corporeality and New Weird   83
    Elif Sendur
6   The Limits of Life: Experimentation, Bodily Consent and Bioethics
    in *Trouble Every Day* (2001) and *High Life* (2018)   100
    Amy C. Chambers
7   Trans-generic Dramas of Non-disclosure: Equilibrium, the 'General
    Viewer' and the Refusal of Meaning in the Films of Clair Denis   121
    Stuart Innes Molloy
8   Writing Female Desire: From *Vendredi soir* to *Avec amour*
    et acharnement   147
    Kristin Hole

CONTENTS

9 In the Cracks: Claire Denis's Cinematic Choreographies   166
   Danica van de Velde
10 Stars and Acting in Claire Denis's Films since 2010   182
   Douglas Morrey
11 Life Imitates Art: The Intimacy of Family in the Work of Claire
   Denis and Yasujiro Ozu   200
   Kate Taylor-Jones
12 'The Stranger and the Surprise': Hospitality, Community and
   Coming to Our Senses in *Vendredi soir*   216
   Jacob Hovind
13 Claire Denis's *Beaux Familles*   231
   Daniel Dufournaud

Index   252

Figures

1.1	Galoup looks over the water	23
1.2	Trebor floats in a mountain lake	25
1.3	Protée showers outside	26
1.4	Manuel relaxes in the pool	27
2.1	Galoup's (Denis Lavant's) gaze as an unreliable narrator	41
2.2	Lionel (Alex Descas) smiles to himself about the prospect of new connections	44
2.3	A death shroud in the opening of *Ratcatcher*	45
3.1	Laure at home	51
3.2	Meeting Jean	57
3.3	Galoup's masculinity	60
4.1	Galoup shaves alone	69
4.2	The cadets crowd the frame	69
5.1	Rivulets of white fluid	84
5.2	The scarred chest	91
5.3	Galoup's throbbing artery	94
6.1	Dr Dibs (Binoche) conducts a pelvic exam on Boyse (Goth), who informs the doctor that she will 'never have kids' and that her 'body obeys' her	101
6.2	Coré from *Trouble Every Day* painting with the blood of a dead thief, and Boyse from *High Life* cradling her leaking postpartum breasts	106
6.3	Dibs's 'dripping' scar; a dribble of Monte's semen on Dibs's thigh; and Boyse's uncontrollable breast milk in *High Life*. Finally, there is a drip of blood in the shower water at the end of *Trouble Every Day*.	108

FIGURES

6.4	Léo in *Trouble Every Day* is positioned here as both scientist and topless specimen on a corporate website detailing his research and the 1990 bioprospecting mission	111
6.5	Dibs mounts a sleeping/drugged Monte to harvest his sperm, which he refuses to donate, and then inseminates the similarly incapacitated Boyse in *High Life*	114
7.1	The figure of the serial killer and the accumulation of perversions/'perversions' – transsexuality in *The Silence of the Lambs* (left) and transvestism in *J'ai pas sommeil* (right)	135
7.2	The complex discovery plot of horror and its destabilisation in *Trouble Every Day* – onset	135
7.3	The complex discovery plot of horror and its destabilisation in *Trouble Every Day* – discovery disrupted.	136
7.4	The complex discovery plot of horror and its destabilisation in *Trouble Every Day* – confirmation refused	136
7.5	The complex discovery plot of horror and its destabilisation in *Trouble Every Day* – confrontation subverted	138
7.6.1	The instantaneous collapse of the bildungsroman in *High Life* – Dibs with the new-born Willow.	139
7.6.2	The instantaneous collapse of the bildungsroman in *High Life* – the teenage Willow lying next to her father.	139
7.6.3	The instantaneous collapse of the bildungsroman in *High Life* – Willow's menstrual blood, abject seal of her embodied maturity.	139
8.1	Superimposition in *Vendredi soir*	152
8.2	Claustrophobic intimacy in *Avec amour et acharnement*	159
9.1	Trebor's horrific visions in *L'intrus* (2004)	173
9.2	The ghostly echoing of Mathilde Monnier in *Vers Mathilde* (2005)	178
10.1	Maria (Isabelle Huppert) from behind. *White Material* (2009)	186
10.2	Marco, sailor (Vincent Lindon). *Les Salauds* (2013)	187
10.3	Monte (Robert Pattinson). *High Life* (2018)	190
10.4	Incongruous outfits: Isabelle (Juliette Binoche) in *Un beau soleil intérieur* (2017)	196
11.1	Akiko in *Tokyo Twilight*	210
11.2	Justine in *Les saludes*: the girl as a last figure on the margins of society	211
12.1	Boni's hyperactive sensory life finding an almost libidinal satisfaction even in his new coffee maker	220
12.2	Laure's secret smile as she inhales the stranger's cigarette smoke pervading her car's newly opened space	227
13.1	Aimée touches Protée's leg	236
13.2	Maria embraces a stranger	239
13.3	Lionel unpacks Joséphine's rice cooker	245

List of Contributors

Rowena Santos Aquino is a film lecturer and critic who teaches courses on film history and theory, with an emphasis on documentary film studies and Asian cinemas. Her research interests include histories and theories of colonial/postcolonial visual cultures and collaborative, performative modes of witnessing, testimony and remembering. Her writings have been published in *Asian Cinema*, *Transnational Cinemas* and *Verge: Studies in Global Asias*.

Kyle Barrett is a Lecturer at the University of Waikato, Aotearoa (New Zealand) and an award-winning filmmaker. His research focuses on global, low-budget production cultures and cinemas, gender representations and creative practice. He has been published in *Directory of World Cinema: Scotland*, *European Journal of Communication*, *The Routledge Companion to Transmedia Studies*, *MECCSA: Special Edition Journal on Screenwriting and Gender*, *Iperstoria: Journal of American and English Studies* and *AMES: Media Education Journal*. He has also directed several documentaries which have been screened internationally and is currently working on several new film projects.

Amy C. Chambers (amycchambers.com/@AmyCChambers) is a science communication and screen studies scholar at Manchester Metropolitan University. Her research examines intersections of entertainment media and the public understanding of science. Recent publications explore astronomy expertise in the movie *Don't Look Up*; medical history and horror in *The Exorcist* (1973); science, race and gender in *Star Trek*; the mediation of women's scientific expertise in mass media; socio-technoscientific imaginaries and SF literature; and women-directed science fiction media properties.

LIST OF CONTRIBUTORS

Helena Gurfinkel is Professor of English at Southern Illinois University Edwardsville, USA. She is the author of *Outlaw Fathers in Victorian and Modern British Literature* and currently at work on a monograph about the Soviet adaptations of Oscar Wilde's works. She has published widely on gender, film, theory, pedagogy and British (especially mid- and late-Victorian) literature. She is the Editor of *PLL: Papers on Language and Literature*.

Jacob Hovind is Associate Professor of English at Towson University. With his most recent articles on the films of Hong Sang-soo and the fiction of Kazuo Ishiguro and David Foster Wallace, he is currently completing a book manuscript on James Joyce's aesthetic theories, ethics and film style.

Stuart Innes Molloy earned his PhD in English and Literary Studies from The University of Western Australia in 2021. He currently works in postgraduate administration at King's College London. He co-edited *Interdisciplinary Perspectives on Torture* (2019) with Lon Olson. Forthcoming publications include 'Bacchus in Bucolic Britain: the textual unconscious of *Sex Education* and a divided United Kingdom' in *The Routledge Companion to Cultural Texts and the Nations* (Sheera Talpaz and Anuradha Needham, 2024).

Douglas Morrey is Reader in French Studies at the University of Warwick. He has published widely on French cinema including several articles on Claire Denis and books on Jean-Luc Godard (2005), Jacques Rivette (2009) and, most recently, *The Legacy of the New Wave in French Cinema* (2020). He also works on contemporary French literature and is currently developing research on the theme of 'toxic masculinity' and the literary establishment in contemporary France.

Elif Sendur is currently working at the Rutgers University-New Brunswick in the department of English as a teaching instructor. She is also the editor of *H-Film*. She received her Ph.D. in comparative literature on the topic of French Marxist film criticism exploring the untranslated post-1968 writings of Cahiers du Cinéma. Her work on global art cinema and weird bodies appeared in venues like *Studies in the Humanities* and *SFRA Review*. Her collaborative chapter with Allison Mackey on Claire Denis's *High Life* compared to Pella Kågerman and Hugo Lija's *Aniara* will appear in *Annihilation to High Life: Feminist Posthumanism and Postfeminist Humanism in Contemporary Science Fiction* edited by Russel Kilbourn and Julia Empey.

Peter Sloane is a Senior Lecturer in Contemporary Literature at the University of Buckingham, UK. He is the author of *David Foster Wallace and the Body* (2019), *Kazuo Ishiguro's Gestural Poetics* (2021), and the co-editor of *Kazuo Ishiguro: 21ˢᵗ Century Perspectives* (2022). His current monograph, *Narrative Displacement: Refugee Writing in the 21ˢᵗ Century*, is due for publication in 2024, and he is currently editing *Cultures of Crises: Representing Refugees in the 21ˢᵗ Century* (2025).

Kate Taylor-Jones is Professor of East Asian Cinema at the University of Sheffield. She has published on topics including colonial Japanese and Korean cinema, cinema and landscape in East Asia and domestic violence and the sex trade. She is author of *Divine Work: Japanese Colonial Cinema and its Legacy* and editor-in-chief of the *East Asian Journal of Popular Culture*. She is co-editor of *International Cinema and the Girl: Local Issues, Transnational Contexts and Prostitution* and *Sex Work in Global Cinema: New Takes on Fallen Women*.

Danica van de Velde is a researcher at the University of Western Australia where she completed her doctoral thesis on the cinema of Wong Kar-wai. Her writing has recently been published in *Refocus: The Films of Michel Gondry* (Edinburgh University Press, 2020) and she is regular contributor to *a Dance Mag*, *Metro Magazine* and *Senses of Cinema*. Danica was the recipient of the *Senses of Cinema*-Monash Essay Prize in 2019 for her essay on the cinematic self-adaptations of French filmmaker and writer Marguerite Duras.

Kristin Lené Hole is the author of *Towards a Feminist Cinematic Ethics: Claire Denis, Emmanuel Levinas and Jean-Luc Nancy* (Edinburgh University Press, 2016). She co-edited *The Routledge Companion to Cinema and Gender* (with Dijana Jelača, E. Ann Kaplan and Patrice Petro, 2016), and has co-authored the textbook *Film Feminisms: A Global Introduction* (co-authored with Dijana Jelača, 2018).

Introduction: Ambiguous Transgressions

Peter Sloane

Claire Denis has been at the forefront of French and world cinema for more than thirty years, since her debut *Chocolat* (1988) was selected for the Cannes Film Festival and met with acclaim by both audiences and critics. Even before taking the helm as director, she worked as an assistant with such luminaries as Wim Wenders, Jaques Rivette (about and with whom she made the documentary *Jacques Rivette, le veilleur* in 1990), and Jim Jarmusch. Though thematically disparate, genre-fluid and geographically eclectic, Denis's films share a fascination with the experience of being on the margins, of what Martine Beugnet describes as 'a foreignness that is simultaneously physical and mental, geographical and existential' (2004, 2). If, as Beugnet remarks, her works show a 'remarkable aesthetic and thematic consistency', that possibly arises from this defining sense of vagrancy, which encompasses both the powerlessness of being the outsider and the observational vantage offered by that state (2004, 2). Regardless of the shifting contexts, the essence of Denis's work draws from a sense of both fearing and desiring transgressions, crossings of borders, of boundaries, not simply those between nations as in *Chocolat* or *White Material* (2009), but between friend and lover/parent, as in *35 rhums* (2008), between scientist and subject, killer and carer in *High Life* (2008) and villain and victim in *Les salauds* (2008). Paradoxically, her films exploit an uneasy and irresolvable tension between simultaneous desire and fear of being both intruded upon and intruder (*l'intrus*), each status involving its own peculiar and ontologically inviolable isolation. Most often, the body is the site of such transgressions, an at once impermeable yet porous ethico-material conduit through which one may both penetrate and be penetrated by others.

In part, and perhaps reductively, one might seek a cause for this preoccupation with marginality in Denis's unique biography. She was born in Paris immediately following the end of the Second World War in 1946 but raised from a young age in French colonial Africa. Her father occupied the ambiguous (even transgressive) position of a pro-independence colonial administrator, moving country every two years. As Andrew Hussey notes, 'Unusually for the 1950s, her father spoke several African languages and was in favour of independence for African nations. He was a personal friend of Félix Houphouët-Boigny, an intellectual and the first president of Ivory Coast' (2010). Denis recalls that 'we grew up somehow with the sense that we didn't belong, that we were outsiders . . . there are things about that way of growing up that never leave you. There is a sense of marginality' (Hussey 2010). Denis's story begins at the centre of the final act of France and Europe's collapsing colonial heritage, a long period of demise that reaches a violent climactic moment, evocatively figured in *White Material*, as Maria Vial (Isabelle Huppert) strains valiantly, futilely, against the inevitable tide of world history. Judith Mayne remarks that 'Denis's films are fully immersed in a world shaped and defined by the aftermath of colonization and decolonization' (2005, xi). Yet she is not defined by any singular experience or form of exclusion, and her films continue to respond to the complexities of twentieth- and twenty-first-century politics and the ongoing fallout of the end of empire and the failure of the cosmopolitan dream. Necessarily, such history raises profound questions about belonging and not belonging. Marjorie Vecchio comments that 'her films prompt us to question how we live, both as individuals and as part of an indefinable social community, where the rules and their scale are not always clear, natural or humane. Her work constantly pushes the concept of personal agency against the boundaries of unquestioned allegiance, nationalism, stupidity, innocence and multi-culturalism' (2014, xv). It is not simply that Denis reflects upon a troubling period of European history, or that she is a postcolonial filmmaker; rather, from her own immersion in this 'sense of marginality', she creates an ontology of isolations and intrusions that is pervasive and fundamentally human, philosophical yet rooted in recent history and lived experience.

With a career spanning over three decades, Denis demonstrates a remarkable longevity in a notoriously fickle industry, as well as a continuing, seemingly insatiable fascination with the possibilities of film as form, as art, as visual language. Simultaneously idiosyncratically French in their deeply philosophical explorations of the (trouble) everyday, yet transnational and multi-ethnic in their sociocultural outlook, her films test traditional boundaries between genres, cultures, fiction and autobiography, perhaps evidencing what Denis herself refers to as her 'dreamy distance with reality'. It is this ongoing challenge of film's plasticity that makes her, as Kristin Hole remarks, 'one of the most challenging and distinctive filmmakers working in France today' (2016, 1). In her fiction films Denis shares the joyful eclecticism that characterises the careers of many great auteurs, from Agnès Varda to Stanley Kubrick, with her explorations of postcolonial, horror, romance, sci-fi and thriller. This deft agility with modes of film manifests a curiosity not simply about what film can do, but also about what film is, and how it has evolved into myriad conventional sub-forms. It is only through a knowledge and subversion of standard themes and tropes that Denis can 'challenge the viewer's expectations by offering feelings and encounters other than the sort they have come to expect at the movies' (Hole 2016, 25). Again, we see in her exploitation of established genres her penchant for transgression, pushing beyond arbitrary but conventional demarcations to unsettle elastic borders.

Denis has also made well received, if more obscure, documentaries focusing on Les Têtes Brûlées (*Man No Run*, 1989), a Cameroonian band on tour; choreographer Mathilde Monnier (*Vers Mathilde*, 2005); and a Chadian refugee camp (*The Breidjing Camp*, 2015). While these might be considered peripheral, or secondary to her fiction films, they work from the same principles and share remarkable similarities in terms of style and theme. As Mayne notes, they stand as 'indications of the primary themes that Claire Denis has explored in her work' (2005, 2). Her first documentary, *Man No Run*, arose during the filming of *Chocolat*, where she met and hoped to work with the band, even referring to herself as a groupie. However, she was unable to include them in that film, but decided instead to follow them during their first tour in France. While this film is more traditional in its subject and realisation, *Vers Mathilde* is an exemplary study in her artistry. The film is a celebration of space, movement and foremost the human body and its possibilities in that space. Once more we see a love of dance, which recurs prominently in every one of her films, from the TV movie *US Go Home* (1994) when Alain (Grégoire Colin) dances alone in his room to the British and US pop music of the 1960s that was so influential on young Denis herself, through the deeply revealing slow dance between Joséphine (Mati Diop) and Noé (Grégoire Colin) in *35 rhums*, to the balletic and finally ecstatic choreography of *Beau travail* (1999), with one of cinema's most powerful endings. Dance is simply one of many elements threaded through the fiction and non-fiction works, but a useful example of the interconnections between the forms. Several chapters in this collection trace the connections between these apparently different modes of filmmaking, teasing out the many ways in which they communicate and cross-seed and through this contribute to the evolution of a single and singularly powerful body of work.

While her films are astonishing in their diversity, their production is grounded in and sustained by long-term working relationships. During her career she has established a cohesive troupe of actors, including Alex Descas, Isabelle Huppert, Béatrice Dalle, Juliet Binoche, Grégoire Colin, Michel Subor, and more recently Robert Pattinson in her English-language debut *High Life* and the forthcoming *The Stars at Noon*. She often works with the same musicians (Tindersticks, or its founding members Dickon Hinchcliffe and Stuart A. Staples), Director of Photography (Agnès Godard), and screenwriter (Jean-Pol Fargeau). While guided by a single creative vision working in the traditions of world cinema (an *auteur* in this sense), Denis's films are also collaborative efforts that exploit the familiarity of the cast and crew. This reliance upon an artistic network lends to Denis's often bewildering films a sense of familiarity, an anchor point, offsetting the unsettling sense of disconnection and thrownness so typical of her films (see Douglas Morrey's chapter for a fascinating discussion of Denis's use of the same actors across her films). One might even suggest that there is something familial in this group, that it provides for both viewer and perhaps more, Denis, the ideated sense of belonging that seems so unattainable beyond the world of film.

Perhaps most notable in Denis's works is a commitment to the idiosyncrasies of film as a visual medium. Her works are imagistic, poetic almost to the degree of Sergei Parajanov, Alexander Sokurov, and others of the Russian 'poetic school', snatching glimpses of a filmed reality but from these elements crafting a unique cinematic language that is only tenuously, coincidentally interested in verisimilitude and only gesturally bound to the temporal necessities of narrative, storytelling. Her films have sparse dialogue, expansive and expressive periods of silence, a camera that, like that of Herzog in his best works or even Joanna Hogg, lingers for just long enough to become, at times, awkward, uncomfortable, tense. That is not to say that nothing 'happens' in her films, or that there are not conclusions. Indeed, many of her films tend like a work of Elizabethan drama to move inevitably towards gruesome deaths – *Trouble Every Day* (2001), *Les salauds*, *High Life*, *L'intrus* (2004), *White Material*, all dissolve into bloody carnage. Yet although there are events, and conversations and gestures towards narrative, the causality of her films is complex, irreducible to any obvious logic. Certain of her films, most notably *L'intrus* and *Les salauds* seem almost perverse in their refusal to adhere to any rationale, to offer any answers. Indeed, in his review of *Les salauds* after its Cannes Premier, David Rooney describes it as 'unrelentingly dour and unnecessarily hard to follow' (2013). One might suggest that this is a misreading, that Denis is uninterested in the idea of 'following' because that implies causality, consequence, chronology and is fundamentally an easy epistemology. As Philip French remarks in his review of *L'intrus*, Denis has dedicated herself to making 'poetic, metaphoric, allusive pictures about people living on the periphery of everyday society' (2005). As emerges in the chapters in this collection, Denis seeks to construct worlds that are more expressionist than rational, as she paints ideas, emotions, concepts on an abstract canvas that has no direction, no forwards or backwards, past or future, evidenced in her frequent use of flashbacks, which disrupt the very idea that things progress uniformly, or that events, images, moments from the past are either left behind or lead directly to effects. Things simply are, or life simply is, she seems to imply, and they are to be (re)encountered in the miasma of trauma and memories of trauma. If you come to Denis looking for answers, for resolution, for logic, messages of hope or redemption, you are in the wrong place.

Yet she does have a series of recurring concerns, ones that bind her disparate body of work in a series of related interrogations. As she has commented, perhaps most immediately visible to a European filmmaker is her focus on non-white characters. Asked by Elena Lazic whether 'the diversity of your cinema something that you achieve consciously?', Denis responded by saying emphatically 'Yes. It is even mandatory. I'm not more intelligent or more responsible than others, but life has always given me the chance to see these people, so they are in all my films' (Lazic 2019). This is part of her ongoing interrogation of the end of empire, the fact of migrations, crossings, and by implication the contemporary cosmopolitan city. The family, another unit of belonging, also comes back time and time again, often in the form of either overly close (*35 rhums*) or overly broken (*Nénette et Boni*, 1996) families (see Daniel Dufournaud's chapter). As Mayne writes, 'virtually all of Denis's films demonstrate a preoccupation with kinship, with family ties and more often, with what takes the place of family ties' (2005, xii). These failing or surrogate ties (work, the foreign Legion) also give rise to that sense of aloneness that seems so typical of her works. The body, usually the male body, has perhaps been the subject of most discussion in her films. But the body is a complex physical, metaphysical, symbolic phenomenon, and Denis's use of it is equally sophisticated. Morrey has argued that 'Claire Denis's films have, for some time now, been tightly focused around bodies, but seem precisely to pivot around an undecideable point on which the body balances between its thick, inscrutable materiality and its diaphanous, symbolic sense' (2008, 12). Perhaps most overtly in *High Life*, we see Denis playing with the body's ambiguity, multiplicity, its brute materiality in the form of bodies cast adrift, its physiological, biological reality in the preoccupation with conception and excretions, its being as the site of but not coextensive with Being conceived existentially. These themes are all related in subtle ways, explored in different degrees and ratios across the body of work, itself ambiguous and fraught with tensions.

Denis's position in or relation to world cinema is hard to place, and it is equally difficult to slot her neatly into a category. Her influences are diffuse, and when she speaks of cinema, she often returns to moments shared with Jarmusch while filming *Down by Law* (1986) or Wenders on *Paris, Texas* (1984). She has also spoken of Shōhei Imamura as having an influence on her work. Notably, these are all part of New Waves, whether German, Japanese or American. She has connections, inevitably, with the French New Wave, Jean-Pierre Melville and with Jean-Luc Godard in particular, even borrowing the character of Bruno Forestier from *Le petit soldat* (1960), a role played in that film by Michel Subor and again in *Beau travail*. Yet her films, while equally experimental, are less playful in their deconstruction of film's form, perhaps even more earnest in their exploitation of editing, narrative uncertainty: that is to say, there is a seriousness to her experiments. But there is also an enduring connection to previous generations, notably Ozu (see Kate Taylor-Jones's chapter here). Given the globality of these figures, one might wonder to what extent we consider Denis a French filmmaker. And, in a global industry, what sense does such a claim now make? It might be more appropriate to consider her a cosmopolitan director, one attuned to cinema's international as opposed to national or nationalist cultural potential. As she said in conversation with Chris Darke, 'I don't think I make the sort of films which have the characteristic traits of French cinema, which is to say a lot of dialogue and a very social focus' (2000). Indeed, dialogue in Denis is rare, her focus rather on the language of colour, movement of camera, subtleties of expression and suggestion. Her works are philosophical in their subject matter and their interrogation of their very being as art, but her characters do not analyse or philosophise about their own circumstances and lack that degree of self-awareness that often intrudes unconvincingly in others' works.

It is worth pausing, too, to think about Denis as a 'female' director, and her role in a cinematic feminist poetics. In part this is tricky, because Denis has been very vocal about not being considered a female or feminist filmmaker. As Hermione Eyre notes, Denis 'has never been interested in being a token this or a minority that. Although she is a product of feminism and is loyal to its ideas, her subject matter is not the battle of the sexes . . . She is a feminist icon by default rather than by design' (2010). In the contemporary period we might want to place Denis alongside Kathryn Bigelow or Kelly Reichardt as the most prominent female filmmakers of the period. Like Denis, 'Bigelow keeps on asserting how she is not a feminist filmmaker as she does not want to be typecast as one' (Sur 2021). Reichardt, too, makes the same point, telling Nathalie Olah that it 'irks me to think about the "woman filmmaker" thing, because if that's the case, *then who are just the "filmmakers"?*' (2017). In her discussion with Kent Jones for the New York Film Festival she speaks very passionately about Chantal Akerman, not because she was a powerful female figure, but because she was always 'fierce', making 'her own films' (Jones 2018). There is then something broader in Denis's engagement with power; as Rosalind Galt has argued, she is an 'anti-neoliberal filmmaker', interested in the ways in which 'race, gender and sexuality [are] central to operations of power and to its opposition' (2014, 98). Denis is renowned for her focus on men, usually black men, although her most powerful figures are often those female leads like Vial in *White Material*, Dr Dibs (Juliette Binoche) in *High Life*, or even Coré (Béatrice Dalle) in *Trouble Every Day*.

Scholarship on Denis has been relatively scant, remarkably so given the importance of her work to contemporary film. However, there are four major works: Martine Beugnet's important and ever-relevant monograph *Claire Denis* (2004); Judith Mayne's impressive *Claire Denis* (2004); Marjorie Vecchio's

INTRODUCTION

creative volume, *The Films of Claire Denis: Intimacy on the Border* (2014), and Kristin Lené Hole's *Towards a Feminist Cinematic Ethics: Claire Denis, Emmanuel Levinas and Jean-Luc Nancy* (2015), which together constitute the foundations of contemporary Denis scholarship. The present study comprises thirteen original works of criticism from world-leading Denis scholars and early career researchers. With contributors from as far afield as Canada and Australia, the collection will also represent a global perspective on Denis's films. Each of the chapters takes a unique approach to a range of films, with each reading themes across several as opposed to single examples, to enable a broader and less film-specific range of questions to be probed. Necessarily, many of the chapters will dwell upon, exploit, uncover similar trends, such as Denis's fascination with the human body, her interest both in genre and in a subversion of genre conventions, and her recurring preoccupation with the status of the outsider (whether that be cultural, existential, linguistic or racial).

We begin in Chapter 1 with Rowena Santos Aquino's unique exploration of the 'iconography and choreography of water in Denis's cinema'. It examines some of the most evocative audiovisual moments in Denis's oeuvre and the intertwined issues of bodies and control through an elaboration of what Adriano D'Aloia has termed 'enwaterment'. Growing out of the author's video essay, this chapter discusses Denis's privileging and praxis of a hydrous and haptic mode of filmmaking wherein images of water serve as a point of departure, motif and tool of analysis of the narrative complexity and layered filminess (with its dual meaning of translucent and muddied) of her films, not to mention their intensely mesmeric rhythm. Stimulating touch and vision simultaneously, Denis deploys the element of water as setting, imagery and mode of camerawork that enters and caresses the actors and lingers on them closely and persistently, and in the process performs a distinct witnessing of the lengths to which people go to exert control over their body and/or others' bodies. From this interlacing of liquid and body, body and image, emerges a singular cinematic language that cuts across her debut *Chocolat* (1988), to *Nénette et Boni* (1996), *Beau travail* (1999), and to her more recent works, *Les salauds* (2013) and *High Life* (2018).

Chapter 2, 'Good Work or Exploitation? *Beau travail* and *35 Shots of Rum* and the Fear of Individualism' offers a comparative reading of Denis and Lynne Ramsay through a class lens, to argue that these two leading female filmmakers challenge and problematise identity in the era of rampant neoliberalisation and individualism (McLaughlin et al. 2006, 5–6). These films depict characters who are outcasts and often exploited by the middle and upper classes (the characters are soldiers, supermarket employees or train drivers, or live in council estates). Furthermore, Denis's films depict characters whose lives are inexorably linked to their professions, and the fear of losing this aspect of their identity has several ramifications. To that extent, it will be posited that the films illustrate elements of Marx's notions of exploitation through capitalism, where both Denis and Ramsay interrogate the abandonment of the working classes (Marx 1887, 153; Wayne 2020, 4). The purpose here is to illustrate how these filmmakers complement one another, despite their drastically different backgrounds.

Helena Gurfinkel, in Chapter 3, 'A Thing on a Friday Night: Objects and Desire in *Vendredi soir* and *Beau travail*', reads *Vendredi soir* from the perspective of Object-oriented Feminism, suggesting that the film explores uninhibited expressions of female sexuality outside of a traditional committed relationship. What is more interesting than the relatively banal plot of the last fling before settling down, however, is the way in which the film establishes a feminist hierarchy between material artefacts and men, in which the latter find themselves at the bottom. The ending of the film is ambiguous, like another tale of powerful desire, *Beau travail* (1999). But whether Laure moves in with her partner, it is going to be a conscious choice, not driven by convention. Besides Jean's body, subsequently abandoned as he remains fast asleep in a hotel room on Saturday morning, the significant objects that revive Laure from her morose acceptance of her romantic fate are everywhere. They include her old car, which she treats like a human, a sexy red skirt, the much focused-upon boxes of books, indicating Laure's intellectual life, the two mirroring sets of keys and space heaters; dancing letters and a smiling pizza. These often-whimsical artefacts grant the protagonist her agency; conversely, men remain mere objects, discarded after having served their purpose. Using Barthes, Heidegger and Brown, the chapter will attempt to see the film through a feminist thing theory lens.

Chapter 4 continues this theme of the solitary and self-possessed. In '"A lover's hand? A breath, An abyss": Aloneness in Claire Denis's, Peter Sloane argues that Denis has a preoccupation with a certain character type, self-isolated, driven by an intense passion, but fundamentally existentially alone: in *Beau travail* we have what Denis describes as the 'lonely legionnaire', a desiring body without recourse to its satisfaction; *L'intrus* follows a reclusive ex-mercenary as he nears the end of a life spent avoiding company and family; *White Material* captures the final days in the deeply solitary life of Maria Vial, a colonial remnant fighting against history; and *High Life* figures the possible end of humanity in a sterile race, the crew of a one-way ship blasted into the image par excellence of isolation, the black hole. The oppressive mood is facilitated by narratives that strive to uncover profound degrees of otherness, but also by the subdued scores of Tindersticks, the low lighting and the lingering long shots, which often hold for just long enough to reveal unspoken emotion. While tracing the various submerged shapes of aloneness explored by Denis, I want also, here, to examine the response, the desire to forge bonds, whether cultural, sexual, familial or of friendship, that sustain characters.

In Chapter 5 Elif Sendur examines Denis from the perspective of 'Corporeality and New Weird'. One of the perhaps overlooked scenes in Claire Denis's 2018 film, *High Life*, takes place in a weird close-up: white skin, wet with mother's milk, follows droplets of this white substance dripping from the nipples down to the belly of Boyse. It is precisely because the camera refuses to move from the close-up to a medium shot that, for a while, the spectator is obliged to stay with this damp skin without recourse to any certainty as to whether this is Boyse who just gave birth or some other curious spaceship fluid. This staying with the body in its fragmented image is one of the ways that Claire Denis explores corporeality in its tangibility. That Claire Denis cinema is corporeal is not a new statement, as observed by Martine Beugnet when she wrote that Denis's cinema is that of senses through its permission to undoing gender, identity and through destabilising the gaze (2004, 169). Similarly, Kristen Hole argues that it is in this primacy of flesh in Denis's cinema, especially with Agnès Godard as her collaborator, that we have an ethics. Here, I uncover how Denis's corporeal cinema works to displace the spectator. By using queer theory, critical disability theories, New Weird framework and technical cinema analysis, I will show that Denis encourages the spectator to sit with the discomfort and the weirdness of the body.

Amy C. Chambers's Chapter 6, 'The Limits of Life: Experimentation, Bodily Consent and Bioethics in *Trouble Every Day* (2001) and *High Life* (2018)', argues that *Trouble Every Day* and *High Life* consider where the boundaries lie in the value of and limits to life – asking characters and audiences to judge whose lives have value, and whether we can justify experimenting on others (both human and non-human animals). *Trouble Every Day* and *High Life* comment on how science and medicine are viewed by society and consider broader fears about humanity's failure to maintain and sustain each other and the planet. The transfusion of fluids (semen and blood) and transplantation of cells are key parts of the two films under discussion here. The films act as spaces of speculation and bioethical discussions of real and imagined bodies, and the borders between self and other. Through both *High Life* and *Trouble Every Day*, Denis shows the legacies of the colonial mindset in the false assumption that science is neutral. The taking and implantation of parts of one body into another (semen and ovum) without consent underpins *High Life* and aligns with the ethical commentary of *Trouble Every Day* where humans are used as sites of experimentation and consumption. These films offer critiques of not only the cultures and systems of science but also the apparently inescapable white, colonial, patriarchal frameworks that govern them. By directing even a notionally science fictional film Claire Denis has changed the way we talk about women-directed science fiction (SF) films. Denis says *High Life* is not SF; this chapter argues, however, that her work should be framed through the notion of SF as mode.

In Chapter 7, 'Trans-generic Dramas of Non-disclosure: Visualising the Refusal of Meaning in *Trouble Every Day* (2001) and *High Life* (2018), Stuart Innes Molloy takes the encounter of the 'general viewer' with the films of Claire Denis, both individually and collectively, as a locus for an exploration of cognition. Upon the map of hermeneutic systems this chapter takes up a position within the terrain of cognitive cultural studies. More specifically, it sees itself as an exercise in cognitive narratology. These broader and narrower points of approach give this chapter its point of difference in the context of scholarship on Denis, making its interpretation of her work unusual and thence hopefully valuable. This chapter is indebted to the work of psychologist Jean Piaget, the source of the term equilibration. The Piagetian understanding of how the mind works is important for the definition of the 'general viewer', who should not be invoked without being defined, although this process is routinely overlooked not just in scholarship on Denis but on film in general. In this regard, this chapter also takes into consideration the impact on the patterns of orientation of Hollywood filmmaking's cultural hegemony. Denis's refusal of meaning is in part a refusal of this hegemony, although this opposition is not counted here as a function of being a francophone filmmaker. With these foundations elaborated, this chapter limns the refusal of meaning in the films of Claire Denis by parsing its effectors, identified as symbolic density and diegetic discontinuity.

In Chapter 8, Kristin Hole focuses on Denis's 'female desire' films – *Vendredi soir* (2002), *Un intérieur* (2017), and *Avec amour et acharnement* (2022) – and their representations of white heterosexual women in midlife, specifically through the lens of adaptation. Denis's screenwriting collaborations with French authors Emanuèle Bernheim and Christine Angot on these films is a departure from her many collaborations with Jean-Pol Fargeau. I examine the ways in which the writing styles and thematic interests of Bernheim and Angot shape the cinematic approach to storytelling in these films, with specific attention to issues of sensory versus dialogue-based storytelling and the shifts in Denis's engagement with issues of race.

Danica van de Velde's Chapter 9, 'In the Cracks: Claire Denis's Cinematic Choreographies', focuses on the documentary work of Denis. In *Towards Mathilde* (2005) Denis unobtrusively captures the creative process of contemporary French choreographer, Mathilde Monnier. Early in the documentary Monnier articulates her approach to dance through a metaphor of spatial conquest: 'Whenever you make an incursion into a space, that space is altered [. . .] It's like a piece of paper that has a mark on it and is no longer blank. There's something dirtying it.' As the film progresses, the camera, wielded interchangeably by cinematographers Agnès Godard and Hélène Louvart, captures Monnier's muscular frame as she attempts to carve and pierce the space surrounding her body. Her movements gesture less towards traditional ideas of dance than to a complex negotiation of space emphasising physical intervention and, at its most extreme, invasion. She is, by her own admission, searching for 'cracks' that allow her to 'invent things within [them]'. Taking *Towards Mathilde* as a springboard for exploring broader ideas of movement, bodies and space in Denis's films, the essay will examine the violent cinematic choreographies featured in *Trouble Every Day* (2001), *Bastards* (2013) and *High Life* (2018). By critically examining the relationship between cinematography, spatial relations and bodies in this trio of films, it will seek to interrogate Denis's unique visual language of devastation and desire that, much like Monnier's 'cracks', unfurls in transgressive interstices.

In Chapter 10, 'Stars and Acting in Claire Denis's Films since 2010', Douglas Morrey takes a unique approach. Since she has become a globally recognised auteur director, Denis has attracted some of the biggest stars of French cinema, notably actors who have accomplished the crossover between popular and art cinema, partly of course thanks to their very work with Denis. Given Denis's predilection for fragmented narrative structure, for generic experimentation and for limited dialogue, her use of stars has often helped, over the past decade, to orient spectators within otherwise difficult and alienating films. Thus Isabelle Huppert's historically recent roles as independent yet intensely neurotic women – particularly her repeated incarnation as almost psychotic mother figures – help to anchor the amoral quagmire of *White Material* (2010); Vincent Lindon reprises in *Les salauds* (2013) the vigilante role that he played in *Pour elle* (2008) and that he would further develop in *Mea Culpa* (2014). Lindon's silent strength lends a dignity to this grubby rape-revenge plot, turning the film into something like a modern *Quai des brumes* (1938). In *High Life* (2018), Robert Pattinson channels something of his iconic role as Edward Cullen from *Twilight* (2008) to incarnate a protagonist who is at once hero and villain, a nurturing father and a dispassionate killer. Finally, *Un beau soleil intérieur* is an exceptional entry in Denis's filmography: a dialogue-driven comedy. It deploys Juliette Binoche's sophisticated but ably self-mocking persona to rich effect, building most of its scenes around moments of acute social awkwardness and relying on Binoche's expressive face and comic timing to carry off the delicately pitched tone.

Kate Taylor-Jones in Chapter 11, 'Life Imitates Art: The Intimacy of Family in the Work of Claire Denis and Yasujiro Ozu', thinks through the significance of Japan's most influential filmmaker and Denis:

> *Late Spring* is very personal for me, very close to that relationship between my mother and my grandfather. I took my mother once to an Ozu retrospective to see *Late Spring*, and she thought it was beautiful – she said, 'I didn't know you could make a film with such a simple story'. So I made up my mind. I wanted to make that film for her. (Claire Denis in Nayman 2009, n.p.)

PETER SLOANE

With her film 2008 film *35 rhums*, Denis was open about her desire to pay homage to Japanese director Ozu Yasujiro. With this acknowledgement, Denis joined the ranks of other global directors such as Hirokazu Koreeda, *Hou* Hsiao-hsien, Wim Wenders, Wes Anderson and Alain Gomis, who have utilised Ozu as both a source of inspiration and a site of reference and homage. Discussions of Ozu invariably focus on his aesthetics, and as I have argued elsewhere, a comparative study of his cinematic aesthetics allows us the potential to draw a clear creative lineage between Ozu's style – both visual, and thematic and the work of Claire Denis. This chapter develops these links further and situates Denis as part of the global legacy of a director who, rather than being a historical figure in Japanese cinema, plays a vibrant and enduring part of global cinema narratives and visions. It explores how Denis's affective engagement with idea of family can find resonance with Ozu's intimate portraits.

In Chapter 12, Jacob Hovind examines '"The Stranger and the Surprise": Hospitality, Community and Coming to Our Senses in *Vendredi soir*'. Building on Claire Denis's work with Jean-Luc Nancy's philosophy of community, heterogeneity and alterity, not just in her meditative adaptation of his memoir *L'intrus* (2004) but in 'Vers Nancy', a short film the two made together for the omnibus project *Ten Minutes Older: The Cello* (2002), Hovind's chapter explores how questions of alterity, cosmopolitanism and openness haunt her entire oeuvre. For both Denis and Nancy, being becomes imagined as a site of openness to 'the idea of intrusion that's contained within every foreigner'. For Nancy, this is most urgently a question of community, envisioning a truly cosmopolitan being-together based on the back-and-forth model of a Blanchodian conversation, one that rejects neoliberal ideals of what is traditionally coded as diversity, in practice usually nothing but templates for cultural homogenisation and the subjugation of alterity within the sameness of the status quo. Nancy's cosmopolitanism, (and Denis's as well) is instead ultimately a kind of Levinasian welcoming of otherness in its perpetual state of otherness, rather than a hospitality that asks the guest to transform into a mirror of their host. Hovind argues that Denis most frequently stages the possibility of such cosmopolitan openness in the private realm of subjective experience before then exploring what kinds of community her visions of cosmopolitan subjectivity might make possible.

In the final chapter in the collection, Daniel Dufournaud looks at 'Claire Denis's *Beaux Familles*'. In the final scene of Claire Denis's most recent film, *High Life* (2018), Monte (Robert Pattinson) and his daughter, the two remaining members of a spaceship that has left Earth's solar system, hurtle towards a black hole – an ending that affirms both Monte's transformation from murderer into a loving father as well as the strength of the intergenerational bond they have formed under most unusual circumstances. Although the film's SF trappings seem to mark a departure from Denis's previous work, this essay suggests that its ultimate focus on a non-normative family formation constitutes something of a through-line connecting this film to her acclaimed early work, and it is only by tracking and analysing this motif across her work that we can appreciate Denis as a filmmaker who interrogates how broad, meta-subjective political issues shape, alter and/or unsettle such an intimate institution of human sociality as the family. For Denis, the family is a site in which the political and social tensions of her narratives find their most dramatic expression, and so this social institution functions as the primary locus of tragedy in her films.

These original chapters constitute a new phase in Denis studies, developing from and reworking existing approaches while also testing new ground, probing new exploratory routes into this unique and still evolving body of work. Necessarily, such studies are always partial, more so in the case of such a fluent, fluid, dynamic and ambiguous artist.

CITATIONS

Beugnet, Martine. 2004. *Claire Denis*. Manchester: Manchester University Press.
Darke, Chris. 2000. '"Desire is violence": Claire Denis on Beau Travail.' *Sight and Sound*, July.
Eyre, Hermione. 2010. 'Claire Denis on Filmmaking and Feminism.' *Prospect Magazine*, 21 June. https://www.prospectmagazine.co.uk/magazine/loving-the-lost-and-monstrous, accessed 25 July 2022.
French, Philip. 2005. 'The Intruder.' *The Guardian*, 27 August.
Galt, Rosalind. 2014. 'Claire Denis and the World Cinema of Refusal.' *SubStance* 43, 1: 96–108. http://www.jstor.org/stable/24540741, accessed 1 March 2023.
Hole, Kristin Lené. 2016. *Towards a Feminist Cinematic Ethics: Claire Denis, Emmanuel Levinas and Jean-Luc Nancy*. Edinburgh: Edinburgh University Press.
Hussey, Andrew. 2010. 'Claire Denis: "For me, film-making is a journey into the impossible."' *The Observer*, 4 July. https://www.theguardian.com/film/2010/jul/04/claire-denis-white-material-interview, accessed 27 July 2022.
Jones, Kent. 2018. 'Claire Denis Discusses her Influences in On Cinema Conversation at NYFF56.' *New York Film Festival*, 12 October. https://www.filmlinc.org/nyff2018/daily/watch-claire-denis-discusses-her-influences-in-on-cinema-conversation-at-nyff56/, accessed 27 July 2022.
Lazic, Elena. 2019. 'No Fear, No Die: an interview with Claire Denis.' *BFI*, 4 June. https://www.bfi.org.uk/interviews/no-fear-no-die-interview-claire-denis, accessed 27 July 2022.
Mayne, Judith. 2005. *Claire Denis*. Chicago: University of Illinois Press.
Morrey, Douglas. 2008. 'Open Wounds: Body and Image in Jean-Luc Nancy and Claire Denis.' *Film-Philosophy* 12 (1), pp. 10–31.
Olah, Nathalie. 2017. 'The Director of *Certain Women* on Sexism in Film & Working with Michelle Williams.' *Refinery29*, 27 March. https://www.refinery29.com/en-gb/2017/02/142090/certain-women-kelly-reichardt-film-director-interview, accessed 29 July 2022.
Rooney, David. 2013. 'Bastards: Cannes Review.' *Hollywood Reporter*.

Sur, Debadrita. 2021. 'How Kathryn Bigelow changed the face of cinema forever.' *Far Out*, 19 July. https://faroutmagazine.co.uk/how-kathryn-bigelow-changed-cinema-forever/, accessed 28 July 2022.
Vecchio, Marjorie. 2014. *The Films of Claire Denis: Intimacy on the Border*. New York, Bloomsbury.

CHAPTER 1

L'eau Life: The Hydrous and Haptic Cinema of Claire Denis

Rowena Santos Aquino[1]

Water is a deceptively simple element in the films of Claire Denis. Fundamentally, it constitutes part of the atmospheric and moody setting of her films' worlds, in the slanted verticality of rain in the opening sequence of *Les salauds* (2013) or in the dusky, wine-soaked shots of the Seine River that bookend *Trouble Every Day* (2001). More strikingly, water is a physical, visual detail of or accomplice to the unfolding of her characters' everyday, which is often marked by struggles over power, desire, hierarchy and identity, within a group, but also simultaneously struggling with their (sense of) self, tested and challenged under specific constrained conditions that are often outside their control. If, on the surface, images of water or scenes of characters framed by water in Denis's films may not always involve heightened emotion or pivotal situations, on closer examination, they in fact constitute not only some of the most evocative moments in her oeuvre but also some of the most markedly audiovisual ways in which to address the intertwined issues of bodies, control and the contested spatialities of the social, political and personal, thematic hallmarks of Denis's cinema.

In its simultaneous weightiness and lightness, water also surreptitiously encapsulates the narrative complexity and layered filminess (with its dual meaning of translucent and muddied) of withholding exposition and privileging play with the less linear structures, fluid camerawork and framing and an intensely mesmeric rhythm of Denis's cinema. Water as substance literally reflects the camerawork and framing choices in Denis's films in that the camera embraces so closely and persistently the materialities and spatialities of her worlds, for spectatorial contemplation and immersion. On still another level, the unique spectatorial experience of Denis's films navigating between the sensual thickness of her world-building imagery, including the raw matter-of-factness of bodies and textures, and a narrative lightness 'loosened from the demands of plot, characterisation and causality' (Walton 2016: 87), aligns with what Adriano D'Aloia terms 'enwaterment' (2012). But if 'enwaterment' for D'Aloia concerns images of water that mimic for the spectator the feeling of being immersed in water, for Denis, it denotes more expansively different facets of her filmmaking, from the image flow, camerawork and framing to her elliptical narratives and thematic preoccupations of border crossing and sensual delineation of the surface–depth of human experiences and interactions.

Taking as a point of departure Saad Chakali's note of *L'intrus*'s (2004) 'oceanic montage', wherein a 'dialectic of the emerged (what we see, knowing that this view is partial) and the submerged (what we guess but do not – or no longer – see)' (quoted in McMahon 2014, note 12) operates, this chapter discusses Denis's 'transgressive political [and cinematic] practice' (Steinberg and Peters 2015, 247) through the lens of a 'visual poetics of water' (Bollington 2021, 263), or hydropoetics. I discuss how Denis deploys the element and qualities of water to help visualise and address the ways in which spatialities (bodily, geographical) are contested, perceived and processed, including the interplay of emerged–submerged, surface–depth and inside–outside, ultimately pointing to the larger context of the personal and public policing of borders and the lengths to which one can/will go to exert control over one's body and/or others' bodies.

SEEING THROUGH WATER

I define a hydropoetics of film as the formal, visual and thematic application of the literal and figurative qualities of water in filmmaking. As a kinetic substance with its own set of shifting spatialities and temporalities and thus possessing an agency that evokes Michel Foucault's theorisation of the heterotopic space (1984), water is a powerful visual and physical matter. Water takes on the appearance of the viewer who looks at its surface, including the space and things that surround her, yet this reflection is shifted, distorted and never exactly the same. It takes on the form or shape in which it is contained, but does not necessarily merge with the properties of the container to become something else. It is a substance that invites immersion due to its cleansing, healing and nourishing capacity as well as aversion due to its unmanageable, engulfing, even contaminant nature. Above water presents a calm exteriority on which to drift and contemplate, while underwater is a turbulent, even terrifying, interiority in which to plunge; inversely, above water can be a site of havoc and danger while underwater a yawning escape. Its uses in ritualistic, religious and everyday life are imbued with meanings, from purification and clarity to transformation and rebirth. A hydropoetics of film is thus constitutive of the larger 'oceanic turn' of the critical invocation of water as image, vessel of meaning, mode of historiography and/or theoretical tool of analysis in the humanities around the turn of the twenty-first century (Hooper 2017, 84).

For example, in her examination of Galician cultural history, Kirsty Hooper suggests reassessing this Spanish region's past and cultural production through the concept of hydropoetics, which she understands as the 'intersection of aesthetics and history with the oceanic and maritime world' (2017, 74). Nodding to a 'shift toward a hydropoetic perspective' (2017, 76) among cultural historians, Hooper examines Galician poetry and geographical literature in the hopes of opening up new avenues of inquiry regarding Galician community and relationships with the past that go beyond the land-bound logic of the nation state and its borders. For Hooper, 'reading hydropoetically' helps to recuperate the 'maritime dimensions' (2017, 75) of the Galician past that was gradually phased out by the emergence of the nation state of Spain, and, by extension, its imposition of an isolating, contracting land-bound approach to history, (re)construction of identity and cultural production. As Hooper's essay demonstrates, however, a (re)new(ed) consideration, even privileging, of the oceanic, coastal and sea runs the risk of creating a simplistic binaristic relationship with *terra firma*, alongside that between the maritime and the national. Nevertheless, Hooper views these connections not as binaries but tensions that invite further examination and elaboration, especially across different fields of study such as cinema.

It is within such a context of productive tension that Amy Suzanne Hough also calls for and theorises a hydropoetic mode of seeing and representation in literature and film that she calls 'liquid visuality'. Taking up Gilles Deleuze and Félix Guattari's challenge of finding or making 'new sensory assemblages', Hough suggests, 'Why not see with water? Why not imagine and explore the potentialities of a liquid eye?' (2019, 7). She takes as her point of departure the idea that vision, 'like matter, can transition into and out of various phases' (2019, 7) and formulates a liquid mode of perception that complements and can transition from (instead of opposing) a 'solid vision' (2019, 4), the latter alone limited in registering the interstitial, subtle aspects of things and relationships in the world. A liquid visuality, then, is at once cognisant and in pursuit of a Deleuzian 'creative becoming' (2019, 18), such that one's vision and perception are, like water, ever moving, changing, and reorienting according to what comes in contact with them and the conditions and actors involved in that contact. In this sense, liquid visuality is also decolonising in that it unmoors the eye from dominant modes of seeing and towards one that is 'more heterogenous and diverse, more intersubjective and relational, than what solid, optical vision allows' (2019, 31). Within the realm of film specifically, Hough proposes that a hydropoetics has been present since film's inception, for 'to explore water as an image was to explore the potentials of the medium' (2019, 32). Like Hooper, Hough avoids slipping into a liquid–solid binary by positioning these different modes of vision complementarily, even while admitting a bias towards the liquid owing to its generative nature of rendering the invisible visible and, by extension, the submerged emerged and inside outside (and vice versa).

Given film's own unique ability to capture and represent multiple spatialities and temporalities, not to mention the fluid way it does so, the growing scholarship of a 'hydropoetic perspective' of film also includes how film and water are creatively reflective of each other. Most notable are the parallels made between the water surface and film screen, the (representation of) worlds that lie beneath/beyond these distinct planes, and the ways in which they raise questions of perception, interiority–exteriority and experience, among other things. D'Aloia also represents such scholarship through his focus on the expressive and thematic uses of water in contemporary narrative cinema that enable an immersive spectatorship and audiovisual capturing of intense emotions and feelings, which he calls 'enwaterment'. Also surveying early films featuring water, D'Aloia notes that they forge

> [an] analogy between the transparency of water and the act of vision, evoking a conception of film viewing as an immersive experience that is capable not only of shocking and astonishing the spectator, but also of inviting and involving him or her into a specific 'sensorial space'. (2012, 88)

For D'Aloia, this immersive 'water-based relationship' (2012, 95) between film and viewer is forged through techniques such as the cross-fade, superimposition, flashback and slow motion, which create narrative moments of heightened emotional involvement and empathetic mirroring. Scenes of submersion and drowning especially demonstrate how water in films has been 'strategically used as a substance capable of marking the passage from one psychological condition to another, and of "hosting" a crucial event' (2012, 92), especially traumatic ones. While D'Aloia does not identify in enwaterment the energy and pursuit of a 'creative becoming' like Hough, his above statement moves towards it. By citing water and film's shared ability to elasticise and pluralise space and time, he gestures towards a hydropoetics that dialogues with Hooper's project for re/considering 'maritime dimensions' and Hough's own in identifying the 'potentialities of a liquid eye' in historiography, literature and film.

The socio-political charge that is largely absent in D'Aloia's notion of enwaterment and only partially developed in Hough's liquid visuality and Hooper's hydropoetic perspective is made explicit in Philip Steinberg and Kimberley Peters's concept of a 'wet ontology', which I find useful in situating a hydropoetics in relation to the interlocking relationships between space, place, bodies and power in Denis's films. In their formulation of a 'wet ontology', Steinberg and Peters look to water and 'its three-dimensional and turbulent materiality, and to encounters with that materiality' (2015, 247–8), as one way towards rethinking the experiences, activities and temporalities of place and space from a geographical perspective. Corresponding to Hough's liquid visuality of rendering visible the more complex twistings and turnings of human interactions and engagements with the world, Steinberg and Peters's wet ontology proposes their own hydropoetic perspective 'of a world of flows, connections, liquidities, and becomings', whereby the 'sea's material and phenomenological distinctiveness can facilitate the reimagining and reenlivening of a world ever on the move' (2015, 248). Through its quality of being 'indisputably voluminous, stubbornly material, and unmistakably undergoing continual reformation' (2015, 248), Steinberg and Peters position water as a productive material and metaphorical lens through which to challenge, on the one hand, 'a terrestrial ontology of bounded zones and emplaced points of power and knowledge' (2015, 253) and, on the other hand, broaden understandings of the 'processes of bordering with a particular intensity not found on land' (2015, 254). At bottom, a wet ontology is a reconceptualised geopolitical approach to the study of the 'complex ways in which power is exercised through, and in, space' (2015, 251) from water's distinct kinetic, shape-shifting perspective. But like Hooper and Hough, Steinberg and Peters are aware of the potential 'dangers in employing the ocean as a "theory machine"' (2015, 257), such as lapsing into fetishisation and romanticisation. They thus emphasise an 'oceanic thinking' predicated on a 'blend of complementarity and opposition', such that a wet ontology not only provides different approaches to constructions of power across varied spatialities and temporalities but also helps to clarify those born from 'land-based thinking' (2015, 257). A hydropoetics of Denis's cinema identifies this same structural principle at work in her films to avoid pitting water against land or body, the fluid against solid, and instead considers the kind of encounters *between* water's materiality and that of the bodies of her actors and the camera, to broaden our understanding of the audiovisual pull of her work.

As theorisations of thinking and seeing through water, I stage a dialogue between D'Aloia's concept of enwaterment, Hough's formulation of a liquid visuality, Hooper's hydropoetic perspective, Steinberg and Peters's proposal of a wet ontology and Denis's filmmaking to elaborate a hydropoetics of her cinema. Through this dialogue, I hope to bring to the surface how water constitutes an important detail to her films' mode of seeing, thinking and representation that discloses and discovers processes, connections, turnings and passages that are not as accessible to solid vision, land-bound as it is and therefore constricted by the 'terrestrial limits' (Steinberg and Peters 2015, 248) of border logics that extend to bodies and interrelations.

L'EAU LIFE: A HYDROPOETICS OF CLAIRE DENIS'S CINEMA

Elaborating a hydropoetics of Denis's cinema may seem like an odd proposition, given that most of her films are set in urban, concrete places or arid, dirt-filled terrain. Yet such a context makes instances of water's presence and qualities in Denis's filmmaking stand out all the more. Furthermore, literature on her oeuvre makes notable references to flow, fluidity and/or drift, if not water directly, relating to rhythm or specific films (Carter 2006; Martin 2006; Mayne 2005; McMahon 2014; Rouxel-Cubberly 2014; Walton 2016). This essay seeks to build on this literature to make explicit the 'intense attraction to the image and aesthetics of water' (Hough 2019, 19) involved in Denis's cinema. Nodding to Gaston Bachelard's study (2003) of the combination of water with other elements or conditions – water and fire, water and earth, water and night – I examine the combination of water and, in the case of Denis, bodies, the camera and filmic language, 'in a blend of complementarity and opposition', to draw out the 'maritime dimensions' of her filmmaking and, in the process, complicate her manner of addressing the social, political and embodied ramifications of border and bodily lines.

Akin to water, Denis's films possess simultaneously a weightiness and lightness, built from the already oft-noted formal and visual characteristics of her films: tight framing, frequent close-ups, lingering camerawork and pace/rhythm, emphasis on the textural qualities of bodies, surfaces and elements, thereby cultivating a 'non-hierarchical visual register, in which human beings seem to have no greater claim to the image than other elements of the décor' (Morrey 2008, 12), and a highly elliptical approach to narrative and characterisation. In this regard, *Nénette et Boni* (1996) presents some of the most caressing, water-like camerawork by frequent collaborator Agnès Godard in Denis's films, as it makes constant contact with the faces and bodies of actors Grégoire Colin and Alice Houri, often when the characters are alone, such as when Boni is in his room engaging in sexual fantasies about the baker and Nénette's introduction. With these characteristics, Denis presents rather insular worlds, grounded in a particular setting, with such insularity part and parcel of what has also been repeatedly noted by scholars of Denis's cinema: the concern with personal and geographical borders of various magnitudes, from French post/colonialism and global financial and communication networks, to differing scales of human migration and inter/personal space and proxemics. Some of the more literal examples of insular, bordered places are the houses of France's family in *Chocolat* (1988) in colonial Cameroon; of Boni's mother, which he inherits and uses as a sensitive boundary between himself, family members and society in general, in *Nénette et Boni*; of Léo and Coré and the constant threat of sexual violence contained therein and projected outwardly with the latter in *Trouble Every Day*; of Trebor within the Swiss countryside in *L'intrus*, fortress-like in its isolation and through Trebor's acute vigilance of the surrounding landscape; and even the spaceship in *High Life* (2018), an organised site whose borders and dimensions never change for its occupants, even as it hurtles through space. Other insular settings encompass the larger borders of a city while focusing on a specific network of activities and actors, as in Marseille and the titular family and immigrant communities who live there in *Nénette et Boni* or the select, nondescript spaces of Paris traversed by the two couples in *Trouble Every Day*, Jean and Laure in *Vendredi soir* (2002), Lionel and Jo's tight social circle in *35 rhums* (2008), and Marco through his investigation of his brother-in-law's suicide and niece's trauma in *Les salauds*. Further expanding upon focused insular borders and more intensely the dialectic of inside–outside are the nation state spaces of post/colonial Africa, as in Cameroon in *Chocolat*, Djibouti in *Beau travail* (1999) and unnamed in *White Material* (2009). These settings set the stage for a close engagement with questions of inside–outside and the kind of relationships and identities that exist and emerge within/between them.

These issues of border and bodily lines are not discoursed upon outright by characters or even disclosed by the narratives in full – at most, occasionally puncturing the surface through inference; hence Rosalind Galt's description of Denis's works as a 'cinema of refusal' (2014). Instead, Denis places this burden of signification chiefly on imagery and form. In this way, Denis's cinema arguably nods to the *Cinéma pur* of the 1920s–1930s French avant-garde, whose experiments with the purely formal and visual qualities specific to cinema led filmmakers towards non-narrative works. However, rather than turning her back on the stuff of the world in favour of the abstraction of forms, Denis applies *Cinéma pur*'s preoccupation with form and imagery precisely towards material realities, notably bodies and water, making such realities banal, compelling and moving all at once, with the viewer 'seduced by the films' poetry, texture, color and style, and simultaneously kept at an arm's length by the narratives' distances and silences' (Carter 2006, 68). Hence the way in which Denis begins her films, a fitting point of departure for elaborating a hydropoetics of her cinema. As examined by Noëlle Rouxel-Cubberley, they are steadfastly marked by movement, manifested visually and formally through a 'meandering' camera; intimate shots of bodies and faces; perspectives from and images of the road and modes of transport; and images of bodies of/and water (2014, 170). If a film's opening moments crucially set the tone for what is to come, they thus establish the correlation between water and film in Denis's cinema through their distinct yet shared kinetic qualities, the movement of images, bodies and camera reflecting the movement of water and vice versa, which enacts a 'meta-cinepoetics' in that these two forms 'speak to [each other's] unique temporality and fluidity' (Hough 2019, 33). For apart from featuring water and often being bereft of dialogue, these opening moments also establish how Denis's approaches to framing, camerawork and editing take on water's contrasting properties, including transparency and opacity. The viewer is compelled to dive head-first into these cinematic worlds and characters without expositional preludes, which nods to how water, '[a]s a reflective entity, also exists as a visual excess that sometimes marks and obscures the image, thereby forcing a partial or refractory spectatorial perspective' (Bollington 2021, 268), while being just as 'capable of directly communicating symbols and meanings to the spectator, reducing the separation between the fictional space on the screen and the psychic space in front of the screen' (D'Aloia 2012, 93–4).

In *Chocolat*, the opening sequence is of the sea in a wide-shot freeze frame as the opening credits roll. After the cast credits and title, the shot unfreezes and a Black man emerges from the sea waves and jogs towards the shore. But he is not alone: what at first appears to be a buoy of some sort is in fact a little boy's arm and, once fully emerged from the sea, the man and boy run around and chase each other at play. They exit frame left and the camera pans 180 degrees right to the shore to introduce in a long shot the adult France sitting on rocks, before she ventures further into Cameroon and revisits the town of her family's colonial home. The next sequence features the same father and son now lying on the shore, as the waves lap around them, while a cut reveals France still seated on the rocks in a closer shot, clearly marking her as distinct and an outsider in relation to the father and son in direct contact with water. In *Nénette et Boni*, the watery title credit segues to the introduction of Nénette via an overhead medium close-up of her in a swimming pool, floating, isolated by the frame. Except at the end after giving birth, she is most at ease here than at any other moment of the film; that is, until an off-screen voice interrupts her reverie. Consequently, she wades towards frame left and a cut shows her emerging from the pool as her makeshift bathing suit is criticised by an instructor. Nénette's contemplative, liquid introduction is succeeded by and in direct contrast to that of her estranged older brother, Boni, who is caught in close-ups and rapid cuts from inside/outside a car with a friend as they burn rubber, which anticipates the siblings' initial antagonistic encounters and ultimately their respective attitudes about Nénette's pregnancy. In *Beau travail*, an early set of lateral tracking shots introduces the legionnaires as a collective unit and Galoup set apart, if only obliquely: after the film's opening shots of a fresco, a dance club and views from a journeying bus, a tracking shot from left to right unfolds images of sand and the legionnaires' po(i)sed bodies, which then cuts to waves churning from the clear perspective of a sailing vessel, over which is then superimposed Galoup's diary and act of writing, which establishes his seafaring perspective.

In *Les salauds*, drenching rain in the opening shots, against concrete walls and streets, shrouds a man sheltering from the rain. Though the rain stops in

Figure 1.1 Galoup looks over the water.

the next sequence, the streets are wet and a young woman who is entirely *deshabillée* walks dazed and disoriented. While seemingly separate, these moments introduce the father and daughter whose tangled sexual, violent relationship constitutes the crux of the film's turn of events. These opening moments, brought into being via water-like ebb-and-flow movements of the camera and with the explicit focus on the 'material surface of bodies and their surrounding environments, rather than character psychology and motivations' (Dooley 2015, 440), in fact perform a process of enwaterment not only to establish the foregrounding of the sensorial in and the unconventional rhythm of Denis's filmic worlds but also to prime the viewer's engagement with these worlds that evokes the feeling of being emerged/submerged in water. In this way, the film performs a dual 'artistic birth' (Rouxel-Cubberley 2014, 170): of a cinematic world and of the viewer's entry into and engagement with that world, both of which are characterised by an altogether different oceanic pacing. As Allan Sekula once said, 'The sea is all about slow time – things move slowly, there's a lot of waiting – and as such it contradicts all the mythologies of instantaneity perpetuated by electronic media' (Sandhu 2012, n.p.). That movement and passage explicitly mark Denis's opening scenes, thereby 'catching her characters on a floating stage' (Rouxel-Cubberley 2014, 170) that in turn are often marked by water, encourages a more extensive consideration of how and where else movement, passage, bodies and water interplay in her films.

On closer inspection, 'catching her characters on a floating stage' is found not just in the beginning but throughout Denis's films. While D'Aloia increasingly finds examples of enwaterment in contemporary films that feature 'crucial scenes that represent immersed and drowning bodies in order to involve the spectators in an enveloping and breathtaking experience' (2012, 88), peppered throughout Denis's films are vignettes or portraits that either introduce the character (at times contained within the opening sequences) or visually convey/observe a mood or state of mind. If the characters are not in direct contact with water, then water is meaningfully nearby through framing choices, camerawork and/or editing, which gives form to 'their predicaments [being] irresolvable and [so] they remain adrift or in precarious or discomforting social situations' (Carter 2006, 68). In *L'intrus*, Trebor is introduced in full nature, in the woods and in the water with his dogs. Though perfectly at peace deep in the forest, he groans out in pain while swimming, as if the touch of water as much as his heart condition is what hurts him. Days later, before venturing out to the city centre, a shot of Trebor lying in his bed cuts to a window that looks out to the lake, denoting it as his object of gaze. While brief, it nevertheless constitutes a charged moment that visually expresses Trebor's character, considering that he is always looking out, surveying the landscape, ever in anticipation of an interloper transgressing the boundaries of his life and body or being surveilled himself, with the body of water framed by the window an indication of origins in one sense and the means by which he will journey throughout the rest of the film in pursuit of a new heart-body, even at the expense of others. This brief moment of Trebor gazing out is repeated in Tahiti, post-operation, this time juxtaposed with a shot of a window framing the docks and water. These vignettes also gesture towards a correlation between the body's volume and boundaries of inside–outside and those of water, such that the 'permeability of the barriers and vessels we have fashioned to keep out water is akin to the fragility of our own borders and is a reminder of the instability of our own individuality' (Isaak 2002, 27), with the human body being one such 'porous vessel' and the 'skin as a very slight and permeable membrane separating us from our surrounding' (Isaak 2002, 29). Is it not the instability of his own individuality through his failing body vessel that characterises and motivates Trebor's seafaring trek from Europe to Asia and to the middle of the Pacific Ocean?

    A comparable sense of instability about one's own bodily border lines in relation to others happens with Shane's rising sexually violent desires towards others in *Trouble Every Day*, Galoup's growing resentment towards Sentain in *Beau travail* and Nénette's advanced pregnancy in *Nénette et Boni*. Denis captures these characters' solitary struggles against physically abject actions towards another or their own body in sequences conspicuously characterised with water. After traipsing through the city and having his wife worry about his whereabouts from their hotel room, a medium close-up shot of the Seine River's waves rendered purple with splashes of red by the setting sun and a wide shot of the same river cut to Shane lying on a stone bench and occupying most of the frame. Yet the top left corner of purple-red water locates him more

L'EAU LIFE

Figure 1.2 Trebor floats in a mountain lake.

specifically at the Seine's embankment. The shot is held for eight seconds, with Shane maintaining a supine position, and the weight of surface observation paradoxically acquires a depth of meaning as to what he is thinking. Following shots of physical exercises and a medium close-up of Forestier, a close-up of Galoup takes over the screen for a full fourteen seconds, with his profile occupying the right side of the screen while a body of water occupies the left side. Interestingly, sounds of the men engaging in physical exercises bridge the cuts, layered over the first five seconds of Galoup's private contemplation. Less than five minutes later in the runtime comes Galoup and Sentain's *duel de regard*. In both of these cases, these characters ultimately decide to cross the bodily borders that separate one from another and perform vengeful acts in response to their desires. In Nénette's case, she acts against her own body when she attempts to abort in Boni's bathroom. Intriguingly, the interiors of Boni's house feature the colour blue (as if to help denote the port city setting), especially the kitchen walls and bathroom, and the start of this three-minute sequence consists of a shot of the bathroom door whose colour and design mimic glistening water. A near reversal of Nénette's introduction in the pool, which births her character, ensues inside the blue bathroom. This time, however, it is Boni who disrupts her floating, using his body to break down the door and then grab Nénette out of the bathtub water.

Steinberg and Peters identify the 'destabilising immanence of liquid' (2015, 256), which for them situates the ocean 'as a means toward unearthing a material perspective that acknowledges the volumes within which territory is practised: a world of fluidities where place is forever in formation and where power is simultaneously projected on, through, in, and about space' (2015, 261). In *Chocolat*, the space and act of showering draw out the bodily and border lines that are operative in the colonial system in three moments

25

spread out across the film, beginning with Protée pouring buckets of water into the barrel for Aimée to take a shower and, once emptied, hurling them down on the ground, as if angered by the waste as the same water gushes down the drain. Later, Protée is shown taking a shower, a shot whose framing foregrounds his body, perspective and subjectivity, since he faces the camera, while Aimée and little France walk towards the front door of their house in the background and away from the camera. Though occupying most of the frame, his intense reaction to hearing them (sheltering himself from view as the water continues to pour down over him and hitting his elbow against the wall) denotes a piercing awareness of his delimited subordinate, subjugated place in the household, in his own country. When Protée finds that Luc (an extended white guest at the household) showers where he showers, he pointedly tells Luc, 'Ici, c'est la douche des boys'.

While these two men share the ability to cross the lines chalked by the colonial system, Protée moving in and out of rooms of the Dalens' house as domestic help and France's designated playmate and Luc going from the house to the domestic staff's living quarters, Protée's strong reaction to Luc's act of showering where he makes gestures at a boiling point of the emotional and psychological toll of the process of appropriating even the minimal living space allotted to him. Strikingly fitting in this context is how the 'ocean[/water] surface is the thinnest of lines between two worlds' (Newman 2021, n.p.), the marking and crossing of them performed by Protée and Luc. Along similar lines, in

Figure 1.3   Protée showers outside.

L'EAU LIFE

Figure 1.4 Manuel relaxes in the pool.

White Material, the first appearance of water dovetails with the brief miniature portrait-introduction of Vial senior in the bathtub in his home (almost as a self-referential nod to Trebor, since Michel Subor plays both characters). A mirroring of this portrait occurs with his grandson Manuel soon after. Though already introduced in a prior scene, much more poignant is the sequence that begins with an upside-down reflection of him in the pool at his parents' house, after which he jumps into it and, for a moment, is bathed in tranquillity, recalling Nénette's introduction. But it is quickly disrupted when he is almost killed by child soldiers looking from a distance and his father enters the scene, prompting him to splash out of the water.

This mirroring of Vial's portrait-introduction in water continues in an increasingly distorted fashion through, first, a panning shot of two child soldiers in the same bathtub, bodily replacing Vial and thus denoting the socio-economic/political implosion happening across the unnamed African country, and second, very brief shots of these children being killed by the military in that same bathtub later still, the redness of their spilled blood mixing with and replacing water and bluntly reinforcing this implosion. While *Chocolat* and *White Material* are two of Denis's 'driest' films, the detail of water in the aforementioned sequences contributes to how the films perform a mode of seeing and representation of destabilising social structures, aided by the detail of water, which is never fully abstracted and is used instead 'with particular attention to its materiality', as a 'volume of vibrant matter that is enlivened and made forceful through its *relation* with human life' (Steinberg and Peters 2015, 256). In this way, too, drawn in combination by her characters' constant movements and relationships struck with each other; the camera's own movement and gaze; and the graphic, material qualities and kinetic presence of water, Denis's cinema presents a *mise-en-abîme* of border and bodily lines, accruing

27

a depth of meaning through concentrated attention on the materialities and spatialities of surfaces during the films' runtimes.

35 rhums is also one of Denis's 'driest' films, yet here too are sequences that could not be more different from each other but are connected by water. One is the famous sequence beginning with the pounding rain and stalled car that prompt Jo, her father Lionel, and friends to change their plans for the night and seek refuge in a local bar instead, and continues into the liquid choreography of the actors' bodies as they dance and change partners and the camera weaves in between and around them to the sounds of 'Night Shift'. The other sequence, less visually expressive though no less memorable, takes place when Jo and Lionel visit her German aunt, who during their conversation recounts memories of Jo's deceased mother:

> I taught her how to swim. She was scared of the water. We're all scared of it. I'm also scared of that sea. So vast, so wide. And when you scream, no one hears you.

Jo and her father then visit her mother's grave and conclude their journey by staying at a beach overnight. Though innocuous in the retelling of those memories and as part of Jo and Lionel's bonding itinerary before the former gets married, the peculiar, seemingly out-of-place words of Jo's aunt speak volumes to the ways in which '[w]ater is simultaneously encountered as a depth and as a surface, as a set of fixed locations but also as an ungraspable space that is continually being reproduced by mobile molecules' (Steinberg and Peters 2015, 252), which understandably provokes fear and uncertainty about one's place and position when in contact with it. Such latent fear and uncertainty even hovers within *High Life*'s spaceship, whose main corridor recalls the hull of a ship and interiors are often bathed in blue underwater-like light, and therefore also among its inhabitants, whose bodies are treated as lab experiments. For in space as in water, following Jo's aunt, no one can hear you scream.

As an ever-moving substance whose shape and borders are also ever shifting, thinking and seeing through/with water 'configures a world that is open, porous, mobile and changing, but concurrently one that can stabilise temporarily' (Steinberg and Peters 2015, 255). Steinberg and Peters thus anchor their formulation of a wet ontology on how the ocean 'creates the need for new understandings of mapping and representing; living and knowing; governing and resisting' (2015, 260–1), which 'suggests that as we turn our attention to the volumes within which politics is practised and territory is produced we must continually rethink the borders that we apply to various materialities and their physical states' (2015, 259). And in Denis's films, the primary materiality towards which they address and enact a rethinking of borders is the human body, perhaps most thoroughly captured by the sequence of Sentain at Lake

Assal in *Beau travail*. When left in the middle of nowhere on his own, as a consequence of Galoup's decisions against him, Sentain encounters the salt lake. Through the wide shot that encompasses a sizeable portion of the lake and most of the frame, Sentain is rendered minuscule as he walks towards it from frame right. A cut then finds him lying on the white salt bed, greatly weakened and stained with salt crystals that seem to be growing on him. In this way, the 'division between body and landscape dissolves' (McMahon 2014, 5), reinforced by the next cut of the lake and surrounding landscape devoid of human figures or even traces of human activity. The next shot pans across the lake's surface from right to left, emulating the direction of the waves, during which the camera discovers Sentain's broken compass, a veritable cinematic imaging of the 'destabilising immanence of liquid' along border and bodily lines.

Alongside direct interactions between the materialities of water and bodies, a veritable iconography of water operates in Denis's films, and not just in terms of shots of the sea in the explicitly water-centric *Beau travail* and *L'intrus*, including maritime subjects such as sailors (the baker in *Nénette et Boni*, who at one point is making a boat out of gingerbread, and Marc in *Les salauds*), or those who have a degree of experience sailing the seas, including the legionnaires in *Beau travail* and Laporte in *Les salauds*. Perhaps knowing spitefully the 'ungraspable space' that the sea presents, Laporte tellingly takes away the son that he shares with Raphaëlle (as punishment for her liaison with Marco) out to sea on his boat, and clues Raphaëlle in on it through a video. In fact, a maritime thread weaves ever so subtly through characters principal and peripheral. Photographs of family at the beach appear in *L'intrus*, through the young man in Tahiti whose office contains a framed picture of himself as a child with his father at the beach and who tells Trebor that 'Ta place n'est pas ici', and *Les salauds*, through the doctor who is treating Marco's niece and whose framed picture of his daughter at the beach catches Marco's attention during their first conversation. It is pixellated footage of someone at the beach amongst the waves playing on the computer in *High Life* that prompts Monte to say, 'These fucking images from earth . . .', which recalls the home movie-like footage of Boni by the sea and two anonymous scuba divers emerging from the water inserted at unexpected moments in *Nénette et Boni*, and also inserts of Paul Gégauff's Tahiti-set and water-drenched *Le reflux* (1965, starring a young Subor) in *L'intrus*. Another highly significant example is in Denis's documentary *Vers Mathilde* (2005), which opens with a forty-second sequence of choreographer Mathilde Monnier walking on the beach. Coming on the heels of *L'intrus*, the rest of the film is less about Monnier's biographical trajectory towards dance and more of a collaborative exploration of movement, spatiality and passage between Denis, cinematographers Godard and Hélène Louvart, Monnier and her dancers. Like the opening sequence's initial focus on the waves creating shapes and spaces around Monnier's feet as she walks along, so the rest of the film captures and performs the rigorous un/making of bodily movements, shapes and lines, which gradually grow in dimensions and rhythm to constitute a piece and meaning. Taken together, this iconography and choreography of water in Denis's cinema expresses a clear fascination with its manifold contrasting qualities, including the way it 'endow[s] her composition with a mutable, textured appearance that shifts between effects of the two- and the three-dimensional' (Walton 2016, 80), of which the viewer finds herself simultaneously inside and outside, submerged and emerged.

CONCLUSION

In this chapter, I have attempted to draw out a hydropoetics of Denis's cinema, or the interlacing of liquid and body, of body and image, touching on its formal, visual, and thematic characteristics that nod to water's 'fluid unknowability' (Steinberg and Peters 2015, 253). In examining Denis's cinema through the perspective of water – its unknowability and ungraspable space as well as communicative capacity and dynamic visual agency – our understanding of the workings of her singular, unsettling cinematic mode of seeing, thinking and representation of bodies, movements, spatialities, and questions of power/control, becomes clearer, at least partially.

NOTE

1. 'Tout cet ensemble mobile, fluide et agité donne le schème directeur du film.' Jean-Luc Nancy.

CITATIONS

Bachelard, Gaston. 2003 [1983]. *L'eau et les rêves: essai sur l'imagination de la matière*. Paris: Livre de Poche.
Bollington, Lucy. 2021. 'Landscapes of desapropiación: Necropolitics and Hydropoetics in Recent Mexican Documentary Film.' *Journal of Romance Studies* 21, 2: 263–90.
Carter, Mia. 2006. 'Acknowledged absences: Claire Denis's cinema of longing.' *Studies in European Cinema* 3, 1: 67–81.
D'Aloia, Adriano. 2012. 'Film in Depth. Water and immersivity in the contemporary film experience.' *Acta Universitatis Sapientiae, Film and Media Studies* 5: 87–106.
Dooley, Kath. 2015. 'Haptic visions of unstable bodies in the work of Claire Denis.' *Continuum* 29, 3: 434–44.
Foucault, Michel. 1984. 'Des espaces autres (1967).' *Architecture/Mouvement/Continuité* 5: 46–9.
Hooper, Kirsty. 2017. 'Ríos, fontes, peiraos, and océanos: Hydropoetics and the Galician cultural imagination.' In *Rerouting Galician Studies: Multidisciplinary Interventions*,

edited by Benito Sampedro Vizcaya and José A. Losada Montero, 73–89. Cham: Springer International Publishing.

Hough, Amy Suzanne. 2019. 'The Liquid Eye: A Deleuzian Poetics of Water in Film.' PhD diss., University of California, Riverside.

Isaak, Jo Anna. 2002. *H2O: Imagination's Matrix*. Geneva: Hobart and William Smith College Press.

Martin, Adrian. 2006. 'Ticket to ride: Claire Denis and the cinema of the body.' *Screening the Past* 20: https://www.screeningthepast.com/issue-20-first-release/ticket-to-ride-claire-denis-and-the-cinema-of-the-body/.

Mayne, Judith. 2005. *Claire Denis*. Urbana and Chicago: University of Illinois Press.

McMahon, Laura. 2014. 'Beyond the human body: Claire Denis's ecologies.' *Alphaville* 7: http://www.alphavillejournal.com/Issue7/HTML/ArticleMcMahon.html.

Morrey, Douglas. 2008. 'Open wounds: body and image in Jean-Luc Nancy and Claire Denis.' *Film-Philosophy* 12, 1: 10–30.

Newman, Cathy. 2021. 'A photographer marries the worlds above and below the water in a single frame.' *NPR*: https://www.npr.org/sections/pictureshow/2021/10/25/1047320224/a-photographer-marries-the-worlds-above-and-below-the-water-in-a-single-frame.

Rouxel-Cubberly, Noëlle. 2014. 'Delivering: Claire Denis's opening sequences.' In *The Films of Claire Denis: Intimacy on the Border*, edited by Marjorie Vecchio, 163–74. London and New York: I. B. Tauris.

Sandhu, Sukhdev. 2012. 'Allan Sekula: filming the forgotten resistance at sea.' *The Guardian*: https://www.theguardian.com/film/2012/apr/20/allan-sekula-resistance-at-sea.

Steinberg, Philip and Kimberley Peters. 2015. 'Wet ontologies, fluid spaces: giving depth to volume through oceanic thinking.' *Environment and Planning D: Society and Space* 33, 2: 247–64.

Walton, Saige. 2016. 'Fabricating film – the neo-Baroque folds of Claire Denis.' In *Neo-Baroques: From Latin American to the Hollywood Blockbuster*, edited by Walter Moser, Angela Ndalianis and Peter Krieger, 76–99. Leiden and Boston: Brill Rodopi.

CHAPTER 2

Good Work or Exploitation? *Beau travail* and *35 rhums* and the Fear of Individualism

Kyle Barrett

The cinema of Claire Denis is perplexing. Each film is a multifaceted, complex text that is grounded in realism but visualised ethereally through an observer's eye. Judith Mayne suggests that Denis often locates details on the periphery, intimate quieter moments that would seem insignificant if created by other filmmakers (2005). Yet these details are the elements that are central to Denis's work: her characters' fleeting moments, gestures and stillness, which we often ignore in the everyday. In essence, Denis's cinema is one of introspection. Since her debut, *Chocolat* (1988), Denis has crafted a distinctive oeuvre that is at odds with both Hollywood and European cinemas, though she has never expressed any aspirations to pursue a career in the former. In fact, for Denis, cinema is universal. Interviewed as part of Mark Cousins's mammoth documentary *The Story of Film: An Odyssey* (2011), Denis states, 'I would love in a second life to be . . . a sort of James Cameron, you know. For me, there is no difference between a James Cameron and a Claire Denis, you know, that wants to make film.' Of course, viewers of both filmmakers' work can certainly discern key differences in their respective creative approaches – the grand visual spectacle of the former as seen in *Titanic* (1997) and *Avatar* (2009) eschews the intimate peripheral details as found in the latter's *L'intrus* (2004) and *Les salauds* (2013). However, Denis's expression of challenging the Hollywood/European cinema divide indicates a belief that film is a universal language, that audiovisual storytelling can be embraced by everyone.

European cinema has been continuously examined, re-examined, dissected and analysed from a variety of perspectives and disciplines in numerous scholarly volumes. The seminal study by the late, great Thomas Elsaesser, *European Cinema: Face to Face with Hollywood* (2005), problematised European cinema to an influential degree, noting that there are multiple 'Europes', split between the East and West, and that it is often held, unfairly, in contrast to its North American neighbour (2005, 9). Since its publication, predominate areas of investigation into European cinema have been notions of identity, its paradoxes and complications that arise from migrant/diasporic narratives and voices (Kaklamanidou and Corbalán 2019, 1). Frequently, European cinema is considered to be in constant crisis, as, indeed, is Europe itself. There have been further complications due to the increase of far right-wing ideologies becoming commonplace throughout the world, while the disastrous Brexit vote that led to Britain leaving the EU has challenged concepts of 'Europeanness' in the twenty-first century (Barrett 2022, 27). At the time of writing, Ukraine has been invaded by Russia, instigating a war that will have far-reaching consequences across the world in the decades to come. Therefore, Elsaesser's astute observations highlighting Europe's constant crises remain relevant.

From the 1970s onward, we have witnessed the rapid transition from collectivism to individualism through neoliberal ideologies. In essence, neoliberalism is a theory of political economics that proposes that 'human well-being can best be advanced by the maximization of entrepreneurial freedoms within an institutional framework characterized by private property rights, individual liberty, unencumbered markets, and free trade' (Harvey 2007, 22). Political leaders such as Margaret Thatcher and Ronald Reagan deregulated the stock market, emboldened business leaders, dismantled the welfare state and actively encouraged the individual to put their needs first above all else at the expense of any community spirit. This strategy has only gained strength, with many of its consequences resulting in much of the turmoil we are witnessing today. In terms of Denis's cinema, she has been an active observer and mirror-holder to the devastation that neoliberalism has had on communities. Denis has a vested interest in the ramifications of the individual pursuit and collapse of collectives. Rosalind Galt brilliantly categorises Denis's work as a cinema of refusal that rejects 'dominant narratives, forms and circulatory mechanisms of global neoliberalism' (2014, 96). Indeed, much of Denis's work focuses on the ramifications of splintering communities, the impact of colonisation and people's inability to communicate effectively with one another. Specifically, the demise of family units and the fear of individualism reverberate across many of her films. Though born in Paris in 1946, Denis was raised in colonial French Africa. Her father was a civil servant who was posted at several locations, including Burkina Faso, Somalia, Senegal and Cameroon (Eyre 2010). Actively encouraged by her father to question France's colonisation of Africa, Denis learned at an early age the meaning of 'white privilege' and its oppressive impact. Speaking in *The Story of Film: An Odyssey*, Denis states:

> I am a white person who grew up in Africa and it is a very powerful experience. We people growing up in a country possessed by white

people but knowing we were not from there and it was wrong make us immensely ... not willing to be giving lessons. (Cousins 2011)

These experiences informed several films, explicitly so in *Chocolat* and *White Material* (2009), but also resonated widely throughout Denis's career. While it may be arguable that her films are lessons to a degree – particularly from a white middle-class perspective – they are, nevertheless, unpatronising and uncondescending towards ethnic and working-class characters. From a gender perspective, Denis, particularly in her early work, is interested in repressed male and female characters and how they navigate their respective environments. For instance, *Beau travail* (1999) and *35 rhums* (2008) feature complex depictions of masculinity and class. The films deconstruct patriarchy in a variety of contexts, where the protagonist in *Beau travail*, Galoup (Denis Lavant), a member of the French Foreign Legion (FFL), trains new recruits and finds his repressed homosexual urges coming to the surface when he finds himself attracted to rebellious young officer Sentain (Grégoire Colin). In essence, the film can be read as an 'interrogation of notions of collective identity – military, patriarchal, national and colonial – within the setting of the FFL, and an exploration of their collapse into difference, disintegration, and obsolescence' (Beugnet and Sillars 2001, 166). To a certain extent, *35 rhums* continues some of these themes. The film finds a single father, Lionel (Decas), and relationship with his daughter, Joséphine (Mati Diop), tested as she pursues her independence. This commences Lionel's questioning of his fathering, life choices and lack of human connection beyond his daughter (Bíró 2009, 39). The perceived collapse of the family unit, or collective (no matter how small), brings a fear of individualism: Lionel living alone challenges his values and human connection. It is one of Denis's most startlingly understated films.

While Denis, to a certain extent, shares many similarities with fellow French filmmaker Agnès Varda, particularly with approaches to character, she shares comparable aesthetic, narrative and class representational approaches with Scottish filmmaker Lynne Ramsay. Released in the same year as *Beau travail*, Ramsay's feature debut *Ratcatcher* (1999) depicts a similarly confused and dispossessed protagonist to Galoup, here twelve-year-old James Gillespie (William Eadie), who harbours mixed feelings of guilt and repression after the death of his friend (Kuhn 2008, 20). *Morvern Callar* (2002) echoes many elements of *Beau travail* and *35 rhums* whereby the titular character (Samantha Morton) drifts aimlessly after the suicide of her partner, questioning her life choices. Lionel presents a mirror image to Callar, who views the separation of his daughter as a 'death' in many regards. Both characters enter a period of self-discovery to comprehend what they truly value in their respective lives.

This essay will explore these films predominately through a class lens to argue that Denis and Ramsay challenge and problematise identity in the era of rampant neoliberalisation and individualism (McLaughlin et al. 2006, 5–6). These films depict characters who are outcasts and often exploited by the middle and upper classes (the characters are either soldiers, supermarket employees or train drivers, or live in council estates). Furthermore, Denis's films depict characters whose lives are inexorably linked to their professions, and the fear of losing this aspect of their identity has several ramifications. To that extent, it will be posited that the films illustrate elements of Marx's notions of exploitation through capitalism, where both Denis and Ramsay interrogate the abandoning of the working classes (Marx 1887, 153; Wayne 2020, 4). The purpose here is to illustrate how these filmmakers complement one another, despite their drastically different backgrounds. While Denis comes from an affluent family, Ramsay grew up in working-class Glasgow. Trained at the National Film and Television School, specialising in photography, Ramsay has also crafted a singular career in contemporary cinema, one that also embraces the peripheral details. A fellow introspective filmmaker, Ramsay delves deep within her characters to unravel their contradictions. Often with minimal dialogue, her characters are constructed through fleeting moments, gestures and stillness. There is no judgement or forced 'lesson' placed on them for questionable ethical and moral decisions. Callar, for instance, places her name on her deceased boyfriend's unpublished manuscript, which later becomes financially lucrative, allowing her to escape the dour surroundings she inhabits. *Ratcatcher* explores guilt, or the possibility of the absence of guilt, in an adolescent who watches (and is perhaps complicit in) his friend's death. What these films offer are not necessarily solutions to the social-cultural conditions in which the characters find themselves but reflective accounts that question our (the viewer's) judgement of morally grey actions. By presenting a comparison between Denis and Ramsay, it can be posited that they exhibit so-called 'European' traditions in their aesthetic choices, yet they are distinctive in contrast with both US and European filmmakers. The art versus popular cinema debate is one that continues, and the former is arguably inexorably linked to European cinema. However, this overlooks several waves and movements of US cinema that challenged mainstream tastes and attitudes with studio support (specifically cinema of the late 1960s/1970s and 1990s/early 2000s). For Denis and Ramsay, they occupy a complex terrain in terms of commercial appeal (even in their respective countries of origin) and maintaining their artistic sensibilities. On the one hand their approaches to cinema challenge certain notions of 'art' cinema and both have dabbled in 'genre' filmmaking – for example, Denis's science fiction drama *High Life* (2018) and Ramsay's neo-noir *You Were Never Really Here* (2017). On the other, they produce works that raise questions as to whether their films are 'politically or aesthetically engrossing, or just self-conscious, complacent artworks made-to-order for cultural elitists' (Çağlayan 2018, 3). This latter notion is intriguing, considering the characters often depicted in their work. An argument can be made that each is exploiting working-class issues for dramatic purposes in order to appease middle- (and upper)-class tastes. Aspects of their practice, as has been indicated, are observational in their cinematography (some might say *documentary*), which captures and distils the working-class characters as they struggle to live and work in a culture of exploitation with little opportunity for upward mobility. And if commercial appeal is raised, who precisely are these films for? These are pertinent questions, and certainly worthy of further investigation. However, here it is contended that because Denis and Ramsay operate in the interstice of art and commercial cinema, their work provides a voice/representation to/of the working-class. Despite Denis's privileged upbringing (which has continuously been acknowledged) and Ramsay's successful career beyond Scotland's borders, these films are crucial texts that are not patronising towards or critical of the characters depicted; they are works that demonstrate the complex realities and the conflicts we all face, regardless of gender, class and sexuality.

GOOD WORK: DENIS AND RAMSAY'S CINEMA

Denis commenced her filmmaking career during a period of significant stylistic change in French cinema. During the 1980s and early 1990s, French filmmakers instigated a period of hyper-stylisation that would become known as *cinéma du look*. This involved an abandonment of narrative realism, shooting in a studio rather than on location, and, visually, 'highly stylized sets, original costumes and carefully designed colour schemes' (Morrey 2019, 45). It was a stark contrast to the 1960s *Nouvelle Vague* (New Wave) that saw the careers of Jean-Luc Godard and François Truffaut skyrocket owing to their innovative methods of location shooting, experimental jump cut/freeze-frame editing and character-driven narratives. Here, the careers of Luc Besson, Jean-Jacques Beineix and Leos Carax began, all of which favoured, arguably, style over substance and a pop culture aesthetic that was reminiscent of the music videos produced at the time. Denis, however, fit neither in the *Nouvelle Vague* or *cinéma du look* categories.

Originally a student of economics, Denis became dissatisfied with her studies and, with the encouragement of her then-husband, a photographer, enrolled in the Institut des hautes études cinématographiques (IDHEC, now known as La Fémis) in 1969. Upon graduating, she began working as an assistant director with an eclectic group of international greats such as Jacques Rivette, Wim Wenders, Costa-Gravas and Jim Jarmusch (Ancian 2002). Working on such diverse projects with renowned directors encouraged Denis to become a filmmaker in her own right, which led to the production of *Chocolat*. The film, semi-autobiographically inspired, depicts a French woman reminiscing on her childhood in Cameroon and the relationship with her family's African servant (Isaach de Bankolé). From the beginning of her career, Denis was already depicting the tensions of the middle and upper classes and the exploited working-class, political elements that can, perhaps, be considered absent from many of her *cinéma du look* contemporaries. Though critically well received, it was overshadowed at the French box office by genre-leaning films such as *The Big Blue* (Luc Besson, 1988), *The Dinner Game* (Francis Veber, 1988) and *The Bear* (Jean-Jacques Annaud, 1988).

Denis followed her debut with a documentary, *Man No Run* (1989), a companion piece of sorts to *Chocolat*, which captures Cameroon musicians Les Têtes Brulées as they tour France. Her next narrative feature, *No Fear, No Die* (1990), explored cockfighting, reunited her with de Bankolé and commenced her long-term collaboration with Descas. Subsequently, *I Can't Sleep* (1994) brought a degree of controversy to Denis with its depiction of a gay serial killer. Denis then made *Nénette et Boni* (1996), a drama that focuses on a brother-and-sister relationship that becomes further strained when the latter reveals she's pregnant. This general overview of Denis's career up to *Beau travail* excludes documentaries, short films and television episodes produced in addition to her narrative features, but collectively it reveals a robust level of outputs in a relatively short period of time.

The French film industry has a particular status within Europe, in general owing to the level of state support it receives. As Patrick Messerlin and Isabelle Vanderschelden explain:

> Over the years, an increasingly complex support framework has emerged in France, in which grants and public subsidies coexist with tax incentives directed at private investors. Supported by state subsidies and partly sheltered from Hollywood hegemony, the French film industry has traditionally been regarded with envy by its European neighbours. (2018, 311)

While its infrastructures and methods of financing are complicated, the frameworks that have emerged over the past few decades have fostered and maintained one of European cinema's richest film industries. Additionally, Brigette Rollet notes that French cinema supports many first-time filmmakers with the aim of renewal, which 'partly explains the high percentage of films directed by women in France relative to other European and North American countries' (2015, 943). In stark contrast, the same cannot be said for the Scottish film industry. Granted, it is inaccurate to compare a small nation such as Scotland to a country the size of France, particularly when film outputs per annum are substantially different. However, if we consider Scottish cinema within the European tradition, it is worth highlighting the contrast. Yet Brexit has complicated this further, with Scotland dragged out of the European Union against its will. This also raises questions as to the contemporary 'European' cinema tradition, in that it moves Elssaeser's arguments into a new debate.

In essence, drawing attention to these completely different industries is fitting when comparing the approaches of Denis and Ramsay. While Denis had a certain degree of continuous support, Ramsay has only produced four narrative features in her career to date. There are a myriad of reasons behind this, but needless to say, Scotland's film industry is minimally supported by the state to foster and indeed finance a filmmaker as daring and poetic as Ramsay. Denis has, for the most part, continued to work and receive support in France; Ramsay has had to seek financing overseas from her native Scotland, crossing over into the US's independent cinema sector with both *We Need to Talk About Kevin* (2011) and *You Were Never Really Here*.

Denis and Ramsay share certain 'realist' sensibilities. This extends beyond their films simply being set in actual locations and settings (Djibouti, Glasgow, Paris, Oban). One of the strongest traditions associated with European cinema is the realist drama. Samantha Lay explains that within Western cinema, there is a dominant mode of realist representation, but 'whilst most Hollywood films, for example, can be regarded as realistic in setting, characterisation, situation . . . they are not necessarily realist texts' (2002, 7). Specifically, 'social realism', a permutation of post-Second World War Italian neo-realism, has found a permanent place within European cinema. Britain particularly fostered social realism after the Second World War; it combined documentary aesthetics with drama, incorporating sociocultural-political themes, predominately focusing on working-class characters. It was also known as the 'kitchen sink' drama, for example *Saturday Night and Sunday Morning* (Karel Reisz, 1960), that influenced future filmmakers, the figurehead being Ken Loach. Indeed, Loach's practices expanded the parameters of social realism, incorporating extensive improvisation, observational camerawork and regional dialects to provide as much 'authenticity' as possible. One continuing adjective that accompanies social realism – where the more miserable (and violent) the images are within these settings, the more 'truthful' they become – is 'gritty'. Loach, and indeed Denis and Ramsay, do not shy away from visualising the grimness of the abandoned working class; they also offer pockets of hope and positivity, predominately through humour. Undeniably, their characters are in dire situations, often in need of escape, but they balance this with moments – fleeting gestures, stillness, contentment – that demonstrate the multifaceted nature of the characters, and our connection with them. In essence, this is a cinema of humility and humanity.

Lay outlines specific caveats for the realist filmmaker, noting that the director 'must have intended to capture the experience of the actual event depicted [and] the film-maker has a specific argument or message to deliver about the social world and employs realist conventions to express this message or argument' (2002, 7). Of course, social realism is not exclusive to Britain alone. Denis's Belgian peers, Jean-Pierre and Luc Dardenne, are certainly filmmakers who have adopted a social realist approach to their work. Highlighting social realism also raises an interesting notion of Marxism through cinema. Certainly, as noted above, depictions of the working-class plight within capitalist societies would pique Marx's interest. However, as will be discussed below, both Denis and Ramsay only adopt aspects of social realism and elasticate its parameters further. Therefore, in a Marxist sense, their films could be considered social 'naturalism', which 'represents an approach to social reality that falls short of realism proper' (Wayne 2020, 168). For instance, Denis's splintering narrative in *Beau travail* – the final scene flashes back to a time where Galoup dances by himself, suggesting a possible dream sequence (such narrative devices are often discarded in social realism as they interfere with the authenticity of a linear story); Ramsay depicts a mouse tied to a balloon drifting off Earth toward the moon in *Ratcatcher*, adding an element of fantasy to the otherwise realist, or naturalist, film.

GOOD WORK: REPRESSED LONGING FOR COLLECTIVISM

Beau travail commences with a panning shot gliding along a wall featuring painted images of soldiers attacking (or can be read as invading) terrain, and stops on the Madagascan flag. On the soundtrack, 'Sous le soleil brûlant d'Afrique' ('Under the burning sun of Africa') plays, sung by FFL Music Band. As the shot cuts to the credits, revealing the cast, we are then taken to a disco. Turkish singer Tarkan's hit 'Şımarık' ('Kiss Kiss') blasts as the crowd dances and gyrates to the beat. The crowd features a few FFL officers who kiss along with the sounds of smacking lips from the song, a not-too-subtle indication of their intentions. Denis shoots the sequence in medium close-up, providing only snippets of the men's faces. The camera drifts in and out of focus when it lands on Sentain, who looks disheartened in his surroundings and stops dancing. From behind his dance partner appears Galoup, who awkwardly sways with the young woman before veering into stilted dance moves.

Both Sentain and Galoup are distinctive from their fellow officers in that they are not engrossed in the evening; they are two men separated by a different desire. Denis then cuts to the window of a train, a shot handheld as the desert dunes of Djibouti pass by. We then see observational shots of passengers as they stare out of the window. These opening sequences are documentary in their approach: Denis is observing these characters as a non-participant. This is representative in the lack of coverage and edits; Denis is capturing moments in time that would be of no consequence to many other filmmakers. However, here, they devise and establish the elliptical tone. Further, this notion is compounded in the first images of the officers proper. As an endurance test, many of them stand in the sun, arms raised. Denis starts by showing their silhouettes – illustrating the officers as a form of shadow puppets – before gliding across their exposed bodies. Some wear shirts, others feel the caress of the sun on their bare torsos. It is an intense gaze, as intense as Sentain's longing look in the disco. This is contrasted with shots of the ocean, where waves crash into one another. The image continues then in an overlay of a pen writing in a journal, an echo of Francis Ford Coppola's *Apocalypse Now* (1979) – another film that deconstructs the male soldier. We learn that what is unfolding are Galoup's memoirs and recollections of his time in Djibouti.

On a boat, we see young officers, captured in close-up. Denis depicts them in brief portraits, with only a short panning shot from one officer to Sentain. The shot lingers, keeping him in stasis, distilling his youth. His gaze fixated on something off screen. Denis then cuts to Galoup who watches over the men, his gaze just as intense. What follows is a training sequence that is reminiscent of Stanley Kubrick's *Full Metal Jacket* (1987). Denis, again utilising observational camerawork, attempts to keep up with the men as they climb over obstacles, all under the watchful eye of Galoup. Sentain, his naked torso baking in the sun, glares at Galoup (who returns an equally intense look) and enters a rivalry with his commander. He dives deep into a pit that Galoup overcame easily and similarly tackles it without much resistance. Denis captures this sequence with no dialogue, aside from the men's grunts. In fact, the first twenty minutes of the film features minimal to little dialogue aside from staccato sentences from Galoup's voiceover.

The crucial element Denis highlights throughout the film is Galoup's gaze and watchful eye. This is compounded during the first section when he announces 'I screwed up from a certain point of view. Viewpoints count.' We are placed very much in his perspective, though it is insinuated (by the dialogue's 'certain point of view') that Galoup may be an unreliable narrator and that his recollections are faulty at best. However, his overseeing of the training is telling in that he wants a unit that is willing to carry out his orders. And, certainly, as with other military forces, the FFL have an established hierarchy. Yet here, aside from Galoup barking orders at the trainees, as with General Sergeant Hartman (R. Lee Ermey) in *Full Metal Jacket*, the remainder of the film has little dialogue. Denis, again, focuses more on his gaze; the officers react as part of a team without the need for verbalisation from Galoup. Additionally, despite the notion of a unit, Galoup is always kept at a distance. This is depicted in the edit: all the young men are seen together, tackling the obstacles with Galoup ahead of them, separated. It maintains the FFL's hierarchy, the chain of command. Mikaela Sundberg's research on the FFL notes:

GOOD WORK OR EXPLOITATION?

More generally, in a greedy organization, interpersonal bonds among members should ideally be defined on the basis of their mutual affiliation with the organization, rather than as affectionate bonds between persons who could potentially interfere with the duties as a member. At the same time as alienation from other members would destroy solidarity, an interpersonally detached and impersonal form of cohesion among members is preferable. (2016, 10)

Galoup is alienated from his fellow officers and certainly impersonal. Throughout the film, he clashes with his subordinates, particularly Sentain; this is insinuated as a longing, repressed desire for the young officer, where 'homoeroticism intersects with colonial power, military violence, and hierarchies of race and gender' (Galt 2014, 99). As seen from the opening sequence, Galoup is awkward around women, and while there is a degree of discomfort in the presence of Sentain, there is an amount of ease in the company of men. Toward the end of the film, there is a confrontation between commander and subordinate. Denis frames this in an extreme wide shot, the men dwarfed by their surroundings.

Both are topless, sweat dripping from their torsos – the homoeroticism is palpable – as they begin circling one another. Denis films this confrontation like a Western duel, yet as they get closer, we are unsure if they will strike or kiss one another. The shot shifts from static wide shot to handheld close-up. The shakes of the camera embody the repressed feelings from Galoup rising to the surface. Cutting to Sentain's close-up, the camera wobbles less; he is now the stable force, the one in command. The scene also concludes Galoup's

Figure 2.1 Galoup's (Denis Lavant's) gaze as an unreliable narrator.

watchful eye. One can interpret Galoup's gaze upon the officers as viewing them as commodities. As Marx states, a commodity is 'in the first place, an object outside us, a thing that by its properties satisfies human wants of some sort or another' (1887, 27). In conjunction with Sundberg, viewing the FFL as an organisation does indicate that the soldiers are there to be exploited. Certainly, their bodies – continuously exposed throughout the film – are treated as labour machines. Galoup's watchful eyes studies and ensures that the men are developing as officers to be exploited later in combat and as an occupying force in Africa. However, as Sentain confronts Galoup, he demonstrates his unshackling of commodification. He is a man, not an object and Sentain's gaze replaces Galoup's. The previous hierarchy is disestablished, and this then leads into the final stages of the film.

As Galoup's tidies his affairs after being court martialled for his actions against Sentain, he is dismissed from the FFL. The final scenes of the film demonstrate Denis's social naturalism. We have been observers of a man coming to the end of his life by his own hand. Taking a gun, he shoots himself in the head. The film brilliantly cuts to Galoup in a disco, smartly dressed, smoking a cigarette. He dances by himself with only a mirror and his reflection as a partner. The dance song classic 'The Rhythm of the Night' by Corona blasts. Denis has commented on this final scene, stating:

> This scene was written in the script that he was going to the nightclub and seen dancing a goodbye to his life as a legionnaire: a dance to death. Then in the script after Marseille he was killing himself, you know . . . but I shot the dance scene in Djibouti before I shoot in Marseille and when we did it, I was so moved. And Denis was moved too, only one take, you know. I said, 'My God, how can I have that scene before, um, him in his bed, taking the gun to shoot himself.' It's not fair, it's better if the last scene comes before and I give this dance scene as his last dream or his last moment he remembers, you know. Something of . . . plenty of life. (Cousins 2011)

However, rather than demonstrating release, Galoup continues to restrain his moves, purposefully repressing his gestures after brief bursts of letting loose. Galoup is tied to his repression, yet when solitary (or alienated, to use Sandberg's word) from the FFL, there are pockets of at least contentment – to feel the rhythm of a life outside a hierarchy, or being a commodity himself.

FEAR OF INDIVIDUALISM

This notion of a unit (organisational or familial) is found throughout Denis's work. The story in *35 rhums* focuses on a small fragile family unit. Widower

GOOD WORK OR EXPLOITATION?

Lionel lives with his daughter Joséphine in a small flat in Paris. Though they are close, Lionel senses it is time for Joséphine, an anthropology student, to pursue her own life away from him. The sense of forthcoming separation spirals Lionel into a deep sense of introspection. The slight narrative of *35 rhums* is an intriguing companion piece to *Beau travail*, not least the similar themes of a man confronting who he is and what he wants in life. Further, Denis delves deeper into a person's relationship with their vocation. Both Galoup and Lionel are inexorably linked to their professions – FFL and train driver respectively – and the dread of losing or leaving their vocations produces further anxieties.

As a single parent, Lionel is the primary income provider and he has much dedication to his work. Denis constructs a cautionary tale through the character of René (Julieth Mars Toussaint), a colleague of Lionel. When René retires, he makes an enigmatic speech remarking that the end of his working life is a 'deliverance', as his now former co-workers watch with concern. More drinks are consumed, and Lionel is asked to drink the remaining sixteen shots of rum. When queried, Lionel claims that it is an old story and that he will not participate. Later, René adrift without employment ends his life, and Lionel discovers his body on the rail tracks. This is parallel to the similar demise of Galoup where without a job, an occupation in the strongest sense, there can be no meaning for existence. Those who emphasise employment as the primary value of their life and make little room for anything else eventually become despondent and lost. This notion haunts Lionel throughout the film, and while it can be argued that some measures are taken to fill the void in his life, such as the possibility of a romance with neighbour Gabrielle (Nicole Dogue), he still prioritises Joséphine (despite being an adult) and his job. Lionel, therefore, is a commodity within a system that will not offer more than a method of making a living to support a life that, now that his daughter is on the cusp of starting her life proper, is somewhat empty. In essence, Lionel represents Marx's notion of work/labour as an 'essential part of what it is to be human . . . Labour is production without which there would be no human progress, no human societies, and no culture' (Wayne 2003, 33). While the family unit (or collective) is, in a manner of speaking, being dismantled, the fear of individualism drives Lionel to find a purpose and more human connection. This can be read as resisting a neoliberal existence, where collectivism and connecting with one another are crucial parts of living.

Stylistically, *35 rhums* can, arguably, be considered closer to traditional social realism, though very loosely. While there are devastating moments throughout the film, such as René's demise, the film would not be considered 'gritty'. However, Denis does place an emphasis on the observational/documentary aesthetics where the camera is often at a distance, establishing a distillation of the fleeting moments, gestures and stillness of these characters. Denis captures this through numerous close-ups that, like *Beau travail*, present Lionel in stasis. Indeed, the film's opening images are the perspective of a train (a 'phantom ride'), which can be 'compared to cinema as a technology of modernity and vehicle of the mobile gaze [that] reinscribes the temporal and sensory experience of labour as fundamental to that system' (Galt 2014, 103). This notion of labour is constantly intertwined with Lionel. Immediately after these opening images, Denis cuts to Lionel smoking a cigarette, staring at trains passing. This demonstrates that even in his spare time, he cannot detach from his job. Later, after René has retired, he is seen in the driver booth of a train with Lionel as he works. René's unwillingness to let go of a vital part of his identity makes his suicide all the more tragic. Denis then challenges our expectations in the final scene. Lionel is ready to consume the 35 rhums after Joséphine is married. The ambiguous nature of this scene, whether he is drinking out of happiness or sorrow, compounds the themes of Lionel's fear of individualism, yet offers 'a recalibration of desire and affection' (Galt 2014, 106). Denis does not explicitly state whether Lionel will suffer the same fate as René, but his fleeting smile indicates the possibility of a positive future where he finds new connections. Indeed, Lionel's profession is in and of itself a perfect metaphor for connection: the rail as a network that brings people together.

Figure 2.2 Lionel (Alex Descas) smiles to himself about the prospect of new connections.

GOOD WORK OR EXPLOITATION?

SCOTLAND'S LOST SOULS: RAMSAY AND THE FAMILY UNIT

Comparatively, Ramsay's debut and second feature, *Ratcatcher* and *Morvern Callar*, share similar themes and visual aesthetics with Denis. *Ratcatcher*, set in a Glasgow council estate during the 1973 bin collectors' strike, depicts the adolescent experiences of James Gillespie as he navigates the destitute world he inhabits. The setting and *mise en scène* compound the abandonment of the working-class, and the squalor they are forced to inhabit. The visualisation – numerous bin bags stacked as high as hills, rubbish spilled across the streets – is dystopic. *Morvern Callar* depicts the title character adrift after the suicide of her boyfriend. Claiming his unpublished novel as her own, she uses the money her boyfriend left behind for his funeral to travel to Spain with her friend Lanna (Kathleen McDermott) to escape her lifeless small-town existence. In both films, Ramsay echoes the need for human connection as seen in *Beau travail* and *35 rhums*. Visually, Ramsay's films are more esoteric than those of Denis, in which everyday objects and images are not what they seem. In *Ratcatcher* the first images are of a net curtain that, in slow motion, twirls around an unseen figure until it becomes tightened. The curtain transforms into what appears to be a shroud when the film snaps from slow motion into reality. The figure tangling the curtain is a young teenage boy, Ryan Quinn (Thomas McTaggart), who is chastised by his mother, Jackie Quinn, for not getting ready to go out. Ryan and James meet and play together at a nearby canal. Ryan drowns and James does not notify or alarm anyone to what has

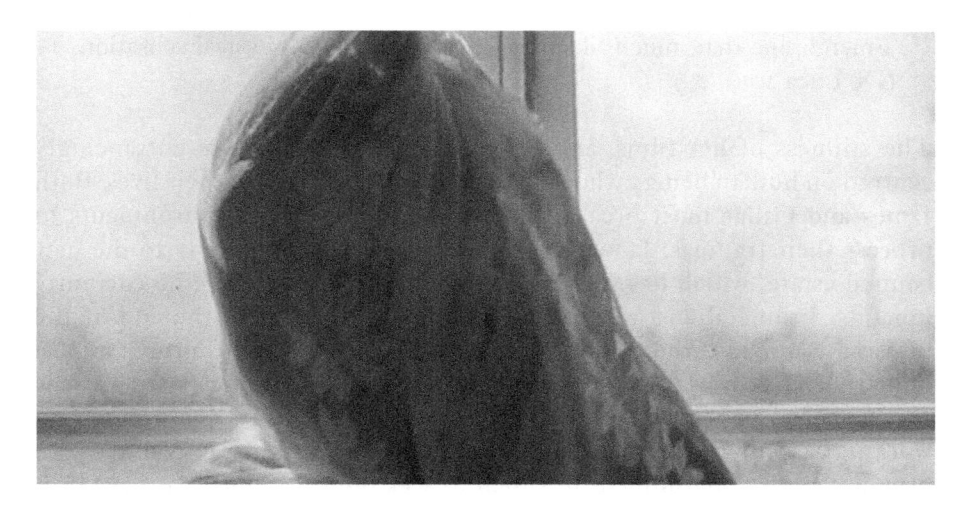

Figure 2.3   A death shroud in the opening of *Ratcatcher*.

45

happened (it is insinuated that he accidentally drowned Ryan while playing). What follows captures how James carries guilt (or lack of) from the incident as his family desperately want to be relocated to a new estate. In many ways, James shares many qualities with Galoup and Callar: all are outliers in their respective environments; all repress much of their emotions and desires. Ramsay crafts many images that place us in James's frame of mind. Many shots linger on the seemingly innocuous (such as a curtain that takes on new meaning as the film unfolds, which resembles a death shroud, as well as the boys' fishing nets).

Similarly, the opening scene of *Morvern Callar* also depicts a death, and the dismantling of a family unit. The off-screen suicide of Callar's boyfriend is eerily subverted when, in a state of shock (or relief – Ramsay keeps Callar's reaction ambiguous), she lies down next to him and begins caressing the lifeless body gently with her finger. The film, based on Alan Warner's 1995 novel, compounds the misery of Callar's existence, setting this early sequence on Christmas morning. While both *Ratcatcher* and *Morvern Callar* can be claimed as very much depicting 'gritty' situations, the films depart from social realism through Ramsay's trademark poetic visual style (Kuhn 2008, 13). Indeed, Ramsay's primary concern is capturing such gestures (the finger caress) in place of any larger set pieces or extravagant action. Like the work of Denis, Ramsay's work demands

> spectatorial attention . . . The screen, Ramsay reveals, is a transitory material – a two-way street – that invites interexchange between its visual matter and spectatorial bodies; her films meditate on the experience of cinema-watching as a visceral affair. These corporeal encounters between images and viewers render the screen into a kind of epidermis, a membrane that, much like human skin, mediates physical sensation. (De Luca 2019, 20)

The stillness of her films, and the characters depicted, are entrancingly centred on human beings who are at constant crossroads in their lives. Both James and Callar must break free from their respective environments to process their traumas. James longs to relocate with his family to the new council estate, which has higher quality houses than the one he currently inhabits. In one almost silent sequence, he takes a bus to the end of the line and wanders through the vacant new houses. Ramsay captures him in numerous close-ups, visualising his wonder and awe at the potential new surroundings in which he might live. Similarly, Callar's departure from working at a supermarket in a small Scottish town and her arrival in Spain provides a new environment in which to seek opportunities that have previously been unattainable. However, in comparison to James, whose father

(Tommy Flannagan) is unemployed (and implied drunk) and mother (Mandy Matthews), who works at an unspecified job, Callar's use of the funds left by her deceased boyfriend provides the escape from her drab existence. Later in the film, she has a meeting with representatives from the publisher she sent the manuscript to who offer her an £100,000 advance, which she accepts. The value of this stolen manuscript is misconstrued by Callar as a means of providing value in her life. This reveals that the 'substance of value is the capacity of labour power to produce social wealth; value is congealed in the products of human labour. Value is thus a very abstract concept' (Wayne 2003, 34). Value, by the film's conclusion, takes on various obscure meanings for the protagonist. Despite a revenue stream that will provide a path to social mobility, therefore a monetary value in her life, it brings her into conflict with Lanna, who wishes to remain in Scotland rather than leave with her friend. There is no growth or progression in Callar, as she remains 'both other and childlike' (Morace 2012, 118). Abandoning her working-class roots then leaves Callar as a solitary figure (what Lionel in *35 rhums* feared), without any connections beyond the publishers, which even then are merely commodifying her stolen manuscript. In effect, social mobility (attained through fraud) has made her a neoliberal ideal, profiting from other people's work for self-gain.

James, however, by the film's end is still stuck within his working-class means. Despite his father becoming a local hero for saving another young boy from drowning in the canal, the family are left in limbo, waiting to get approval for relocation to the new estate. Throughout the film, James becomes more desensitised to his reality. Ramsay captures this visually by specifically choosing close-ups of seemingly innocuous events where attention is placed on the 'tactile materiality of the domestic realm, with an emphasis on daily routines and the things that surround James and his family in their everyday lives' (Kendall 2010, 183). For instance, we see James toying with his mother's stocking as she sleeps, her toe protuding from the rip. Later, he plays with sugar spilled on the table, his finger making shapes. Ramsay takes pains to stretch time in these sequences, dragging them out for as long as possible, accounting for the mundanity that can cause a person to detach from reality. This is acute at the film's end. James, seemingly conceding to his living conditions (and therefore class status), plunges into the canal. Ramsay then cuts to a wide shot of a field where his family carry objects from their house to the new estate. The shot lingers and far behind them emerges James. Ramsay ends on a close-up of the boy's face as he smiles at the camera. As with Denis's ambiguous endings, Ramsay neither confirms or denies whether James is dead or this is a dream, which in many ways echoes *Beau travail*'s conclusion, with Galoup's last 'memory' of him freeing himself through solitary dancing.

CONCLUSION

This chapter has discussed Denis's work in the relation to class representation. Distilling these films within the auspices of European traditions (social realism) and class struggles, there are recurring themes and motifs throughout her work. In a comparison with Ramsay's films, it can be argued that both directors are interstitial with regards to categorisation. Neither operates within the bounds of either commercial or exclusively 'arthouse' cinema but both craft texts that occupy an interstitial space. Indeed, this is also depicted through their characters, who are often in a similar state of 'in-betweenness'. As has been argued above, Denis's characters are intertwined with their vocations: Galoup succumbs to despair by his dismissal from the FFL; Lionel fears a life of individualism and losing a job he prides himself in. Ramsay, perhaps stemming from her own upbringing, provides a 'still life' (Kendall 2010, 184) capturing of working-class life in both a period and a contemporary setting. *Ratcatcher*'s dystopic vision of a 1973 Glasgow estate establishes a terrain in which the adolescent protagonist wishes to leave, yet he and his family are denied an expedient avenue of escape through council relocation initiatives. This takes its toll on James and he becomes adrift within this reality. Callar manages to escape by committing fraud, and more concerningly, dismembering her boyfriend's dead body and burying him in the Scottish mountains, never to be found. By pursuing an escape from her circumstances, without confronting or acknowledging her trauma, Callar reshapes and recalibrates the values in her life. She is finally left with only her money and a life without friends or family. Perhaps Denis and Ramsay's cinema is one that articulates the complexities of living in fear and in contrast to neoliberal existence. *Beau travail*, *35 rhums*, *Ratcatcher* and *Morvern Callar* are all texts that display the problems of repression, individualism, abandonment and social mobility as a primary value in people's lives. Yet both filmmakers at least offer a sense of positivity, one fostered through continuous human connections and forming new collectives.

CITATIONS

Ancian, Aimé. 2002. 'Claire Denis: an interview.' In *Senses of Cinema*, last modified December 2002. https://www.sensesofcinema.com/2002/spotlight-claire-denis/denis_interview/.

Barrett, Kyle. 2022. 'Still shite being Scottish? *T2: Trainspotting* and the "Scottish European".' In *The Routledge Companion to European Cinema*, edited by Gábor Gergely and Susan Hayward, 26–35. Abingdon/New York: Routledge.

Beugnet, Martine and Jane Sillars. 2001. '*Beau travail*: time, space and myths of Identity.' In *Studies in French Cinema* 1, 3: 166–73: DOI: 10.1386/sfci.1.3.166.

Bíró, Yvette. 2009. 'A subtle story: *35 rhums*.' In *Film Quarterly* 63, 2: 38–43. DOI: 10.1525/FQ.2009.63.2.38.

Çağlayan, Emre. 2018. *The Poetics of Slow Cinema: Nostalgia, Absurdism, Boredom*. Cham: Palgrave Macmillan.
Cousins, Mark. 2011. *The Story of Film: An Odyssey*. Glasgow: Hopscotch Films.
De Luca, Raymond. 2019. 'Dermatology as screenology: the films of Lynne Ramsay.' *Film Criticism* 43, 1: 1–29. DOI: 10.3998/fc.13761232.0043.102.
Elsaesser, Thomas. 2005. *European Cinema: Face to Face with Hollywood*. Amsterdam: Amsterdam University Press.
Eyre, Hermione. 2010. 'Claire Denis on filmmaking and feminism.' In *Prospect*, last modified 21 June 2010. https://guides.unitec.ac.nz/chicagoreferencing/webpages.
Galt, Rosalind. 2014. 'Claire Denis and the World Cinema of Refusal.' In *SubStance* 43, no.1, Iss.133: *French Cinema and the Crises of Globalization*, 96–108. DOI: 10.1353/sub.2014.0009.
Harvey, David. 2007. 'Neoliberalism as creative destruction.' In *The Annals of the American Academy of Political and Social Science* 610, 1: 22–44. DOI: 10.1177/0002716206296780.
Kaklamanidou, Bettry and Ana Corbalán. 2019. 'Introduction: Contested terms, the European Union contribution, and a financial crisis.' In *Contemporary European Cinema Crisis Narratives and Narratives in Crisis*, edited by Betty Kaklamanidou and Ana Corbalán, 1–19. London/New York: Routledge.
Kendall, Tina. 2010. '"The in-between of things": Intermediality in *Ratcatcher*.' *New Review of Film and Television Studies* 8, no. 2: 179–97. DOI: 10.1080/17400301003700327.
Kuhn, Annette. 2008. *Ratcatcher*. Basingstoke: Palgrave Macmillan.
Lay, Samantha. 2002. *British to Social Realism: From Documentary to Brit Grit*. London: Wallflower.
Marx, Karl. 1887. *Capital: A Critique of Political Economy – Volume I Book One: The Process of Production of Capital*, translated by Samuel Moore and Edward Aveling, edited by Frederick Engels. Moscow: Progress Publishers.
Mayne, Judith. 2005. *Claire Denis*. Urbana/Chicago: University of Illinois Press.
McLaughlin, Janice, Mark E. Casey and Diane Richardson. 2006. 'Introduction at the Intersections of Feminist and Queer Debates.' In *Intersections Between Feminist and Queer Theory*, edited by Diane Richardson, Janice. McLaughlin and Mark E. Casey, 1–18. Basingstoke: Palgrave Macmillan.
Messerlin, Patrick and Isabelle Vanderschelden. 2018. 'France's protected and subsidised film industry: is the subsidy scheme living up to its promises?' In *Handbook of State Aid for Film Finance, Industries and Regulation*, edited by Patrick Murschetz, Roland Teichmann and Matthias Karmasin, 311–32. Cham: Springer.
Morace, Robert. 2012. 'The devolutionary Jekyll and post-devolutionary Hyde of the two *Morvern Callars*.' *Critique: Studies in Contemporary Fiction* 53, no.2: 115–23. DOI: 10.1080/00111619.2012.623475.
Morrey, Douglas. 2019. *The Legacy of the New Wave in French Cinema*. New York: Bloomsbury Academic.
Rollet, Brigitte. 2015. 'French women directors since the 1990s: trends, new developments, and challenges.' In *A Companion to Contemporary French Cinema*, edited by Alistair Fox, Michel Marie, Raphalle Moine and Hilary Radner, 941–86. Chichester: John Wiley.
Sundberg, Mikaela. 2016. *A Sociology of the Total Organization: Atomistic Unity in the French Foreign Legion*. London/New York: Routledge.
Wayne, Mike. 2003. *Marxism and Media Studies: Key Concepts and Contemporary Trends* London: Pluto Press.
Wayne, Mike. 2020. *Marxism Goes to the Movies*. Abingdon: Routledge.

CHAPTER 3

A Thing on a Friday Night: Objects and Desire in *Vendredi soir*

Helena Gurfinkel

On a Friday night in Paris, the protagonist of *Vendredi soir* (2002), Laure (Valérie Lemercier) is packing up her apartment to move in with her partner, François. She has trouble parting ways with her independence and her material possessions, which, in many cases, stand in for independence. Laure spends her last night of freedom with a stranger named Jean (Vincent Lindon). Like Denis's much later film, *Un beau soleil intérieur* (2017), *Vendredi soir* explores uninhibited expressions of female sexuality outside of a traditional committed relationship.[1] What is more interesting than the relatively banal plot of the last fling before settling down, however, is the way in which the film establishes a feminist hierarchy between material artefacts and men, in which the latter find themselves at the bottom. The very embodiment of solid domesticity, François winds up a disembodied voice on an answering machine and a note on a set of keys, thereby downgrading domesticity to the lowest level of priorities. The sensual Jean is an object of desire, discarded once, after a night of gastronomic and sexual satiation, Laure gains energy, mirth and a measure of control over her life. Whether or not Laure moves in with her partner, it will be a conscious choice, not one driven by convention.

The ending of Denis's earlier and perhaps most famous film, *Beau travail* (1999), is similarly ambiguous. The villainous protagonist, Galoup (Denis Lavant), a senior officer of the French Foreign Legion stationed in Djibouti, attempts to commit suicide, but, shortly after, is shown dancing alone with uncharacteristic abandon at the same Djibouti nightclub where the film starts. The solitary dance removes Galoup from the heteronormative context in which he and Laure are equally uncomfortable.

A THING ON A FRIDAY NIGHT

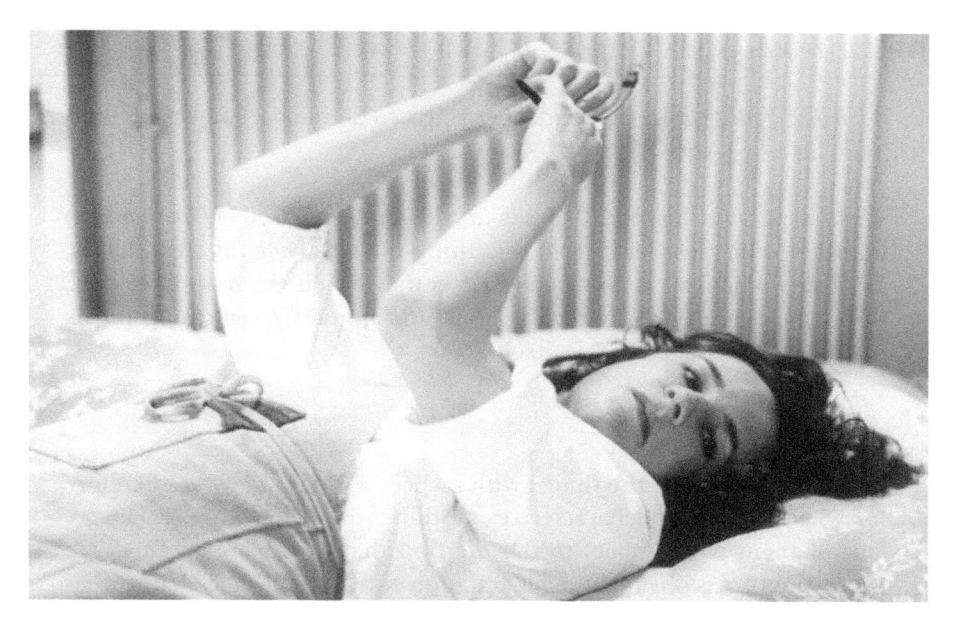

Figure 3.1   Laure at home. Credit: Photofest.

In the 2002 film, Jean remains fast asleep in a hotel room on Saturday morning. There is no dialogue between the lovers: Laure half-heartedly attempts to say goodbye, and Jean does not respond. Conversely, the significant objects that wake Laure from her initial morose acceptance of her romantic fate are everywhere. These include her old car, to which she talks lovingly, as if it were human; a sexy red skirt; the much focused-upon boxes of books, the prime indicators Laure's rich, albeit unspoken intellectual life; the two mirroring sets of keys and space heaters (in her apartment and in her and Jean's hotel room); dancing letters and a smiling pizza. The often whimsically filmed artefacts grant the protagonist her agency and become 'things'; men, however, remain mere objects, discarded after having served their purpose.

In the case of Galoup, the acknowledgement of his (homoerotic) desire, which remains illicit in the context of the rigid military environment, leads him in the opposite direction. He must transition from treating human bodies (specifically, those of Rahel, his African romantic partner, and Gilles Sentain, the legionnaire with whom he is obsessed) as objects to recognising them as 'things'. Using primarily Heidegger and Brown, this chapter will attempt to see the films through a feminist and queer thing theory lens. *Vendredi soir* is the central focus of this chapter, while *Beau travail* provides a contrasting queer male angle.

OF THINGS AND OBJECTS

In *What is a Thing?*, Martin Heidegger starts to define his subject (or object?) with the help of Kant:

> With respect to this, Kant speaks of 'the-thing-in-itself' (*Ding an sich*) in order to distinguish it from the 'thing-for-us' (*Ding für uns*), that is, as a 'phenomenon'. A thing-in-itself is that which is *not* approachable through experience as are rocks, plants, and animals. Every thing-for-us is a thing and also a thing-in-itself. (1967, 5).

He writes further:

> [W]e want to look at the things with respect to their *thingness*, therefore for what presumably characterizes all things and *each* thing. When we look at them with respect to this we find that things are singular ... Being singular is obviously a general, universally applicable characteristic (*Zug*) of all things. If we look closely, we even discover that these single things are just these (*je diese*) the door; the chalk, this now and here, not those of classroom six and not the ones from last semester. (1967, 18)

'This' as the descriptor of things, Heidegger further explains, is completely subjective:

> It is now clear: to go straight to the things cannot be carried out, not because we shall be stopped on the way but because those determinations at which we arrive and which we attribute to things themselves – space, time, and 'this' – present themselves as determinations which do not belong to the things themselves. (1967, 27)

What we discern here is the 'subjective' attributes ascribed to objects at our disposal. It is hard to arrive at the 'truth' of the thing, which is the truth only insofar as we can use and comprehend it (Heidegger 1967, 27). In relation to Denis's feminist cinematic reification of things and their truth, I would argue that the seemingly arbitrary material objects that Laure encounters or possesses acquire a singularity and uniqueness through their imaginative visual animation. The seemingly unique human beings, Jean and François, are 'reduced' to the status of things without a 'this'; they become disposable objects, for which the female protagonist has limited and temporary use. The process proceeds in the opposite direction for Galoup, Rahel and Sentain. The seemingly disposable younger woman and man rise to the dignity of things to which the specific 'this' can be attached.

Bill Brown, working through Heidegger's definition of the 'Thing' in *What Is a Thing?* and especially in *Being and Time*, argues that a Thing 'really names less an object than a particular subject–object relation' (2004, 4). In other words, for Brown, a Thing is a completely subjective 'threshold between nameable and unnameable' (2004, 5). Indeed, when it comes to material objects, specifically tools of labour, *Being and Time* establishes a relationship between Being and Thing based on perception and interaction, rather than on stand-alone qualities of a Thing:

> The ready-to-hand is not grasped theoretically at all, nor is it itself the sort of thing that circumspection takes proximity as a circumspective theme. The peculiarity of what is proximally ready to hand is that, in a readiness to hand, it must, as it were, withdraw . . . in order to be ready-to-hand quite authentically. That with which our everyday dealings proximally dwell is not the tools themselves . . . On the contrary, that with which we concern ourselves primarily in the work – that which is to be produced all the time; and this is accordingly ready-to-hand too. The work bears with it that referential totality within which the equipment is encountered. (2008, 99)

Heidegger deemphasises 'circumspection' and, instead, stresses the 'referential', interactive totality that constitutes the reality of the Being–tool interaction, a tool being, of course, only one example of a material object available to a Being.

Graham Harman likewise interprets the Heideggerian Thing as subjective, with the subjectivity emerging in a relational space between it and a human (2007, 64). Of everyday tools, on which Heidegger dwells in *Being and Time*, Harman writes, 'We do not think of them as random things of plastic and metal, but either ask an expert to explain them, or turn away in boredom and despair' (2007, 64). Susanne Kűchler objects to the notion that '[t]hings are allowed back into the analysis of culture, but only as long as they serve as target for a mind eager to project itself onto mirrorlike surfaces' (2005, 207). Things reflect the human face back to itself. The household and street objects on which Denis's film focuses intently, enter precisely the kind of subject–object relation with Laure that makes a Thing out of an object, whereas the men, who are disembodied or discarded, are reduced to the status of an object. Conversely, in Galoup's relationship to the Other's body, whether that of a colonised woman or a younger, subordinate man, this body must rise to the status of the Thing, instead of being reduced to the object. Leaving the French Legion, with its attendant ideologies of colonialism and homophobia, like Laure's (temporary?) abandonment of patriarchy, makes the transition possible.

The idea of an object, or objectification, bears, obviously, an important relation to feminist theory. According to Katherine Behar (2016), OOF (Object-oriented Feminism) not only questions the perennial oppressive objectification of women, but also dislodges the white male Enlightenment-based concept of the subject and makes space for a non-anthropocentric universe of objects, without sacrificing female interiority. Though Behar does not always agree with Ian Bogost, her words resonate with his assertion that 'humans and the world are inextricably tied together, the one never existing without the other' (2012, 4). In the case of OOF, women's link to the material world takes precedence. I argue that Denis's attention to the universe of the non-human object, concurrent with the effort to empty out and render insignificant human male subjectivities, exemplifies a uniquely feminist approach to cinematography and characterisation. Brown asks, 'What are the rhetorical strategies by which fiction works to convince us not just of the visual and tactile physicality of the world that it depicts but also of that world's significance?' (2003, 14). The same question can be asked of film, and Denis's playful visual rhetoric of animating inanimate objects into things; Laure's verbal communication with them, as well as the disembodied/insignificant patriarchal presence constitute a feminist answer to Brown's question, which is congruent with Behar's definition of OOF.

We also observe the connection between the sparse dialogue in *Vendredi soir*, and the protagonist's peculiar propensity to speak to things and be largely silent with men. Lorraine Daston distinguishes between talking and silent things: 'Talkative things instantiate novel, previously unthinkable combinations. Their thingness lends vivacity and reality to new constellations of experience that break the old molds' (2004, 24). While things themselves do not 'talk' to Laure (though some of them flash neon and 'make faces'), she talks to them. The things that invite conversation, whether one-sided or not, have a vital role in encouraging Laure's agency and decision-making, while the 'human males' do not have any meaningful communication with her. In the emotionally reserved, or stunted, homosocial/homoerotic world of *Beau travail*, intersubjective/objective conversation is minimal; it is self-reflection conveyed by an internal monologue and diary writing, as well as the kinetic power of dance, that help Galoup break free.

OF THINGS AND BODIES

Several critics have noted that *Vendredi soir* starts with panoramic, greeting-card-like views of Paris, both during the day and at night-time, thus making the city a character in the film, and its protagonist a sexually uninhibited *flâneuse*.[2] The potential of becoming a Parisian *flâneuse* makes Laure a feminist riff on Baudelaire's iconic francophone cultural figure. But the City of

Lights is not necessarily the focal point here. Before seeing Paris, we take note of mundane objects that fill Laure's soon-to-be-former single person's domicile. The camera zooms in on boxes that are, in turn, filled with more objects, namely books. We see at least two boxes of *livres*; one of them additionally includes documents ('*docs*'). Later, while stuck in traffic, Laure rescues three more books from a box of possessions slated for donation. One of them is a book of poetry, while the other two visibly older books, illustrated with what looks like medieval tapestries, appear to be academic titles or textbooks. These books suggest that Laure has lived an intellectually engaged life and is likely highly educated. The protagonist's intellect becomes apparent to us not through (mostly absent) dialogue or (barely there) plot, but, instead, through objects to which we must pay careful attention in order not to miss this important part of her characterisation.

Laure's insinuated intelligence and education make her transition into conventional heteronormative and reproductive domesticity – represented hilariously by her friends Bernard and Marie and their baby, as well as, eerily, by the absent François – even more jarring and difficult. Significantly, she makes the decision to keep the books, and thus part of her intellectual or professional identity, under the watchful eyes of two women from a car nearby: a grey-haired woman of about sixty and a red-headed girl of about fifteen. Denis the feminist replaces the male gaze with the watchful gaze of women, reminding Laure of the passage of time and the importance of retaining a measure of control over her life. This female homosocial communication symbolises Denis's commitment to intellectual collaborations between women. The director has made films loosely based on works by male authors: for example, Roland Barthes's philosophical work *A Lover's Discourse: Fragments* (1977) serves as the foundation of *Un beau soleil intérieur* (*Let the Sunshine In*) (2017),[3] while *Beau travail* (1999) is a rather loose adaptation of Herman Melville's 1891 novella *Billy Budd*. The script of *Vendredi soir* was co-written by Denis and Emmanuèle Bernheim and sticks closely to the eponymous novel. In other words, just as Laure's small-scale intellectual awakening is prompted by the female gaze, the director's larger-scale collaboration emphasises the importance of female creativity.

In addition to women's eyes, on at least two occasions, Laure is watched by blinking neon signs that are shaped like glasses and apparently used to advertise an optician's office. The film undoes the (male) gaze in two ways: it grants women the ability to look, as well as turning the gaze into a parodic object, one more example of men reduced to the status of objects. Bookish Laure is a modest dresser, with barely visible make-up and hair that she washes and absent-mindedly blow-dries in her car. Her plain appearance, clearly not calculated to please the male gaze, distinguishes her not only from the thoroughly domesticated Marie, but also from the two women subtly competing for Jean's attention, when he suddenly appears, looking for a ride, a casual companion or both. One of them is an attractive, overtly feminine blonde woman, visibly younger than Laure, who smiles dreamily and puts lipstick on, hoping that Jean will join her in her car. The other is an even younger woman, possibly in her late teens, with a stylish pixie haircut and nipples provocatively showing through a t-shirt, who plays a foosball machine at the fateful 'Le Rallye' café, and whom Jean nearly picks up when the suddenly jealous Laure decides to rejoin him. She instantly makes a choice to pursue Jean, instead of letting him choose which woman to objectify for the night.

Our intellectual, somewhat dowdy and gaze-resistant heroine, then, is set to make a transition into a life of monogamous coupledom, and Denis makes this transition complicated. Laure has a difficult time relinquishing her agency; more precisely, she retains her agency by noticing and respecting several material objects ('things' in the Heideggerian sense) that come whimsically to life, and by treating men as disposable or invisible objects. Back in the apartment, in the early 'packing' sequences, Laure has a thought-provoking moment of asserting her sexuality through a Being–Thing interaction. She decides to keep a bright red skirt that hugs her hips and has a long slit revealing almost her entire leg provocatively. She puts the skirt on, and tells it, 'I will keep you'. At that moment, Laure wears a simple white dress and an eggshell-coloured apron, indicating impending domestication. The red skirt clashes with the 'homemaker' outfit and represents the conflict inside the protagonist. Speaking to the skirt, animating it, and retaining the memory of carefree single sexuality is at least as significant as the tryst with Jean. In fact, I would argue that having sex and sharing a meal with Jean for a night is a less bold move when it comes to Laure's sexual autonomy.

She barely converses with Jean and reduces him to a sexual fantasy that fades in and out, as well as to objects (that is to say, he is akin to, or even beneath, a smiling pizza, or a ten-franc condom from a machine). She leaves him sleeping (or pretending to) in a tawdry hotel room on Saturday morning. While Elizabeth Newton (2008), Noëlle Rouxel-Cubberly (2014) and Kiva Reardon (2017) note Denis's conspicuous focus on materiality and corporeality in *Vendredi soir*, they do so mainly in relation to the human body. My analysis seeks to emphasise the predominance of object things. In that regard, it is akin to Troy's (2020) brilliant Heideggerian reading of the human–thing relationships in Denis *35 rhums*,[4] except that Troy focuses on race and diasporic belonging, while I concentrate on gender and sexuality.

During her adventure, Laure speaks to, and animates, several physical artefacts that belong to her and uphold her identity. When a man in a nearby car, also stuck in traffic, tells her that she is 'crazy' to ask fifteen thousand francs for her car (which has a 'for sale' sign on a window), Laure whispers, 'Poor little

A THING ON A FRIDAY NIGHT

car', and gently cleans up the space near the glove compartment. In a film set during a public transportation strike in Paris (that had actually happened some seven years earlier), cars become part of one's identity, mobility and safety. While two men caught in an accident, observed by Jean and Laure, fight almost to the death because of damage done to their cars, Laure indicates the importance of her car to her selfhood, safety and independence by talking to it. She banishes Jean from it when she feels that his control of it becomes excessive. The aforementioned scholarly books also belong in the space of a car, and she gives the tomes a verbal promise to keep them.

Meanwhile, Jean, a handsome stranger to whom Laure gives a ride, admonished by a radio announcer reporting on the strike, barely converses with Laure. Lindon plays the 'strong silent type' (almost a parody of it) to perfection, sending us back to the 1950s cinema (a young Jean Gabin or a Kirk Douglas, the audience can take its pick). He drives expertly, does not speak much, eats heartily, smokes heavily, pays for dinner and the hotel room and makes love with phallocentric confidence. Yet from the outset, he signals his status as an object. When Laure asks where she can take him, he says that she can 'leave [him] anywhere [she] wants'. The broad hint of his disposability emerges early on. He only offers his generic name, Jean, after Laure introduces herself. The camera subtly objectifies Jean by treating us to two sideways shots of his naked body. We do not see his penis, but, in a visual synecdoche, he is reduced to it when

Figure 3.2 Meeting Jean. Credit: Photofest.

57

he buys condoms from a machine in a café. Laure sees the machine when she makes a phone call and notices the delightful, if on-the-nose, instruction 'push all the way in' on it. The visual and verbal puns establish their relationship as sexual, and Jean as the phallic (but not dominant) object in it. In the hotel room, Laure lays out Jean's watch, a wrapped condom and a pack of cigarettes on a bedside table. These objects paint a picture of the physicality and limited temporality of the relationship, as well as replacing the man with a synecdochic trio of objects, marking the passing of time and timed transgressions.

During the post-coital meal at a nearby Italian restaurant, Jean's object-hood manifests itself in two ways. First, while sitting across the table from him, Laure fantasises about Jean without saying a word to him. The camera fades into her imaginings of Jean making out, first with herself and then with another female customer in the restaurant bathroom. The shot holds in it both the 'real' Jean and the fade into the fantasy, thereby reducing the importance of Jean to Laure. There is no hint of emotion or possessiveness. Laure barely murmurs a response to Jean's question whether she is thinking about him. It does not help matters that the woman in the bathroom is part of another simultaneously sad and comical representation of committed coupledom: freezing and exhausted from walking through the paralysed city, the husband and wife fight and refuse food, while the casual lovers, Laure and Jean, experience fleeting but uninhibited and peaceful pleasure.

Both Laure and Jean order a Neapolitan pizza. When the two pies appear, one of them whimsically imitates a smirk and a lifted eyebrow on Jean's face. The meal and the man acquire an equal status of a tasty material object to be consumed to sate passing hunger. In the morning, Laure calls Jean by his name, perhaps to say goodbye, but he is asleep and she leaves him in the room, like an object, without much emotion or regret. She utters nothing like 'I will keep you', previously addressed to inanimate objects.

If Jean's body acquires the kind of materiality that Laure desires on what is presumably the last night of her single life, the man who forecloses her access to singlehood and freedom, her partner, François, does not appear on screen. The first object that represents him is a gaudy sparkly heart-shaped keychain, to which a note is attached: 'François, our place, tomorrow.' The sheer tastelessness of the keychain, which does not reflect Laure's unpretentious aesthetic as we have seen it so far, is an ironic, tacky representation of monogamous bliss. The necessity of a note, reminding Laure of such an important change of life, hints at a certain reluctance, or hesitation, with which she makes the move. After calling François, Laure repeats 'Chez nous' (a phrase that also appears on the piece of paper, as if trying to remind or convince herself of the necessity of the move).

François appears next as a disembodied voice on an answering machine, as Claire calls to update him of her plans to have dinner with friends, just before she cancels the dinner and spends the night with Jean. While, as a plot point, it is somewhat strange for François to be unavailable to answer the phone on a momentous evening, philosophically it makes sense that this stand-in for traditional patriarchy has less embodiment and agency than a casual lover, a book or a skirt. Both central male characters, then, bear generic first names and are truly disposable, as Laure decides on Saturday morning. The decision itself, I would argue, remains equivocal. The ending of *Vendredi soir* is a signature Denis masterwork of ambiguity. Laure is suspended between sexual freedom and domesticity. Having abandoned Jean in a hotel room, Laure skips along an empty early-morning street, smiling. The smile is mysterious. It is not clear, to me in any event, whether Laure, having had her last fling, is ready to meet her movers and merge her life with her partner's, or whether she has made the decision to rid herself of the cumbersome thought (and action) of being in a monogamous live-in relationship. No matter the interpretation, however (and the former appears to be more common), the two men, placed below, or on the same level as, a pizza pie, a condom, an ugly keychain and a voicemail recording, have had little or nothing to do with the decision.

The film represents the domestic space itself as precarious, using pairings of household objects and spaces. When leaving the apartment for the evening, Laure keeps a space heater on; shortly beforehand, she packs a lamp and a lampshade that will go to her and François's apartment. Jean and Laure briefly make the inside of her car their pseudo-domestic refuge. As they settle into the hotel room, a virtually identical space heater remains on for most of their one-night stand. As one of Denis's more whimsical directorial decisions, a lampshade flies onto the hotel lamp and has the lamp light go on by itself, not only duplicating the lamp and lampshade at home, but also, literally, shedding light onto Jean, casually lying down and smoking on a well-worn red bedspread. The film draws visual, material parallels between the solid and domestic and the casual and ephemeral, thus undoing the moral and aesthetic superiority of the former over the latter. In her ninety-minute feminist meditation on female sexual, social and intellectual agency, Denis privileges objects over human characters and makes a uniquely material(ist) statement about a woman's quest for fulfilment and independence. The unabashed visual fancy that animates and empowers the things is also an artistic statement against the conventional plot structure and characterisation.

The ending of *Vendredi soir* is not Denis's best known. The honour belongs to *Beau travail*, a ninety-minute visual poem about a group of soldiers and two commanders: the Commandant, Bruno Forestier (Michel Subor), and Adjudant-Chef Galoup. Both senior commanders pay especially close attention to a recent recruit, the twenty-two-year-old orphan Gilles Sentain (Grégoir Colin). The mysterious Forestier holds secrets from the time of the Algerian War (is it his sexuality, or his connection to the Soviet bloc? A little noticed detail of Forestier's characterisation is his fluent Russian, shown in a conversation with a Russian legionnaire). Galoup is inwardly seething, quiet, disciplined and involved in a torturous triangle: Forestier is affectionate towards the good-looking, courageous and popular Sentain; Galoup strives to earn the Commandant's approval and is consumed by his intermingling feelings of desire and envy for the young, brave Billy Budd-like foundling.

No less tortuous is the heterosexuality of the Legion's outpost in Djibouti. The film begins in a nightclub in which soldiers dance, and presumably form sexual relationships with, local women. Christine Brinckmann (2014) notes the feminist aesthetic of the film: the women in the night club freely objectify and express attraction for the (mostly white) French soldiers. The frequently seminude bodies of the young legionnaires receive loving treatment from the female filmmakers. Rahel (Loula Ali Lotta), a young local woman, is in a presumably consensual casual relationship with Galoup. While all of it is true, heterosexual desire, insofar as it is attended by economic inequality and the quasi-colonial presence of the French soldiers, is forced and uncomfortable. Forestier awkwardly refuses the services of a female sex worker ('a coloured girl'); neither Sentain, nor any other young soldiers for that matter, ever appears on screen coupled up with a woman, let alone in an explicit sex scene. Galoup is the only male character appearing in a post-coital sequence. His relationship with Rahel

Figure 3.3 Galoup's masculinity. Credit: Photofest.

is an example of a forced objectification. In general, the film links local women to objects. We witness a casual but detailed conversation about the quality, symbolism and price of multi-coloured prayer mats between two women in a store: one younger (the maker of the mats), and the other middle-aged (the customer). The conversation, seemingly incidental to the plot, demonstrates the link between (African) femininity and quotidian material objects. The way in which the women interact with the material object is agentic: they participate in producing, buying and selling the mat, as well as in placing it in the sociocultural and religious context of their country.

The French soldier–material object–African woman triangulation that Denis's film limns next is quite different. Of particular interest are two objects on which Galoup focuses his attention, and which are more important to him, at least initially, than the subordinate human beings, Rahel and Sentain, with whom they are interchangeable. To perform the final liberating dance, Galoup needs to leave the system that downgrades abject human bodies to the status of objects. This is a departure from the interpretations of the film, such as Grant's (2004), or Dooley's (2013), which valorise the female and homoerotic gaze as counter-objectifying and, therefore, subversive forces. In a sequence in the middle of the film, Galoup tries to buy a small bottle of perfume for Rahel from a street vendor. He holds and inspects it for a long time, strangely hesitant to purchase a small and clearly inexpensive object. Having turned it over in his hands a few times, the officer buys the perfume. We subsequently see him and Rahel, after sex, completely alienated from one another by this calculated encounter, which may give the woman some financial assistance in exchange for shoring up the man's heteronormativity.

A shot of Rahel's swivelling dancing head, in a dance club neon spotlight, fades into Galoup, smoking with his back to the camera. The separation of the woman's body from her head dehumanises her, while the man's inability to meet the camera's gaze alienates him. After sex, Galoup puts the perfume bottle in the lifeless hand of Rahel, who is silent and, apparently, half-asleep with a grin on her face. Like Lindon's Jean on Saturday morning, she seeks to avoid the emotionally untenable (and, in her case, possibly physically awkward) encounter. Galoup claims to 'beg for a word [. . .] . . . a gesture'. He calls for Rahel ('ma douce, ma douce'), as an incantation of sorts, and receives no response. It is as if he attempts to convince himself of the authenticity of heteronormative enjoyment for both parties. The repetition makes the enjoyment itself feel traumatic (it is reminiscent of Laure's reluctant, and recurring, 'chez nous', describing her and François's future home). The effort to push the perfume vial into Rahel's lifeless hand, as well as her lack of agency in the scene, makes her effectively equal in value to the bottle of perfume: exotic, necessary, ostensibly appropriate. In Heideggerian terms, this lack of meaningful interaction between the two downgrades Rahel to the status of the object. The Eurocentric patriarchal structures, which eventually drive Galoup to commit a crime and attempt suicide, both treat women in this way and, by their sheer phallocentric force, entrap the officer in the heteronormative setting of the bedroom.

We see Rahel's subtle and clear-eyed view of the relationship, when she discusses her 'boyfriend' with an older woman. Although she claims that the affair is going well, Rahel tells her friend that he 'make[s] [her] laugh', implying that the relationship is in no way meaningful. Galoup's heterosexuality is so precarious as to be laughable (an interpretation supported by Rahel's constant smile, which hardly results from enjoyment). It requires props, human and inanimate. Viewed from a different angle, however, Rahel's vitiation of the relationship through laughter begins to unshackle both herself and Galoup. Female homosocial cross-generational bonding depicted in the scene harkens back to the two women's conversation about a mat, as well as foreshadowing Laure's empowering encounter with women stuck in traffic.

Denis's and Godard's feminist camera also focuses on the desirable and seemingly submissive male body of Gilles Sentain. The young and charming soldier causes a storm of emotions in Galoup and invites Forestier's quietly eroticised appreciation. Attached to the mysterious commander and jealous of the fellow legionnaires' admiration of the younger man, Galoup takes revenge, using a material object that, initially, comes to symbolise, or be identified with, Sentain, in the same way as the perfume vial is identified with Rahel.

The officer first provokes Sentain's act of insubordination in defence of a fellow soldier (another Black body devalued by Galoup, albeit in a non-erotic manner) and then gives him an old rusty broken compass, using which the banished Sentain travels in the wrong direction and almost dies in a salt plain. A local family saves his life and moves his body to safety; Forestier quietly discharges Galoup, instead of subjecting him to a steeper punishment. The compass (Galoup's broken moral compass) functions to cover up, or kill, the illicit desire for a male body. To attempt a difficult combination of Heidegger and Wilde, the object 'kills the thing [Galoup] loves'. The former officer returns to France and shows contrition. In an austere and solitary room in Marseilles, he attempts suicide; however, we do not see his corpse. The film's ending has invited much speculation. Does Galoup punish himself for untenable desires? Does he regret nearly killing Sentain? Are both versions equally plausible?

In the film's poetic and ambiguous concluding sequence, reflecting either a post-mortem fantasy or the film's diegetic 'reality', dressed in black civilian clothes, Galoup performs a wild dance. He returns to Djibouti but, presumably, as a private citizen, untethered from the rigid codes and quotidian drabness of the French Legion. He is alone on the dance floor, unencumbered by male 'competition', or possibly unwelcome female desire. The tacky early-1990s club hit 'The Rhythm of the Night' by the Italian pop outfit Corona inexplicably serves as the musical backdrop to the dance: perhaps, the 'rhythm of my life' lyric signals the character's ability to live his life on his own terms.

Matt Mazur (2010) underscores Galoup's queerness throughout the film. In concert with his reading, and given the literary basis of the film, Melville's *Billy Budd*, the interpretation of liberated homoeroticism sheds light on the film's ending. Both the joyfully leaping Laure and the fitfully dancing Galoup have set their desires free and changed their relationships to human flesh. While Laure engages intensely with material objects instead of male bodies, Galoup, in his sexually uninhibited performance, acknowledges the importance of the desired and desiring body, while repenting the attachment to the material weapon of attempted murder. Simultaneously, the ideology of the subjection and objectification of the female body of colour in the name of Eurocentrism and heteronormative appearance leaves his life and body, as he moves alone in a club previously occupied by forces representative of this ideology. Both equivocal endings hold a promise of freedom through a changing relationship with objects.

NOTES

1. Like Laure, the protagonist of the 2017 film, the artist Isabella (Juliette Binoche) pursues relationships with married men and expresses her sexuality freely.
2. See Hardwick (2010) and Archer (2008), for a detailed analysis of Laure as a *flâneuse*, as well as the relative insignificance of male characters. Unlike mine, Hardwick's and Archer's respective readings do not focus on material objects. Beugnet also emphasises the special status of the cityscape 'reciprocating Laure's gaze' (2008, 221). Likewise, Mayne's (2005) seminal comparative analysis of *Trouble Every Day* and *Vendredi soir* includes a discussion of the special significance of the depiction of Paris. My goal is to shift the focus to smaller, ostensibly less significant objects and locations.
3. For this script, Denis also had a woman co-writer, Christine Angot. *Beau travail* is also a collaboration between Denis and her long-time camerawoman, Agnès Godard. See Brinckmann (2014) and Smith (2018).
4. In Troy's interpretation of Denis's film, material things (again, in the Heideggerian sense) signify African immigrants' attempts to forge communities, family ties and belonging in France.

CITATIONS

Archer, Neil. 2008. 'Sex, the City, and the Cinematic: The Possibilities of Female Spectatorship in Claire Denis's *Vendredi soir*.' *French Forum* 33, 1–2 (Winter/Spring): 245–60.
Barthes, Roland. 1977. *A Lover's Discourse: Fragments*, translated by Richard Howard. New York, NY: Hill and Wang.
Behar, Katherine. 2016. 'An Introduction to OOF.' In *Object-oriented Feminism*, 1–36. Edited by Katherine Behar. St Paul, Minneapolis: University of Minnesota Press.
Bernheim, Emmanuèle. 1998. *Vendredi soir*. Paris: Gallimard.
Beugnet, Martine. 2008. 'Re-enchanting the World: Pascale Ferran's *Lady Chatterley* (2007) and Claire Denis's *Vendredi soir* (2004).' *Australian Journal of French Studies* 45, 3: 212–24.
Bogost, Ian. 2012. *Alien Phenomenology, or What It's Like to Be a Thing*. St. Paul, Minneapolis: University of Minnesota Press.

Brinckmann, Christine. 2014. *Color and Empathy: Essays on Two Aspects of Film*. Amsterdam: Amsterdam University Press.
Brown, Bill. 2003. *A Sense of Things: The Object Matter of American Literature*. Chicago: University of Chicago Press.
Brown, Bill. 2004. 'Thing Theory.' In *Things*, edited by Bill Brown, 1–19. Chicago: University of Chicago Press.
Corona. 1993. 'The Rhythm of the Night.' *The Rhythm of the Night*. DWA/ZYX/WEA.
Daston, Lorraine. 2004. 'Preface: Things That Talk.' In *Things That Talk: Object Lessons from Art and Science*, edited by Lorraine Daston, 7–24. New York, NY: Zone Books.
Denis, Claire, dir. *Beau travail*. 1999. New York, NY: The Criterion Collection, 2020. DVD.
Denis, Claire, dir. *Vendredi soir*. 2002; New York, NY: Arena Films, 2002. VHS.
Denis, Claire, dir. *Let the Sunshine In*. 2017. New York, NY: The Criterion Collection, 2019. DVD.
Dooley, Kath. 2013. 'Foreign Bodies, Community and Trauma in the Films of Claire Denis: *Beau travail* (1999), *35 rhums* (2008) and *White Material* (2009).' *Screening the Past*, accessed 11 April 2022. http://www.screeningthepast.com/issue-37-aesthetic-issues-in-world-cinema/foreign-bodies-community-and-trauma-in-the-films-of-claire-denis/.
Grant, Ben. 2004. 'On the Margins of *Beau travail*.' *Journal of European Studies* 34, 1/2: 60–81.
Hardwick, Joel. 2010. 'Transports Privés: *Vendredi soir* and the Mobile Urban Woman in French Cinema.' *French Cultural Studies* 21, 3: 192–201.
Harman, Graham. 2007. *Heidegger Explained: From Phenomenon to Thing*. Chicago, LaSalle, IL: Open Court Press.
Heidegger, Martin. 1967. *What Is a Thing?* Translated by W. B. Barton Jr. and Vera Deutsch. Analysis by Eugene T. Gendlin. South Bend, IN: Gateway Editions, Ltd.
Heidegger, Martin. 2008. *Being and Time*. Translated by John Macquarrie and Edward Robinson. Foreword by Taylor Carman. New York: Harper Perennial.
Kůchler, Susanne. 2005. 'Materiality and Cognition: The Changing Face of Things.' In *Materiality*, 206–30. Edited by Daniel Miller. Durham, NC: Duke University Press.
Mayne, Judith. 2005. *Claire Denis*. Champaign, IL: University of Illinois Press.
Mazur, Matt. 2010. 'Control: An In-depth Look at Claire Denis's *Beau travail*.' *ICS: International Cinephile Society*, 4 November, accessed 11 April 2022, https://icsfilm.org/reviews/control-an-in-depth-look-at-claire-denis-beau-travail/.
Melville, Herman. 2017. *Billy Budd, Sailor*. Mineola, NY: Dover, 2017.
Newton, Elizabeth. 2008. 'The Phenomenology of Desire: Claire Denis's *Vendredi soir* (2002).' *Studies in French Cinema* 8, 1: 17–28.
Reardon, Kiva. 2017. 'Discourses of Desire in Claire Denis's *Vendredi soir*.' *Cléo: A Journal of Film and Feminism*, 19 December, accessed 3 September 2021. https://cleojournal.com/2017/12/19/discourses-of-desire-in-claire-denis-vendredi-soir/.
Rouxel-Cubberly, Noëlle. 2014. 'Delivering: Claire Denis's Opening Sequences.' In *The Films of Claire Denis: Intimacy on the Border*, 163–74. Edited by Marjorie Vecchio. New York, London: I. B. Taurus.
Smith, Imogen Sara. 2018. 'Beautiful Work: The Female Gaze in *Beau travail*, *La France*, and *The Romance of Astrea and Celadon*.' *Film Comment*, 24 July, accessed 10 April 2022, https://www.filmcomment.com/blog/beautiful-work-female-gaze-beau-travail-la-france-romance-astrea-celadon/.
Troy, Eddy. 2020. 'Intersubjectivity and the Cinematic Thing: Diasporic Being-with in Claire Denis's *35 rhums*.' *Studies in European Cinema*, ahead-of-print, 1–16, accessed 14 September 2021. DOI: 10.1080/17411548.2020.1848095.

CHAPTER 4

'A lover's hand? A breath, An abyss': Aloneness in Claire Denis

Peter Sloane

Despite being dispersed across a remarkably diverse body of work, which includes forays into the semi-autobiographical, postcolonial, horror, romantic drama and even science fiction, Claire Denis's films all capture characters in various degrees of solitude, frequently encountered as their precarious worlds unravel. Her films, disparate in tone, setting and form, each foreground their subjects' profound cultural, romantic and existential isolation, a mood enhanced by a distinctive cinematography (usually Agnès Godard's) that lingers suggestively on or tracks languidly over often desolate, unpeopled topographies, atmospherically accompanied by the subdued, wistful soundscapes of her long-time musical collaborator, Stuart A. Staples. The kinds of aloneness explored in Denis's genre-fluid oeuvre take many forms, each arising from the peculiarities of their unique sociocultural situation. A biographically inclined viewer might read Denis's artistic interest in solitary being as evidence of an ongoing attempt to grapple creatively with her own experience of feeling like an outsider. It is well documented that she was raised in various African nations – including Cameroon, Djibouti and Burkina Faso – by her father, a colonial official, before returning with polio at thirteen to a Paris that seemed to the displaced youngster like a foreign country. A white European in Africa and ostensibly a stranger to France, she confided to Gavin Smith (in the past tense, as if such hope had been abandoned) that 'I was always ready to be inside, because I never felt inside' (2006). Being 'drawn to ciné-literate genre appropriation', as Tim Palmer notes, Denis rarely visits the same territory twice, and yet many of her characters are confronted with the same fundamental questions: how is one to live with Being alone?; and, how is one to live with Others? (2022, 3). Some seek temporary solace in illusions of physical or emotional intimacy (*Vendredi soir*, *Un beau soleil intérieur*); adopt, even appropriate, the cultures of others (*Chocolat*, *White Material*); or take comfort in family (*Nénette et Boni*, *35 rhums*); others, like René in *35 rhums* shortly after his retirement from his work as a train driver, despairing in a solitude stretching as inexorably as rail tracks into a barren future, commit suicide. For most, certainly those discussed here, isolation is cultivated.

In readings of *Beau travail* (1999), *L'intrus* (2004), *White Material* (2009) and *High Life* (2018), films that feature aggressively solitary figures, I suggest that, for Denis, aloneness is often the result of, even a price paid willingly for, a passion or obsession that goes beyond that for companionship, love, family or community. Her protagonists are usually already in enclaves (colonial, penal, military) that are themselves typified by facultative difference from their enclosing wider social settings. As Judith Mayne writes, all kinds of 'Strangers populate the films of Claire Denis . . . exiles who live sometimes on the margins, sometimes in the shifting spaces of the geographies of race and gender and colonization' (2005: 80). These strangers with whom we become so fleetingly familiar in these brief but intense encounters are often intrusive foreign bodies, outcasts on distant outposts or islands, whether figurative or literal. It is not, however, the simple fact of their strangeness that marks them as remarkable, but the fact that they strive to perfect their sequestration within these stratified concentric spaces. In this sense, the films are not about the lonely, isolated, excluded or marginalised, but about the profoundly and voluntarily ontologically apart. Here, I focus on the forceful figures at the (faltering) heart of their often-solipsistic narratives; the landscapes that frame, enforce, symbolise their isolations; the fleeting moments of intimacy that temporarily irrupt within and offer ultimately illusory or unsatisfying alternatives to their aloneness; and finally, the ways in which each film witnesses its precarious subject in a moment of things – life, colony, humanity, comradery –collapsing. I want also to think through the significance of motion and stasis, velocity and inertia ('are we rushing forward, are we standing still?' as Robert Pattinson croons questioningly in Staples' *High Life* soundtrack), the delicately balanced torsional forces between which play such a crucial role for Denis's characters. Regardless of the shifting contexts and the ostensibly different lives portrayed, Denis's films are united by an almost pathological idio-alienation that proves, ultimately, to be fatal.

BEAU TRAVAIL

Arguably her most critically regarded film, *Beau travail* is a creative interpretation of Herman Melville's eponymous posthumous novella *Billy Budd* (written 1891, published 1924), enriched with music from Benjamin Britten's opera.[1] Set in a French Foreign Legion camp in Djibouti, the film follows Adjudant-Chef

Galoup (Denis Lavant) as he trains a small troupe of soldiers in the scorching northeast African deserts. The action surrounds the handsome young recruit Gilles Sentain (Grégoire Colin), who is popular with his peers but attracts the ambiguous attention of Commandant Bruno Forestier (Michel Subor reprises the role he played in Godard's *Le petit soldat* (1963)). We know from Galoup that Bruno, whom he admires, or even desires, had been 'dogged' by unspecified rumours after leaving his post in Algeria. We might surmise that these rumours had to do with his homosexuality, captured, or at least implied, in the taut triangulated gaze between Galoup, Bruno and Sentain in a structure of interdependent and antagonistic desires that echoes those in Jean-Paul Sartre's *No Exit* (1944). Envying Sentain, Galoup contrives to cause his death but is expelled from Djibouti and repatriated to France. The narrative is drawn from Galoup's journal as he recounts the events while awaiting court martial in Marseille. However, the film is not a confession, or an acknowledgement of and request for forgiveness for transgressions. Neither is the film merely about not belonging *to* something (family, nation, land) in a transitive or relative sense; Denis wanted to explore the ontology of foreignness, 'the feeling of ... being a foreigner to one's life'.[2]

'Drenched in myth', the Legion has romantic connotations, certainly in popular culture; its eclectic recruits are often stateless, or possibly fleeing dubious pasts (Beugnet and Sillars 2001: 166). The implication for many is that civilian life has somehow gone wrong, that other systems (social, familial) of care and support have failed. But it is as a result of its indifference to origin and its elision of cultural, racial and political differences that the Legion comes to act as a redemptive or reclamatory space for the emergence of an elective community of the otherwise alone. At various moments we see the men methodically setting camp, uncoiling a perimeter of barbed wire that keeps them in and others out. The barricade, symbolic rather than pragmatic in the absence of conflict, is a porous but corporeally hazardous boundary, one that, like the cinema screen itself, is susceptible to visual but not physical penetration. These mobile spaces act as a fittingly shifting home for the itinerant accretive family. Even Galoup, alone in exile, acknowledges in his journal that 'They're your only family. You're a father looking out for your sons.' Sentain himself is described as an orphan who was found 'utterly abandoned in a stairwell'. *Beau travail* draws our attention to the ways in which marginalised individuals come to form bonds: the synchronous combat training balletically choreographs the single bodies in harmonious unity while also once more foregrounding the now purely formal dimensions of training for theoretical combat (martial arts becomes modern dance); shared labours, communal living, bathing and eating as a corpus bring the group together in the everyday maintenance of life. In one scene a black soldier is on punishment (ostensibly but mistakenly) for abandoning his post; as another black soldier approaches to protest, Galoup reminds him that 'you are not African anymore, you are a legionnaire'. Uniquely, the Legion is the only French unit that swears allegiance not to a national flag but to the Legion itself. When they join, as Thomas Elsaesser comments, a 'curious and deliberate transubstantiation takes place, which we could describe as the taking in of the world's outcasts or abjects, in order to give them a sacred mission' (2012, 720). Such devotion represents both a means of abrading bonds arbitrarily imposed by race or nationality while braiding an equally artificial but chosen one with problematic historical associations. Beugnet astutely argues that 'such integration is predicated on the unquestioning acceptance [of the] values of the French nation' (2004, 107). Indeed, after its creation by Louis Philippe in 1831, the Legion was initially based in Algeria, playing a vital role in colonial 'pacification'.

Most of the film dwells on either the youthful recruits' boyish physical play or the undramatic, mundane, seemingly endless domestic chores that occupy so much of their time, often under Galoup's hostile gaze. Although he too is muscular, athletic, Galoup seems somehow different: they are all shorn, tall; he is short, with comparatively long hair, the prerogative of rank. All the tasks carried out by his wards he performs alone: while he shaves apart, they do so pressed together, joyously crowding the mirror's frame while the film frame reinforces and becomes complicit in Galoup's exclusion from what becomes, finally, a facsimile of a family portrait captured in the frame within the frame. His own mirror reflects his aloneness, his position beyond the family frame, as it will again with stunning effect at the film's end (more of which below). It would be easy to assume that Galoup has *been* excluded, but he maintains his exclusion. Fatally, as Beugnet and Sillars remark, 'the eruption of desire in this closed system ruptures its unity, destabilises its authority and reveals its internal divisions' (2001, 166). Sentain's developing intimacy with Bruno disturbs the equilibrium of distance established by Galoup, his transgression is one that erodes carefully maintained boundaries between selves, identifying them as dangerously permeable. Indeed, the destabilised community reveals itself to be a utopian dream, subject to the inequalities and tensions that characterise the modern cosmopolitan metropolis. The failure of this micro utopian space, then, gestures obliquely but powerfully towards a wider series of integrative societal failures that are also implicated in the colonial and postcolonial context of the film.

Galoup's isolation is however broken by passing moments of intimacy that take place beyond camp with his girlfriend, Rahel (Loula Ali Lotta). Their relationship is painted economically in a few sparse shots scattered like idyllic oases across the film's otherwise romantically barren terrain. Yet, and somehow, these quasi-domestic moments and their obvious mood of transient convenience serve only to heighten as opposed to alleviate Galoup's aloneness. The film's overt homoerotic imagery, its insistence on revealing as fleshy object the exposed male body while the female form remains covered, creates a further degree not simply of sexual ambiguity but dissatisfaction, as if, envisaging a different form of desire, Galoup plays the role of the conquering masculine libido. Because they

'A LOVER'S HAND? A BREATH, AN ABYSS'

Figure 4.1   Galoup shaves alone.

Figure 4.2   The cadets crowd the frame.

are painted by Denis as momentary transgressions across and between racial and ideological borders, a kind of seediness colours the interactions between the soldiers and local women, as if a transaction is taking place under the transparent and reciprocal ruse of affection. Gift giving, which seems rather a price paid than an act of unmotivated kindness, reinforces this unsettling feeling. Indeed, the film's opening sequence in the Djiboutian dancehall plays in sophisticated symbolic ways with these implications; the space is populated with the casually erotic undulating bodies of expectant young women caught reflected in a net-like mirror as if in a market space, on offer, before the soldiers enter and select a partner. Although these instances of (physical) intimacy between local and colonist momentarily gesture towards the possibility of a crossing of the boundary between intruder and intruded, their superficiality breeds yet deeper and irresolvable cultural and even metaphysical differences between the transient occupier and the stationary occupied.

Beau travail's evocative setting works as an objective correlative to the mood of aloneness: the vast desert evokes heat-distorted visions of nomadic solitary wanderings, hazy mirages all enhanced by Godard's poetic imagistic shots. It seems likely that Denis took inspiration from Werner Herzog's hallucinatory *Fata Morgana* (1971), an elegy to the desert as space, concept, cultural and poetic imaginary composed mostly of long tracking shots over the expanse of the Sahara, with a soundtrack of François Couperin, Handel, Mozart's *Coronation Mass* (which brings to mind Denis's use of Britten), and even Leonard Cohen (which finds an echo in Denis's use of Neil Young).[3] If the Legion embodies the idea of foreignness, the desert is the symbol of erosion, abrasions, shifting time, anonymity. Although the desert is a permanent backdrop, it becomes more prominent when Galoup sends Sentain on a punishment trek, giving him a broken compass. Thinking that he is heading home, Sentain wanders the featureless desert with increasing urgency, shedding clothes and gear in a sequence that reads like a life shot in reverse, a return to unburdened childhood, before eventually collapsing on the stark rim of a vast salt flat (likely the northern shores of Lake Assal in the Danakil Desert). The desert is already inhospitable, yet Sentain beaches like a shipwreck on the shores of an even more desolate desert island, like a deep-ocean brine lake, a further symbolic refinement of all that the film poetically limns. Sentain appears to die on his bed of salt, but like the artefacts the recruits later find in the market (including the infamous compass, casting suspicion on Galoup), he simply becomes crystalised by the land before being resurrected, reclaimed as something precious. Galoup's final scenes on a single bed in Marseille are placed in dialogue with Sentain's, as he travels almost like an infant, a foundling once more, tenderly cared for by the young women who rescue him, to begin a new life, a third life perhaps.

L'INTRUS

Denis's narratologically disconcerting *L'intrus* pursues reclusive ex-mercenary Louis Trebor (Michel Subor) as he travels from France for a black-market heart transplant in Korea before moving on to Tahiti in the ultimately unrealised hope of locating a son he has never met. It is based, at least conceptually, on Jean-Luc Nancy's enigmatic essay of the same name, in which the philosopher meditates on the physical and metaphysical implications of his heart transplant, his post-operative sense that 'In me there is the *intrus*, and I become foreign to myself' (2002, 9). Once more we return to *Beau travail*'s interest not simply in being an outsider, but in the ontology of aloneness, the phenomenology of feeling like a 'foreigner to one's life'. Trebor lives on the margins of a small border town in the Jura Mountains between France and Switzerland. Metaphors of transgressions open the film in a series of night-time border crossings captured in the jerky headlights of a slowly moving car as Tindersticks's oddly jazzy yet quasi-dystopian soundtrack throbs and pulses menacingly over the credits. These territorial incursions are figured almost biologically, as if the migrants were pathogens entering and infecting the national bloodstream in a manner that gestures towards the troubling anti-migration (and even post-Brexit) rhetoric of refugee 'crises', 'plagues' and 'swarms'. Trebor appears content in the utter solitude of a life in the wilderness accompanied only by his dogs (which he eventually abandons) and the occasional visits of his lover (Bambou, abandoned too). Unlike Galoup, Trebor has no loyalties, no ideologies, no community, but in his retirement comes to refine the techniques of living off grid that would have been part of his working life (we might read Galoup as the origin story for Trebor, and see him not committing suicide on a single bed in Marseille, but enduring). As Wim Staat remarks, he is a 'somewhat unsympathetic loner [whose] motivations are seldom articulated' (2008, 196). Although alone, he never seems lonely, and even his interactions with his part-time lover are pointedly pragmatic; they alleviate his need for sex and, because she is the local pharmacist, provide his heart medication. It is only after suffering a minor cardiac arrest while swimming alone in an isolated lake that he embarks on the search for his son.

If *L'Intrus* is remarkable for the impact of its visual poetics, one particularly startling moment sees an excised heart discarded on a dramatically contrasting background of pure white snow. The bodiless organ acts as both a jarring corporeal confrontation and a point of radical exegetical uncertainty within the film's ambiguous significatory matrices: is it Trebor's failing heart; his donor heart in cellular stasis on a protective bed of ice; the heart of the victims of his profession as a hired killer; the heart torn by dogs from the frozen corpse of the young man he kills with a knife in a forest; an objective manifestation of love as a concept; a material realisation of the many failures of love and care portrayed in the film? The unresolved polysemy contributes to the film's aggressive interrogation of meaning, foregrounding its deconstruction of epistemological desire through which, as Rosalind Galt remarks, even the 'most basic expectations of narrative payoff are thwarted' (2014, 106). Using what Kristin Hole describes as 'interruptive scenes that refuse to close or fix the meaning of the film', Denis shows not that the heart might be any *one* of these possible things, but that the enigmatic cinematic object is simultaneously *all* and, by virtue of this uncertainty, *none*, that it both (re)solves and (de)stabilises the film's various complex narrative and visual threads (2016, 6). Yet the visceral image gestures most poignantly towards the necessity for connections beyond the organ in isolation. If, as Deleuze and Guattari enigmatically propose in their perpetually obscure discussions of the 'body without organs', persons are a 'connection of desires, conjunction of flows, continuum of intensities' which are metaphorically 'plugged into other collective machines', then this organ without a body, which Nancy describes in his essays as a 'deep red, muscular mass with pipes sticking out of it', is unplugged, dissevered from any system, and neither supports nor is supported by those complex integrated and interdependent arterial networks of family, friendship or love (Deleuze and Guattari 2005, 161; Nancy 2002, 3). That is to say, the abstracted organ ceases in any meaningful sense to be an organ, defined by the function it serves in the entelechy of the body, much like a person might be considered simply one element of a wider community.

As Sentain is cast adrift and washes ashore on an island of salt, so Trebor comes finally to the image par excellence of his own self-made solitude, a small (Crusoe-esque desert) island in a South Pacific archipelago. The island is the natural negative of the lake in which he almost dies: that is a single point of water in an expanse of land, this a single point of land in an ocean of water. In some ways the image of inaccessible individual islands in a vast sea is a little obvious, suggesting John Donne's plea that 'No man is an island entire of itself; every man / is a piece of the continent, a part of the main'. Trebor's island is barren, the remnant of a life, or perhaps even lives abandoned. We are of course encouraged to speculate about what *kind* of life; did Trebor once envisage a South Sea paradise, a new Eden, and if so what events or what in himself prevented its realisation. A clue is revealed when he uncovers a gun buried in the sand, a sign of both the genuine danger of his profession and his paranoia. Katrin Pesch draws attention to the fact that 'Trebor's island refuge has fallen apart, so that by the time we get to see more of the island, it is too late' (2017, 243). As he approaches his death, as awareness of his mortality emerges, he (re)builds something of a home in the expectation that a facsimile of the domestic will create the conditions necessary for that long-lost family to emerge or return from the sea (or perhaps not return, as I suggest below). Yet no one comes, inevitably, as Trebor lies in wait on the geographic manifestation of a life spent avoiding closeness, family, responsibility. The divided islands, fragments of a once larger whole drifting tectonically apart over geological time, become the perfected image not simply of isolation, but of a deepening and irreversible separation of a once single body, like the solitary excised and dying heart in its sea of snow.

Oddly, Trebor's other son, Sidney (Grégoire Colin), and grandchildren live locally, although he spends no time with them and shows little affection on the single accidental encounter we witness. Denis plays a characteristic game, here: in *Beau travail* Colin is Trebor's ward; here, they recreate something of the structure of that relationship (in the same way that Colin and Alice Houri appear as brother and sister in *US Go Home* and *Nénette et Boni*). One wonders why Trebor is so committed to his quest to find an unknown offspring, and why he leaves his wealth to someone who is, in the end, purely speculative. Tatjan Gajic sees Trebor is 'a heartless man who goes in search of, or on a hunt for, his heart or hearts' (2015, 405). In this reading he seeks something of himself, a lineal continuation in the vicarious bond with his offspring. Trebor is clearly disappointed in Sidney, a stay-at-home father with little ambition beyond being a good parent and husband, while the other son, 'like Trebor when young, is a sailor' (Gajic 2015, 404). In this sense Sidney (who we assume was raised by the mother, who never appears in the film) is the opposite of Trebor, a genetic anomaly. Yet the fact that Trebor seeks a son he has never met, who is perhaps mystical, mythical, a fabrication (despite suggestions that he is in and has been adopted by the community), gives rise to the possibility that he does not in fact seek to find him, only that as his life nears its end, he goes in search of something he knows not to be there. The film's central paradox then is that Trebor hunts his lost son precisely because he is unfindable, enigmatic; his absence suggests that he, unlike Sidney, is at home with his solitude in the wilderness like his father. If he were to arrive, to demonstrate by implication a desire for a relationship with his long-lost father, this would signal to Trebor that he was, finally, simply human, and would therefore constitute a profound disappointment, the failure we attribute to Sidney. Trebor thus travels not in the hope of meeting his son, but in the hope of proof that he is not needed by his son; his end-of-life quest does not then reveal to us a profound change (of heart or mind), a search for redemption in the recognition of a misspent life, but merely a further and final proof that Trebor remains ontologically committed to a life utterly singular.

In the end we come to see that his transplant involved a high price, when it is revealed that his new heart was taken from the murdered body of Sidney, exposed on the cold steel of a mortuary table and bearing a scar identical to that borne by Trebor himself. Laura McMahon remarks that, in the suggestion that Trebor's new heart has been taken from his son, 'the film explores a violent reversal in the expected logic of patrilinear transmission' (2008, 466). This should be a moment of epiphany, regret, although Trebor seems to be undisturbed by the result of his own desire for a young heart. In a terrible but poignant irony, Sidney's heart rejects the body of the father who rejected him, refuses to sustain such a life. As the two bodies co-mingle in the tactile closeness of transplant, the film proposes various failures of parenting. Streiter comments that 'The philosophical work of Jean-Luc Nancy and the films of Claire Denis resemble each other strikingly in the way both of them link the question of community, of the impossibilities and necessities of being together, to the body and to touch' (2008, 53). Sidney is simply one more casualty of Trebor's single-mindedness, his indifference to community, responsibility, others.

WHITE MATERIAL

Denis returns to French colonial Africa (the location of her debut) in *White Material* which, along with *35 rhums*, is amongst her most conventional films. If her first African outing 'was like writing a journal until [she] decided to add fictional elements to it', *White Material* is much less biographical and perhaps more directly a comment on the colonial mentality (Reid 1996). The film sees Maria Vial (Isabelle Huppert) as the ex-wife of André (Christopher Lambert), a coffee plantation owner in an unnamed African country, desperately trying to complete a final harvest during revolution and war between rebels and government forces. André and Maria live, or perhaps more accurately coexist, on the plantation with their surly teenage son, Manuel (Nicolas Duvauchelle), and André's seemingly terminally ill father (Subor once again). In its tight focus on a female character, *White Material* is something of an outlier in Denis's works, which as Mayne remarks, 'are more about men than they are about women' (2005, 26). We follow Vial (very literally, as Morrey notes in his paper, with much of the focus being on Huppert from behind) over the final few days and weeks of the French presence, and ultimately the era of colonialism, as she attempts through shear will to hold on to the land and by implication a past that has become deeply problematic and practically untenable. The film is sophisticated and ambiguous in its evocation of sympathies: on the one hand Vial is the sole female protagonist frustrated by and working against an unfair patriarchal system, surrounded by idle and incompetent but empowered men; yet on the other she is an agent of racial injustice, an incarnation of oppressions past and present. Denis offers no simple colonial morality tale here, and an already ethically nuanced situation becomes still more ambiguous when, after hearing that he has signed away the plantation that she hoped to inherit, Vial brutally murders her father-in-law with a machete.

In many ways the spatiality of the film echoes that of *Beau travail*, situating the invasive foreign enclave within the heart of an occupied country. Vial though, perhaps like Denis herself, appears to feel at home here, and has expectations of inheriting the farm from her father-in-law, unaware that André is gradually losing it to the local mayor. Vial is a white French outsider, not welcome by either the government forces or the rebels intent on retaking the land, and even encouraged to leave by the retreating French army, which abandons what is by this point an already tenuous hold on the country. Like Galoup and his troupe in Djibouti, Vial is a trespasser in a land that is inhospitable to the remaining echoes of the colonial past. As Andrew Hussey remarks, although 'Maria feels that she belongs in Africa because she works the land', she is 'alone, vulnerable and white in a country where the majority population is black' (2010). But the film's engagement with the question of belonging is by no means didactic, and there is no clear or at least no obvious or superficial sense that Vial is 'morally wrong', to use a crudely reductive expression. It is rather a study of a legacy colonist who does recognise herself as such, despite the many expectations that she has of the locals as essentially a labour force. At one point when stopped by a group of rebels on the road demanding payment, she attempts to appeal to them *as if* they were the same, by reminding them that she knows their families, their pasts. Yet as Andrew Asibong notes, 'Again and again in her encounters with African people in this film, Maria seems to grasp clumsily for a connection . . . that seems altogether unlikely to be forthcoming' (2011, 161–2). If their paths previously intersected, they did so within the imbalanced infrastructures of oppression. The degree of resistance that Maria faces, though, draws our attention to the fact that she is fundamentally alone, separate from family, country, culture, the locals, and that her unwillingness to countenance her own difference reinforces her deeply solipsistic indifference and insensitivity to the local community. Vial's dilemma is that the land is not hers but the country's, the plantation is not hers but her father-in-law's and she cannot harvest the crop herself and so must, though utterly determined to be self-reliant, rely on others to complete the harvest.

Like the compounds of Djibouti, its salt islands, or like Trebor's Haitian island, the plantation represents a further refined space of isolation, an island surrounded by a boundary fence and locked iron gates. At various key moments this barrier is very literally transgressed when a group of child soldiers pierce the fence (one that recalls the unfurled barbed wire of *Beau travail*) to assault Vial's son, who is stripped, shaved, and possibly sexually molested. This is simply the climax to a series of incursions as the children invade the sanctity of the enclave to observe, or to steal 'white material'. Like those border crossings in *L'intrus* and the barbed wire in *Beau travail*, trespass is a key theme in this film, although it is ambiguous precisely who is transgressor/intruder and who is transgressed/intruded upon. Vial's social environment is black, the culture African, and so she and her family already sit awkwardly, even anachronistically within a space of selected isolation, forcing on the locals a presence that acts as a reminder of a brutal past. The plantation is self-sustaining, well stocked, a recreation of the military compound, the long-distance (space)ship, a micro-colony exploiting black labour within the otherwise liberated nation.

Although one might expect instances of care to emerge between Vial and her son, like Trebor with Sidney, she shares little with him, and even remarks 'You disappoint me . . . I don't know what happened. I can't believe you're my son! I feel like a total failure . . . Letting yourself go, Manuel, is the vilest thing a boy can do. It's loathsome.' But it is with the Boxer (Isaach de Bankolé) that she shows a more tender side. One may wonder why she finds some comradery here. However, he represents all the things that she prides in herself, but more importantly all the things she finds absent in the men around her, most notably her son; he is brave, dedicated, motivated, driven single-mindedly. There is a commonality, here, as Streiter suggests: characters in Denis's films 'are like planets, each one a compact and impenetrable composition of forces and elements. Each one has a drive, a rhythm of existence, an individual way of traversing time and space' (2008, 57). In one scene, Vial finds her son lounging apathetically in bed and asks with distaste 'how can you spend all day in bed?' This scene has a mirror, when she finds the Boxer alone, wounded and bleeding in her son's bed, and so cares for him because he, like her, is alone in meaningful and deliberate ways, enigmatic and adrift, but the engine for change. They speak little, but very clearly a bond forms between them in the newly unstable space of the under-siege compound:

> Vial: It's no longer safe here for someone like you.
> Boxer: For someone like you either.
> Vial: This is my son's room.
> Boxer: Why didn't you leave with your son?
> Vial: I'm a good fighter too. How could I show courage in France? It would be absurd, no rhyme or reason. I'd slack off, get too comfortable.

In many ways The Boxer, in her son's room, becomes for a moment the son she would have wanted, in the same way that the ever absent lost child of Trebor is his ideal son (by virtue of that absence). Vial and the Boxer are not simply people assailed by but taking arms against a space that is variously inhospitable, yet defined by, revelling in, nurtured by the antagonism of their situation. Vial makes explicit her motivations here: to be independent, to show courage, to resist – in this sense, although these final weeks appear to represent a catastrophe, for Vial they create the perfect environment for her to explore the depth of her ontological aloneness. In this moment then, amid the catastrophic collapse of her world, Vial glimpses the possibility of a real family, united not by cause but by passion and self-reliance, and this moment mirrors that in which Trebor lies alone in bed, comforted not by the presence but rather the absence of his lost son.

HIGH LIFE

High Life is Denis's first science fiction film, but not of course her first genre movie. The narrative follows Monte and his crewmates on a spaceship headed towards a distant blackhole. Monte and his colleagues are prisoners, originally sentenced to life behind bars, or to death, but offered the redemptive opportunity to take part in an ill-conceived trip to harness energy from a blackhole (inspired by the theories of Roger Penrose). Again, there is a sense of excision, as if expelled like a virus, the felons have been forced from a body that they were harming. Denis remarked in interview with Pamela Hutchinson that the film began with the question of 'where can you throw away people you don't want anymore on Earth?' (2019, 22). As with many of her most iconic films, Denis exploits the temporal and spatial disorientation of a non-linear narrative interspersed with frequent flashbacks, some of which feature moments from the characters' lives, while others provide some explanation about the film's socio-political context.[4] As Katharine Asals has remarked of Denis's style, her 'narratives are loose – based more on impressions and small moments than plots [relying on] gesture and expression' (2007, 2). There are scenes evoking a 1970s television documentary aesthetic; grainy, set on a train (a tube-like facsimile of the spaceship) passing through industrial landscapes as a scientist explains to a journalist the necessity for such exploratory travel while also discussing the ethical implications of sending prisoners into space. The film has much in common with Godard's *Alphaville* (1965), Trumbull's *Silent Running* (1972), Tarkovsky's *Solaris* (1972), Fassbinder's *World on a Wire* (1973), and even Boyle's *Sunshine* (2007). Most notably in this film, as Erika Balsom remarks, Denis constructs a pressured environment to explore the 'eternal problem of living together' (2019, 61). Eventually, through various forms of foul play, the rest of the crew die, are killed or kill themselves, and as Monte sends the bodies into space we see a 'transition to a new order of aloneness', until finally Monte remains alone with his daughter, Willow (Wilson 2019).

Like *Beau travail*, there is a hierarchy in this small carceral community: Dr Dibs (Juliette Binoche), a Medea-like killer of her own children, appears to have some authority, mostly because she controls the ship's supply of narcotics. She too enforces a dance-like exercise regime to keep the crew's bodies healthy so that she can experiment with fertility in space.[5] Her only success comes after she drugs and rapes Monte before using his sperm to inseminate Boyse (Mia Goth), who gives birth to Willow. Despite the connection established between the crew by their shared situation, Monte, 'the last man', remains aloof, an outsider even among outsiders, refusing either to form friendships or to participate in the experiments in reproduction carried out by Dibs (Hutchinson 2019, 25). In one scene, Boyse taunts Monte with the lyrics of Johnny Cash's 'Always Alone': 'Always alone, alone and blue I've got no one to share [*sic*] my troubles to / No one to care to call my own it seems that I must always be alone.' This is a provocation to a seemingly impassive, even inert Monte, who at times appears to be giving an unconvincing performance as a person. Peter Bradshaw ponders in his review whether 'Monte is capable of love', or if events have not rendered the 'emotion of love obsolete' (2019). Although Denis suggests that 'Loneliness was also one big factor' in the film's conception, Monte seems immune to such human responses (Hutchinson 2019, 23). We might find a clue in a remarkably similar moment to that in *L'intrus* (with which it shares many concerns), when, in a flashback, we see Monte as a child holding the heart of a friend he'd killed (for killing his dog) before dropping the still-bleeding organ it into a well. The exposed heart provides a rationale for Monte's isolation, his unwillingness to form bonds, to be vulnerable, to love. The image, as in *L'intrus*, also demonstrates what Mayne sees as a desire in Denis's films to explore a 'sense of displacement, of choosing to move around an object or a theme or a person, instead of moving in directly' (2005, 29). Monte's commitment to his own purity marks him out. Indeed, there is something of the ascetic, the hermit, in his refusal of either sensual gratification or companionship. As Monte remarks, he chose 'abstinence overindulgence . . . chastity was a way of making myself stronger'. Stronger for what, one might wonder, given the hopelessness of his situation.

If the salt pans of Djibouti, Trebor's destination of a tiny island, and Vial's imperilled plantation represent psycho-geographical spaces of radical and radically concentric isolation, what greater image exists for absolute aloneness than a small ship adrift in the endless oceans of space, a capsule surrounded by vacuous, lifeless blackness. Indeed, at one point, unbelievably, miraculously, Willow and Monte, the sole survivors of the mission and of humanity, come across another ship, adrift, and it acts like another island in the archipelago, another planet and the past. Of course, a limited space occupied with those sentenced to death is little more than a thinly covered metaphor for our predicament on a dying planet surrounded by hostile space. Raymond Deluca, in a fascinating essay on the significance of hair in Claire Denis, suggests that 'These characters cling to hair, refusing to "admit" the disappearance of their earthly reality. Monte literally preserves his facial clippings' (2021, 19). Although bodily shedding and decay, greying hair, captures materially the mortality at the film's heart, Monte seems unconnected with his past or planet. But, like many of Denis's films, this focus on grooming draws attention both to the body and to those rituals and routines that create the veneer of civilisation, and Monte seems here to be playing a very specific role, to have reinvented himself as a kind of religious recluse.

Despite having no landscape as such, *High Life* repeatedly gestures toward the now lost earth, even in the soundtrack, a lullaby for a girl born and to die in space, asking where she is hiding now, perhaps in the dappled light of a forest, along a beach. Not only will Willow never see such sights, but the clear implication is that they no longer exist. The earth is drawn in negative. But with no knowledge of these remnants of a vanished society beyond the images still received from earth, they evoke no sense of loss in Willow. Many scenes take place in the ship's garden, a staple of long-distance sci-fi films, most notably of course *Silent Running*. The space is again a further space of isolation in the concentric isolations of the film, and may also be the final patch of earth in the universe. It is also an Edenic space, more so when we see Monte and a young Willow among the vegetation. Here, the two are alone but not lonely, and neither gives any indication that anything is missed or missing. Here, Denis forcefully reiterates her interest in those who are deeply self-sufficient, ontologically apart. Of course, Monte and Willow have one another, and there is a developing sense in the film of Willow's growing sexual curiosity, in tension with both Monte's own abstinence and of course the ultimate taboo of society.

ENDINGS

Although these diverse characters arise from remarkably different circumstances, they are unified by the shocking intensity of their passions, by the claustrophobia of the pressured spaces in which they thrive. Each not only enjoys but exacerbates, nurtures, actively seeks a profound and ontological isolation even within the exclusion of their already besieged communities. Each is characterised by an utter commitment to an ideal, a vision, whether that be of the self-sufficient soldier, the detached hermit, the solitary colonist or the celibate father by immaculate conception. They are also united by being in seemingly perpetual motion. As Anja Streiter argues, Denis's characters are often 'in a transit, movement, travel, gliding and drifting' (2008, 57). Possibly, though, they are aware that to be still is to die. Galoup is always moving, for the duration of the film, and always alone, ahead of the pack. Yet our voyeuristic transgression into the deeply personal final reflections of Galoup, 'the lonely legionnaire', facilitates for him a moment of sharing – alone in Marseille awaiting court martial, he has no willing interlocutor, and his anonymous audience represents the only contact with a confessor, a listener, even a friend (Romney 2000). This plays on the tension between film as a communal act of cinematic voyeurism and film as a lone act of solitary viewing; either way, there is a peering in, a one-way encounter that gestures towards the absence of reciprocated attention, interest, care. Finally, we find him in a single room, on a single bed, static, simply waiting or about to commit suicide, depending on the generosity of our readings. When we finally catch up with Trebor he is seen running, cycling, swimming, hunting, driving, travelling to Korea, then Tahiti. Again, it is here that he finally takes to a bed, and as he stops so he dies: motion is associated with life, stillness with death. Vial moves, rapidly; from the film's opening shots we track her on motorcycles, in buses and trucks, running, walking swiftly, but never simply sitting or lying. Indeed, every character that lies down or takes to a bed in this film dies, often while lying: we see the army cutting the throats of the child soldiers found asleep in Vial's home; her son, eyes closed, drifting in a pool, about to be killed with a spear; her sickly father-in-law prone in a hospital bed (like Trebor). *High Life* very explicitly plays with motion, or the illusion of motion, on a ship that travels at almost the speed of light. Indeed, the lullaby 'Willow' has the line 'are we rushing forward, are we standing still?' In this film, too, to take to a bed, more a single bed, is to be vulnerable: Boyse is raped in bed, and Monte too is drugged and raped by Dibs. The single bed within these already isolated states is symbolic, an island within an island.

Each of the films discussed here captures our protagonist as the worlds collapse; that is to say, they are interested in endings. Trebor lies alone awaiting a son who never comes on a fragment of earth broken from a larger whole in the middle of a vast ocean; Vial is, presumably, either burned alive or killed at the centre of her own decaying empire in the middle of a foreign culture; Monte, already deeply alone on earth and then in space, enters the event horizon of a black hole in the depths of space; Galoup, lying alone and thinking back fondly to his own isolation amongst the community of the Legion, in the unfamiliar setting of a France abandoned years before, holding a handgun with the suggestion that he is about to commit suicide: as he remarks, he is 'Unfit for life', before the qualifier 'Unfit for civil life'. The ending of *Beau travail* is one of cinema's most captivating. We return to the dancefloor, the disco of the opening, whether in Galoup's imagination, some past point or even some redemptive future. He stands alone, cigarette in hand, leaning on the tessellated mirror watching himself. This is an image of self-sufficiency, but also one of possibility. He seems relaxed, unwatched, his military body becomes a dancer's and he, in his civilian clothes, gives in to an impulse to move with a fluid freedom that is in stark contrast to the rest of the film. There is no choreography, no symmetry, no function, no design, simply a body in motion that appears both oddly jubilant and elegiac. As Susan Hayward observes, he is 'frantically caught in the mirror, caught, one suspects, in the web of his own imaginings and desires. He alone can witness his own abjection, cast out of the company of men, about to be repatriated' (Hayward 2002, 48). Oddly, the diamonds of the dancehall mirror recall the barbed wire of the earlier scenes. Galoup's frantic performance also mirrors the energetic solitary dancing of Alain (Colin) in *US Go Home* (1994). But Galoup is not abject here, and he was never in the company of men; he stood apart, deliberately so. To come back to the image of the heart, the physiological metaphor, in one of the film's final moments the camera dwells on a single pulsing artery in Galoup's underarm, a sign of life, vitality, but also tracing a line back to the source, a metonym for the heart. But if these films give us the end of single lives and moments of history, *High Life* represents the end of humanity as Monte and Willow abandon their ship to head into the black hole, brings us back to the earlier scene with the heart held over and dropped into a dark well: the heart suspended over the circle of the well's rim is reframed as the two hearts heading into the circle of the blackhole, the earlier image a foreshadowing. The black hole, circular, also represents the perfected image of the human egg awaiting fertilisation, the phallic ship heading towards the opening of space before releasing its cargo to enter the egg. Again, the image is also reminiscent of an island, visually it has a centre and what appear to be shores, perhaps those endless circling salt flats of Djibouti, the island upon which Trebor dies, Vial's plantation. Yet if the earlier image foreshadows a single heart dropped into nothingness, here there are two hearts beating in unison, and it is this fact that invests that final scene, the end of humanity, with a moment of optimism. Perhaps such optimism is misplaced. Denis does not offer morals, her films are not parables, warnings or offers of redemption: that is to say, there is nothing to be learned here, no secret message, only film and the viewer alone in the darkness of cinema's solitary encounter.

NOTES

1. The title inherits a tradition of using the word 'beau' in films about the legion, including *Beau Geste* (1926, 1939, 1966, 1982), *Beau Sabreur* (1928), *Beau Ideal* (1931), and Laurel and Hardy's *Beau Hunks* (1931).
2. This idio-alienation coincides with *L'intrus*, Jean-Luc Nancy's meditation on his heart transplant, which inspired Denis's film of the same name: his sense that, with another's heart keeping him alive, 'In me there is the *intrus*, and I become foreign to myself' (Romney 2000, 9).
3. Popular music has been instrumental in Denis's life and career, from the Animals in *US Go Home* (1994) to the use of a Frank Zappa song title for *Trouble Every Day* (2001).
4. There are some arresting crossovers between this and *L'intrus*, not least the repeated association of exposed hearts and canines (as dogs eat the heart on snow, this heart is removed as revenge for the killing of a dog).
5. She also employs a 'fuck box', in a sequence that recalls Walerian Borowczyk's erotic fantasy, *La bête* (1975).

CITATIONS

Asibong, Andrew. 2011. 'Claire Denis's Flickering Spaces of Hospitality.' *L'Esprit Créateur* 51, 1: 154–67. http://www.jstor.org/stable/26290036.

Asals, Katharine. 2007. 'The silent, black centre in the early features of Claire Denis.' *CineAction* 71, 2 (Winter): 7.

Balsom, Erika. 2019. 'High Life Review.' *Sight and Sound* 61: n.p. https://www2.bfi.org.uk/news-opinion/sight-sound-magazine/reviews-recommendations/high-life-claire-denis-robert-pattinson-space-sci-fi-human-taboos, accessed 26 October 2022.

Beugnet, Martine. 2004. *Claire Denis*. Manchester: Manchester University Press.

Beugnet, Martine and Jane Sillars. 2001. 'Beautravail: time, space and myths of identity.' *Studies in French Cinema*, 1, 3: 166–73.

Bradshaw, Peter. 2019. 'High Life Review.' *The Guardian*, 8 May.
Deleuze, Gilles, and Felix Guattari. 2005. *A Thousand Plateaus: Capitalism and Schizophrenia*. Translated by Brian Massumi. Minneapolis: University of Minnesota Press.
Elsaesser, Thomas. 2012. 'European Cinema and the Postheroic Narrative: Jean-Luc Nancy, Claire Denis and *Beau travail*.' *New Literary History* 43, 4: 703–25. http://www.jstor.org/stable/23358664, accessed 1 March 2023.
Gajic, Tatjana. 2015. '(Re)Moving the heart: interiority and intrusion in María Zambrano, Jean Luc Nancy and Claire Denis.' *Journal of Spanish Cultural Studies* 16, 4: 397–413.
Galt, Rosalind. 2014. 'Claire Denis and the World Cinema of Refusal.' *SubStance* 43, 1: 96–108. http://www.jstor.org/stable/24540741, accessed 1 March 2023.
Hayward, Susan. 2002. 'Claire Denis's "Post-colonial" Films and Desiring Bodies.' *L'Esprit Créateur* 42, 3: 39–49. http://www.jstor.org/stable/26288385.
Hole, Kristin Lené. 2016. *Towards a Feminist Cinematic Ethics: Claire Denis, Emmanuel Levinas and Jean-Luc Nancy*. Edinburgh: Edinburgh University Press.
Hussey, Andrew. 2010. 'Claire Denis: For me, film-making is a journey into the impossible.' *The Guardian*, 4 July.
Hutchinson, Pamela. 2019. 'Heavenly Bodies.' *Sight and Sound*, June.
Mayne, Judith. 2005. *Claire Denis*. Chicago: University of Illinois Press.
McMahon, Laura. 2008. 'Figuring Intrusion: Nancy and Denis.' Contemporary French and Francophone Studies 12, 4: 463–70.
Nancy, Jean-Luc. 2002. *L'intrus*. Éditions Galilée. Trans. Susan Hanson, Michigan State University Press.
Palmer, Tim. 2022. *Modern & Contemporary France* 30, 1: 1–17.
Pesch, Katrin. 2017. 'Ecologies of debt in Claire Denis's *L'intrus/The Intruder* (2004).' *Studies in French Cinema* 17, 3: 236–51, DOI: 10.1080/14715880.2017.1314147.
Reid, Mark A. 1996/2006. 'Claire Denis interview: Colonial observations.' *Jump Cut* 40: 67–72.
Romney, Jonathan. 2000. Claire Denis interviewed by Jonathan Romney. *The Guardian*, 28 June. https://www.theguardian.com/film/interview/interviewpages/0,6737,338784,00.html, accessed 1 March 2023.
Smith, Gavin. 2006. 'Interview: Claire Denis.' *Film Comment*, January–February.
Staat, Wim. 2008. 'The Other's Intrusion: Claire Denis's L'intrus.' *Thamyris/Intersecting* 19: 195–208.
Streiter, Anja. 2008. 'The Community According to Jean-Luc Nancy and Claire Denis.' *Film-Philosophy* 12, 1: 49–62.
Wilson, Emma. 2019. 'Love Me Tender: New Films from Claire Denis.' *Film Quarterly* 72, 4: 18–28.

CHAPTER 5

Claire Denis, Corporeality and New Weird

Elif Sendur[1]

A scene that can easily be overlooked amidst the fusillade of corporeal scenes in Claire Denis's 2018 film, *High Life*, occurs in an extreme close-up: the camera is on the surface of white skin, wet with a milk-like liquid that we can only vaguely guess to be mother's milk. This thickish white substance flows down in two streams towards what we can perhaps recognise as someone's belly until a quick cut finally shows another close-up of the face of one of the main characters (Boyse's), with her nipples freely lactating. The camera stays with this leaky body for a while, with Boyse's hands touching her damp belly, to finally shift to a medium shot where she meekly gazes on her own half-naked torso with milk mellifluously flowing from her nipples towards her belly, yet without a baby nearby. At this juncture, we may hesitantly conclude that she must have given birth to a healthy baby, especially if we consider a previous scene in which we are shown one. Still, this is not simply a scene of a new mother with her baby, a trope that would be easy to codify and understand: in lieu of such a mother, this scene depicts a body lost in milk, a body that is alien and uncomfortable to Boyse, and through her, to the spectator. It is precisely because the camera refuses to shift to a medium shot sooner that the spectator is obliged to stay with this damp skin without a more comfortable space that might lead to a meaningful understanding of this seemingly simple scene. Claire Denis does not give us that comfort; she wants us to stay with this fragmented dampness and leakiness instead of perceiving this body as a whole. Like Boyse confronted with her own inescapable viscerality, the viewer is forced into a sustained confrontation with the body as a becoming and not as an object to appropriate.

This encounter with the body in its fragmented fleshliness is one of the ways Claire Denis explores corporeality in its weird tangibility. From the naked chests

ELIF SENDUR

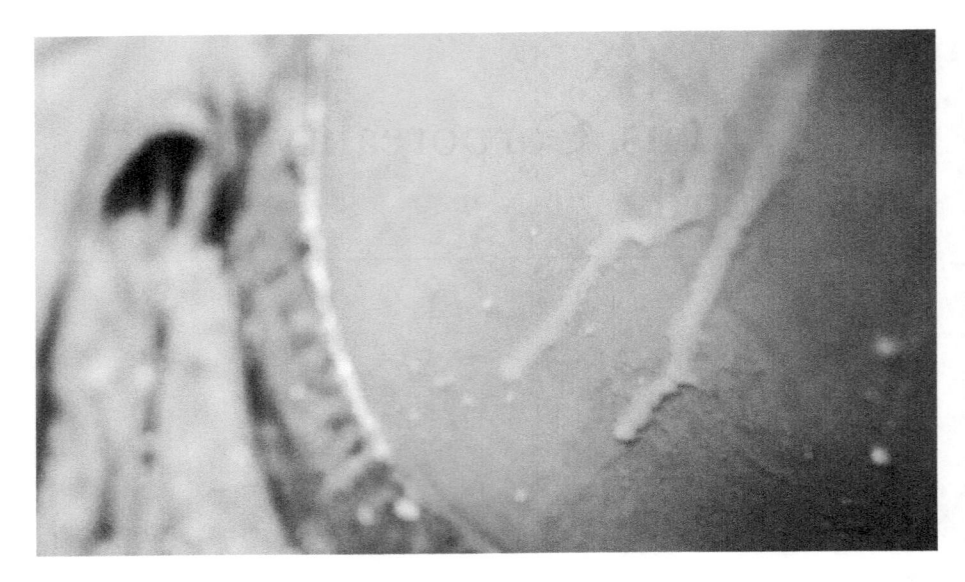

Figure 5.1   Rivulets of white fluid.

and arms of disciplined bodies in *Beau travail* (1999) to the much-discussed wounds of a heart transplant in *L'intrus* (2004), from the erotic encounters in *Nénette et Boni* (1996) to carnal sexuality in *High Life* (2018), Denis displaces our encounter with bodies towards a fragmented, weird space by creating disorientation that revokes the spectator's epistemological grounding. Leo Bersani, for example, in his reading of *Beau travail*, presents this displacement as a foreignness manifested on the surface of the bodies as these skins and these bodies become impenetrable to the viewer (Bersani 2010, 102). In a similar vein, James Williams underlines that Denis denies suture by playing with the conventional forms of shot–counter shot by 'elongating and even suspending the flow of time' (2016, 235). In other words, by denying the framing and closure of scenes, for example in the case of the long, unexplained close-up of Boyse's milk, the scene refuses to provide the spectator with a sense of unitary meaning where the spectator can find themselves in it.[2] This impossibility of reading the film as such seems to happen especially through what I will tentatively call the *weirding* of the body in Denis.

That Claire Denis's cinema is corporeal is not a novel idea, as observed by many scholars in the field. Her cinema places bodies at the centre of cinematic experience in a way that estranges the spectator from the experience of bodies as a given object. By preventing the view of the wholeness of the body as a totality, by technically holding the camera on the skin and the body, Denis is performing what Thomas Elsaesser designates as 'cinema of abjection' (2018, 133) or what Kristin Lené Hole argues for an 'aesthetics of alterity' (2016, 2).

In many of these corporeal readings, theorists underline the displacing, othering, layering quality of Denis's work within the fields of ethics and aesthetics. Adding to this body of work from another point of view, this chapter will concentrate on a set of bodily encounters in Denis's cinema, to expand these ethical and aesthetic placements into ontologies where the weirdness of these bodies provides a space to question the 'being' or more accurately, 'the becoming'. One major framework to pose the question of the ontological movements that Denis's bodily configurations create is through the cinematic and literary genre Weird. Precisely because Denis's cinema asks us to sit with the body in its flesh, in its texture, in its tactile affect without necessarily using the body as an object to comprehend or to appropriate as such, we may find ourselves in a weird experience of being in which in lieu of understanding or perceiving the world differently, we may experience the impossibility of individuating the body as a purely epistemological or aesthetic entity. In other words, through corporeal disruptions and weird disorientations created by Denis's cinema, we may conceive the all-becoming of the body as an experience of excess and utter deterritorialisation.

WEIRD. WHAT IS WEIRD? WHY WEIRD?

After writers like China Miéville, Jeff VanderMeer and John Harrison revived the genre of the New Weird in the early 2000s, it gained prominence in academia owing to the abundance of literary and cinematic works that subsequently appeared.[3] The New Weird was, and today still is, especially open to ecocritical and post-humanist readings that made the genre especially attractive to the academics now involved in those questions owing to the imminent climate and species crisis. The Weird genre is not new and be can very loosely categorised under the large umbrella of science fiction (SF). Yet the discussions surrounding its definition differ widely. For example, one of the New Weird's most prolific writers, Jeff VanderMeer, traces it to both H. P. Lovecraft's 'Weird' of the early twentieth century and the New Wave of the 1960s while providing a style-based definition that underlines its 'visceral' and 'not overtly political' quality. On a different note, China Miéville's understanding of the Weird is less about definitions and more about its *affects*, the possibilities it creates, as well the impossibilities it relinquishes. Miéville asserts that 'The Weird's unprecedented forms, and its insistence on a chaotic, amoral, anthropoperipheral universe, stresses the implacable alterity of its aesthetic and concerns. The Weird is irreducible' (Miéville et al. 2016, 112). This definition of the Weird may sound ominous and perhaps even confusing, but the emphasis here is its power to radically alter the way perception and cognition are assumed to function. Based on this definition, for example, Boyse's damp, creamy, tangible skin with her leaky nipples refuses at first to render itself to any precise meaning as we are thrown off, veered away from the often-comfortable space of human-centric perspectives. We must remain with the skin in its awkward angle, with this wetness that we cannot make sense of, as the concept of motherhood is not there to help us leave a close-up surface in its place. In this sense, the Weird escapes and estranges stability, and along with it any recourse to a static individual being or meaning while promoting a dynamic individuation.[4]

The Weird with its 'slippery and elusive' character aims to create an *affect* in an ontologically and aesthetically displacing way (Luckhurst 2017, 1042). Hence the primary movement of the Weird is one of change or *becoming* instead of an epistemological and cognitive being. This becoming eventually threatens boundaries between normal and abnormal, opening up the possibility of another way of being, another way of understanding and living that can be beyond the norm. For example, Alison Sperling epitomises Weird's affective movement as 'a kind of willful and unruly corporeality, an often fatalistic . . . sense of dread over becoming, of transformation, of finding in oneself . . . that the outside is and has already been within' (2019). This realisation of the uncontrollability of the body's limits, of not knowing where the body begins and ends, the undoing of outside and inside of the corporeal assurance, is where the becoming is experienced in lieu of merely being comprehended, which takes away any and every epistemological security. Claire Denis's corporeal cinema builds precisely on this epistemic insecurity and demands a corporeal relation with her films.

CORPOREAL CONVULSIONS AND WEIRD SHUDDERS: *HIGH LIFE*

An instance of this lack of epistemological comfort as comprehension is what we can tentatively name the becoming-animal scene that takes place in Denis's 2018 science fiction film, *High Life*. This film follows the hopeless journey of ten criminals in a box-like, leaky spaceship that aims to reach a specific black hole to experimentally extract energy for already-annihilated earth in exchange for the commuting of their sentences. While the film plays with science fiction genre tropes, with a nod to Andrei Tarkovsky's 1972 chef d'oeuvre *Solaris* and with Denis's insistence on collaborating with physicist Aurélien Barrauto ensure an accurate account of black holes (Hammond), it does not reverberate around the adventurous black hole journey as do many films of the same genre.[5] Instead, Denis's film veers from SF, displacing the genre's conventions to explore something about parenthood and reproduction. Indeed, instead of an exciting journey hunting black holes, we follow the everyday lives of Monte (Robert Pattinson) and his daughter Willow, born onboard the spaceship as a result of the incessant reproductive experiments of Dr Dibs (a mad scientist and *Medea*-inspired murderer of her own children acted by a sensual, long-haired Juliette Binoche). Already weirding the SF genre into something out of its boundaries, Denis confuses SF-savvy spectators by providing them with a spaceship that looks like a coffin, with unclean, rudimentary interiors that evoke hospitals with a touch of prison discipline, while keeping the classical SF story – the voyage to the black hole – on the margins.[6]

In this move towards weirdness, bodies play a central role in the epistemological discomfort of the spectator. Dr Dibs's masturbation scene epitomises this cognitive abandonment when she enters a special machine, a 'fuckbox', which stands with its rectangular shape reminiscent of a mechanical horse with a metallic vibrator on top. Dr Dibs places a condom on the metallic penis, slowly strips down and we witness a long, weird, disorienting masturbation scene where we encounter fragments of her body convulsing, twisting and turning on the machine, with the camera constantly moving from one surface to another, always in close-up or medium shots with accelerated cuts which, in lieu of a sense of rhythm, evoke a vertiginous feeling of losing control. With the Tindersticks soundtrack moaning in the background, the camera shows Dr Dibs's naked back then moves to her breasts from above, then suddenly switches to following a large scar across her lower abdomen, which breaks the smoothness of her skin and is reminiscent of her murdered children. With the camera constantly moving on her body while she trembles, shakes, wriggles and pulsates, with her hands holding two ropes that seem to hang from the dark ceiling, we see sections of her sweating skin, messy pubic hair, gaping mouth, convulsing, twisting and turning flesh while her body breaks into multiple fragments. This oneiric scene reaches its climax when the machine that she is riding becomes an animal: a close-up of her hand shows her caressing what looks like light brown fur. She merges with the animal, finally finishing her convulsions. This merging with the animal and the machine ends with the metallic machine being automatically cleaned while oozing a black, sticky substance.

What happens in this scene is a plethora of sensations and blurring of the lines. As academics, we may rush to read this scene immediately with a transgressive merge of the animal with the human via the Deleuzian notion of 'becoming-animal'. Indeed, becoming-animal explains this utter lack of comprehensive respite, as in the process of becoming-animal, 'all forms come undone, as do all the significations, signifiers and the signified, to the benefit of an unformed matter of deterritorialized flux' (Deleuze et al. 1986, 13). Even if one can discern diverse elements in the moment of deterritorialisation, for example, the rapid cuts to the parts of the body with close-ups, which, in theory, allow us to notice that there is pubic hair here and the back of Dr Dibs there, they do not cohere into an epistemological narrative.[7] The persistent cuts to Dr Dibs's body, with rhythmic pulses and close-ups, do not reterritorialise into meaningful stability until the end of the scene. Even then we are not certain of what has really happened.[8] Hence, while becoming-animal explains the form of the event as a moment of utter flux, and our experience of the scene can be named deterritorialisation, this remains one affect among many that Denis offers.

Concomitant with this utter deterritorialisation, which removes the possibility of making sense of the experience of watching this scene, we can think about how we experience the body through and beyond the senses. In her treatise on French cinema of transgression, Martine Beugnet observes that in Denis's films,

> the remapping of the body appears coextensive with a remapping of the cinematic territory, where the function and use of the close-up, in particular, mark a desire to do away with the usual binarisms and blur the frontiers between the inside and outside, masculine and feminine, figurative and abstract, sensory and conceptual, subjective and objective. (2007, 207)

Beyond the easily recognisable idea of masturbating with a prosthesis, the scene does not allow the spectator to appropriate it; it is not a proper masturbation scene, partly because we cannot see it in its entirety owing to cuts, unusual camera angles and close-ups. While the body becomes, the cinema becomes something else. The body does not remain intact, unitary, in-itself, but instead bifurcates into animality and machinery rendering the subject–object relation an attribute that the spectator may attach to the scene only after the fact. In this sense, understanding the scene or this body is not given but something to work towards and without any guarantees.

This lack of guaranteed sense is one of Weird's gestures par excellence. When referring to the 'tentacularity' often associated with the Weird, Miéville makes this lack of meaning very clear, 'a weird tentacle does not "mean" the Phallus; inevitably we will mean with it, of course, but fundamentally *it* does not "mean" at all' (2008, 112, Miéville's emphasis). We can understand that there is a body masturbating, this scene is not meant to provide a sense: it refuses, first and foremost, to be reduced to one sense by refusing to mean as such. On another register, the fragmentation of these masturbating bodies (the amalgamation of Dibs, the animal and the machine) also transgresses a unitary, stable self where Dibs's self can be separated from the relations that she is entering through this ultimate sexual act. We are caught in a weird space where we can recognise the parts of the body, of the machine and of the animal, yet when put together, they do not provide us with a picture of a body, a dildo or an animal. Hence, we may perhaps note that this weird cinema demands an ontological encounter with the viewer that is beyond comprehension.

WEIRD TEMPORALITIES ON SKINS

In the 2004 film, *L'intrus* ('The Intruder'), Denis adapts Jean-Luc Nancy's short essay on his own heart transplant.[9] Shot in 35mm, the film follows an old mercenary, Louis Trebor, acted by Michel Subor, who lives a secluded life in his cabin in the Jura Mountains located near the France–Switzerland border. Trebor spends his days in quasi-solitude swimming in the mountain lake, sunbathing naked in the forest with his dogs, making love with his pharmacist lover, and occasionally stabbing an intruder, who could be (although we can never be certain) one of the illegal immigrants /Europe's uninvited guests/ intruders crossing the border in the darkness of night. Noticing that he needs a heart transplant, he abandons his beloved dogs by releasing them into the wild and goes to Korea for a black-market heart transplant. After insisting on receiving a young, male heart from organ smugglers who seem to act as both the provider of his new organ and the judge of his right to keep it, he finally goes to Tahiti, trying to find and reconnect with his estranged son.

While this summary makes it appear that the film is shot in a linear fashion, in fact, the film, just like the essay that inspired the film, is dispersed in time and composed of lines of intensities where Denis questions what it means to cross a border, to be an intruder and to have someone else's heart inside one's body in very tangible, carnal encounters with both Trebor's body and its radical otherness. Beugnet affirms this corporeal strangeness when evaluating this film as a form of film-essay, as she explains, 'in its cinematographic and in its literary expression, the theoretical preoccupation with foreignness is mapped out on the very body of the narrator/character, as well as in the wording of the written text and on the material surface of the film's images – imprinted, as it were, in the flesh of the text/film' (2016, 69). This primacy of the foreign and the strange flesh, this carnal exposition of the weird sensation of the stranger is epitomised in two main moments.

A wide-angle long shot shows a white, snowy hill with two men carrying what seems to be a corpse wrapped in white, bloodstained sheets. This view from a distance quickly cuts to a handheld camera looking down on the snow in a close-up following what appears to be human footmarks. At the end of this shaky walk, the camera shows a human heart covered in red blood, which seems to have been surgically and recently removed from a body, standing in the middle of this endless white snow. From this bleeding close-up of the heart without a body, the handheld camera turns left – perhaps to search for the owner of this stand-alone heart, improperly placed on the snow. The camera then shows the corpse of a woman, soaked in blood, lying on the snow. Soon enough, Trebor's Akitas, now abandoned by their companion, who is in search of another heart in another country, arrive and start nibbling on the heart. As in *High Life*'s lactation scene, this close-up of a detached heart first remains strange and weird. How and why is this heart surgically removed like this, in the middle of nowhere, in snow, and for what purpose? Denis does not sensationalise this moment. Instead, the camera stays with the heart, which seems too unreal and weird, while showing a very real and blood-covered corpse without explication, without recourse to any kind of pity or interiority. Is this the body of an immigrant who was crossing the border or is this the job of the organ mafia? Denis does not answer. What might a heart chewed by dogs mean? Why these dogs? We are left with this flesh in its strange appearance, a flesh that should not be there. Once again, to satisfy our academic need to anchor a meaning, we may quickly run to Nancy's own essay to find a reference to quench our thirst for easy and singular meaning. Throughout the essay, Nancy thinks about intrusion as an event where the strangeness of one's own life becomes clear. Thinking about the heart transplant itself, Nancy asserts, 'organ transplant imposes the image of a passage through nothingness, of an entry into a space emptied of all property, all intimacy' (2007, 9). Perhaps this is the image of this very nothingness where the heart is no longer the property of this corpse, and perhaps this heart is an organ without property revealed to the eye of the spectator. Yet such an explication does not account for this weird object, this heart, that appears in its out-of-place being; hence while being perfectly recognisable as a heart, this organ appears strange and alienating.

We can examine this estrangement with Mark Fisher's definition of weird objects that are

> so strange that it makes us feel that it should not exist, or at least it should not exist here. Yet if the entity or object is here, then the categories which we have up until now used to make sense of the world cannot be valid. The weird thing is not wrong, after all: it is our conceptions that must be inadequate. (2016, 15)

Fascinating in Claire Denis's cinema is precisely this ability to render bodily objects as weird: whether it is milky nipples or a human heart on snow, when these objects appear, the validity of the categories of inside/outside, subject/object are useless – if not detrimental – to the effect of the scene. We may want to desperately cognise the function and the meaning of this heart, this nipple, this becoming-animal. However, any cognitive framework that we bring up will not affect the existence of the weirdness of this object that we can no longer comprehend.

Is this heart lying bare on the snow, outside of its usual borders, in nothingness, simply a transgressive moment then? In other words, how can this loss of making sense of the world as such function? For Beugnet for example, playing with borders like inside and outside can move beyond usual perception towards the 'multi-sensory' kind that is freed from the 'omniscient gaze' (2007, 107).

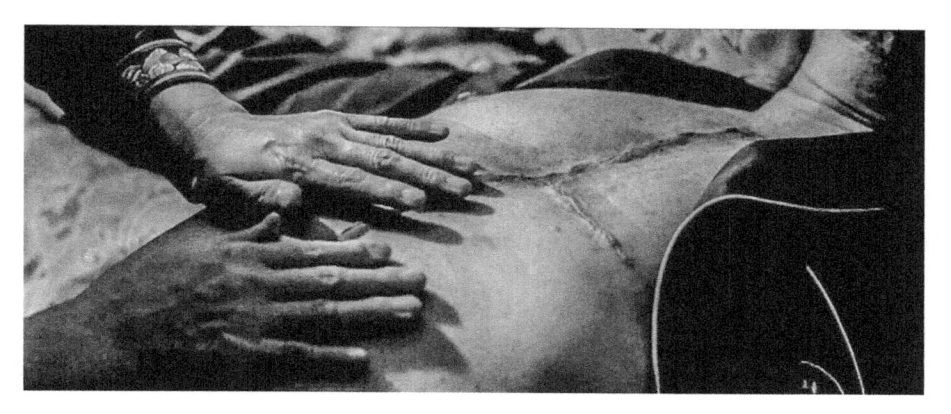

Figure 5.2 The scarred chest.

This all-knowing gaze is indeed lacking in Denis, where many interpretations, many knowledges and many sensations are all present at the same time, leaving the spectator in a state of an affective disorientation without the possibility of making sense that would secure any transgression back inside the known limits.

The function of this corporeal, weird disorientation becomes an experience in borders when we examine another scene in which we encounter the hands of a blind masseuse in a dark, dingy hotel room massaging Trebor's scar via an extreme close-up. Here, despite the open curtains, the room remains tenebrous, and we follow the hands of a petite woman exploring Trebor's head. The camera concentrates on Trebor, who is lying on his side, yet suddenly shifts to his feet as if clumsily checking whether they exist or not. This vertiginous scene with a camera that jumps from one section of the body to the other is in fact the meeting of these two skins: the woman's hands with Trebor's skin. The massage becomes a meticulous scanning of Trebor's post-operation body with someone else's hands as if the masseuse is perceiving this broken body with her fingers rather than her eyes. Finally, the masseuse turns Trebor on his back. Yet the camera stands at the edge of the bed as if peeking at his body from the corner of an eye. Trebor turns in pain with his belly and chest now visibly cut, a deep, swollen line of skin forming a scar. A tumescent wound with fresh, long, reddish stitches reminds us of the intrusive operation that disperses the smoothness of this body from the thorax to the belly. The scarring of this skin is reminiscent of pain, of the heart that is missing and the new intruder that is there. But this skin also makes us uncomfortable because the intactness of the body is now breached, and the scar is the proof of this missing unity. The lack of unity is mentioned by Sara Ahmed as she defines skin as what 'feels . . . purifies and expels' (1998, 51). Ahmed also marks the skin as temporality, as 'the skin remembers: It transforms itself in the passing of time' (1998, 51). The freshness of the wounds reveals both the pain and the time of the event, while threatening the integrity of the body. Indeed, besides dividing this body, besides fragmenting its proper unity, the scar is supposed to function as a marker of a before within the filmic time.

Yet Denis does not give us a before and after as temporal markers. The film is loosely linear, events and scenes are rather shown in various temporalities almost synchronously. Denis does not show changing seasons with *mise en scène* or perform continuity editing to tell us what happens when. Instead, many events happen at once where the order of things is not given. If and when we have a sense of time, then this is marked by the bodies incorporating change: this protuberant scar tells us that an 'after' the operation happened. The function of our corporeal encounter becomes a fragmented, weird time that is never completely mastered.

Yet this is not the only function of this weirding of the body. Ahmed reminds us, 'The scar demands and negates the integrity of the body: its form is a rem(a)inder of the failure of such integrity yet keeps in place the desire of integrity as the measure of well-being' (1998, 47). The ultimate disturbance accompanied by these weird sensations appears with this loss of integrity of the body: the masseuse goes over the scar with her fingers leading Trebor to moan in pain. The touching of his pinkish scar by these wandering hands leaves no space for making sense: besides the unsettling nature of the masseuse's blind touch providing a disquieting sensation, what remains in this scene are a lack of borders, the porosity of the body and the possibility of intrusion all felt in one hand stroke that asks us to reconsider the body and its borders.

CLOSELY WATCHED VEINS

From Dr Dibs's scars to Trebor's, from machine to animal, the body becomes a constantly moving terrain where any stable, unitary, intact line immediately dissolves into something uncomfortable, often through close-ups that refuse to provide the spectator with a full picture of the body. Roger Luckhurst underscores this undoing of borders in Weird as the genre's 'principal purpose' (2015, 1055). While he gives examples of territorial borders, we can very well see these porous, fragile, untenable delineations in Claire Denis's bodies. An accelerated montage as in the masturbation scene, or a handheld camera defying stabilisation, reflects the refusal to mean something by making every object, every image, more than itself and transgressing its proper borders. Hole considers these fragmentations as possibly another ethics, one that reintroduces the other in a way that does not subsume its alterity into the same. She observes an interruptive gesture in Denis's form when she says these films 'privilege fragmentariness in content and form, refusing wholeness and closure, having neither a definitive origin nor an endpoint, and continually expose their own limit/frame' (Hole 2016, 45). One of the effects of this fragmentation, besides encountering the other as Hole suggests, is to deprive the spectator of any feeling of cognitive mastery over the scene, instead of forcing them to stay with a multitude of affects and multiple cognitive explications that are all perfectly valid yet not proven at the same time.[10]

One of the final scenes of *Beau travail* can perhaps enlighten this impossibility of landing on a precise line of thought while revealing this fragmentation of bodies and borders. This film, perhaps the most known of Denis's works placing her in every syllabus in academic film studies, takes place among French legionnaires in Djibouti where we encounter soldiers training and their half-naked bodies that are exercising, swimming, bleeding and dying with the self-reflexive voiceover of a sergeant Galoup (Denis Lavant), whose unending jealousy of beautiful newcomer Gilles Sentain – acted by Denis's favourite, Gregoire Colin – costs him his career and possibly his life. From its opening scene, where an eerie Tarkan song mimicking a kiss encases the slow dancing bodies of Djibouti women seen on the mirror of a local discotheque frequented by the legionnaires, to the exercising bodies of soldiers, *Beau travail* uses the tangibility of the bodies as the main surface of the filmmaking.

Before the infamous final dance, where we watch Galoup's contorted, haunting and weird solitary dance in the dingy discotheque that opened up the film, Denis places the camera in Galoup's bedroom in a weird shot that never lets the spectator see the whole room to comprehend the space. First, carefully framed in a medium shot, we watch Galoup making his bed with a semi-static camera from an angle that enhances the bedmaking rather than the character. Galoup sits on the now perfectly made bed, and while we perhaps expect to look at his face, a very quick cut takes us out of the room to a long shot where all his legionnaires are standing in front of the sea as if posing for a picture. At first, this quick cut may seem like a photograph that Galoup perhaps holds in his hands, yet the wind on the scene tells us that it is a film-image, possibly a memory. When we come back from this live image, the camera is no longer in the claustrophobic bedroom; it is in an awkward place, outside of Galoup's green window panels, looking into the bedroom. From this clandestine place, we see him bend down to take his gun and lie down on his bed, his head and face now obscured by the window frame. His body is already fragmented by the room, the frame of the window, and the impossible angle of the camera. We cannot see this body, this man, who seems to attempt suicide.

Galoup holds the gun next to his body and a quick cut takes us back to the room to finally resume in an extreme close-up to his hand holding the gun, calmly resting on his naked abdomen. We remain very close to the body of this man for a while without being able to move back to see his face – as with Boyse's breasts – to perhaps understand his feelings. This weird proximity to the body, this weird angle is what Elsaesser uses to define him as an 'abject hero', a hero that throws the spectator off as the latter

> have to experience . . . a 'being with' that breaks with almost all the conventional spectator positions, such as voyeur or invisible fly on the wall, participant-observer or aggressively implicated addressee. Instead, all possible forms of affective and perceptual responses to the protagonist have to be reassessed by the spectator. (2018, 183)

Here we are with Galoup, on his body, on his skin, without the wholeness of the body that could make this awkward angle bearable. Instead, we are asked to be affected by him and with him, and to come up with all the possible actions he may take, and the reasons why this body might be here this way. In this fragmented corporeal space, all explanations are equally valid and sound. This very excess once again asks us to move from a cognitive comfort towards an affective discomfort, from knowing things properly to understanding the improper displacements of everything in its largest sense.

This scene ends with another extreme close-up, this time to his chest, specifically on top of his left nipple where we read a tattoo that asserts his motto 'serve la bonne cause et meurs' ('serve the good cause and die'), which Galoup's voiceover reads in the background. The camera slowly moves upon his body, brushing over his built biceps to centre finally on one single artery throbbing with the rhythms of his heart. As he has been serving the good cause for a while now, is it his time to fulfil the motto and die? Does the vein tell us that he is alive, or will it stop moving? These questions remain

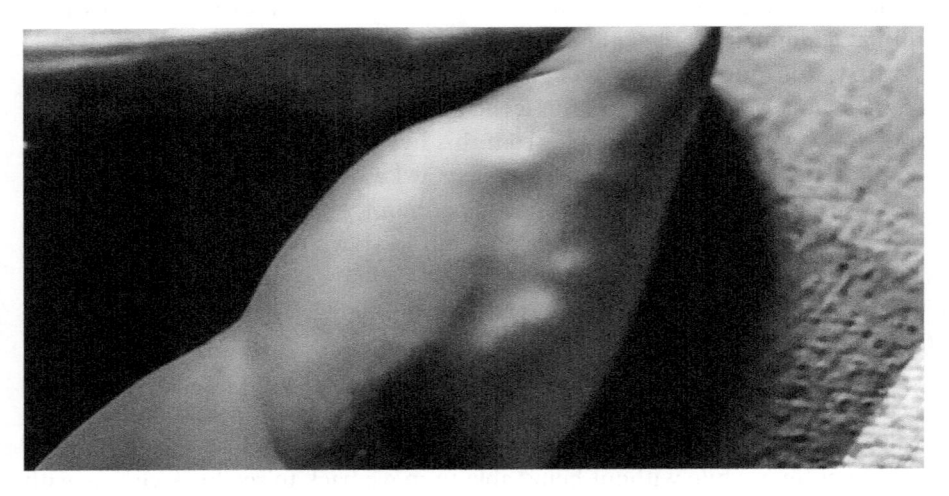

Figure 5.3 Galoup's throbbing artery.

unanswered, with a slow crescendo of Corona's song 'Rhythm of the Night', followed by a violent cut that takes us to the fragmented mirrors of the first scene. Just like the scar, the vein divides the smooth surface of the skin to mark the temporality and the ambiguity of the flesh: is this the end of the line for Galoup? Is the next scene perhaps a memory, or really a proof of his will to live? As in the case of Trebor, this vein marks an empty temporality that pinpoints change without giving the time. Once again, while all explications are completely plausible, Denis does not answer our quest for epistemic certainty, leaving us with this fragmented, weird bodily space where we are not allowed to appropriate this body as a body to know; instead, she insists that we encounter the body as site of becoming again and again, in its divisions, dispersions, veins, scars and leaks.

FRAGMENTED BODIES AND WEIRD ONTOLOGIES

How is this encounter with the body through fragmentations weird, and why can't we capture this weirdness with the old notion of uncanny? Precisely because encounters with these bodies are not really moving from something familiar, now estranged, that would place them in the centripetal force of the uncanny. Instead, here we have a centrifugal force: an affect of something that is out of place, a wrong within the given order that escapes from the centre contaminating the known towards the peripheries. We have access neither to the repressed desires nor to the deep psychology of any character in Denis to account for the uncanny – including the possible desires of an assumed spectator or addressee. In fact, rather than a familiar within the strange gathering a moment of unhomely feeling, we have an act of dispersion and expulsion from home happening through the body. For example, in *Nénette et Boni*, Denis's 1996 film exploring the relationship between a pregnant sister and an alienated brother who takes care of them, there is a very quick scene where Nénette, lying in bed under her comforter, lifts her comforter to look at her belly. The strange camera of Denis suddenly takes the place of her head, under the wraps, looking down at her swollen, naked, pregnant belly and her two legs, bent as if to give birth, resting on the bed. As with Galoup's body, we are at an impossible angle, looking at this round skin now resembling a peachy hill where we notice an abrupt move from inside. Is this a baby kicking or muscle spasm? This surprising angle changes not only the conception of the pregnant belly codified as such within an aesthetic and ethical order, but also demands that we accept the impossibility of ever conceiving a body as a being by revealing its instability. Here, we are not simply haunted by the echoes from the past, a familiar pregnancy now becoming unhomely: we are asked to reconsider the very conditions of possibly even understanding this pregnancy as such.

Yet just because we experience the weirdness of the body as centrifugal, dispersive force is not enough to claim an ontological encounter with these bodies. Why can't we leave Denis's corporeal cinema as another way to be estranged cognitively? In fact, if we follow Darko Suvin and many other SF theorists, cognitive estrangement, the state of not being able to immediately make sense owing to the experience of the strange in SF, is the gesture par excellence of the genre. So perhaps then, these fragmented bodies, claustrophobic close-ups, disorienting temporalities, are ways in which cognitive estrangement leads to a higher cognition.[11] Yet as I have argued throughout this paper, cognition becomes one minor and often uncertain affect among many in Denis's cinema. We may desire to come up with an excess of explanations for why and how we have this corporeal encounter, and we may perhaps attempt to make a stable meaning out of it. Yet these scenes move beyond simple cognitive estrangement and towards a weird space, as if there is something essentially wrong with the way we experience the world. We are at the wrong close-up, looking at the vein throbbing, with the wrong hands, touching the wrong scar as this close-up does not do what it is supposed to do: it is supposed to provide us with some interiority, some explanation, yet in its lieu, it leaves us in the wrong world.

Hence Denis, by using these extreme close-ups to fragment bodies, reveals a fundamental wrong in our experience of our own being in the world. By weirding our experience of the body as dispersive, moving and becoming instability, she makes us understand that the conception of a unitary, intact, stable body, as imagined by modern Western thought, does not belong here. This wrongness stems from this encounter with the weird as Fisher indicates where the weird 'is a signal that the concepts and frameworks which we have previously employed are now obsolete' (2016, 13). For example, in showing the scar of the heart transplant in *L'intrus*, Denis does not merely show the pain of intrusion or traces of a heart transplant. This scar pinpoints the uncontrollable becoming of the body as such where 'the body has always been porous, at risk, and imbued with a strangeness such that it was never properly bonded to begin with', and hence these scenes ask for another relationship with this body as the other (Hole 2016, 51). The body is no longer a property of the self, and precisely because it cannot be appropriated by this self the body becomes something weird and monstrous. Margrit Shildrick underlines the importance of this relation between the self and the body when she asserts that, 'to be a self is above all to be distinguished from the other, to be ordered and discrete, secure within the well-defined boundaries of the body rather than actually being in the body' (2002, 42). In other words, by undoing the borders of the body, and showing it as a constant becoming, Denis threatens the being of the self that can no longer hold on to this body.

In this excessive sense, the Weird is useful in rethinking Denis's corporeal expositions. Weird happens when we are affected by what we watch and see in a strange way. In this experience of the sense of weirdness, despite our mnemonic and automatic gesture of trying to attribute sense to a scene, we are opened up to a radical alterity in a more or less ontological sense. Miéville asserts this quality as 'a never-avowed-nor-disavowed – an abcanny' (Miéville et al. 2016, 201). An *abcanny*, unlike 'uncanny', is a centrifugal force that alienates by refusing meaning. We can agree with Miéville and/or we can call this centrifugal force *a becoming*. Yet what Denis's veins, skin, hair and flesh ultimately succeed in doing is escaping the ultimate epistemological and ethical comfort of the mind in order to ask for a disturbance to the very being of the body. Indeed, in an interview with Claire Denis, Jonathan Romney indicates this disturbance regarding *Nénette et Boni* when he says, 'we don't know where we are in this film and we have to find ourselves, we have to find the story', and asks whether this disorientation is a conscious decision that Denis made (2000). Denis, in turn, explains that her choices are both conscious and unconscious and she adds, 'but for me, cinema is not made to give a psychological explanation, for me cinema is montage, is editing. To make blocks of impressions or emotion meet with another block of impression or emotion and put in between pieces of explanation, to me it's boring' (2000). In response to how to find a way in a film where the spectator is 'lost', Denis chooses to respond by loving that sense of loss.

Denis's corporeal cinema claims the impossibility of appropriating the body as a totality, which would permit us to perceive it as whole, to control it and to put it in its proper place. Reconsidering these corporeal encounters that Denis creates, we can notice the novelty and excess of Denis's approach to bodies, not as a lack because bodies are weird and fragmented, but as an excess where any meaning we attribute to these scenes, from the otherness of the body as ethics (Hole) to the cinema sensation of Beugnet, is epistemologically plausible and yet not enough to exhaust all the possible epistemological, aesthetic and ontological possibilities. Her weird cinema is first and foremost a strange affect that disorients and veers off the road to get lost, and a corporeal cinema that undoes the familiar categories of meanings in order to transform the comfort of meaning into the discomfort of becoming.

NOTES

1. 'Again, I am not trying to make it difficult but I think, as a spectator, when I see a movie one block leads me to another block of inner emotion, I think that's cinema . . . But I think we also have a dream world, the brain is also full of image and songs and I think that making films for me is to get rid of explanation. Because there is, I think, you get explanation by getting rid of explanation. I am sure of that.' Claire Denis.
2. Originally a Lacanian concept, cinematic conception of suture is developed by Jean Pierre Oudart in his two-part article published in *Cahiers du Cinema* titled 'Suture 1' and 'Suture 2'.

Oudart introduces suture as a way for the filmic subject or the spectator to add itself to the signifying chain of the film. One of the most thorough explications of Oudart and suture can be found in the second volume of Daniel Fairfax's book *The Red Years of Cahiers Du Cinéma (1968–1973)*. Fairfax explains that suture is related to the possibility of reading the film as 'it is the suturing function that allows the viewing subject to "read" a succession of filmic images not as isolated, atomized spatiotemporal units but as articulated with one other, as operating within the same imaginary field' (Fairfax 2021, 668) By weirding the time and space of the bodies, Denis denies such meaningful reading of the film.

3. In an interview with Mike Bould, China Miéville asserts this rebirth through New Weird: 'It took the New Weird not to create but to strengthen and allow a field of possibility where the Weird, as a serious phenomenon and subset of literature, could be examined' (Bould 2016, 25).

4. When I use the concept of individuation in this article, I am specifically referring to Gilbert Simondon's (1995) concept of the individual and individuation, where the individuated being is understood as a *becoming*, a process. In *L'individu et sa genèse psycho-biologique* (1995), Simond asserts, 'the individual is not a being but it is an act and being is individual as the agent of this act of individuation through which it manifests itself and exists' (my translation, 186); 'l'individu n'est pas un être mais un acte, et l'être est individu comme agent de cette acte d'individuation par lequel il se manifeste et existe'.

5. In addition to Barrau, in 2014 artist Olafur Eliasson and filmmaker Claire Denis met to discuss their common fascination with black holes 'and their shared interest in abstraction'. We can see *High Life* as part of that fascination: https://olafureliasson.net/archive/watch/MDA116523/contact-a-film-by-claire-denis.

6. Jean Sebastian Chauvin indicates, 'Genre, in Claire Denis, resembles a wandering-infiltrating process. It has less to do with the perverting of cinematic modernity than with providing it with a wider horizon' (quoted in Beugnet 2007, 126).

7. Raymond DeLuca (2021) examines hair follicles and hair in Claire Denis as markers of space and time, which is an interesting conception of the body as a site of temporality.

8. I would like to thank Douglas Morrey for his suggestions of additional interpretations of this scene including the idea of the fetish, which is another way of reterritorialising it.

9. Denis explains that after reading Jean Luc Nancy's text, she began adapting it while talking with Nancy, who tells Denis that she 'never did an adaptation of the book. You adopted the book. That's different' ('Claire Denis Introduces *L'intrus*').

10. Here I would like to thank Peter Sloane for his discussion of Claire Denis suggesting that, beyond refusing to mean something proper, we can actually notice an excess of explications that are all valid at the same time.

11. I am specifically referring here to Darko Suvin's definition of cognitive estrangement. He borrows the terms from Bertolt Brecht to apply it to SF so as to elevate it into a literary genre that generates thought through cognition. Suvin's intentions in doing so are varied, including rendering SF as a high literature igniting thinking, but my emphasis here is on the cognitive activity that such estrangement carries. For Suvin, SF is *the* 'literature of cognitive estrangement' (1972, 372). Hence, *High Life* would count as SF if and only if it estranges us cognitively, which it does, among other things.

CITATIONS

Ahmed, Sara. 1998. 'Animated Borders: Skin, Colour and Tanning.' In *Vital Signs: Feminist Reconfigurations of the Bio/Logical Body*, edited by Margrit Shildrick and Janet Price, 45–65. Edinburgh: Edinburgh University Press.

Bersani, Leo. 2010. 'Father Knows Best.' *Raritan* 29, 4: 92.
Beugnet, Martine. 2007. *Cinema and Sensation: French Film and the Art of Transgression*. Edinburgh: Edinburgh University Press. https://doi.org/10.3366/j.ctt1r2d8p.
Beugnet, Martine. 2016. 'The Practice of Strangeness: L'Intrus – Claire Denis (2004) and Jean-Luc Nancy (2000).' In *The Essay Film: Dialogue, Politics, Utopia*, edited by Elizabeth Papazian and Caroline Eades, 68–85. Columbia: Columbia University Press.
Bould, Mark, and China Miéville. 2016. 'Not Just Some Viggo Mortensen of Desolated Left Politics: An Interview with China Miéville.' *Global Weirding, a Special Issue of Paradoxa* 28: 15–40.
Deleuze, Gilles, Félix Guattari and Réda Bensmaïa. 1986. *Kafka: Toward a Minor Literature*. Translated by Dana B. Polan. Theory and History of Literature. Minneapolis: University of Minnesota Press. http://www.kafkasocietyofamerica.org/.
DeLuca, Raymond. 2021. 'Hairy Screens, Filmic Follicles: The Uses of Hair in a Selection of Films by Claire Denis.' *Canadian Journal of Film Studies / Revue Canadienne d'études Cinématographiques* 30, 1: 1–24.
Denis, Claire. 'Claire Denis Introduces L'Intrus'. https://metrograph.com/claire-denis-introduces-lintrus/.
Denis, Claire. 1996. *Nénette et Boni*.
Denis, Claire. 1999. *Beau travail*.
Denis, Claire. 2004. *L'intrus*.
Denis, Claire. 2018. *High Life*.
Elsaesser, Thomas. 2018. *European Cinema and Continental Philosophy: Film As Thought Experiment*. New York: Bloomsbury Academic.
Fairfax, Daniel. 2021. 'Jean-Pierre Oudart and Suture.' In *The Red Years of Cahiers Du Cinéma (1968–1973): Volume II, Aesthetics and Ontology*, 665–94. Amsterdam University Press.
Fisher, Mark. 2016. *The Weird and the Eerie*. Watkins Media Limited.
Hole, Kristin Lené. 2016. *Towards a Feminist Cinematic Ethics: Claire Denis, Emmanuel Levinas and Jean-Luc Nancy*. Edinburgh: Edinburgh University Press.
Luckhurst, Roger. 2015. 'American Weird.' In *The Cambridge Companion to American Science Fiction*, edited by Gerry Canavan and Eric Carl Link, 194–205. Cambridge: Cambridge University Press.
Luckhurst, Roger. 2017. 'The Weird: A Dis/Orientation.' *Textual Practice* 31, 6: 1041–61. https://doi.org/10.1080/0950236X.2017.1358690.
Miéville, China. 2008. 'M. R. James and the Quantum Vampire Weird; Hauntological: Versus and/or and and/or Or?' In *Collapse: Concept-Horror*, edited by Robin Mackay, Re-issue edition. Falmouth: Urbanomic.
Miéville, China, Benjamin Noys and Timothy S. Murphy. 2016. 'Morbid Symptoms: An Interview with China Miéville.' *Genre* 49, 2: 199–211. https://doi.org/10.1215/00166928-3512333.
Romney, Jonathan, and Claire Denis. 2000. 'Claire Denis Interviewed by Jonathan Romney.' *The Guardian*, 28 June. https://www.theguardian.com/film/interview/interviewpages/0,6737,338784,00.html.
Shildrick, Margrit. 2002. 'The Self's Clean and Proper Body.' In *Embodying the Monster: Encounters with the Vulnerable Self*, 48–67. SAGE.
Simondon, Gilbert. 1995. *L'individu et sa genèse psycho-biologique*. Paris: Jerome Milon.
Sperling, Alison. 2019. 'The Weird and the Queer.' *Collateral: Online Journal for Cross Cultural Close Reading*. https://www.collateral-journal.com/index.php?cluster=16#d-fn1.
Suvin, Darko. 1972. 'On the Poetics of the Science Fiction Genre.' *College English* 34, 3: 372–82.
Williams, James S. 2016. *Space and Being in Contemporary French Cinema*. Reprint edition. Manchester, UK: Manchester University Press.

CHAPTER 6

The Limits of Life: Experimentation, Bodily Consent and Bioethics in *Trouble Every Day* (2001) and *High Life* (2018)

Amy C. Chambers

INTRODUCTION

High Life (2018) is a space- and science-based film that uses the mode of science fiction (SF) to explore not only the edges of the unknown reaches of space, but also the limits to sustaining human life beyond the constraints of Earth-bound ethical and historical frameworks. But *High Life* is not the first of Claire Denis's works to engage with the fictions of science. Her earlier work *Trouble Every Day* (2005) explores the uncontrollable subject of medical experimentation and the discussions of bioethics that *necessarily* limit scientific exploration. *Trouble Every Day* and *High Life* consider where the boundaries lie in terms of the value of and limits to life – asking characters and audiences to judge whose lives have value, and whether we can justify experimenting on others (human and non-human animals) to serve a greater good. Experimental subjects include a medical student and a doctor's wife in *Trouble Every Day* and death row murderers in *High Life*. Both films explore the ethics of bodily consent and the limits and value of 'life' in the medical sciences where the body can be reframed as a resource that is a mere 'collection of separable, detachable, exchangeable and re-incorporable objects' (Zwart 2016, 152). This science-based approach also allows Denis to continue to interrogate interests in whether we can truly disentangle human stories from the heritage of the incessant desire to colonise and exploit bodies, lands and futures. Whereas *Trouble Every Day* explores the limits of the body in terms of taste, control and survival, the desolate lifelessness of the vacuum of space in *High Life* exacerbates the inconsequential futility of human stories while both questioning and critiquing the ethics of maintaining and prolonging human 'life' while facing inevitable earthly extinction.

THE LIMITS OF LIFE

Figure 6.1 Dr Dibs (Binoche) conducts a pelvic exam on Boyse (Goth), who informs the doctor that she will 'never have kids' and that her 'body obeys' her.

In *High Life* the imagined future is both a narrative space and a discussion of the ethics of procreation and sustaining life. Life is presented as hierarchical with bodies and body parts becoming central to the focus of the film's scientist character, Dr Dibs (Juliette Binoche, Figure 6.1). She analyses her cast of fellow prisoners as if they are subjects in a lab to be used in the pursuit of creating life in space. The convict-crew are sent on a one-way mission to collect data on harvesting energy from black holes (testing the Penrose Process theory[1]), but Dibs also harvests eggs and sperm from the inmates in unwanted, perhaps unsanctioned but necessary experiments – in terms of long-term generational space habitation – into sustaining foetal life in often-sterilising, irradiated conditions. Dibs's fertility experiments eventually have limited success as she inseminates an unwilling female prisoner (Boyse/Mia Goth) with sperm stolen from her favoured male specimen, Monte (Robert Pattinson). The resulting child, Willow (Scarlett Lindsay) is first introduced in the film's opening sequences alongside Monte, who was made her father with neither his knowledge nor consent. Willow's future is already decided as she will become the last human, left with the choice of living out her days with her father and then alone, or shuttling into the abyss of the black hole that is presented simultaneously as a death sentence and a hopeful journey into the unknown.

Death and fear of unknown futures also haunt *Trouble Every Day*, an erotic narrative of medically induced cannibalism told across the intertwined stories of two couples: American newly-weds Shane and June Brown (Vincent Gallo and Tricia Vessey), and older, long-married Parisians Léo and Coré Sémeneau (Alex Descas and Béatrice Dalle). Coré and Shane apparently share an illness that is linked to experimental research on psychoactive plant extracts conducted by neuro-biochemist Léo. Shane once worked for Léo as a medical student on a bio-prospecting mission in tropical Africa that had been focused on finding possible cures for ailments including 'problems of the libido' as a barely glimpsed website informs us (see Figure 6.3). Shane uses his honeymoon in Paris as a guise for tracking down the Sémeneaus and soon discovers that Léo has been banished from a clinical research project on human libido for being unethical. It is unclear as to whether Léo intentionally used Shane, but it soon becomes clear that his wife Coré is an experimental subject. Shane and Coré have a cannibalistic afflic-tion that makes desire for sex and for flesh indistinguishable. Shane has refused to consummate his marriage for fear of literally consuming his new bride, June. Coré, however, is locked away every day at the Sémeneaus' home/laboratory but she occasionally escapes and devours the objects of her lust. Léo has failed to find a way to regulate the lethal libido of his wife and almost lovingly cleans up after her. Like *High Life*, the film's opening scene is the end of the film's narrative. It shows an unknown copulating couple, limbs indistinguishably intertwined in the back of a car, their semi-public lust veiled in shadows. The man wears a necklace of molars that take on new resonance by the end of *Trouble Every Day* as those teeth shift from being a metaphorical reference to sexual hunger, to the realisation that these are grotesque bio-object trophies akin to the hunter's safari souvenir. The couple are never seen again, but the scene and its disembodied teeth presents the lingering suggestion that this contagion has spread.

This chapter will argue for a reading of *High Life* and *Trouble Every Day* as science-based fictions. I position SF as a mode rather than a genre as it allows for interrogations of the body in relation to medical and imagined futures of science. These films align with the tropes of Denis's cinema that replay and rework the colonial narratives of desire for other peoples, places and resources and the recurrent colonial and 'nominally postcolonial' stories of 'rape, breed-ing, desire, kinship, and love' that hold Denis's works in close communion (Asibong 2011, 159). This will feed into analysis of *Trouble Every Day* and *High Life* as films of experimentation that dissect and reassemble discussions of bio-ethics and imagine the medical and ecological futures of humanity. Denis does not envisage a future where we will cure or escape our dying planet; humans have already consumed/cannibalised too much of the Earth *and* each other.

Despite their distinctive engagement with and reception through genre, these films correlate in their presentation of science (including medicine) and its relation to bodies past, present and future. This chapter positions science fiction as a mode rather than a genre where discussions of 'secondary "fuzzy" characteristics' are sidestepped to focus on the intersections of fiction and science (Menadue et al. 2020, 1). The following section begins by discussing science on screen and laying out the ways science, medicine and Denis's screens work together.

HEALTHY DOSES OF SCIENCE, MEDICINE AND CINEMA

As a creative space, SF allows for speculation, extrapolation and interrogation of the present day and imagined futures of what it is to be human. *High Life*, in comparison to *Trouble Every Day*, is the most clearly science fictional of the two, due to the tropes or characteristics it is seen to align to, including spacesuits, spaceships, black holes and long-term space travel. In an interview for High Life's press pack, Denis (Lefort 2018, 6) exclaims: 'Above all, and I must insist, High Life is not a science fiction film even if there are healthy doses of fiction – and science.' Notably, Denis accepts that her work includes 'doses' of science alongside the fiction, but is seemingly unwilling to consider her work as part of the wider and predominantly Anglo-American mainstream of SF cinema. Interrogation of science and medicine and speculation about the future are central to *High Life* as well as contemporary understandings of the mode of SF. Science fiction, as Brooks Landon argues, 'has moved in the twentieth century from being only a literary category to being a set of attitudes and expectations about the future' (2002, 4). Critical, fanatical and scholarly approaches have also expanded to consider the different ways of understanding and defining the term as mode rather than using the SF label that seems to cause serious 'auteurs' such trouble.

Claire Denis rejects the SF genre marker, perhaps suggesting a response like author Margaret Atwood's disavowal of the term. Atwood chose the more fluid and elusive, for non-academic publics, term speculative fiction – a distinction that holds little sway with SF authors, fans and scholars who accept the interconnections between these terms. Ursula Le Guin was famously frustrated by Atwood's apparent snobbery, and her 'arbitrary restrictive decision' to reject SF (Le Guin 2009, n.p.). Atwood made a clear distinction between *genre* fiction and the *literary* (Bechtel 2016), defining SF as mainstream 'sci-fi', tantamount to fantasy, and stingingly noting that 'if it is plausible or realistic, it is not science fiction' (Atwood 2011, n.p.). Le Guin's definition, however, was far more expansive and aligned to accepted scholarly approaches to SF as a speculative, sociotechnical imaginary where stories are based in reality rather than in fantasy. SF as a label can be read interchangeably as speculative fiction and science fiction. Atwood's expectations of 'talking squids in outer space' were drawn from schlocky stereotypes and fears that her promotion or even mere acceptance of the label would limit audiences and the sophisticated reception that was expected and desired. Leading to questions as to whether Denis's assertion that her work is not SF is a similar attempt to distance herself and her art from 'lowbrow, fluffy, escapist entertainment' and maintaining it as the filmic equivalent to 'literary fiction [that] is more serious, realistic, and sophisticated' (Bechtel 2016, 117).

Key SF theorists including Damien Broderick have argued for the reframing of SF as 'mode rather than genre' (1995, 23). This distinction allows for discussions of what SF *does* rather than what it looks like, and sidesteps those 'fuzzy characteristics' conversations altogether (Menadue et al. 2020, 1). Defining SF as ways of knowing and producing meanings 'about the contemporary world of global capital, information overload, techno-scientific imperialism, and geopolitical upheaval' allows for a broader understanding of SF (Hollinger 2014, 141). It is also one that incorporates and illuminates Denis's thought experiment films, or what Kath Dooley considers her 'graphic art house films' (2015, 435). Rather than reading these films through narrative, this approach focuses on patterns and themes as being 'of paramount interest' (2015, 140). In developing and releasing films like *Trouble Every Day* and *High Life*, Denis has not suddenly jettisoned her phenomenological concerns. Instead, these films offer a speculative space that almost intensifies some of the commentaries on the inescapability from humanity's imperialist desire, and disregard for their contemporaries and their world by positioning them beyond her viewers' lived experiences yet simultaneously in a realistic, plausible, speculative realm that allows the philosophical considerations to be centre stage through and *with* science.

Despite the startling accuracy achieved in *High Life* – the precise presentation of the black hole (photographic evidence was published after the film's release) and the theory surrounding black hole energy extraction (Penrose Process) – Claire Denis's attention to science is not entirely consistent. Darko Suvin's definition of SF surrounds the novum or the writer/reader's 'interest in strange newness' and the genre's potential for serious critical engagement with science and society (1972, 373–5). Denis's engagement with science is focused on the novum of the black hole and extracting energy from it, but is selective elsewhere. She shows little interest in the pragmatics of her trip into space despite having the crew and cast spend time at the European Space Agency (ESA) working with space scientists and astronauts. She is more interested in the lived bodily experience of outer space habitation on her characters. Either nonchalantly or disruptively (and perhaps simultaneously), Denis includes some scenes that would not be acceptable in high/hard SF. For example, in the opening scene the main character Monte (Robert Pattinson, already unexpected in both SF and a Claire Denis film) is fixing part of the spaceship only for him to drop his spanner; the spanner falls instead of floating off. *High Life* is a break from the traditional Claire Denis film, but also a break from the rules of SF in terms of believability and accuracy. Science and the 'strange newness' of SF is seemingly only of central interest when it is aesthetically or phenomenologically relevant. Gravity be damned.

THE LIMITS OF LIFE

When discussing science on screen, it is not possible to categorise discussions within a single film genre. Eva Flicker uses the label 'fiction film with a scientific theme' to indicate films that 'are set in a scientific milieu' (2008, 242). Here, I will use the shorter-term 'science-based' to indicate a similar concept. This is an approach to understanding interrogations of science and medicine where science itself becomes 'a genre, theme, or conventional representation in fiction' (Kirby 2003, 263). Science and the analysis of the spaces, systems and ethics of this field and cultural sphere in fiction extend beyond single genres, thus functioning as a mode of interrogation rather than simply a marketable genre.

SCIENTIFIC AUTHORITY AND TRANSFUSION CINEMA

Claire Denis and the creators of *High Life* showed clear interest in science by working with scientists in pre-production. French physicist and philosopher Aurélien Barrau was the cosmic consultant for *High Life*, and the images produced for the film of the black holes were strikingly accurate – but as Barrau has noted it was 'moving' but 'probably not a revolution because it basically looks like what [scientists] expected' a black hole to look like (Tayag 2019).[2] Filmmakers essentially 'borrow [the] scientific authority' of their science advisors to give their movies an aura of realism and believability (Kirby 2003, 264). Part of the marketing of *High Life* drew on discussions with and about Barrau, and space advisor Laura André-Boyet and the cast and crew's visits with her at the ESA. The ESA excursions included immersive experiences of working with 'real procedures, protocols, and equipment . . . to discover why we need to produce Space environment scientific data for the future of Human Spaceflight' (Epstein 2018, n.p.). Spaceship 7 is both a prison and a laboratory as it contains and collects the type of data required for potential future space habitation. Although the use by Dr Dibs of the societally discarded, docile inmate bodies in *High Life* aligns with Denis's previous features, where bodies are 'unstable, sinister, fragmented, eroticised or torn apart', the framing in *High Life* is distinctly science-based (Dooley 2015, 434).

Trouble Every Day and *High Life* comment on how science and medicine are viewed by society. They engage with these ideas through their presentation of not only the consequences but also the spaces and processes of science including the medical lab and the research ship (Figure 6.2), and the processes of dissection and analysing cells under a microscope. Representations of science and medicine on screen 'can impact how people understand scientific ideas, practices, and ethics' (Chambers and Skains 2022, 349). For example, both films prominently feature Dr Frankenstein-inspired medics with ethical frameworks corrupted by power, pleasure and murder. Drs Dibs and Sémeneau align with the original novel version of Dr Victor Frankenstein and his 'eugenics-based motive . . . to use science to create the perfect human rather than defeating death' (Kirby 2007, 86). But like many adaptations of Mary Shelley's original novel (1818), the focus in both films is on the ethics of experiments with the body, the limits of our conception of life and, in the case of Dibs, creating life from what she sees as raw materials rather than the bodies and fluid belonging to and part of distinct people. The connection between body and soul was a major theological concern of the early nineteenth century when Shelley imagined her modern Prometheus. But in these contemporary transfusion and transplant myths, there is little concern for individual preservation or the saving of souls; instead *Trouble Every Day* and *High Life* consider broader fears about humanity's failure to maintain and sustain itself and the planet.

The transfusion of fluids (semen and blood) and transplantation of cells are key parts of the two films under discussion here. These medical themes can be seen to align this discussion with what Hub Zwart defines as transplantation cinema – a narrative form that expands across genres including horror, SF, drama and even comedy to explore individual and cultural responses to the 'the cutting up and dismemberment of the body through medical power' (Zwart 2016, 159). As Ruth Penfold-Mounce explains, *Frankenstein* 'lies at the heart of transplantation myths origins', spawning a subgenre of horror and later parodic comedies where transplanted limbs and organs become possessed bio-objects that retain the nature of past owners (e.g. *Mad Love* [Freund, 1935], *The Beast with Five Fingers* [Florey, 1946], *Body Parts* [Red, 1991], *The Animal* [Greenfield, 2001]) (2018, 45). These films act as spaces of speculation and bio-ethical discussions of real and imagined bodies, and the fluid borders between self and other.

The apparent fluidity, unpredictability and vulnerability of borders and bodies recurs as a theme throughout *Trouble Every Day* and *High Life*, with blood, semen, milk and water taking central visual roles. With every act of circulation, exchange, excretion and extraction, these potentially life-giving and sustaining fluids connect the characters but also often appear in extreme moments of pleasure and pain. Of course, blood is vital to *Trouble Every Day*, but in its excessive presentation its meaning is unfixed and even lost as blood

Figure 6.2: Coré (L) from *Trouble Every Day* painting with the blood of a dead thief, and Boyse (R) from *High Life* cradling her leaking postpartum breasts.

THE LIMITS OF LIFE

cannot always be attributed to specific bodies or aligned to neat ethical frameworks. Images of Coré (Figure 6.2) in a blood-soaked negligée, including provocative images taken from scenes of her painting with the blood of one of the thieves who breaks into her home, dominated the promotional material for the film. Denis questions the value placed on the lives of criminals: is Coré's mutilation and murder of the intruder justified in this film as she *needs* blood to survive and the victim *chose* to rob her? Similarly in the space prison of *High Life*, is Boyse's forced insemination nullified morally by the crimes that brought her to death row?

Boyse is non-consensually impregnated in her drug-induced sleep. But the next scene shows her postnatal and separate from the incubated baby dribbling milk from the corner of its mouth. Neither the pregnancy nor the birth is shown; instead Boyse is presented in a tender, emotional and yet sexually redolent scene with her breast milk streaming across her topless torso (Figure 6.2). Her milk is an expression of her complex emotional response to the child she never wanted and a reminder that her body does not always 'obey' her. Close-ups of milky drips mirror earlier shots of Dibs's abdominal – likely caesarean section – scars and Monte's semen dripping down Dibs's thigh (Figure 6.3). Notably this also visually references *Trouble Every Day*'s closing scenes where close-ups of blood drips intermingled with shower water are shown after Shane eats (out) a maid; Shane invites June into the shower but the bloody drips reveal his infidelity to her and to his vow to resist his cannibalistic urges (Figure 6.3). Attempts to wash away the evidence of the affliction are also seen as Léo cleans up a murder scene and then tenderly sponge bathes a bloodied Coré. Water is also a potent fluid in *High Life* as several scenes include shots of the wastewater processing system that Dibs uses to drug the other inmates. The inmate-crew are human waste to be recycled – as Monte defines them – drinking purified (recycled) yet simultaneously contaminated (drugged) water that allows them to become Dibs's specimens. Akin to the plants and organs that are dissected in the lab in *Trouble Every Day*, the human specimens in both films are cut up and consumed by the camera in tightly framed shots that replicate either the medical gaze or a lustful hunger (and sometimes both, as Dibs's desire for Monte's fluids is both clinical and carnal). Fluids and cells are transfused and transplanted between bodies and across experiments as controllable bio-objects, but they cannot be fully severed from the messiness of their human donors or recipients.

Medical training and licences give Drs Dibs and Sémeneau power over the bodies of those they care for and ultimately disrupt. When considered through transplantation and transfusion medicine, 'the intimate interior of our bodies contains a set of valuable items that other humans (craving subjects) lack' (Zwart 2016, 152). Blood and organs are craved most explicitly by Shane and Coré in *Trouble Every Day*. But the clinician characters in both films show fascination with the 'valuable items' contained within the bodies they use for

107

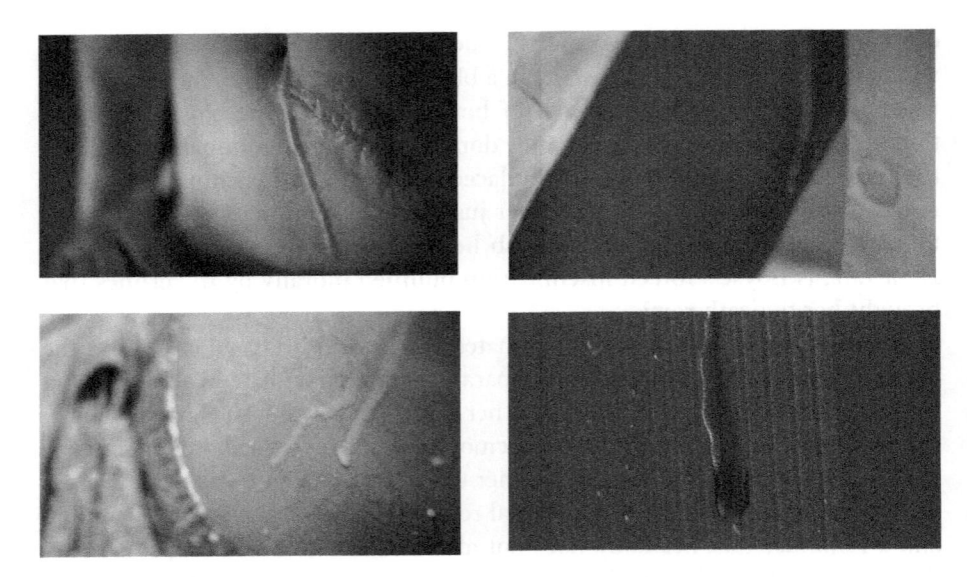

Figure 6.3 Dibs's 'dripping' scar (top left); a dribble of Monte's semen on Dibs's thigh (top right); and Boyse's uncontrollable breast milk in *High Life* (bottom left). Finally, there is a drip of blood in the shower water at the end of *Trouble Every Day* (bottom right).

their experiments. For example, in *High Life* Dr Dibs uses her clinical focus on reproduction framed as collecting valuable environment scientific data to justify rape and forced insemination. She is a craving subject who desires Monte not simply as a sexual object but as a medical one, who is letting his 'parts' go to waste through his own self-imposed celibacy. Monte is raped for his 'valuable items' (sperm), but is unable to consent to Dibs's (medical) advances. Dibs attempts to ethically neutralise her interventions as they are consistently presented under the guise of medical progress.

The removal and reinsertion of body parts – via transplantation cinema – has been part of the history of Anglo-American/Hollywood filmmaking since the 1910s and the release of Edison Studio's adaptation of *Frankenstein* (1910). Stories of mad scientists, possessed body parts and illegal organ markets and theft abound, but Gurvinder Kalra and Dinesh Bhurgra (2011) argue that post-2000 transplantation cinema marked a change in representation with more nuanced responses that considered the ethics of donation when the donor is not able to consent. They highlight *My Sister's Keeper* (Casavettes, 2009) as a key example that 'raises the ethical question of consent and how far one can go to save the life of a terminally ill individual, while risking that of the other' (Kalra and Bhurgra 2011, 97). In this film, a girl is conceived through in vitro fertilisation (IVF) as a saviour sister and raised to be a resource of transplantable organs for her terminally ill older sister. In response to her sister's desire for release from the cycle of surgeries that prolong rather than cure her condition the younger sister sues her parents for medical emancipation. *Never Let Me Go*, both Kazuo Ishiguro's 2005 novel and the 2011 film adaptation, imagines a future of clones who are created as 'spare parts persons' to be used up by their originals as oblivious and thus non-consenting donors (Schweda and Schicktanz 2009). Denis's own *L'intrus* (2004) also aligns with this cinematic turn as it 'creates elliptical evocation of the postcolonial transnational zeitgeist that is literally incarnated in the body of [the main character]', who predatorily buys illegal organs for transplantation into his own body that turn out to be from his estranged (cut off) and murdered (cut up) son (Beugnet 2007, 86).

Transplantation cinema, like science-based fiction more generally, offers a narrative framework for several genres. When asked to write this chapter as a discussion of Denis's engagements with SF, I was far more drawn to her uses of science not only in *High Life* as the most obvious example but also the underpinning of cannibalism in *Trouble Every Day* as a medically rather than supernaturally induced phenomena. Claire Denis is known as a filmmaker who 'blurs the frontiers of genre' as she rarely fits into a neat categorisation, instead finding 'a rhythm of variation to carry her through themes and genres' (Beugnet 2004, 84; Wilson 2019, 27). Denis has experimented with genre across her films with examples ranging from her true-crime/noir film *J'ai pas sommeil* (1994) to her romantic comedy *Un beau soleil intérieur* (2017). Unlike the realistic framing of the other genres she has explored, the films under discussion in this chapter seemingly offer and often disrupt identifiable genre spaces with the excessive horror gore of *Trouble Every Day* and the imagined future SF space-setting of *High Life*. There is a dissonance between the expectations of the genre being played with and the expectations audiences have of Claire Denis as an arthouse filmmaker. Does this perhaps suggest that Denis is herself functioning as the genre here, as neither *Trouble Every Day* nor *High Life* deviates from Denis's fascination with 'the dramas and desires of the human, tracked through an unremittingly tactile focus on the dynamics of vulnerable, exposed and wounded bodies' (McMahon 2014, 94)? Bodies in both *High Life* and *Trouble Every Day* are subject to the ravages of medical experimentation and the consequences of blurring the ethical concerns of consent. So, regardless of their generic genealogy, Denis's work consistently considers the ethical edges of where humans value their own or imagined future lives over the lives of others.

COLONISING SPACE(S) AND BODIES

Akin to her (dis)regard for genre boundaries and neat, marketable labels, Denis 'does not offer a clear and easy presentation of the plot and characters' in either

High Life or *Trouble Every Day* (Taylor 2007, 23). Audiences are left to make connections between flashbacks, diegetically present-day conversations and their own reactions to the experiences and situations in which the actors/ characters are placed. As Denis explains it, her films have 'a deconstructed form' moving elliptically across time and place (quoted in Talu 2018, 31). There is a consistent blurring of the lines between object and subject, 'object and idea, and what is seen and felt' (Dooley 2015, 223). The spaces that are used as settings across these films are also important in relation to these apparently fluid ideas around how bodies are understood. Claire Denis's characters (and their bodies) are often 'isolated but also integrated into space' and caught in the in-between of being part of society and an object outside of it (Price 2021). People become objects to be controlled, contained and/or concluded.

Trouble Every Day and *High Life*, through their narratives of exploration and experimentation, the ethics of consent and individual and institutional desire for resources and territories can be understood as what Andrew Asibong considers 'only nominally post-colonial spaces' (2011, 159). Many of Denis's films are actively positioned in colonial histories and legacies, including *Chocolat*, *Beau travail* and *White Material*. But those that are seemingly beyond the scope of these colonial discussions – and most explicitly *High Life*'s imagined future of outer space – still replay and repeat the themes of the 'alienating colonial mechanisms' found across her directorial oeuvre (Asibong 2011, 160). The science-based *High Life* does not offer a fantasy postcolonial future, arguing that it is impossible to fully disentangle human stories from their colonial pasts. Historically, science (including medicine) was presented 'as a positive enterprise that merely accompanied – and did not aid or support – a rapacious colonialism' (Seth 2009, 373). Denis, through both *High Life* and *Trouble Every Day*, shows the legacies of the colonial mindset in the false assumption that science is neutral.

The African bioprospecting mission that takes and mutates African resources, and the investigations into harnessing the power of black holes and colonising space as *caelestia nullius*, are not explicitly discussed as political actions even though they have wide-ranging consequences.[3] Léo and the infected Shane are followed back to France by a cannibalistic affliction as 'a reminder of a colonial past that cannot be shaken off' (Dooley 2015, 436). This biocolonial extraction is a representation of 'new imperial science' as defined by Laurelyn Whitt (2009, xiv). The extraction of local knowledge and resources is 'marked by the confluence of science with capitalism', where indigenous knowledge is often used to the benefit of large pharmaceutical companies (xiv), and thus 'a continuation of the oppressive power relations that have historically informed the interactions of western and indigenous cultures' (2009, 1). The neo-colonial mission of spaceship 7 in *High Life* is futile and shows only a replication of the deadly white desire to colonise and control – in the end,

THE LIMITS OF LIFE

space offers only death rather than riches and glory. As noted above, people and places become objects to be controlled, contained and/or concluded in Denis's films just as colonial subjects and the valuable resources of their homelands have been, and neo-colonially continue to be seen, as neutral objects to be consumed.

In *Trouble Every Day*, Léo is 'infused with the legacy of the French colonial past' (Taylor 2007, 26). Although he is of African heritage, this black scientist is associated with missions to discover and remove plants natural to Africa. As a Western/French researcher he uses local knowledge and foreign money to take African resources for the betterment of Western experiences and quite literally to cure Western impotence. Shane, a white former medical student of Léo's, is infected (perhaps purposely by Léo). Notably, but unsurprisingly, Denis frames this as being not the fault of Africa (like the mystification of AIDS as African [Patton 1999]), but of the scientists who take and mutate the plants. Where violent consumption of other bodies in *Trouble Every Day* might be read as both a punishment for and a continuation of French colonialism, the futility of *High Life* can also be read in conversation with the postcolonial. *High Life* offers a critique of prolonging human life and colonising outer space when the earth has been allowed to die. Space exploration in the anthropocene is a 'technofix for capitalism's destruction of planet earth, and thereby as an expression of human exceptionalism and isolationism' (O'Key 2019, 251). It does not address the systemic imperialist desires of humans or interrogate why the earth has been allowed to be so thoroughly assaulted and over-consumed.

Figure 6.4 Léo in *Trouble Every Day* is positioned here as both scientist and topless specimen on a corporate website detailing his research and the 1990 bioprospecting mission.

III

Trouble Every Day includes a bioprospecting (new imperial science) mission that aligns the film with Denis's ongoing post/neo-colonial critiques. *High Life* also includes not only the narrative of space colonisation and manifest destiny but also that of biocolonial control. Following the subversion in *Trouble Every Day* where a black African-heritage scientist represents French colonial arrogance, the incarcerated/enslaved pregnant subjects in *High Life* are white women. Women's bodies are increasingly 'resources and a major site of colonization and profitmaking' as incubators for stem cells and bio-by-products (e.g. from abortions) that can be used for research into cloning and reproductive technologies (Hawthorne 2007, 319). The use of the cells and internal organs of the women in *High Life* employs similar logic to *terra nullius*, which justified land occupation via the belief that apparently barren spaces were destined to be occupied and cultivated (Kemball 2022). Pregnancy is viewed through an imperial and scientific/medical lens here because to successfully colonise space, which requires long-term space habitation, women astronauts' reproductive capacities must be harnessed, with women, their organs, and their progeny considered 'property' (a future *partus sequitur ventrem*[4]) of the ongoing colonising mission.

Just as colonised and enslaved women were necessary to deliver the next generation of human chattel, the women on generational ships (also termed 'world ships' or 'colony ships': see Hein et al. 2020, 3–4) are necessary to permit long-term interstellar travel. As Denis explains: 'if you want to get somewhere a lifetime is not enough', and thus 'reproduction is important in a story about time. [It's] really something that belongs to science fiction, in a way, because it belongs to the future of travelling into space' (TIFF Originals 2019). Spaceship 7 is not a generation ship, but the exo-solar fertility experiments are as important as attempts to exploit black hole energy. The death row inmates who occupy the ship, including a woman doctor who killed her own children, are at the outer edges of ethical, legal and moral frameworks akin to the imperial attitudes held to the binary construction of the to-be-colonised Other. They are there to be used and/or dispatched for the progress of those who see themselves as inherently worthy of the Other's oppression and unconsented sacrifice.

High Life is set on a spaceship that is also a penal colony where prisoners are used as scientific subjects. *High Life* draws upon existent trends in SF literature, film and television that imagine the future of incarceration with off-planet penal colonies (*The Moon is a Harsh Mistress* [Heinlein, 1968]; *Alien*[5] [1992]); spaceship prisons (*The 100* [2014–20]; *Intergalactic* [2021]); and prisoners as medical subjects (*A Clockwork Orange* [1962/1971]; *Woman on the Edge of Time* [Piercy, 1976]). *High Life* aligns with the latter two tropes, as spaceship 7 is a prison ship of death row inmates given the choice between execution and imprisonment as test subjects on a one-way mission of deep space exploration from a devastated

THE LIMITS OF LIFE

Earth. As detailed in the press kit for the film, *High Life* is in American English not only because it is one of the international languages spoken on the International Space Station but also because the director wanted 'the spectator to recall a country where the death penalty still exists' (Denis quoted in Lefort 2018, 3). This imagined future US maintains the death row system, and retains the image of being a country where human life has value only as long as it serves a political purpose. As Monte explains 'we were scum, trash, refuse that didn't fit into the system, until someone had the bright idea of recycling us to serve science'. As prisoners they were already isolated, but as astro-convicts they are entirely cut off from the world they knew and any hope of release or pardon. They are experiments for both the penal institutions in terms of dealing with overpopulation and the resident medic whose fertility trials might give hope for long-term interstellar travel to escape mass extinction.

DOSES OF MEDICAL EXPERIMENTATION UNDER INCARCERATION

The medical narratives in *High Life* and *Trouble Every Day* do not revolve around consenting living subjects or cadaveric donors but unwilling participants (Monte and Boyse; Coré and Shaun). The victims of *Trouble Every Day* are two-fold as the ravenous Coré and Shaun are themselves subjects of experimentation, with their desires framed as impotence through illness (Taylor 2007, 23); they are victims alongside the people they eat. All the characters in *High Life* can be understood through the frame of experimentation as the entire convict-crew is on a one-way data-collecting mission where information about the impact of long-term space habituation on civilian astronauts (and their offspring) is perhaps as beneficial as the black hole data.

In *High Life*, Dibs sees the other inmates as subjects, as bodies to be disassembled and reconstituted in the service of creating new life (*à la* Dr Frankenstein). She coerces them into donating (sperm and ovum samples) and receiving sex cells without the sex. Dibs rapes Monte (Figure 6.4) in a disturbing scene where the sleeping subject (drugged by Dibs through the water) is mounted by the medic. The scene mirrors an earlier sequence in the unsubtly named 'fuckbox', where inmates are encouraged to relieve their sexual tensions on sterilised stationary sex aids. Dibs and her writhing body are central to both scenes; she is explicitly shown reaching orgasm in the blackened sterility of the fuckbox and later forcing Monte to ejaculate by mounting and stimulating him in the surrounds of the spaceship's white, clinical living quarters. Partnered sex for either pleasure or impregnation is not part of the imagined future of *High Life*.

Without consent, Dibs steals a sperm sample from Monte and almost immediately inseminates Boyse as they both sleep (Figure 6.5). They are both

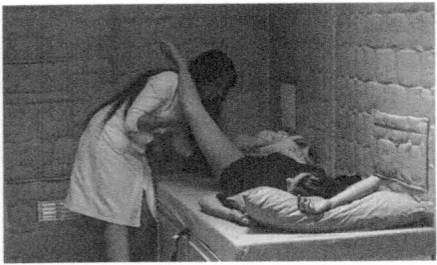

Figure 6.5 Dibs mounts a sleeping/drugged Monte to harvest his sperm, which he refuses to donate (L), and then inseminates the similarly incapacitated Boyse (R) in *High Life*.

raped. The previous subjects in Dibs's fertility trials have died, but both Boyse and the foetus survive the pregnancy. As Rene Almeling notes in their fantastically titled book *Sex Cells: The Medical Market for Eggs and Sperm*, we have moved from discussions of 'sex to cells' when it comes to the medicalisation of reproduction through assisted reproductive technology (2011, 10). *High Life* extrapolates this further as mothers and fathers (as gametes then zygote) and the hoped-for-foetus are valued for their cellular processes and scientific data rather than their lived experiences and future possibilities. The foetus has value only during incubation and its initial survival. Willow – the surviving child of Boyse and Monte – is destined to live a hard life and to die without reproducing (unless incestuously); the futures of these children are not considered here as they are essentially bio-by-products of successful experiments. Dibs (and an assumed governmental/international institution funding the mission) does not care for these discarded carceral bodies, and her filicidal history further compounds the reading of the character as unnatural (Frankenstein-like) and uncaring (a child-consuming witch).

The Foucauldian (1995 [1975]) docile, carceral body is relevant here as it is framed through notions of bio-power where there has been 'an explosion of numerous and diverse techniques' – and indeed technologies – 'for achieving the subjugations of bodies and the control of populations' (Foucault 1978 [1976], 140). The prisoner is redefined in terms of what it is to be human, and Dibs's repositioning of the inmates as reserves and vessels to be plundered and filled aligns with justifications for prison treatment, experiments and SF narratives concerned with incarcerated patients (Glenn et al. 2020; Nellis 2013).[6] In the carceral space, bodies are ethically aligned with non-human animals (also used in experimentation and for 'purpose breeding'), and even deemed un-human in order to create conditions that justify them being seen as disposable or even killable (Morin 2017). As death row inmates on spaceship 7, Monte and Boyse's bodies have value in their usability (recyclability) and the prison becomes a laboratory, at least in Dibs's mind. Historically, the medical abuse of patients is not restricted to the atrocities of the Nazi Holocaust and Stalin's Gulag, with experiments common and officially sanctioned in US prisons during most of the twentieth century (Washington 2006). As Karen M. Morin surmises, 'there are serious ethical problems with suggesting that captive prisoners could ever be "free" to consent' to clinical and experimental testing (2017, 1325). Even though the convict-crew in *High Life* technically donated their bodies to a scientific mission they did so to avoid death at the hands of the state (execution).

The only African-American male prisoner in *High Life*, Tcherny (André Benjamin/André 3000), explains to Monte that the only reason he agreed to the mission was 'to turn [his family's] shame into some type of glory'; his consent is conditional and, as it turns out, rejected as 'bullshit' by his wife. Without explicit consent the donor body is victimised regardless of who is saved or sated by its consumption. Margrit Shildrick argues that 'donor altruism' and 'gift of life' discourses are central to clinical and public narratives surrounding the donation of fluids and organs (2022, 55). Recipients are connected to their donors as they are made aware that the implanted organ/fluid is 'not simply a circulating spare part' but a gift given by consent of a donor that the recipient is 'effectively indebted' to (Shildrick 2003, 55, see also Shildrick 2013). It is a 'commodification of the body – a process in which economic value is assigned to bodily services or goods', but one where part of the value is consent (Almeling 2011, 10). The gift economy narrative allows for people to overlook the reality of the disintegration of the body and the extraction and reuse of bloody body parts (Sharp 2006, 12). Although *Trouble Every Day* explicitly shows cannibalism, *High Life*'s Dibs's 'strange harvest' (Sharp 2006) of bodily parts and fluids can be analysed through what bioethicist Stuart J. Youngner terms 'nonoral cannibalism', where body parts being removed from host bodies are implanted in and thus cannibalised (2003, 707). The ethical line is created by consent, and public discourses frame reused body parts as gifts willingly given and graciously received.

Organ transplant is seen as a cannibalistic act in another of Denis's early 2000s films: *L'intrus*. In this film the main character, Louis Trebor (Michel Subor), buys a heart on the organ black market to save his own life. Rather than being a willing participant, the donor is murdered (preserving life without consent) for those desired parts, a disregard that is also seen in the genre-framed films *Trouble Every Day* and *High Life*. The taking and implantation of parts of one body into another (semen and ovum) without consent underpins *High Life* and aligns with the ethical commentary of *Trouble Every Day*, where humans are used as sites of experimentation and human bodies are consumed. Whereas literal cannibalism could perhaps be deemed *necessary* for survival for the human medical experiments in *Trouble Every Day*, the life created in *High Life* is futile: Monte and his daughter are the only survivors on a one-way space mission. But then again, Dr Dibs's obsession with creating life at any cost – including stealing body parts and bodily autonomy by forced donation and forced insemination – may be positioned more ethically fluidly than the need for human flesh and blood in *Trouble Every Day* that results from Dr Léo Sémeneau's work. In the medical lab space of the spaceship in *High Life* the inmates are imprisoned like lab rats, sent out on a one-way mission because they are deemed ethically disposable. Their deaths are given apparent meaning as they are sacrificed by the state and 'save' other scientists from needing to become martyrs to missions to save the dying planet. Hero scientists are not needed here, but there is still a need for scientific intervention and medical care that explains Dibs's inclusion on the mission even though it is revealed that she murdered her own children. A chilling revelation for a character so obsessed with procreation on a mission to save the future of humanity.

CONCLUSION: THE LIMITS TO LIFE: BODIES OUT TIME, SPACE AND REALITY

In *High Life*, the inmate-astronauts are little more than 'specters from a dying world', memories of a world in turmoil and light years ahead in time, meaning that Monte and Willow are not only the last alive on the *7* but also perhaps the last of humanity (Wilson 2019, 19). They are bodies out of time, space and our lived reality. Stories of difficulties between Denis and the original screenwriter, Zadie Smith, abound with the revelation that Smith wanted the journey to be one of return. A suggestion to which Denis responded, 'What the fuck do you mean, going home? There's no one alive there anymore' (Erbland 2018, n.p.). In *High Life*, the isolation of space allows character analysis but also makes comment on the climate crisis and Denis's apparent acceptance of the inevitability of the sixth mass extinction.[7] Similarly, through the spectacular frame of *Trouble Every Day*, Coré and Shane's affliction leads to the insatiable colonisation/consumption of other bodies that is brought about by the constant use and misuse of natural resources. The spreading of the affliction that is warned of at the beginning of the film essentially suggests that this disregard for nature and its intended use/home is the beginning of the end of humanity. People are literally consuming each other following humanity's rapacious overconsumption and overpopulation of the planet. These eco-disaster elements align these films to what Mark Bould (2021) identifies as 'the anthropocene unconscious', where contemporary media have become 'pregnant with catastrophe' and imagined futures of climate disaster.

The doses of science, fiction and reality in Claire Denis's 'graphic arthouse' films *High Life* and *Trouble Every Day* do not correlate with a science fiction/fantasy genre frame (Dooley 2015, 435). They instead privilege patterns and themes over genre characteristics and narratives, offering critiques of not only the cultures and systems of science but also the apparently inescapable white, colonial, patriarchal frameworks that govern some human behaviours. Science is more than a plot point, but part of the way these films are structured through discussions of the ethics of experimentation on unwilling participants for the greater good, building on notions of control and lack of control over bodies and their interiors and ultimately questioning the trust placed in the medical establishment and scientific institutions whose commercial motivations overshadow the need for collective efforts to save our future by saving our planet. Science fiction as a mode provides a socio-political commentary on where humanity may be heading, and as such it reveals an elevated creative form where the speculative is more than fictional.

NOTES

1. 'Above all, and I must insist, *High Life* is not a science fiction film even if there are healthy doses of fiction – and science.' Claire Denis (quoted in Lefort 2018: 6).
2. Research published in 2020 and 2022 after the 2019 release of *High Life* confirms the underlying physics of this theory/method of energy extraction from black holes proposed by mathematical physicist Roger Penrose in 1969. See Faccio and Cromb (2020); Cromb, et al. (2020); Braidotti, et al. (2022). A fascinating coincidence alongside the strikingly accurate representation of the black hole discussed later in this chapter.
3. The first direct visual evidence of a super-massive black hole and its shadow located in the galaxy Messier 27 was released in April 2019 (Lutz 2019). It was strikingly like the image rendered for use in *High Life*.
4. *Caelestia nullius*, meaning 'celestial bodies belonging to no one', is drawn from the Latin term *terra nullius* ('the land of no one'), previously used in international law to define territories as belonging to no one and thus legally uninhabited (despite indigenous populations), and therefore open to be claimed by sovereign nations. *Terra Nullius* deprived indigenous people of their property rights and was used to justify colonisation. See Fitzmaurice (2007) and Temmen (2022).
5. *Partus sequitur ventrem* translates as 'that which is brought forth follows', and was a legal doctrine that declared that slave status was passed through the mother regardless of the father's race or position. If a mother was a slave, then so was her child (see Cowling 2013, 53–5; Turner 2017).
6. For example, the science fiction prison drama *Fortress* (Stuart Gordon, 1992) is focused on reproductive futures as people are imprisoned for having more than one child, and all prisoners are fitted with 'intestinators' that cause extreme pain or explode if behaviour *needs* to be controlled. In the novel (Burgess, 1962) and film adaptation (Kubrick, 1971) of *A Clockwork Orange*, medicine becomes the jailor as the main character Alex DeLarge becomes an experimental subject in apparently rehabilitative aversion therapy. State violence is seen as at least equivalent, in *A Clockwork Orange*, to the violence perpetrated by the convicts themselves.
7. The sixth mass extinction is underway; human overconsumption and overpopulation has caused a 'biological annihilation' of wildlife in the last few decades that threatens ongoing survival of humanity (Ceballos et al. 2017; see also Kolbert 2014).

CITATIONS

Almeling, R. 2011. *Sex Cells: The Medical Market for Eggs and Sperm*. Berkely: University of California Press.

Asibong, A. 2011. 'Claire Denis's Flickering Spaces of Hospitality.' *L'Esprit Créateur* 51, 1: 154–67. https://doi.org/10.1353/esp.2011.0008.

Atwood, M. 2011. 'If it is plausible or realistic, it is not science fiction.' *Gizmodo* 6 October. https://gizmodo.com/if-it-is-realistic-or-plausible-then-it-is-not-science-5847421

Bechtel, G. 2016. 'Our Villains, Ourselves: On SF, Villainy, and . . . Margaret Atwood?' *The Word-Hoard* 5: 115–30.

Beugnet, M. 2004. *Claire Denis*. Manchester: Manchester University Press.

Beugnet, M. 2007. *Cinema and Sensation: French Film and the Art of Transgression*. Edinburgh: Edinburgh University Press.

Bould, M. 2021. *The Anthropocene Unconscious: Climate Catastrophe Culture*. London: Verso.

Braidotti, M. C., F. Marino, E. M. Wright, and D. Faccio. 2022. 'The Penrose process in nonlinear optics.' *AVS Quantum Science* 4: 010501–13. https://doi.org/10.1116/5.0073218.

Ceballos, G., P. R. Ehrlich and R. Dirzo. 2017. 'Biological annihilation via the ongoing sixth mass extinction signaled by vertebrate population losses and declines'. *PNAS* 114, 30: E6089–E6096. https://doi.org/10.1073/pnas.1704949114

Chambers, A. C., and R. L. Skains. 2022. 'Science and Technology.' In *The Routledge Handbook to Star Trek*, edited by L. Garcia-Siino, S. Mittermeier and S. Rabitsch, 348–56. London: Routledge. https://doi.org/10.4324/9780429347917-53.

Cowling, C. 2013. *Conceiving Freedom: Women of Color, Gender, and the Abolition of Slavery in Havana and Rio de Janeiro*. Chapel Hill: University of North Carolina Press.

Cromb, M., G. M. Gibson, E. Toninelli, M. J. Padgett, E. M. Wright, and D. Faccio, 2020. 'Amplification of waves from a rotating body.' *Nature Physics* 16: 1069–73.

Dooley, K. 2015. 'Haptic visions of unstable bodies in the work of Claire Denis.' *Continuum* 29, 3: 434–44. https://doi.org/10.1080/10304312.2015.1025360

Epstein, S. S. 2018. 'Claire Denis's Science Consultant Talks About *High Life*.' *Sloan Science & Film/Museum of the Moving Image*, 14 November. http://www.scienceandfilm.org/articles/3169/claire-denis-science-consultant-talks-about-high-life

Erbland, K. 2018. '"High Life" Director Claire Denis Explains Why Novelist Zadie Smith Departed Film: "There Was Not a Word We Could Share".' *IndieWire*, 3 October. www.indiewire.com/2018/10/high-life-claire-denis-zadiesmith-left-robert-pattinson-1202009125/.

Faccio, D., and Cromb, M. 2020. 'Could we extract energy from a black hole? Our experiment verifies old theory.' *The Conversation*, 26 June. https://theconversation.com/could-we-extract-energy-from-a-black-hole-our-experiment-verifies-old-theory-141464

Fitzmaurice, A. 2007. 'The genealogy of Terra Nullius.' *Australian Historical Studies* 38, 129: 1–15. https://doi.org/10.1080/10314610708601228

Flicker, E. 2008. 'Women scientists in mainstream films: social role models contribution to the public understanding of science from the perspective of film sociology.' In *Science images and popular images of the sciences*, edited by B Hüppauf and P. Weingart, 241–56. New York: Routledge.

Foucault, M. 1978 [1976]. *The History of Sexuality: An Introduction Volume One*, translated by Robert Hurley. New York: Random House.

Glenn, J. E., A. M. Bennett, R. J. Hester, N. N. Tajuddin A. and Hashmi. 2020. '"It's like heaven over there": medicine as discipline and the production of the carceral body.' *Health Justice* 8, 5. https://doi.org/10.1186/s40352-020-00107-5.

Hawthorne, S. 2007. 'Land, Bodies, and Knowledge: Biocolonialism of Plants, Indigenous Peoples, Women, and People with Disabilities.' *Signs: Journal of Women in Culture and Society* 32, 2: 314–23. https://doi.org/10.1086/508224.

Hein, A. M., C. Smith, C. Marin and K. Staats. 2020. 'World ships: feasibility and rationale.' *Acta Futura* 12: 75–104.

Hollinger, V. 2014. 'Genre vs. Mode.' In *The Oxford Handbook of Science Fiction*, edited by R. Latham, 140–52. Oxford: Oxford University Press. https://doi.org/10.1093/oxfordhb/9780199838844.013.0012.

Kalra, G. G., and D. Bhugra. 2011. 'Representation of organ transplantation in cinema and television.' *International journal of organ transplantation medicine* 2, 2: 93–100.

Kemball, A. 2022. 'Biocolonial pregnancies: Louise Erdrich's *Future Home of the Living God* (2017).' *Medical Humanities* 48:159–68. https://doi.org/10.1136/medhum-2021-012250.

Kirby, D. A. 2003. 'Scientists on the Set: Science Consultants and the Communication of Science in Visual Fiction.' *Public Understanding of Science* 12, 3: 261–78.

Kirby, D. A. 2007. 'The Devil in Our DNA: A Brief History of Eugenics in Science Fiction Films.' *Literature and Medicine* 26, 1: 83–108.

Kolbert, E. 2014. *The Sixth Extinction: An Unnatural History*. New York: Henry Holt.

Landon, B. 2002. *Science Fiction After 1900: From the Steam Man to the Stars*. London: Routledge.

Lefort, G. 2018. 'Interview with Claire Denis.' In *High Life* press kit, Wild Bunch International Sales, 2–6. URL: https://www.wildbunch.biz/movie/high-life/.

Le Guin, U. 2009. 'The Year of the Flood by Margaret Atwood.' *The Guardian*, 29 August. https://www.theguardian.com/books/2009/aug/29/margaret-atwood-year-of-flood.

Lutz, O. 2019. 'How Scientists Captured the First Image of a Black Hole.' *NASA Jet Propulsion Laboratory*, 19 April. https://www.jpl.nasa.gov/edu/news/2019/4/19/how-scientists-captured-the-first-image-of-a-black-hole/.

McMahon, Laura. 2014. 'Rhythms of Relationality: Denis and Dance.' In *The Films of Claire Denis: Intimacy on the Border*. London: I. B. Tauris.

Menadue, C. B., K. Giselsson, and D' Guez. 2020. 'An Empirical Revision of the Definition of Science Fiction: It Is All in the Techne. . .' *SAGE Open* 10, 4: 1–18. https://doi.org/10.1177/2158244020963057.

Morin, K. M. 2017. 'Carceral space: Prisoners and animals.' *Antipode: A Radical Journal of Geography* 48, 5: 1317–36.

Nellis, M. 2013. 'Future punishment in American science fiction films.' In *Captured by the Media: Prison Discourse in Popular Culture*, edited by P. Mason, 210–28. New York: Routledge.

O'Key, Dominic. 2019. 'Animal Borderlands: An Introduction.' *Parallax* 25, no. 4, 351–7.

Patton, C. 1999. 'Inventing "African AIDS"'. In *Culture, Society and Sexuality: A Reader*, edited by P. Aggleton and R. G. Parker, 387–404. London: University College London Press.

Penfold-Mounce, R. 2018. *Death, The Dead and Popular Culture*. Bingley: Emerald Publishing.

Price, Y. 2021. 'Transplanted Territories: Claire Denis's 'L'Intrus' (2004).' *MUBI Notebook Feature* [online]. 25 March. https://mubi.com/notebook/posts/transplanted-territories-claire-denis-s-l-intrus-2004.

Schweda, M., and S. Schicktanz. 2009. 'The "spare parts person"? Conceptions of the human body and their implications for public attitudes towards organ donation and organ sale.' *Philosophy, Ethics, and Humanities in Medicine* 4, 4. https://doi.org/10.1186/1747-5341-4-4

Seth, S. 2009. 'Putting knowledge in its place: science, colonialism, and the postcolonial.' *Postcolonial Studies* 12, 4: 373–88. https://doi.org/10.1080/13688790903350633.

Sharp, L. A. 2006. *Strange Harvest: Organ Transplants, Denatured Bodies, and the Transformed Self.* Berkeley: University of California Press.

Shildrick, Margrit. 2003. 'Relative Responsibilities.' *Women: A Cultural Review*, 14:2, 182–94. DOI: 10.1080/09574040310104.

Shildrick, M. 2013. 'Re-imagining Embodiment: Prostheses, Supplements, and Boundaries.' *Somatechnics* 3, 2: 270–86. https://doi.org/10.3366/soma.2013.0098.

Shildrick, M. 2022. *Visceral Prostheses: Somatechnics and Posthuman Embodiment*. London: Bloomsbury.

Suvin, D. 1972. 'On the Poetics of the Science Fiction Genre.' *College English* 34, 3: 372–82.

Talu, Y. 2018. 'The Space Between Us: Claire Denis Talks About Finding the Melody Between the Notes.' *Film Comment* (May–June): 31.

Tayag, Y. 2019. 'How "High Life" Created a Black Hole That Looks Just Like the Historic Photo.' *Inverse*, 20 April. https://www.inverse.com/article/55087-high-life-claire-denis-aurelien-barrau-got-black-holes-right.

Taylor, K. 2007. 'Infection, Postcolonialism and Somatechnics in Claire Denis's *Trouble Every Day* (2002).' *Studies in French Cinema* 7, 1: 19–29. https://doi.org/10.1386/Sfci.7.1.19_1.

Temmen, J. 2022. 'Writing Life on Mars: Posthuman Imaginaries of Extraterrestrial Colonization and the NASA Mars Rover Missions.' In *Life Writing in the Posthuman Anthropocene*, edited by I. Batzke, L. Espinoza Garrido and L. M. Hess, 205–23. Cham: Palgrave Macmillan.

TIFF Originals. 2019. *Claire Denis on sex as an escape – in space! | HIGH LIFE | TIFF 2019* [video]. https://www.youtube.com/watch?v=1pMowXy77O4.

Turner, S. 2017. *Contested Bodies: Pregnancy, Childrearing, and Slavery in Jamaica*. Philadelphia: University of Pennsylvania Press.

Washington, H. 2006. *Medical Apartheid: The Dark History of Medical Experimentation on Black Americans from Colonial Times to the Present*. New York: Doubleday.

Whitt, L. 2009. *Science, Colonialism, and Indigenous Peoples: The Cultural Politics of Law and Knowledge*. Cambridge: Cambridge University Press.

Wilson, E. 2019. 'Love Me Tender: New Films from Claire Denis.' *Film Quarterly* 72, 4: 18–28. https://doi.org/10.1525/FQ.2019.72.4.18.

Youngner, S. J. 2003. 'Some must die'. *Zygon* 38, 3: 705–24.

Zwart, H. 2016. 'Transplantation medicine, organ-theft cinema and bodily integrity.' *Subjectivity* 9, 2: 151–80.

CHAPTER 7

Trans-generic Dramas of Non-disclosure: Equilibrium, the 'General Viewer' and the Refusal of Meaning in the Films of Claire Denis

Stuart Innes Molloy

The first Claire Denis film I watched was her most recent release at the time, *High Life* (2018), a tale of single fatherhood located within the generic boundaries of sci-fi. It is adrift in space that Monte must raise his daughter, Willow. The second Claire Denis film I watched was her debut, *Chocolat* (1988), a story of twinned experiences that does little to indicate its belonging to any genre. What unfolds is a French girl's complicity in colonial oppression and a Cameroonian man's oppression by colonialism. Prima facie, the two appear to have little in common. But since *Chocolat* I have watched Denis's other films roughly chronologically, and I am struck by their aesthetic and philosophical coherence as a whole (although I do not consider chronological viewing as important in this regard). The best simile I can muster is that the cinema of Claire Denis is like the poetry of Emily Dickinson: idiosyncratic, impressionistic, illuminating. Using the image rather than the word, Denis, like Dickinson, has an extraordinary capacity for aphorism. She achieves in her films a distillation of experiences and ideas that goad for explanation while in the same moment intimating the redundancy of that very thing.

Other salient features of Denis's work that contribute to its sense of unity include her habit of long-running collaborations. Denis has collaborated with prolific cinematographer Agnès Godard on ten films; she has also collaborated ten times with screenwriter Jean-Pol Fargeau; English alternative rock band Tindersticks have worked on the soundtracks of seven of Denis's films; and Denis has worked again and again with a set of actors who are especially striking in appearance, most notably Isaach de Bankolé, Alex Descas, Grégoire Colin, Vincent Gallo, Béatrice Dalle and Juliette Binoche.

It can also be said without tautology that Denis's is a pointedly visual body of work. Every cinematic text visualises things, of course; cinema is a visual medium. But Denis embraces and prioritises the image and its movement with arresting intensity. Borrowing a phrase from Elena del Río, what the viewer finds in the films of Denis is an 'extreme attachment to the surface of the image' (2003, 186). Indeed, much critical attention given to Denis cites prioritising the visuality of her medium as her signature, a feature of her work typically highlighted alongside the minimisation of dialogue in her filmmaking (Beugnet 2016; Carter 2014; Mayne 2005).

Closely allied with the intense visuality of Denis's cinema is her fascination with corporeality, a feature of her work that draws attention to her collaboration with striking actors and vice versa. The domination of the *mise en scène* by their embodiment of character underpins what Laura McMahon calls Denis's 'unremittingly tactile focus' (2014, 1). From *Chocolat* to *High Life*, bodies are topographies; they are settings in and of themselves (cf. Dooley 2015; Deluca 2021; Hole 2015).

Most salient of all is a viewing experience of bewilderment. I invariably get to the end of a Denis film feeling perplexed about the contents of the preceding two hours, an ambiguous affective response, neither negative nor positive. This chapter is an attempt to understand my sense of misunderstanding, a venture seemingly at odds with itself. Why is disclosure so elusive from *Chocolat* to *High Life*? The answer that I offer is at once personal and, I suggest, general if not universal.

This chapter takes the encounter of the 'general viewer' with the films of Claire Denis, both individually and collectively, as a locus for an exploration of cognition. Upon the map of hermeneutic systems this chapter takes up a position within the terrain of cognitive cultural studies. More specifically, it sees itself as an exercise in cognitive narratology. These broader and narrower points of approach give this chapter its point of difference in the context of scholarship on Denis, making its interpretation of her work unusual and thence hopefully valuable. This chapter is indebted to the work of psychologist Jean Piaget, the source of the term equilibration. The Piagetian understanding of how the mind works is important in the definition of the 'general viewer', who should not be invoked without being defined, although this process is routinely overlooked not just in scholarship on Denis but on film in general. In this regard, this chapter also considers the impact on patterns of orientation of the cultural hegemony of Hollywood filmmaking. Denis's refusal of meaning is in part also a refusal of this hegemony, although such opposition is not counted here as a function of being a francophone filmmaker. With these foundations elaborated, this chapter limns the refusal of meaning in the films of Claire Denis by parsing its effectors, identified as symbolic density and diegetic discontinuity.

The parsing of symbolic density and diegetic discontinuity takes shape through a survey of Denis's cinematic releases gathered up as trans-generic dramas of non-disclosure. This means that the auteur's fourth film, *US Go Home* (1994), is discounted because it was made for television. Her fourteenth, meanwhile, *Both Sides of the Blade* (2022), must be excluded as it is still to be released in the UK at the time of writing. Gathering up Denis's cinematic releases as trans-generic dramas of non-disclosure signals an organisational focus on genre, something that Denis by turns both abandons and embraces. It is possible to arrange the thirteen films referenced here into two categories, non-generic and generic, at a ratio of 8:5. Denis's non-generic titles are: *Chocolat* (1988); *S'en fout la mort* (1990); *Nénette et Boni* (1996); *Beau travail* (1999); *Vendredi soir* (2002); *L'intrus* (2004); *35 rhums* (2008); and *White Material* (2009). Her generic titles are: *J'ai pas sommeil* (1994); *Trouble Every Day* (2001); *Les salauds* (2013); *Un beau soleil intérieur* (2017); and *High Life* (2018). Since these twinned claims cannot go unsubstantiated, there will be a return to the respective absence and presence of genre later. Suffice to say for now that the former will be worked out by inquiring into how this categorisation might be made more nuanced and insightful than it currently stands using the rather insipid term 'non-generic'; the latter will be worked out by identifying the genres at play.

There are three interlinked reasons to leverage genre organisationally. First, genre is a useful tool for thinking through narrative in general. As such, second, considering the operation of genre in narrative provides access to the relationship of storytelling to the realities reflected and refracted in stories together with our relationship to those realities. As John Frow asserts, genre is 'a universal dimension of textuality' that goes so far as to 'actively shap[e] the way we understand the world' (2015, 2). Third, following on, genre has specific importance relative to equilibration and non-disclosure, notions circulated in this chapter as crucial to its argument. Genres, in Piagetian parlance, are schemata. More on this in due course.

Opting for a survey has its limitations, chiefly the sacrifice of depth for breadth. Umberto Eco has cautioned that a corollary of this choice is susceptibility to deleterious omissions (2015). This possibility is compounded in the current context. It is especially challenging to address a filmography as extensive and rich as that of Denis in a space as brief as a single chapter. Mitigating this, and hopefully counteracting any omissions immediately detectable here if not excusing them, is this chapter's appearance as one of many in a volume dedicated to the work of Denis. There is depth in the collective.

The richness of Denis's filmmaking has yielded heterogeneity in endeavours to interpret it. Given Denis's colonial upbringing in various African countries and the consequent inflection of many of her films by diasporic experience, issues of colonialism and postcolonialism have long been attended to in scholarship about the cinema of Denis and continue to be. Cáit Murphy recently revisited *Beau travail*, triangulating the auteur's exilic background with Hamid Naficy's notion of accented cinema and the postcolonial theory of Homi K. Bhabha (2021). At the same time, considerable critical range has been achieved. Consider the imbrication of thing theory in a reading of *35 rhums* by Eddy Troy, who homes in on the function of everyday items as mediators of intersubjectivity (2020).

Committing to a sustained analysis of the films of Claire Denis by approaching them through the lens of cognitive cultural studies remains atypical. The value of this point of difference is sharpened precisely because seeing and tracking in Denis's work a refusal of meaning, or some variation thereof, is not a unique perspective. Quite the opposite, critical attention to her filmmaking often takes stock of this facet of her work. This chapter echoes Martine Beugnet, who talks about 'the refusal of closure' in 'The Practice of Strangeness' (2016, 69). Beugnet is discussing *L'intrus*, which she summarises as a 'deliberately mystifying narrative', parsing it as an 'essayistic project' if not exactly an essay film, but the refusal of closure and the concomitant mystification of the viewer is certainly not limited to Denis's adoption of Jean-Luc Nancy's essay of the same name (2016, 76 and 69). Mia Carter identifies the structuring presence of the refusal of closure in *Nénette et Boni*, a site where 'the viewer is seduced by [visual] poetry, texture, color [while] simultaneously kept at an arm's length by the narrative's distances and silences' (2014, 68). Lisa Coulthard and Chelsea Birks also speak of a variation of the refusal of meaning in their discussion of *Trouble Every Day* as an instance of new extremist cinema (2016, 461–76); so too Kath Dooley in connection with characterisation in Denis's oeuvre (2015, 435); and also del Río, who in fact passingly invokes cognition before pursuing a Deleuzian line of interpretation (2003, 185–97). As Emma Wilson puts it in a retrospective piece on Denis published by *Film Quarterly* in 2019, 'her films have consistently retained ambiguities of narrative [that] produc[e] a sense of looking in on a world not fully understood . . . fostering doubt and paranoia in viewers' (2019, 18). This chapter, to reiterate, offers nothing new in pursuing non-disclosure in the films of Claire Denis. Its novelty, rather, lies in limning that facet of her work with an emphasis on cognition.

The terrain of cognitive cultural studies is latitudinous. Narrowing down its position, and echoing David Herman in 'Narrative Theory and the Second Cognitive Revolution', this chapter belongs more specifically to cognitive narratology insofar as it focuses 'on the nexus between narrative and mind' (2010, 155). Situating itself within cognitive narratology impacts on the kind of viewer – the 'general viewer' – that this chapter adduces in advancing its argument that Denis visualises the refusal of meaning through symbolic density and diegetic discontinuity. Before this receives elaboration, however, expanding on the underlying debt to the psychology of Piaget is in order. Indeed, Piaget's conceptualisation of how the mind works is so essential here that his name and adjectival inflections of it are used metonymically. Calling Denis's storytelling anti-Piagetian is tantamount to submitting that the way Denis packages stories is contra-cognition. This is on account of its disruption of apperception.

Apperception is no longer a fashionable term, but it serves nevertheless as a useful shorthand for the computational operations of the mind as articulated by Piaget. The phrase 'computational operations of the mind' is not intended to imply that the mind is a computer. Rather, it is to say that 'the mind is a kind of computer', following Steven Pinker (2015, 271). This might seem a pedantic interjection, but the minutiae of equating the two or resisting the equation has formed an intellectual battleground of some rancour. Piaget held an agentic view of the human subject, asserting that every individual is actively involved in constructing their own reality (cf. Fischer and Kaplan 2005). Fundamental to such agency are two yoked commitments definitive of Piagetian thinking: the first is that cognitive development is divisible into four stages; the second is that people build mental models in order to make sense of the world (cf. Carey et al. 2015).

The particulars of the four stages, which can be found in *The Psychology of the Child* (1969), are not presently important except to point out that neo-Piagetians have subsequently remarked on the degree to which neuroscience corroborates the staged nature of development hypothesised by Piaget, observing that neural networks in the brain undergo successive reorganisations (Fischer and Kaplan 2005). The insights of Piaget, in other words, cannot be dismissed as anachronisms but remain relevant and productive.

That said, what is presently important is the building of mental models. A mental model in Piagetian vocabulary is a schema, 'a collection of basic knowledge about a concept or entity that serves as a guide to perception, interpretation, imagination, or problem solving' (APA 2022). Collected within the schema 'dog' might be details such as four legs, fur and a tail. These details, of course, also describe a cat. People ordinarily in contact with dogs and cats learn early on that they are not the same thing. Learning to distinguish between the two not only involves a linguistic component, the acquisition of a new noun, but also a computational one, the creation of the new schema 'cat'. For the distinction to be durable, new information must be added to one of the two schemata or both. The schema 'dog' comes to include four legs, fur, a tail, *and friendliness* while 'cat' becomes four legs, fur, a tail *and aloofness*.

Two processes govern the formation, reformation and proliferation of schemata over the course of a lifetime. Assimilation, the incorporation of external data into a person's way of thinking, is how schemata grow in number and complexity (O'Donnell 2018). Accommodation, the modification of existing schemata into a new and better way of thinking, is how schemata are organised in relation to each other (O'Donnell 2018). Assimilation and accommodation work in concert to maintain or restore a cognitive state devoid of conflicting schemata. This process is known as equilibration in Piagetian theory (APA 2022). Properly speaking, Denis's storytelling disrupts equilibration by frustrating assimilation and accommodation, the computational operations glossed here by the single if unfashionable term apperception.

The thesis that the stories encountered in the films of Claire Denis activate a state of disequilibrium rests on the consensualness of the schema 'story' as inclusive of logically sequential structure, but is it reasonable to assume such a consensus? For proponent of cognitive cultural studies Patrick Colm Hogan, the logically sequential construction of diegeses – the idea that x should lead to y should lead to z – is not merely a general expectation of storylines but a universal one. Discussing storytelling as a transcultural and transmodal practice, Hogan describes it as the articulation of 'causal sequences of nonbanal events involving human agency (with banality defined relative to culturally specific expectations) . . . for aesthetic enjoyment' (2010, 45). Causal sequencing is not evacuated in Denis's cinematic oeuvre, but it is minimised. From *Chocolat* to *High Life*, storylines do not consistently take the viewer somewhere that clearly makes sense of where they have been taken, the dilution of causality being an inflection of diegetic discontinuity in her work.

Still, recruiting Hogan does not guarantee that the logical sequential construction of diegeses is in fact an expectation that people universally have of storylines. As Hogan himself admits in paraphrasing Noam Chomsky, 'one of the first tasks for researchers who study universals is to overcome habituation' (2010, 45). If an appeal to universality is tenuous, how then to sustain the argument that Denis's deployment of diegetic discontinuity works as an effector of non-disclosure based on sewing cognitive disequilibrium in the mind of the viewer? The answer is habituation itself. Appealing to generality is sufficient.

It is possible that wanting to know what happens next and why it is happening based on what has gone before it is a feature of the neural architecture of all human beings, and it is against this that Denis's dilution of causation acts. What is certain is that this relationship to narrative is a culturally internalised pattern of orientation determinative of the schema 'story' in the context within which Denis's films are produced and consumed. Here is where the impact of this chapter's claim to be a piece of Piagetian cognitive narratology on the kind of viewer adduced comes to receive elaboration.

In 'Navigating – Making Sense – Interpreting', Maria Mäkelä explores cognitive narratology as a particular hermeneutic. Mäkelä initially classifies it as a species of post-classical narratology. Its antecedent is, naturally, classical narratology, itself forerun by structuralism. Post-classical narratology becomes interchangeable with cognitive narratology as Mäkelä's exploration progresses and classical narratology becomes interchangeable with structuralism. With the emergence of such interchangeability in her essay, Mäkelä goes on to point out that while both structuralism and cognitive narratology 'speak of sense-making', their respective advocates conjure discrete sense-makers (2012, 139). That is, they conceptualise the figure of the reader very differently. Moreover, the reader – or the viewer, in dealing with screen narratives – is complicit in whatever advocacy is afoot. As Mäkelä puts it, '[t]he common denominator of . . . reader figures is that they are . . . interpretive constructs, synthetic constellations of hypotheses about the actual reading process' (2012, 140). The reader/viewer stands in at once for the critic and their addressee, servicing the argument of the first by compelling the second to concur on the basis of implicit collectivisation. Invoking 'the reader'/'the viewer' denies the *I*-ness of a viewpoint, insisting instead on *we*-ness. The invocation allows the critic to say tacitly to their addressee 'this is not my view of a text but everyone's, including yours as a member of everyone, even if you were not previously aware of it until it was pointed out'. The reader/viewer conceptualised by structuralism, returning to Mäkelä, 'is an industrious yet somehow doomed performer of higher thinking, reaching for the ultimately unattainable (the "meaning")', while the reader/viewer conceptualised by classical narratology 'is a languid "general reader" who opts for the primary, the likely, the coherent and the familiar' (2012, 139–40). The viewer conjured in this chapter is indeed the latter, but not just in keeping with the cognitive narratological position.

There is reason to mobilise such a figure beyond posture, a clue to which is in the language used by Mäkelä. Languid viewers who opt for the primary and the coherent, or the immediately apperceptible, are general figures indeed. They are widespread. Despite the negative connotations carried by both commonness and languidness, this is not to be derogatory. In fact, the possibility of derogation in this setting is foreclosed following the mechanics of agency described by Piaget. It is natural for people to seek out order, universally human to organise the contents of reality. Even without reference to Piaget, the naturalness of order-seeking is accepted and acceptable. It is seconded by Terry Eagleton, for example, who connects cognitive consonance and necessity when he speaks of 'our need for coherence' in discussing our engagement with texts (2005, 45). It is as good as axiomatic that people should gravitate to immediately apperceptible narratives, that preference for the primary and the coherent not only be typical of readers/viewers but in fact typify the figure of 'the reader'/'the viewer', the idealised instantiation – or synthetic constellation, to echo Mäkelä – who is a metonym for a majority.

The natural typicality of the cognitive narratological version of the viewer is insured by habituation courtesy of the cultural hegemony of the classical Hollywood style in filmmaking. Any discussion of this mode would be incomplete without mention of Robert Kolker, whose treatment of it in *Film, Form, and Culture* (2016) stands out as authoritative. According to Kolker, the chief aim of the classical Hollywood style, or continuity style, of filmmaking is to entertain, and 'entertainment means unobstructed access to story and character' (2016, 39). A key ingredient of films made in the classical Hollywood style is invisibility of form. Invisibility sounds a curious constituent for a visual medium, but it refers not to the image per se, the foundational formal property out of which screen narratives are fashioned, so much as the successive organisation of the image's multiplication – that is, the fashioning process. What must be invisible is the grammar of cinematic storytelling, and indeed it is. Who when watching a movie at the cinema or a TV series on Netflix ordinarily pays attention to the types of shots or the length of takes on the screen before them? Enthralled by the apparently seamless unfolding of the story, it takes conscious effort to attend to these things.

Something Kolker takes for granted, interestingly, is that the seamless unfolding of the story in classical Hollywood-style films requires more than the construction of a diegesis the constructedness of which is submerged from view. Assembling the assimilable is also a requisite. Proving at once the habituating influence of Hollywood and the blinding effect of habituation, Kolker recognises only tacitly that the most invisible film grammar is for nought if the formal continuity it provides is without contiguity in the psychological sense. A case in point is Kolker's elaboration of the opening ten minutes of *Casablanca*. Specifics of the sequence cited by Kolker include the close-up of the sign 'Rick's Café Américain' followed by the tracking of the camera down to the door, an invitation to enter the café realised by a cut to its interior. However fragmentary this piece of the film, it is representative of the assembly of the assimilable. The diegetic construction is such that the viewer can put two and two together on a continuum. This is not unique to *Casablanca* but ubiquitous in classical Hollywood films, which are themselves ubiquitous. A significant function of this ubiquity is that the schema 'film' – sitting within the schema 'story' – contains easily accessible arrangement based on logical sequencing, and arguably has done for almost a century since the establishment of Hollywood's major studios.[1]

Having established the Piagetian cognitive orientation(s) of the 'general viewer' (hereafter the viewer) invoked in this chapter, and arguably all scholarship on Denis fascinated by the refusal of meaning in her work, it remains to parse the effectors of non-disclosure: symbolic density and diegetic discontinuity. What is meant by the first in the present context? How does it connect with the central concern of the refusal of meaning and indeed effect it? Symbolic density codes for the paradoxical fact that non-disclosure in Denis's cinema is in large part a matter of proliferation. The refusal in question occurs not by absenting meaning but by fragmenting it. Meaning is not vanished in Denis's films, made impossible to see. It is exploded, rendered kaleidoscopically. Analysis of her debut serves as a representative case in point.

Chocolat begins by positioning a white woman as voyeur. Hers is the gaze as the camera takes in a father and son, both black, playing in the shallows of a tropical ocean before sunbathing on its beach. The unusualness of this viewpoint, derived from its subversion of the phallocentrism typical of film (Mulvey 1975), signals to the viewer that they are embarking on an unconventional narrative journey.[2] It heralds at the same time, with the benefit of hindsight, the start of a career in storytelling notable for an unconventional approach to telling stories, an approach organised around a fascination with bodies and the treatment of them as topographies. Extending the unusualness of *Chocolat*'s opening scene is the absence of explanatory intertitles or contextualising dialogue. Yet through nothing more than the accumulation of images it is deducible that the voyeuristic woman, the witness to whom the viewer is witness in a multiplication of voyeurism, is a former colonial subject alienated in a now postcolonial space and time. This is to concur with Carter, who notes that '[i]n most of Denis's films, the *mise-en-scène* tell the story' (2014, 69).

What is meant here by 'colonial subject' is not that the character was one subjected to colonialism. Rather she is one whose subjectivity formed during colonialism, in its midst both historically and geographically, like that of the film's director. This deduction is made possible by the cinematographic articulation of the autochthony of the two African characters. For they are in fact not black-skinned so much as they are coloured like the landscape. They merge with the place in which they are encountered signifying that they are of that place. In contrast, the nativity of the white woman watching them is inescapably foreign. This is coded by a cluster of separations: her whiteness, of course; her femininity; and her distance from them, seated liminally where the beach turns to jungle.

In the following scene, the father and son notice the woman walking down the side of the road as they drive along. They offer her a lift, which she accepts, and it transpires through their conversation that the woman's name is, rather pointedly, France Dalens. France has returned to Cameroon to visit, having lived in the country as a little girl before it gained independence. It transpires too that the father and son are not Cameroonian, they are American. This complicates the earlier assumption about their autochthonous status, but it does not collapse it. However ambiguous this detail renders their Africanness, it does not subtract it from them or them from it. They remain profoundly of Africa, their voluntary return to their ancestral homeland a quiet reversal and rebuttal of imperialism and slavery. The father and son, on their way to Limbe, drop France off in Douala. Between the beach and the Cameroonian capital, in the lull of conversation, France recollects a portion of her childhood in Mindif.

The remembrance of things past – for the analeptic turn is indeed sudden and consuming in the manner of Proust's involuntary memory – is anchored most of all by France's relationship with Protée (de Bankolé), the Dalens' houseboy. The character's name is a rendering in French of Proteus, the figure from Greek mythology famous simultaneously for his omniscience, his reticence to share his knowledge and his ability to shapeshift. As France is France, Protée is Proteus. They are personifications: the one of an imperial and post-imperial nation state confounded by its own imperialism (cf. Beugnet 2016: 69); the other of a godlike being that sees everything but prefers to say nothing and who can exercise that preference so long as he remains physically unrestrained. Memorably, Aimée Dalens, France's mother, who desires Protée, attempts to take hold of him. She attempts, that is, to realise a taboo yearning for the houseboy that is at once sexual and epistemological. Oddly crouched against the wall, Aimée reaches for Protée's ankle as he adjusts a curtain. Unlike Menelaus in *The Odyssey*, however, Aimée fails to hold onto her Proteus. He pulls away decisively, keeping equally and contiguously intact the possession of his body and the privacy of his omniscience.

More than for this intertextual echo, Protée is Proteus because he is protean – not directly in the sense of being a shapeshifter, but indirectly in the sense of the primordiality associated with the ability to shapeshift. The primordial is essentially formless, and as such polymorphic. The primordial is also what came first, something that existed from the beginning. Calling the character of the houseboy Protée/Proteus/protean asserts his incorporation of originality. His name encodes his state of belonging as the African encountered in Africa, a fold in the symbolic substance of the film that takes the viewer back to its beginning, with its visualisation of the autochthony of African bodies through their coalescence with the African landscape.

Analysis could continue, but the meandering nature of the foregoing close reading has made, gesturally, the key point: the movement of meaning in a Claire Denis film is emphatically multidirectional. It is explosive, radiating outward everywhere at once; it is like the kaleidoscopic image, possessed of a centre to which the eye always returns only to depart from it once more, a canvas where order and disorder can be seen to merge. This is what is meant by symbolic density, disruptive of equilibration – although not beyond it – because it precipitates the proliferate activation of schemata, pressuring the viewer's capacity for apperception.

Symbolic density is one effector of non-disclosure identified in this chapter, effecting the refusal of meaning in Denis's films by interfering with the viewer's capacity for equilibration. The other is diegetic discontinuity. This has a number of inflections, including diegetic discontinuity per se, moments when Denis structures her diegeses through non-sequitur. The opening of *Trouble Every Day* relative to the rest of the film provides an example. It begins with a relentless close-up. The camera focuses on two lovers kissing passionately in a car, lingering on them with unbroken attention for fifty-four seconds. This long take eventually ends with a cut to black, which itself lasts at length. This is broken by a dissolve to a close-up of the play of light on water (a kaleidoscopic image). The unbroken attention given to the lovers positions their characters as desiderata. Despite this initial assignment of importance in the mind of the viewer, however, the two lovers never appear again. Instead, they inexplicably give way to the film's actual protagonists: Shane Brown (Gallo) and his wife, June, and Léo Sémeneau (Descas) and his wife, Coré (Dalle).

The opening of *Trouble Every Day* also provides an example of a second inflection of diegetic discontinuity: languorous temporality. The persistence of the gaze as it focuses on the diegetically redundant lovers, watching them for almost a minute, is a common feature in Denis's construction of narrative. Long takes are a staple of her oeuvre. This is also noted by Wilson in 'Love Me Tender: New Films from Claire Denis' (2019), from whom the term languorous temporality is adapted. Such persistence is perverse in popular filmmaking, structured as it is by the internalisation of the classical Hollywood style, a diegetic grammar internalised by filmmakers and viewers alike. As Kolker highlights in *Film, Form, and Culture* (2016), the gaze is highly segmented in popular filmmaking: 'the average shot length of an American film is about nine seconds, usually shorter, occasionally longer, but rarely by much' (85). Encounters with languorous temporality in Denis's films are prominent because they are relatively dissonant experiences for the viewer.

A third inflection of diegetic discontinuity that the viewer encounters in Denis's films is paradoxical structuration. Denis succeeds, remarkably, in not showing something by showing it. Or, in more theatrical terms, she renders something obscene by staging it. Consider a scene from *White Material* as a case in point: the mass slaughter of the child soldiers while they sleep. This grisly passage is constructed as a montage of close-ups. The gaze positions the viewer so close to the action, in fact, that they are spared from being able to take it in. There is obscenity in seeing knives pulled from sheaths and red blood spattering over white walls. Necessary as this act of self-censorship is, the scene remains both profoundly disturbing and disorienting.

A fourth inflection of diegetic discontinuity, one mentioned previously, is the dilution of causality. Recall the assertion that Denis's storylines, from *Chocolat* to *High Life*, do not consistently take the viewer somewhere that clearly makes sense of where they have been taken, a breach of general if not universal fundamentals of storytelling. The figure of Monsieur Luminaire provides a particularly memorable locus for the dilution of causality in *Nénette et Boni*. The character is rather reprehensible because of his remoteness as the father of the eponymous protagonists, but he is otherwise unremarkable. Yet he is endowed with a thoroughly remarkable death: he leaves the gym after a workout with his lover; he takes the driver's seat as they get into the car; he opens his window before pulling out of the parking spot; two men on a motorcycle suddenly pull up alongside the car; the passenger points a gun through the open window and Monsieur Luminaire has his brains blown out. This irruption of violence is cryptic. The viewer is forced to assume that the character must have done something to someone at some time to earn such a murderous amount of ire, but what he did, when he did it and to whom remain unknown. Perhaps the scene is a fantasy of patricide harboured by Boni (Colin), but if so, it is entirely indistinguishable from reality within the film.

The disruption of expectation is a fifth inflection of diegetic discontinuity. It is closely related to the dilution of causality and, for that matter, to diegetic discontinuity per se. In fact, although all the inflections are glossed here discretely, they are often operationally inseparable. The example of Monsieur Luminaire's assassination as a dilution of causality also constitutes a disruption of expectation, while the example of the false opening in *Trouble Every Day* as diegetic discontinuity per se is exactly that because it constitutes a disruption of expectation. Disrupting expectation, after all, is intrinsic to non-sequiturs. Yet the disruption of expectation can also be decoupled from these other inflections, and here it is mobilised in and of itself primarily in relation to genre. One of the critical dimensions of genre, returning to Frow, is that generic boundaries pose a '*structure of implication* [that] both invokes and presupposes a range of background knowledges, and in so doing sets up a certain complicity with the reader' (2015: 10). In other words, genre relies on expectation, initially in terms of establishment and thereafter in terms of maintenance. Immersed in and conditioned by a screen culture predominated not only by the structural conventions of the classical Hollywood style but also by its map of generic boundaries, the viewer expects to encounter certain sets of tropes when watching action movies/horror movies/romcoms, et cetera for their billing as such to be confirmed. Cognitively speaking, this is the process of accommodation.

Five of Denis's thirteen films overtly harness genre, invoking and presupposing a range of background knowledges across the construction and consumption of narrative. These generic films are: *J'ai pas sommeil*; *Trouble Every Day*; *Les salauds*; *Un beau soleil intérieur*; and *High Life*. However, the activation of sets of tropes in these films is typically imperfect. Genre offers Denis ways of constructing and deconstructing stories, ways of arranging and refusing meaning. Genre, in Denis's oeuvre, provides a site for the disruption of expectation.

Based on the murders committed by the Monster of Montmartre, Martinician émigré Thierry Paulin, *J'ai pas sommeil* is a crime drama. More specifically, the film can be classified as a work of serial killer fiction, a subgenre exemplified by Jonathan Demme's adaptation of *The Silence of the Lambs*, released three years before *J'ai pas sommeil*. Tropes definitive of the subgenre apparent in Demme's film are replicated in that of Denis, with a prominent exception.

First, the narrative is *not* structured as a whodunit. Its trajectory is not governed by arrival at the identity of the perpetrator as an endpoint. Comparing the films of Demme and Denis, it is true that the perpetrators' identities are not known to law enforcement – the FBI in *The Silence of the Lambs*; the Parisian police in *J'ai pas sommeil* – but they are known to the viewer. The viewer is aware, respectively, that Jame Gumb and Camille are the serial killers for whom law enforcement is looking. Such dramatic irony is common in the construction of serial killer fictions, as Leonard Cassuto corroborates in *Hard-Boiled Sentimentality* (2009), and it is for this reason that examples of the subgenre are sometimes referred to as whydunits.

Indeed, serial killer fictions are character studies, imaginative explorations of psychopathology. On that note, it is tropic for the perversity of serial killing to be merged with other 'perversions', often along lines of gender and sexuality. Instantiated in cultural forms, cued by psychiatric discourse, the serial killer figures a cluster of comorbidities. In the case of *The Silence of the Lambs*, Gumb is guided in his murderous actions by a fantasy of transsexuality; in *J'ai pas sommeil*, Camille is depicted as a homosexual transvestite (Figure 7.1).

The serial killer's accumulation of perversions/'perversions', both in serial killer fictions and in real life, is typically further merged with and exacerbated by a history of familial dysfunction, often of considerable severity. Cassuto states: '[c]riminologists, psychiatrists, and novelists have all sought the killer's motivation in his upbringing. And what they all find is an abused child grown up' (2009: 259). Cassuto's formulation echoes the aphorism of Mark Seltzer in *Serial Killers:* 'wounded as a child, wounding as an adult' (1998: 4). *The Silence of the Lambs* and *J'ai pas sommeil* are both candid in characterising their serial killers as traumatised. Gumb is assigned the trauma of momism; Camille suffers not only from a dysfunctional family, indicated by the character's difficult relationship with his brother, Theo (Descas), but also from what Frantz Fanon might call the trauma of being black (2019).

Where Denis departs from convention, thereby disrupting expectation, is in the final handling of Camille's character. Serial killer fictions are typically resolved by an agent of law enforcement uncovering the serial killer's identity and lethally confronting them. In *The Silence of the Lambs*, Clarice Starling realises that Gumb is Buffalo Bill and kills him in the gunfight that ensues. This trope is abandoned in *J'ai pas sommeil*, which features no such triumphant vanquishing of the serial killer. It is not an agent of law enforcement who realises that Camille is the perpetrator but Daiga, the maid in the hotel where Camille stays. Daiga does not confront Camille but instead breaks into his room and steals the loot he himself has stolen from his victims. Admittedly, the police do ultimately identify Camille as the perpetrator, but the final confrontation expected by the viewer is displaced by an interview between the police and Camille's brother, Theo, suspected of involvement. The absolutism of *The Silence of the Lambs*, paradigmatic of serial killer fictions, is missing from *J'ai pas sommeil* despite its signalling itself in multiple other ways to be a serial killer fiction. Denis, jarringly, avoids representing the defeat of evil by good based on the latter's dual possession of certain knowledge and clearcut moral righteousness.[3]

Noël Carroll elaborates at length on the tropes of horror in *The Philosophy of Horror* (2003). Carroll points out that horror derives its name from the affect it intends to produce. Accordingly, a basic test for classifying a text as such is to ask: 'Does it produce a sense of horror?' Asked of *Trouble Every Day*, which bloodily depicts the cannibalistic compulsions of Coré and Shane during sexual arousal, the answer is emphatically yes. Another test for classifying a text as horror is the presence of monstrosity. However, as Carroll cautions, the mere presence of monstrosity is an insufficient criterion for establishing that a story is a *horror* story since several genres routinely mobilise monsters, for example fantasy and sci-fi. The mobilisation of monsters in horror contributes specifically to what Carroll calls 'the drama of iterated disclosure' (2003, 182). This is the core of the complex discovery plot typical of horror and parsed by Carroll as having four stages: onset; discovery; confirmation; confrontation.

Consider Steven Spielberg's *Jaws*: a woman swimming at night is attacked (onset – the awareness of a monstrous presence forms extradiegetically at first, located with the viewer); the woman's remains are found on the beach (discovery – awareness of the monstrous presence becomes intradiegetic but highly localised, the knowledge of only one or two characters); more attacks occur, the shark overtly terrorising swimmers (confirmation – intradiegetic awareness of the monstrous presence becomes generalised, known to all characters); finally, Brody, Hooper and Quint set out to find and destroy the shark (confrontation – typically ending in favour of the heroes of the diegesis to the relieved satisfaction of the viewer).

Mapped against this formula, *Trouble Every Day* is a drama of iterated disclosure, but not one that proceeds neatly through the four stages of the complex discovery plot. Onset: the viewer watches Coré seduce a truck driver, a sequence made enthralling and dreadful by the predatory energy of Dalle; her murder of him is not witnessed, but it is evident – her mouth and face are bloodstained and, as with the mangled limbs on the beach in *Jaws*, the body of the truck driver lies face down in a nearby field (Figure 7.2). (Disruption of) discovery: Léo finds Coré but, shockingly for the viewer, her gruesome homicidal behaviour is not shocking to his character; rather, Léo embraces Coré, returns her to their home, and tenderly washes the gore from his wife's body, a series of actions that comes to constitute a routine for the pair (Figure 7.3). Refusal of confirmation: a consequence of Léo's actions is that there is no intradiegetic spread of awareness regarding Coré's monstrosity; there is iterative disclosure of her monstrosity, but it remains extradiegetic, located with the viewer, who goes on to witness her sexual cannibalism in action when a young man tries to free her from domestic imprisonment (Figure 7.4). Subversion of confrontation: the monster that is the cannibalistic Coré is confronted and indeed destroyed, but her confrontation and destruction are not enacted by a hero but by another monster, Shane, who has prior knowledge of Coré's condition and who suffers from it himself (once more disrupting discovery and refusing confirmation) (Figure 7.5). Such multiplication of monstrosity again conforms to the trope of iterated disclosure, but in simultaneously evacuating heroism it forecloses the possibility of achieving relieved satisfaction for the viewer. Indeed, relieved satisfaction is rendered quite impossible by the closing scenes: Shane seduces and cannibalises a chambermaid in the basement of the hotel where he and his wife are honeymooning before returning to his room to take a shower, his monstrousness undiscovered, unconfirmed, unconfronted within the world of the story.[4]

As with *J'ai pas sommeil* and *Trouble Every Day*, Denis's remaining three generic films also disrupt expectation by both retracing generic boundaries and deviating from them. The background knowledges by turns embraced and abandoned in *Les salauds*, *Un beau soleil intérieur* and *High Life* can be limned succinctly with recourse only to common sense. *Les salauds* centres on Marco

Figure 7.1 The figure of the serial killer and the accumulation of perversions/'perversions' – transsexuality in *The Silence of the Lambs* (left) and transvestism in *J'ai pas sommeil* (right)

Figure 7.2 The complex discovery plot of horror and its destabilisation in *Trouble Every Day* – onset.

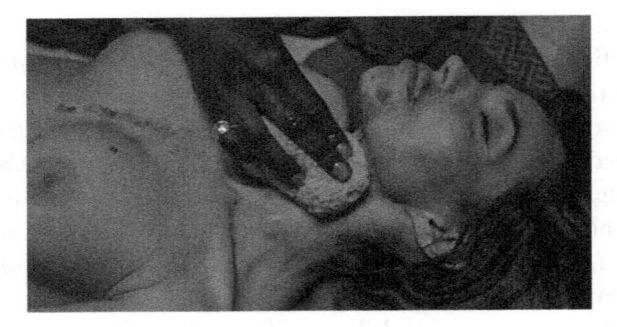

Figure 7.3 The complex discovery plot of horror and its destabilisation in *Trouble Every Day* – discovery disrupted.

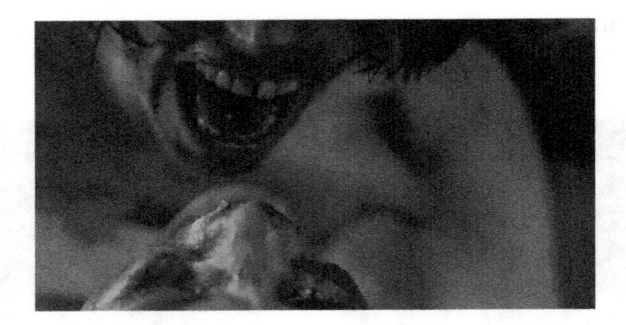

Figure 7.4 The complex discovery plot of horror and its destabilisation in *Trouble Every Day* – confirmation refused.

Silvestri, a ship's captain recalled to Paris following linked tragedies: the brutal rape of his niece and the suicide of his brother-in-law. The film is billed as a thriller and bears hallmarks of the genre, Marco positioned as private detective cum vigilante. He enters a *noir* world populated by amoral characters, such as the pimp Xavier (Colin), and headed by the psychopathic mogul Laporte, whose estranged wife Raphaëlle instantiates the femme fatale. It transpires that Xavier facilitated the rape of Marco's niece, orchestrated by Laporte to produce a sickening piece of pornography, and Marco resolves to carry out vengeance. But the revenge narrative fails. Marco is shot and killed by Raphaëlle when he launches an attack on Laporte. The unexpected failure of the revenge narrative is of course attended by the unexpected failure of vigilante justice, with Laporte free in the end to carry on being *un salaud*, a bastard.

Similarly, it is failure that punctuates and indeed finally punctures *Un beau soleil intérieur*. The film stars Binoche as Isabella, a middle-aged artist and divorcée stuck in a series of dead-end relationships. For much of the film, the protagonist's tragicomic plight appears isomorphic with the shape of the romcom. With that isomorphism comes the expectation that the character will in the end find love and be granted a 'happily ever after'. But there is no such ending for Isabella. There is instead a confounding meeting with a psychic, whose own romantic affairs are in a state of disrepair, a meeting cryptic in its temporality. The viewer is left to wonder whether they have just witnessed the unfolding of the psychic's predictions or whether his predictions, which bear remarkable resemblance to the diegesis's series of events, are still to unfold, implying rather bleakly – and contra the film's title – that Isabella is doomed to the iteration of romantic failure.

High Life is a tale of single parenthood that foregrounds paternity set in space. It is also the site of multiple disruptions. Several of these cluster around the villainous Dr Dibs (Binoche). The setting of the film insists on its status as a sci-fi while its focus on fatherhood simultaneously destabilises that classification. This is not to say that fatherhood does not figure in science fiction. The *Star Wars* franchise, paradigmatic of the genre, not only contains but is considerably arranged by the mythical trope of father–son conflict. But no such oedipal dynamic charges *High Life*. It is the story of a man, Monte, trying to raise his daughter, Willow, adrift in a spaceship. As such, *High Life* exemplifies Denis's fascination with life as it is: disparate; ongoing; and filled with agents but absent or uncertain of heroes (cf. Elsaesser 2012). This only increases its distance from sci-fi qua popular culture, where it is pretended that life is containable and teleological through the organising force of heroic action.

Complicating the classificatory process further is the inclusion and collapse of the bildungsroman. Through the presence of Willow there is the possibility that a coming-of-age arc might inflect the diegesis. However, in a move that pairs with diegetic discontinuity per se, Willow's maturation is elided by a jarring non-sequitur. The viewer is privy to her neonatal form held aloft by Dibs (Figure 7.6.1); next the viewer sees her nestled against Monte, her father, but Willow is suddenly a teenager (Figure 7.6.2) and her menstrual blood has stained the sheets (Figure 7.6.3).

It is partly for this abject seal of embodied maturity that the non-sequitur is so jarring. But it is also jarring because her mature body, juxtaposed with that of Monte, positions her as his lover. When it is resolved that she is his grownup daughter, by his shoeing her out of his bunk, this raises the spectre of incest. Indeed, it is the incestuous undercurrent of the situation that seems to disgust Monte and spur him into action.

Finally, there is also the intrusion of horror elements – in fact not intrusive per se. It was noted earlier that the presence of monstrosity is as common in sci-fi as it is in horror. Its intrusiveness, rather, is derived from the unexpected appearance of the monster, Dibs, whose beauty is incongruous with monstrosity, typically connotative of grotesque xenomorphism. The monster, following Jeffrey Jerome Cohen, is 'harbinger of category crisis' (1996, 6). Much

Figure 7.5 The complex discovery plot of horror and its destabilisation in *Trouble Every Day* – confrontation subverted.

of Dibs's monstrousness comes from her synthetic characterisation. She is a killer of children and finds one of her prototypes in Medea; she is also a mad scientist, conducting experiments in artificial insemination on the crew; raven-haired, she is visualised as a witch, but not as a crone; and, lastly, Dibs is a rapist. It is through her rape of Monte that Willow is begotten, a plot point that disrupts expectation by divorcing sexual violence from masculinity.

Moving to a survey of Denis's non-generic titles, *Chocolat* is a story of twinned experiences: France's complicity in colonial oppression and Protée's oppression by colonialism. It is also a story in which the chronotope is divided along temporal lines. The setting for the bulk of the narrative is the Cameroon of the colonial past, when the character of France is a child, but the action therein plays out parenthesised by her movement as an adult in the Cameroon of the postcolonial present. These features draw attention to a sixth inflection of diegetic discontinuity common in Denis's films that might be dubbed unresolved stereoscopy. Operationally inseparable from disruption of expectation, unresolved stereoscopy is a duplication of perspective that thwarts rather than produces a complete – or three-dimensional – way of seeing. Of course, the division of a diegesis spatially and/or temporally into two or more strands is itself unremarkable. Countless films mobilise a number of plotlines across multiple times and spaces. Especially memorable examples from cinematic history of the last twenty years come from Christopher Nolan, notably *Memento* (2000), *The Prestige* (2006), *Inception* (2010), *Dunkirk* (2017) and *Tenet* (2020), to say nothing of Nolan's trilogy of Batman blockbusters. Usually, however, as in the case of the films just cited, the multiplicity of spatially and temporally

TRANS-GENERIC DRAMAS OF NON-DISCLOSURE

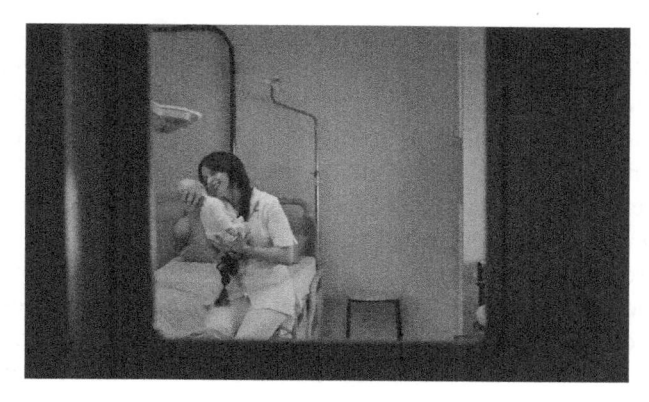

Figure 7.6.1 The instantaneous collapse of the bildungsroman in *High Life* – Dibs with the new-born Willow.

Figure 7.6.2 The instantaneous collapse of the bildungsroman in *High Life* – the teenage Willow lying next to her father.

Figure 7.6.3 The instantaneous collapse of the bildungsroman in *High Life* – Willow's menstrual blood, abject seal of her embodied maturity.

varied plotlines converges; their relationship each to the others is resolved. The ultimate unity of the chronotope eventually affords the viewer equilibriation. In an arrangement of reinforcement, the schemata 'film' and 'story' both have multiple plotlines and settings that interact meaningfully by the end. Denis's diegeses disrupt this formula, eliding its critical latter half. Denis's 'films' and 'stories', then, have multiple plotlines and settings, the effect of which is to leave the viewer in a state of cognitive dissonance.

The unresolved stereoscopy of *Chocolat* is that its depiction of France Dalens in the present, the past and then again in the present deflates the expectation carried in this proleptic return of marked revelatory insight. The viewer is never supplied the satisfaction of an 'aha' moment; they can never say to themself 'I see why we journeyed into the character's past'; they are left only with the opportunity for ambiguous speculation, 'Perhaps the protagonist has realised that as a European woman with an African upbringing she belongs nowhere, is condemned to chronic alienation.' But this is an attempt at equilibriation that is only possible with knowledge of Denis's biography and what Beugnet succinctly calls the director's 'double experience of foreignness' (2016, 69). It is not the sort of knowledge the viewer would be expected to possess.

Unresolved stereoscopy is an inflection of diegetic discontinuity also evident to varying degrees in *S'en fout la mort, Nénette et Boni, Beau travail* and *L'intrus*. *S'en fout la mort*, like *Chocolat*, is also a story of twinned experiences: two émigrés, Dah (de Bankolé) and Jocelyn (Descas), fighting for survival in Paris – metaphorised constantly by the spectacle of cock fighting by which they make a living – and the unsavoury lordship of Pierre, the native Parisian who owns the venue where the fights take place. There is no analepsis in the film; time, in the form of the present, remains constant. Prima facie, there is spatial constancy too. Significantly, however, although the characters occupy the same part of Paris, they exist in very different spaces, spaces only commensurable through conflict: the battling of the roosters and, (in)conclusively, the fatal confrontation between Jocelyn (Descas) and Michel, Pierre's son. This is (in)conclusive since, on the one hand, it supplies the denouement while, on the other, it resists closure. There is no justice for Jocelyn following his murder, and Dah is left to embrace itinerancy. The final scene, which is without finality, depicts Dah riding in a taxi on the motorway, ultimately condemned to a state of going. Through such encodings of dissonance, the viewer encounters another anti-Piagetian ending.

Nénette et Boni is another story of twinned experiences: the eponymous protagonists, sister and brother (Colin), each floundering in a world divested of parental guidance while they themselves must face the enormity of parenthood. Their lives converge, of course, but only to underline their profound alienation each from the other, suggesting the mutual foreignness of masculine and feminine subjectivities beyond the characters' instantiations of those positions.

Intensifying this formulation of unresolved stereoscopy is the intrusive presence of the siblings' father, named after his shop, Monsieur Luminaire, and the punctuation of the narrative by forays into the shared life of the baker (Gallo) and his wife, who remain anonymous. Monsieur Luminaire is a highly ironic name, for there is nothing enlightening about his character. Quite the opposite, and in a deepening of irony, his character is a point of incursion for a noire element that results (if that is the right word) in the perverse and cryptic comedy of a lamp salesman getting shot in a gangland-style execution. The baker and his wife, meanwhile, embody a disruption of equilibration through their very anonymity, the nomination of things crucial to the formation and organisation of schemata.

Beau travail harnesses a doubling of perspectives once more. The film reimagines Herman Melville's unfinished novella, *Billy Budd, Sailor*. It offers Galoup, who refigures Claggart, and Sentain (Colin), who refigures Budd, as viewpoints into life in the French Foreign Legion, and charts the inexorable collision between them, an oedipal struggle between 'father' and 'son' complicated by homoeroticism. Like *Chocolat*, *Beau travail* divides the chronotope along temporal lines, and further divides it spatially. The bulk of the action takes place in the Djibouti of the past, but it is intercut with scenes of Galoup in the Marseille of the present, whence he writes his memoir chronicling his conflict with Sentain. It is striking that Galoup's attempted murder of Sentain is contingent on the older man's tampering with the younger man's compass, a denial of orientation that maps onto the whole of Denis's work and indeed the viewer's experience of it. The compass finds its cognitive cognate in apperception, the process by which reality is navigated. Sentain's broken compass, then, is a concise metaphor for the breakdown of apperception. Ironically, the obvious premeditation of Galoup in engineering Sentain's demise signals his abundant possession of direction in the Djibouti of the past. In contrast, the character is profoundly directionless in the Marseilles of the present, signalled by his consumption by memory and by his riding a train to nowhere. Like Dah in *S'en fout la mort*, Galoup is left in a state of going, but one further problematised in being divested of a future to which to look forward. Bonded to the character in the end, entranced by the dizzying lines traced by his dancing body in the unforgettable coda, the viewer is ultimately bound to Galoup's disorientation.

L'intrus, arguably the opaquest work in Denis's oeuvre, also features a version of unresolved stereoscopy. *L'intrus* is the story of a retired mercenary, Trebor, who buys a heart on the black market to replace his own failing organ and so prolong his life. Of course, the protagonist, despite appearing pathologically egocentric, does not populate the world of the story by himself. The viewer is also given glimpses into the life of Sidney (Colin), Trebor's son, and is served visions of the ferally charged Queen of the Northern Hemisphere (Dalle). As the oddity of the name of the latter character suggests, *L'intrus* is saturated by oneiric affect. Proceeding in a dreamlike fashion, the organisation of the diegesis is such that its pieces never exceed a relationship of suggestive juxtaposition. Depictions of the mutilated body of Sidney alongside the surgical scars borne by Trebor hint that the father's life has been bought through the son's death, but the surreal structure of the film eschews final disclosure regarding this gruesome suggestion. *L'intrus*, in sum, toys with the viewer's cognitive compulsion to correlate, and, from correlation, to locate causation.

Diegetic discontinuity, particularly in the form of unresolved stereoscopy, is less obviously a feature of the three remaining non-generic films in Denis's oeuvre. In fact, *Vendredi soir*, *35 rhums* and *White Material* enjoy notable chronotopic stability. But this is not to say that diegetic discontinuity disappears altogether from these stories. The narrative in *Vendredi soir* is contained by a passionate chance encounter made possible by a traffic jam. The foundational function of gridlock, of course, means that such narratological neatness is predicated on inertia. Just as cars and the characters they contain and conjoin literally go nowhere in the film, so there is nowhere to go cognitively for the viewer.

It is with deceptive simplicity that *35 rhums* tells the story of widower Lionel (Descas) and his daughter Josephine, who live together in a Parisian apartment building also inhabited by Gabrielle, a taxi driver, and Noé (Colin), who, as a young man, subverts the cultural archetype of the old cat lady. While the diegesis is not structured by inertness, as in *Vendredi soir*, movement remains highly circumscribed in *35 rhums*. Its characters possess only a mobility of inevitability. This is succinctly symbolised by the motif of travelling along train tracks, the viewer inhabiting the point of view of Lionel, a train driver. Eventually, or indeed inevitably, Josephine and Noé marry. But the narrative closure that heteronormative union typically provides is collapsed by the film as it lingers finally on Lionel, ageing and alone in the apartment he once shared with his daughter.

White Material, third, stands out as the most conventional of Denis's films insofar as it observes narrative coherency as a given of filmmaking within the schema 'film' (although it avoids categorisation by genre). The story of a white coffee-farming family in an unnamed francophone African country sliding into deadly civil unrest, *White Material* comprises and is comprised by diegetic *continuity*. The coalescent arrangement of characters and plotlines is nowhere more evident than in the coordination of the prologue (x) and epilogue (z) that parenthesise the bulk of the film (y). The prologue depicts a young white man condemned to die in a burning building guarded by a military force; the epilogue depicts the mother of the young man encountering his charred remains and vengefully murdering her father-in-law, who is complicit in his grandson's immolation; the bulk of the film joins the dots, depicting the young man's entanglement with a rebel militia and their decimation by the military force representative of the government. This progression, x to z to y, is easily reconfigurable in the mind of the viewer as a sequential movement from x to y to z. Here is storytelling, posited as a universal practice, defined by Hogan (2010): a causal sequence of non-banal events involving human agency. Its very coherence a fissure within a framework patterned by fissures, *White Material* is, in the final analysis, the exception that proves the rule.

Attention to Denis's non-generic films has so far passed over their categorisation as such. That none of them do much to mark themselves out as belonging to a particular genre constitutes another inflection of diegetic discontinuity. Within such schemata as 'film' and 'story' sits the schema 'genre', which itself branches into numerous sub-schemata – 'comedy', 'horror', 'sci-fi', 'thriller', et cetera. However tautological as an exercise in nominative determinism, it bears stating that Denis's non-generic films are anti-Piagetian because they refuse accommodation not only in the schema 'genre' but also, more precisely, in any of its sub-schemata.

Resistant to equilibration as these films are, they are not beyond it. Indeed, the very act of categorising them as 'non-generic' is an equilibriative effort by way of assimilation, the process by which schemata grow in number and complexity. On account of its insipidness, though, 'non-generic' offers only a weak execution of assimilation. A more robust formulation might be found by adducing the work of Kathryn Hume, who coined the notion of 'aggressive fictions' (2012). An 'aggressive fiction' is not a fiction that contains violence, as the term implies, although the graphic depiction of violent action can count toward qualifying a text as an 'aggressive fiction'. Rather, an 'aggressive fiction' is one that *does violence*. That is, the text itself is violent.

An 'aggressive fiction' is violent essentially because it abrogates the millennia-old contract between author and reader – or indeed director and viewer. This contract stipulates that a fictional work should be pleasurable and insightful, following Horace's insistence that poetry (covering all creative texts) 'is properly *dulce* (entertaining) and *utile* (useful, informative)' (Hume 2012, 1). To be pleasurable and insightful, Hume goes on, a fiction ought to be apperceptible. Hume, incidentally, proceeds on the side of cognitive cultural studies in *Aggressive Fictions*, citing such stalwarts of psychological criticism as Norman N. Holland and Lisa Zunshine, although Hume does not explicitly declare such allegiance in her monograph. In other words – and Hume borrows those of Holland – a Horation fiction or general fiction can be identified by possessing a high level of conformity to the reader's 'mental patterns' and 'inner templates' – what Piaget called schemata (2012, 3). The aggressiveness of the category proposed by Hume emanates from the fact that the fictions that fit into it are xenomorphic. They are strangely shaped, refusing conformity with the shapes of expectation. This, ironically, makes Hume's aggressive fictions isomorphic with the non-generic films of Denis. The consonance between the two is readily appreciable, so much so, indeed, that the labelling of the first can supplant the labelling of the second. In a further inflection of irony, this enables Denis's 'non-generic films', disruptive of equilibration, to be assimilated as 'aggressive fictions' – that is, a schema that recognises the disruption of schemata as a qualifier for inclusion.

Denis's is an anti-Piagetian cinema. It is a cinema of cognitive assault. The thing under attack more than any other is equilibration – the mental movement from a state of dissonance to one of consonance through the processes of accommodation and assimilation. This attack is not limited to the filmmaker's aggressive fictions – *Chocolat*, *S'en fout la mort*, *Nénette et Boni*, *Beau travail*, *Vendredi soir*, *L'intrus*, *35 rhums* and *White Material* – but is also perpetrated by her generic ones – the serial killer fiction *J'ai pas sommeil*, the horror *Trouble Every Day*, the thriller *Les salauds*, the romcom *Un beau soleil intérieur* and the sci-fi *High Life*. All these titles, by way of symbolic density and diegetic discontinuity, frustrate an apparatus of apperception – the mind of the 'general viewer' – constructed to detect causality and further conditioned to that task by the psychological contiguity underlying the hegemonic continuity style of filmmaking. From *Chocolat* to *High Life*, across an oeuvre reminiscent of the poetry of Emily Dickinson, aphoristic and cryptic in its distillation of experiences and ideas, the films of Claire Denis surveyed together form a set of trans-generic dramas of non-disclosure.

NOTES

1. Rosalind Galt (2014) offers a fascinating analysis of Denis's contrary position relative to the dominance of Hollywood and its embeddedness in global neoliberalism.
2. For a substantial treatment of the gaze of the white woman in Denis's debut, see Céline Philibert (2002). A counter to asserting the primacy of France's/the white woman's gaze in Denis's debut is offered by Levilson Reis (2013).
3. For a sustained reading of the disruption(s) staged in *J'ai pas sommeil*, see Nikolaj Lübeker (2007).
4. Alternative analysis of the ways *Trouble Every Day* works within and against the horror genre is provided by Coulthard and Birks (2016), specifically 470–2.

CITATIONS

APA Dictionary of Psychology. 'Equilibration.' Accessed 29 May 2022. https://dictionary.apa.org/equilibration.

APA Dictionary of Psychology. 'Schema.' Accessed 29 May 2022. https://dictionary.apa.org/schemas.

Beugnet, Martine. 2016. 'The Practice of Strangeness: *L'intrus*, from Jean-Luc Nancy (2000) to Claire Denis (2004).' In *The Essay Film: Dialogue, Politics, Utopia*, edited by Elizabeth

Papazian and Caroline Eades, 68–85. New York: Columbia University Press. ProQuest Ebook Central.
Carey, Susan, Deborah Zaitchik and Igor Bascandziev. 2015. 'Theories of Development: in dialogue with Jean Piaget.' *Developmental Review* 38: 36–54.
Carroll, Noël. 2003. *The Philosophy of Horror: Or, Paradoxes of the Heart*. Florence: Taylor & Francis. ProQuest Ebook Central.
Carter, Mia. 2014. 'Acknowledged absences: Claire Denis's cinema of longing.' *Studies in European Cinema* 3, 1: 67–81. https://www.tandfonline.com/doi/abs/10.1386/seci.3.1.67/1, accessed 1 March 2023.
Cassuto, Leonard. 2009. *Hard-Boiled Sentimentality: The Secret History of American Crime Stories*. New York: Columbia University Press.
Cohen, Jeffrey Jerome. 1996. 'Monster Culture (Seven Theses).' In *Monster Theory: Reading Culture*. Minneapolis: University of Minnesota Press.
Coulthard, Lisa and Chelsea Birks. 2016. 'Desublimating monstrous desire: the horror of gender in new extremist cinema.' *Journal of Gender Studies* 25, 4: 461–76.
Del Río, Elena. 2003. 'Body transformations in the films of Claire Denis: from ritual to play.' *Studies in French Cinema* 3, 3: 185–97. https://doi.org/10.1386/sfci.3.3.185/1.
Deluca, Raymond. 2021. 'Hairy Screens, Filmic Follicles: the uses of hair in a selection of films by Claire Denis.' *Canadian Journal of Film Studies* 30, 1: 1–24.
Dooley, Kath. 2015. 'Haptic visions of unstable bodies in the work of Claire Denis.' *Continuum: Journal of Media & Cultural Studies*, 29, 3: 434–44. http://dx.doi.org/10.1080/10304312.2015.1025360, accessed 1 March 2023.
Eagleton, Terry. 2005. *Literary Theory: An Introduction (Second Edition)*. Oxford: Blackwell.
Eco, Umberto. 2015. *How to Write a Thesis*. Translated by Caterina Mongiat Farina and Geoff Farina. Cambridge, MA: MIT Press.
Elsaesser, Thomas. 2012. 'European Cinema and the Postheroic Narrative: Jean-Luc Nancy, Claire Denis, *Beau travail*.' *New Literary History* 43, 4: 703–25. https://www.jstor.org/stable/23358664, accessed 1 March 2023.
Fanon, Frantz. 2019 [1952]. *Black Skin, White Masks*. London: Penguin Classics.
Fischer, Kurt and Ulas Kaplan. 2005. 'Piagetian Theory, Development of Conceptual Structure.' In *Encyclopedia of Cognitive Science*, edited by Lynn Nadel. Hoboken: Wiley.
Frow, John. 2015. *Genre* (second edition). Oxford: Routledge. ProQuest Ebook Central.
Galt, Rosalind. 2014. 'Claire Denis and the World Cinema of Refusal.' *SubStance* 43, 1: 96–108. https://www.jstor.org/stable/24540741, accessed 1 March 2023.
Herman, David. 2010. 'Narrative Theory after the Second Cognitive Revolution.' In *Introduction to Cognitive Cultural Studies*, edited by Lisa Zunshine, 155–75. Baltimore: Johns Hopkins University Press.
Hogan, Patrick Colm. 2010. 'Literary Universals.' In *Introduction to Cognitive Cultural Studies*, edited by Lisa Zunshine, 37–60. Baltimore: Johns Hopkins University Press.
Hume, Kathryn. 2012. *Aggressive Fictions: Reading the Contemporary American Novel*. Ithaca: Cornell University Press.
Kolker, Robert Phillip. 2016. *Film, Form, and Culture (Fourth Edition)*. London and New York: Routledge. ProQuest Ebook Central.
Lübeker, Nikolaj. 2007. 'The Dedramatization of Violence in Claire Denis's *I Can't Sleep*.' *Paragraph* 30, 7: 17–33.
Mäkelä, Maria. 2012. 'Navigating – Making Sense – Interpreting (The Reader behind *La Jalousie*).' In *Narrative, Interrupted: The Plotless, the Disturbing, and the Trivial in Literature*, edited by Markku Lehtimäki, Laura Karttunen and Maria Mäkelä, 139–52. Berlin: De Gruyter. ProQuest Ebook Central.

Mayne, Judith. 2005. *Claire Denis*. Champaign: University of Illinois Press.

McMahon, Laura. 2014. 'Beyond the Body: Claire Denis's Ecologies.' *Alphaville: Journal of Film and Screen Media* 7: 1–18.

Mulvey, Laura. 1975. 'Visual Pleasure and Narrative Cinema.' *Screen (London)* 16, 3: 6–18. https://doi.org/10.1093/screen/16.3.6.

Murphy, Cáit. 2021. 'The Complexities of Exile, the Other, and the Postcolonial Predicament in *Beau travail* (Claire Denis, 1999).' *Film Matters* 12, 2: 9–21.

O'Donnell, Angela M. 2018. *Educational Psychology (3rd Australian Edition)*. Hoboken, New Jersey: Wiley. ProQuest Ebook Central.

Philibert, Céline. 2002. 'From Betrayal to Inclusion: The Work of the White Woman's Gaze in Claire Denis's *Chocolat*.' In *White Women in Racialized Spaces: Imaginative Transformation and Ethical Action in Literature*, edited by Samina Najmi and Rajini Srikanth, 207–26. Albany: State University of New York Press.

Pinker, Steven. 2015. *Language, Cognition, and Human Nature: Selected Articles*. Oxford: Oxford University Press.

Reis, Levilson. 2013. 'An "other" scene, an "other" point of view: France's colonial family romance, Protée's postcolonial fantasies and Claire Denis's "screen" memories.' *Studies in European Cinema* 10, 2–3: 119–31. https://www.tandfonline.com/doi/abs/10.1386/seci.10.2-3.119_1, accessed 1 March 2023.

Seltzer, Mark. 1998. *Serial Killers: Death and Life in America's Wound Culture*. New York and London: Routledge.

Troy, Eddy. 2020. 'Intersubjectivity and the cinematic thing: diasporic *Being-with* in Claire Denis's *35 rhums*.' *Studies in European Cinema*: 1–16.

Wilson, Emma. 2019. 'Love Me Tender: New Films from Claire Denis.' *Film Quarterly* 72, 4: 18–28.

CHAPTER 8

Writing Female Desire: From *Vendredi soir* to *Avec amour et acharnement*

Kristin Hole

From her earliest films, desire has been recognised as a major facet of Claire Denis's work, driving her exploration of bodies and their stories. While her early work was noted for its focus on men and male bodies, after more than a decade of directing Denis made *Vendredi soir* (2002), which at the time was consistently described as an outlier in her oeuvre for its focus on a (desiring) female character. The film also signalled a departure from the bulk of her earlier work in that it focused exclusively on two white characters. But rather than remain an anomaly in her career, the exploration of heterosexual female desire in front of the camera has become a more prominent concern for Denis, recurring in recent films such as *Un beau soleil interieur* (2017), and *Avec amour et acharnement* (2022).[1] These explorations of female desire mark a shift from the desiring gaze of the camera/filmmaker as it traverses the male (and often non-white) body predominant in the first decade or so of Denis's career. Scholars have read her early films, such as *Chocolat* (1988), *S'en fout le mort* (1990), *J'ai pas sommeil* (1994) and *Beau travail* (1999) through the concept of the postcolonial desiring gaze, but the dynamics of race and the impact of colonial legacies are noticeably less prominent in much of her recent output.[2] While Denis has continued to cast non-white actors in the majority of her films, they are peripheral to the films' white leads (*Vendredi soir*, *L'intrus* [2004], *Les salauds* [2013], *High Life* [2018], *Un beau soleil interieur*, *Avec amour et acharnement* and *Stars at Noon* [2022]). Her most sustained exploration of black female desire occurs in *35 rhums* (2008), but in general, at this juncture, Denis's more consistent examination of female desire has seemed to coincide with a stronger foregrounding of white female characters.

Denis has been ambivalent towards, if not outright rejecting, the label of 'woman director'. Her early films never treated stereotypically female subjects and she rightfully resisted readings of her work through a lens that would reduce her storytelling to an essentialised notion of the 'female gaze'. As Judith Mayne notes, at other times, Denis explicitly invokes a feminine way of seeing in interviews, nodding to the relevance of gender without allowing it to define the meaning of her work (2005, 27–8). In some sense her stubborn, opaque female characters parallel her own persona as a filmmaker: she refuses to be pinned down and insists on making the films that she wants to make, regardless of larger trends or critical expectations. That said, now that Denis is comfortably enshrined as one of the most important living directors, she seems to have given herself the freedom to explore female desire in front of the camera, and to do so through genres that have historically been dismissed as feminine and too popular for the art cinema world that is her milieu. In her more recent films with Juliette Binoche, Binoche seems to act as a muse through which she explores specifically midlife female desire and sexuality. Denis is no longer a director who 'lies in wait among men', as fellow director Catherine Breillat once noted (Mayne 2005, 26).[3]

Notably the three most significant films to date in this newer trajectory – *Vendredi soir*, *Un beau soleil intérieur*, and *Avec amour et acharnement*– were co-written with important French authors (both women), a departure from Denis's many screenwriting collaborations with Jean-Pôl Fargeau. In what follows, I examine these collaborations, along with the source material for the films, and the ways in which they shape Denis's exploration of female desire on-screen. Denis collaborated with Emmanuèle Bernheim (who passed away in 2017) to adapt her novel *Vendredi soir* to the screen, and has worked with Christine Angot on three projects to date. She adapted one of Angot's novels into the short film, *Voilà l'enchaînement* (2014) and cowrote *Un beau soleil intérieur* and *Avec amour et acharnement* with Angot. The latter film is based on Angot's novel *Un tournant de la vie* (2018).

VENDREDI SOIR

Prior to adapting *Vendredi soir*, Emmanuèle Bernheim had contributed to the script for *Trouble Every Day* (2001).[4] Unlike Angot, Bernheim had strong ties to cinema before her collaboration with Denis, and is generally recognised for the links between cinema and literature across her career. Previously, Bernheim had written television movies, in addition to co-writing the film *L'Autre nuit* (1988) with director Jean-Pierre Limosin, and François Ozon's *Sous la Sable* (2000). After *Vendredi soir*, Bernheim worked on two further scenarios with Ozon, *Swimming Pool* (2003) and *5x2* (2004).[5] In fact, Bernheim has worked on more screenplays than she has finished novels, having written only six novels in some thirty years. *Vendredi soir* is her only collaboration that adapts one of her own novels into a fiction film scenario.

Bernheim's relationship with film extends further into her biography: in 1980, she began managing the photo archives at *Cahiers du Cinéma* and was encouraged to write for the journal by Serge Daney himself (she abstained). Her husband, Serge Toubiana, currently the president of Unifrance, headed La Cinémathèque française from 2003 to 2016 and was chief editor of *Cahiers du Cinéma* for over a decade prior to that. Her personal and professional life were thus deeply enmeshed with the cinema. For Bernheim, her books were her mode of filmmaking: 'When I started writing, my influence was the cinema. Novels are my way of making films' (2017).[6] As Sonia Assa notes, 'Her narration seems to emulate the great diegetic articulations of cinema: the zoom, the fade, synchrony and asynchrony, etc., which she transforms into fundamentally literary techniques' (2007, 54). Assa argues that *Vendredi soir*, the novel, 'refers more to cinema than to literature', referencing Wong Kar-wai, Alain Resnais and *film noir* (Assa 2007, 59). Bernheim is known for her minimalist style, and thus, her economic use of language (her novels are typically around a hundred pages), and for an approach 'that makes space for silence and the unsaid'.[7] These qualities make her writing conducive to Denisian adaptation. Additional affinities between her work and Denis's filmmaking include 'the absence of commentary, of "psychology" and embellishment, the refusal to explain, to justify or condemn' (Assa 2007, 58).[8] Like Denis, she evokes sensation while at the same time sharing the 'least possible interiority' (2007, 54).

Denis wanted *Vendredi soir*'s adaptation to stay as close to the novel as possible. Its story is simple: a woman, Laure (Valerie Lémercier), packs up her apartment as she prepares to move in with her partner the following day. She leaves to have dinner with friends but gets stuck in a traffic jam, due to a transit strike. Drivers are encouraged to pick up stranded commuters and Laure gives a ride to Jean (Vincent Lindon). Desire grows between them and they end up spending the night together in a hotel. The many shots through car windows that reflect the bouncing light of the dark streets render the world oneiric and ephemeral, yet smell and touch are invoked to insist on the materiality of Laure's experience. At the film's end, Laure is seen running from the hotel through streets lined with parked cars, a smile on her face. The film follows the dreamy drift of a night that feels unreal, a state of exception in which the whole city is effectively immobilised, and Laure crosses over from the known to an unscripted future.

Vendredi soir contains many of Denis's trademark elements – an open ending, momentary glances towards the periphery of the narrative and haptic camerawork. Regarding the periphery, for example, early in the film, Denis includes a scene not present in the novel. The cleaner at Laure's apartment building takes out the trash and discovers that Laure has discarded some usable lampshades. The camera lingers on the caretaker as she declares the lampshades worth keeping and takes them back into the building with her. We never see this character again, and, typical of Denis's filmmaking, she represents one of many brief moments in which our gaze is directed elsewhere, reminded of the many stories that are not being told right here and now in this film – gesturing at another possibility that lies beyond the frame.

With almost no dialogue (a trait it shares with the novel), the cinematography, *mise en scène* and sound evoke spaces of warmth and cold, smells of leather and tobacco, textures of skin and hair. Near the beginning of the film we cut from Laure drying her hair with the car's heating vent to a shot outside the vehicle. The prominent sounds of humming motors and grinding machinery induce a visceral response. Smoke billows up, presumably from an exhaust pipe, and then the film cuts back inside to a view of Laure's rain-dabbled windshield. The hum of the motor and gust of the heater are dominant on the soundtrack, accompanied by a bristling sound as Laure begins to finger comb and shake her hair, viewed in close-up. We can feel the warmth and wind of the heater, the womb-like enclosure of the car and the wetness of her hair, and are just as startled as Laure is when a hand knocks loudly on her window, interrupting our immersion in a world of sense.

The film also showcases long-time Denis collaborator Agnès Godard's sensual and haptic camerawork. The love scenes share continuity with the sex scenes in Denis's previous film, *Trouble Every Day*, where in lieu of discernible shots of one character performing an act on or with another character, sequences that in conventional cinema highlight the woman's breasts, buttocks or limbs, we are brought in close to the bodies, seeing hands, feet and hair, but lacking clear visual markers of who is where and what exactly is happening to whom. The viewer is forced to let their vision give way to other senses: the textures, the breaths and the smells that the image opens onto. This mode of filming moves away from the male gaze as a mastering gaze and towards a different kind of spectatorship, one in which the spectator is implicated in a much more bodily way, and the gendered body is displaced as the primary site through which to cognise physical intimacy on-screen (Hole 2016, 142–4). The scenes in *Vendredi soir* in which Jean and Laure embrace, kiss and/or make love, rely exclusively on diegetic sound, so we hear textures rub against one another, breathing and the hum of a hotel room heater, adding to the tactility of the experience. Because I want to contrast this with the sex scene in *Un beau soleil* specifically, I note here the duration of these wordless scenes: their first embrace on the street alone lasts almost three minutes.

More so than Bernheim's other film collaborations (for example, with Ozon), which did not stem from her literary work and rely more heavily on dialogue, *Vendredi soir* follows a series of impressions and thoughts expressed almost completely without language from a woman's point of view. The novel is written in free indirect discourse – describing the world around Laure and her actions, while giving us access to her interiority, what she smells or hears and where her imagination wanders. For example, at one point Laure is convinced that Jean has absconded with her car while she made a phone call. The text describes, 'She threw her head back and breathed in the cold air. Despite the exhaust fumes, she felt she could still perceive his odour' (1998, 31).[9] She imagines him finding a red skirt that she was planning to donate in the car:

> He'd definitely bring it home. He'd give it to the woman he lives with and she'd try it on in front of him. She would no doubt be thin and tall, the skirt would be too big and too short. He'd look at her long legs and then come closer to her' (1998, 31).[10]

The film translates this written style visually through various techniques, which could be labelled impressionistic. Laure's playful imagination is shown, for example, when a licence plate's letters move around in time to the music that she dances to in her car, or when she looks down at her pizza and a pepper forms a mouth smiling up at her. Visual techniques, such as irised transitions, dreamy superimpositions, slow and fast motion photography and editing that elides space and time, all combine with close-ups on Laure's regarding face throughout the film to focalise the narrative through her subjectivity. While I have emphasised continuity with Denis's previous work, in many cases these techniques are new for Denis and some haven't been featured since (for example, the use of irises and the playful trick photography). It is as if Denis is seeking out a new visual vocabulary not only to translate the novel to the screen, but also to privilege a woman's gaze and interiority. Irises are used, for example, to transition momentarily to a scene in which Laure humorously imagines a scenario where she invites Jean along to her dinner plans that evening. Her friend asks Jean to put out his cigarette because of the baby and the two sit awkwardly on the couch holding their whiskeys. In another instance, superimpositions indicate Laure's daydreams: as the couple eat pizza, her face is superimposed with images of her and Jean making love.

Mariah Devereux Herbeck does well to point out the parallels between Germain Dulac's *The Smiling Madame Beudet* and *Vendredi soir*, which echoes many of the impressionist techniques used in the earlier film.[11] Both films draw on cinematically specific means to represent a woman's interiority, yet Laure's interiority is never fully transparent for the audience, as she maintains a degree of Denisian opacity, in contrast with the legibility of Mme Beudet. Unlike *Madame Beudet*, *Vendredi soir* features significant mobile camerawork, which is central to the film's politics of desire. As Maud Ceuterick argues, the moving camera, '"magically" offers Laure the wandering gaze that cinema offers to women. Laure meta-cinematically becomes empowered to look without being looked at, without her female body being identified as a problem for "public" spaces' (2020, 65). At a leisurely pace, the camera pans across Laure's car, the

Figure 8.1   Superimposition in *Vendredi soir*.

metal reflecting the movements of other cars caught in the traffic jam. After moving upwards to show us her face, a superimposed track over a neon sign slowly replaces Laure's visage. This sign is a pair of spectacles, playfully indicating that Laure's perspective drives the film. It is directly after this that we get our first shot of Jean, a close-up of his direct gaze that hints at the embodiment of Laure's fantasy that he represents. In *Vendredi soir*, the turn to a feminist impressionist visual vocabulary reinforces that Denis is doing something new in her work here: exploring visual modes for representing female desire on-screen in a sustained way.

With the shot/reverse shots from Laure's perspective through the window (screen) of the car, parallels can be drawn between the immobility of the traffic-arrested drivers and the cinematic apparatus. Neil Archer reads the character of Laure, 'not so much as a "real" being, but as the identificatory figure through which the play of feminine cinematic pleasure, experienced as a parenthesis in social reality, can take place' (2008, 256). Judith Mayne also discusses the film through its representation of women's gaze as knowing, observing, questioning and desiring (2005, 124). It is specifically through the lens of spectatorship and the gaze that the film can add a medium-specific commentary to the already cinematic novel. I emphasise readings of the film that see it as a kind of manifesto of female desire connected with an exploration of the possibilities of the female gaze and spectatorship, because this contrasts with the interests of Denis's films with Angot. Where *Vendredi soir* sees female desire generating lines of flight that break, at least momentarily, with the everyday order, as something that alters the quotidian experience of the real, the films made with

Angot are not interested in exploring the politics of female spectatorship and mobility.

In summary, despite the thematic shifts in Denis's oeuvre that *Vendredi soir* represented at the time of its release and its experimentation with new cinematic techniques, in retrospect, the film feels more continuous with Denis's previous filmic style than would her subsequent work with Angot, perhaps in large part due to the affinities of the source material with her own approach to narrative.

FROM *VOILÀ L'ENCHAÎNEMENT* TO *UN BEAU SOLEIL INTÉRIEUR*

Examining *Un beau soleil intérieur* does not invalidate much of what has been written about *Vendredi soir*'s exploration of female desire, but it does show Denis eschewing the notion that to represent female desire is to move away from language, as some critics argued.[12] In the latter film, the playful impressionist techniques are absent, no doubt owing in part to the differing source material and co-scenarist. The source material for *Un beau soleil* is disputed – a point I will return to – and the film was written with Denis's more recent collaborator, the author Christine Angot. Angot is a prolific writer (twenty-two novels and ten plays to date), known for her provocative works of autofiction, several of which examine the sexual abuse she suffered at the hands of her father. She also mines her romantic relationships for her material, notably her high-profile romance with French rapper Doc Gynéco (Bruno Beausir), and, after their relationship ended, her partnership with Beausir's best friend, the Martiniquan musician Charly Clovis. These relationships are the subject of the novels for two of her collaborations with Denis. As mentioned, *Les Petits* (2008) was the source material for the short film *Voilà L'enchaînement*, and *Un tournant de la vie* (2018) for *Avec amour et acharnement*. *Les Petits*, based on Clovis's relationship with his ex, was the object of a public legal battle. Clovis's former partner accused Angot of *atteinte de la vie privée*, i.e. publicising personal details of her and her children's lives in a transparent way in the text. Angot lost the case.[13]

Les Petits explores the power dynamics between Hélène and Billy, who have four children together in addition to Hélène's child from a previous marriage. Hélène is a white middle-class woman and Billy, a Martiniquan musician in a position of economic and racial disadvantage vis-à-vis Hélène and within French society at large. The novel charts the ways in which Hélène begins to assert dominance within the relationship, using her relative systemic privilege to push Billy out of the children's lives. It narrates moments of fetishisation or insensitivity that cross the threshold of racist behaviour: Hélène wants their child to have dreadlocks and Billy does not; she wants Billy to tattoo her name on his body, which reminds him of being branded like cattle; she calls him a 'stud' (*ètalon*), a word he has heard only in reference to the selling of slaves. Words are loaded with a history of racial oppression that Hélène ignores. Ultimately, Billy becomes, like so many non-white men, a victim of the penal system. Trapped in a dysfunctional dynamic, Billy is at a complete disadvantage if an argument erupts and the police are called. He ends up in prison. The short film pulls key scenes from this text, focusing on the moments that document the racial and class inequalities that inflect and enable the power dynamics of the couple. The short film feels experimental for Denis in its almost exclusive focus on dialogue. There is almost nothing in the way of *mise en scène* beyond the characters themselves (they are clearly on a soundstage, with a door representing a bathroom or a mattress standing in for a bedroom). Also shot by Godard, the visual minimalism directs focus on the two characters' speech. *Voilà l'enchaînement* prefigures the more dialogue-heavy nature of Denis's feature collaborations with Angot, in marked contrast to a film like *Vendredi soir* and Denis's previous work in general. It also forms a link with the source material for *Avec Amour et acharnement*, which is based on Angot's relationship with Clovis and the re-emergence of Beausir in their lives. *Voilà l'enchaînement* is somewhat different from the feature films I am discussing here in that it is focused not on female desire but on domination and power as they traverse the most intimate domains of our lives.

If *Vendredi soir* offered Laure the perfect fantasy in Jean, *Un beau soleil* forces its female lead to deal with the reality of men. In the film, we observe Isabelle (Juliette Binoche), an established painter, as she passes through a series of actual and would-be lovers. The film feels as if it could start and stop arbitrarily at any point in Isabelle's life – there is no telos towards which we move and it is unclear whether Isabelle has grown as a person or is in a better place at the film's end. The lack of resolution is playfully reinforced by the extension of the action throughout the closing credits. Gerard Depardieu plays a psychic who (self-interestedly) counsels Isabelle on her romantic future, their conversation continuing throughout the ending credit sequence as if to emphasise that romantic longing does not fit itself into a traditional beginning, middle and end structure. Although not based on a text by Angot, Denis notes, 'We decided that dialogues will be the architecture of the film . . . instead of location or situation'.[14] This is a marked contrast with her description of her writing process with Jean-Pôl Fargeau:

> When Jean-Pol Fargeau and I write, we write sensations. We even describe odours – the smell of a forest in summer when you're naked in the heat with two dogs. In a script you need to understand the ellipses. Sometimes they come later, little by little but often they impose themselves from the start. (Romney 2005, 42)

Where Denis may have been drawing on Bernheim's descriptive and sense-based writing in *Vendredi soir*, this style was continuous with her previous writing approach. With Angot, Denis moves away from the notion that exploring female desire necessitates an abdication of language and a move towards the body.

Despite *Un beau soleil*'s focus on desire, there is only one sex scene in the film, which is markedly different in terms of how it is shot from scenes in films like *Trouble Every Day* and *Vendredi soir* (despite sharing Godard as DP).[15] The film opens on a striking overhead medium shot of Isabelle lying in bed, her breasts visible and her face in a state of arousal. The camera rotates as it views her from above; heavy breathing and light non-diegetic music comprise the audio. The image cuts to a side view: a medium close-up of her lover, Vincent (Xavier Beauvois), tilts down to include Isabelle, who lies underneath him. The camera stays on their faces as he thrusts and heaves, and as the camera alternates between overhead and side perspectives on the action, it becomes apparent that Isabelle is tired and bored. For a moment the camera shoots the couple from a perspective looking down their horizontal bodies from the tops of their heads; if the take were longer, the viewer might get lost in the movement of bodies in close-up, their grunts and adjustments. But Isabelle quickly becomes frustrated with Vincent's slowness to orgasm, and the camera moves back again to a side view. Dialogue begins within a minute of the scene's start, with Isabelle directing Vincent to orgasm and assuring him she is satisfied (compare this with the many minutes of dialogue-less touching and caressing on the street in *Vendredi soir*). Vincent asks Isabelle, insensitively, whether she came easily with her previous 'friend' and she slaps him, rolling over and crying, so that only her back is shown. Throughout the sequence the camera ultimately gives us a more *external* visual perspective, perhaps because it is here representing something quite different from Laure's desire being consummated. Instead this is a frustrating and fruitless interaction for Isabelle, one of many the film will document. But it is also emblematic of Denis's heavier reliance on dialogue in her work with Angot and the way in which it shapes the cinematography. The scene is not asking us to get lost in sensation, but invites recognition of a situation of physical intimacy, sexual expectations and frustrated desire.

This early scene is followed by one in Vincent's home, shot in one long take, so both characters are visible as they manoeuvre through the space. The dialogue is without pause, as physically, Isabelle moves around Vincent's upscale apartment. Again, the camera chooses an external view, most advantageous for seeing the dynamics between the speaking parties. This scene is followed by another involving the same two characters at a bar. The cinematography is quite self-conscious here – the sequence has few cuts – and highlights the effect of Vincent's domineering and slightly sadistic personality on Isabelle.

To capture this, the camera stays close to their faces for most of the scene, continuously moving around one face and then panning to the other, back and forth, as if to highlight the psychological and emotional exchange between the two, in particular the impact of Vincent's words on Isabelle. Incidentally, he is torturing her with what we find out is an unfounded rumour about a relationship between her ex-husband and her current gallerist.[16] As I've described, throughout the film the cinematography works to highlight the relations between speaking subjects. The dialogue shapes the visual strategies and much less time is allowed for silence than in most of Denis's previous work. This even becomes a gag at one point in the film, when Isabelle declares to a new lover (an actor in the theatre) as they embrace, 'I couldn't bear it anymore. It feels so good to stop all that talking.' Of course, they continue to talk – and to not quite understand one another – as they kiss their way to the bedroom.

Upon its release many reviewers wrote that the inspiration for *Un beau soleil intérieur* was Roland Barthes's *A Lover's Discourse* (1977).[17] In interviews, Denis denies this, admitting that the producer's initial request was for an adaptation, yet she and Angot realised, as women of a certain age, that they had a vast catalogue of their own sexual and romantic experiences from which to write. In interviews about the film, Denis repeatedly tells the story of having obsessively read Barthes's book in her early twenties during a difficult time in her life. She describes her well-worn copy of the monograph, confessing that she would cry when reading it (Yoonsoo Kim 2018). Denis recounts telling her producer that the only film she could make based on Barthes's text would be called 'Agony' (2018). Despite her claim that 'not a fragment' of Barthes appears in the final film, the text slips in occasionally, perhaps unconsciously.[18] For example, in one more blatant moment of reference, Isabelle yells at Vincent, 'I want the last word'. In his discussion of 'Making Scenes', Barthes notes that 'Each partner of a scene dreams of having the *last word*', and he goes on to elaborate this desire as a key characteristic of 'making a scene', one of his figures of the lover's discourse (1977: 207). That said, I am not interested here in a reading of *Un beau soleil intérieur* that looks at which of Barthes's figures are being invoked through the dialogue and *mise en scène* of various sequences, but rather in considering the form of the text in relation to the developments in Denis's style in this film, particularly as she represents female desire.

A Lover's Discourse is a series of fragments, or what Barthes calls figures. It is organised alphabetically by terms that stand in for the ideas or dispositions expressed in each figure, from *s'abimer* (to be engulfed) through *déclaration* (declaration) and *dépendance* (dependency), ending with *vouloir-saisir* (will-to-possess). The figures are meant to offer not a complete picture of the lover, but a series of thoughts, preoccupations and emotions that are often present in any love situation. They are structural, in that they are features of the state of being in love, common to any lover regardless of who the lover loves. In *A Lover's Discourse*, as in *Un beau soleil*, some moments or figures are more fleshed out and others are necessarily incomplete. The film, regardless of stated intention, does seem to echo this cataloguing of facets of desire. It consists of a series of fragmented scenes; the glimpses of narrative do not integrate into a larger coherent arc (Barthes emphasises that his text is non-syntagmatic and does not progress to a larger 'point'; the structure is arbitrary). While Denis is always elliptical, here it feels much more Barthesian: scenes in themselves, or an agglutination of scenes with one specific love interest, function to illustrate a personality type, a form of romantic dilemma or another common situation that one might find oneself in while navigating the terrain of romantic life. This is unique to the film and not typical of the structure of Denis's films in general.

While the lover may occupy a structural position (the figures are common), Barthes notes that each love is singular and each beloved loved for their *thusness*. The tendency of Denis's films to foreground characters' singularity or to expose them to the viewer in a manner that fails to fully grasp them, bears an affinity with Barthes's emphasis on the singularity of the loved one. For Barthes, and for *Un beau soleil*, while love's failures may resemble one another, the beloved themself is always 'incomparable', always singular: 'it is in their difference, that I find the energy to begin all over again' (1977, 103). In many ways Barthes's lover's discourse articulates what was already at practice in Denis's films – her refusal to thematise, master or to make fully visible her characters is much like the lover's attitude according to Barthes. In this sense, Denis's filmmaking practice is itself a kind of lover's discourse. Denis often brings up the relationships of love and trust that she builds with her actors, most of whom she works with repeatedly. She said of casting Isabelle's lovers in *Un beau soleil* specifically, 'Not partners in acting only, I wanted them to be partners for me too. Men I could trust, [that] I knew. So they were also, in a way, *my* partners.'[19] The desire that has been evident in her work from her earliest films, particularly as it directs the gaze of the camera onto the male body, has coincided with a refusal to fully put into language who her characters are. Instead, they are *this* smell, *this* gesture, *this* body as it moves to the music, *this* hand clasping. 'The other must become in my eyes pure of any attribution; the more I designate him, the less I shall utter him . . . Thus, the lover will say: *you are thus, thus and so, precisely thus*' (Barthes 1977, 221). Ironically, in Denis's work with Angot, language has come to be much more dominant in determining the narrative structure and characterisation in her films. This is not to say that language is used to offer a transparent psychological portrait of her characters, but that dialogue has come to greater prominence in these films, perhaps at the expense of the sensory as a form of exposure without mastery.

AVEC AMOUR ET ACHARNEMENT

Denis's next collaboration with Angot, *Avec amour et acharnement*, is notable not only for continuing the patterns I've noted in their work together, but also, as a film based on one of Angot's novels, it allows a closer inspection of the possible relationship between the style of the text and its adaptation. In this discussion, I also want to further examine the treatment of race in Denis's 'female desire' films.

The film charts the relationship between Sara (Juliette Binoche) and Jean (Vincent Lindon), who have been together for nine years. Jean has spent time in prison, but we are not told why. His son, Marcus (Issa Perica) lives in the suburbs with his grandmother (Bulle Ogier); Marcus's mother has returned to Martinique. One day on the street, Sara sees François (Grégoire Colin), her former lover and a close friend of Jean, for the first time in years. She is deeply unsettled. The film examines Sara's enduring desire for François and the toll it takes on her relationship with Jean, who has gone back into business with François scouting rugby players. François's character has few redeeming qualities: he seduces Sara, a willing participant, and then shows her amorous text messages to Jean, telling him to leave her. In the end, Jean does. The narrative is incredibly elliptical, focused mostly on intense verbal exchanges between Sara and Jean, occasionally between Sara and Francois, and sometimes between Jean and his mother or son. The film moves from the couple's declarations of love to Sara repeatedly questioning Jean about his actions and feelings (he is characteristically withholding), to Sara and Francois's declarations of love, and by the film's end, to intense arguments between Sara and Jean as their relationship falls apart. As previously mentioned, the focus on verbal exchanges between characters is shaped by Angot's writing, which is heavily rooted in dialogue (most of the dialogues are taken directly from the novel). *Un Tournant de la Vie* includes brief moments of description – straight external observations that tend not to be poetic or unexpected in their use of language, while dialogue and the reportage of the narrator shape the story, as opposed to sensations, smells and sounds. For example,

> He got out of the shower. He was wrapped in a large towel, which he held in front of him with two hands. He shivered. A second towel was around his head. His eyes were red, his teeth chattered:
> 'You were reading there, am I disturbing you?'
> 'I'm listening.' (2018, 11)

The relationship in the film is depicted in claustrophobic terms. Unlike the novel, in which the narrator has two close female friends she calls on regularly to process her love triangle, in the film the couple seem to have no real lives outside of each other, with Jean's only other regular contact being his mother, whom he hardly visits.[20] The beautiful opening shots of the film monumentalise Jean and Sara's love for each other, as they are depicted frolicking in a clear blue sea framed by rocky cliffs. Their isolation in these earliest frames sets the tone for the rest of the film. The claustrophobia of their relationship is emphasised by obsessive close-ups and handheld camera work (this is Denis's first film with DP Éric Gautier, with whom she also shot *Stars at Noon*). When not in tight close-up the couple is usually in frame together: at times the camera tracks their conversation without cutting away, further compounding the sense of containment. Visually, they separate more when François re-enters their lives. Once Sara and François start an affair, François begins to receive the cinematographic treatment previously reserved for Jean in his sequences with Sara. When Sara and Jean argue and she tells him that he is controlling and constantly surveils her, there's been nothing to support this claim in the elliptical plot. Seemingly unsubstantiated by the narrative, the cinematography may be hinting at the confining nature of their relationship.

Many reviewers note that the film shows the reality of the Covid pandemic in that masks are a prominent part of the *mise en scène*. One wonders if this pandemic backdrop is part of the reason that the characters are portrayed in such an insular fashion in the film, yet at the same time, they attend opening parties and press events for François's agency, suggesting that there is opportunity to interact with a larger world. The claustrophobic emphasis on the couple is not necessarily a problem, although the lack of third parties, through which Sara can articulate her experience, perhaps contributes to the less successful aspects of the film – she is not so much opaque as unlikeable, seemingly betraying Jean for something she doesn't need from someone who can't give it to her, and gaslighting Jean throughout the film about his legitimate feelings. Where the novel is as interested in the power dynamics between the two men as in

Figure 8.2 Claustrophobic intimacy in *Avec amour et acharnement*.

exploring the narrator's desire, the film centres on Sara's powerful attraction to François. The novel's protagonist isn't necessarily a saint, but we are given the opportunity to better understand her motivations and her experience of her lover's manipulation through her first-person narration and the conversations she has with her friends throughout the story. This has the effect of adding a significant amount of complexity to what the text relates, which could only strengthen the film's representation of female desire. Of course, as a work of autofiction, the narrator in the novel is a writer, whereas in the film Sara is a radio host. This also shines light on why the couple's isolation in the film feels somewhat unnatural. In the film, Sara hosts a radio programme where she interviews real-life guests – Hind Darwish on the 4 August explosion in Beirut, and Lilian Thuram, former soccer star and commentator on race in France, with whom she discusses the problem of whiteness. Thuram declares himself a Fanonian, in that he sees race as primarily an issue of psychology, of individuals being fixed in their racial identities. These guests gesture to a backdrop of significant historical events occurring beyond the pandemic in 2020 – the explosion in Beirut and mass protests against racial injustice. Yet unlike *Voilà l'enchaînement*, where the intimate relationship is clearly shaped by issues of class, nationality and race, it is unclear what the connection is here between Sara's job and her private life, or how including a commentary such as this on race meaningfully relates to the relatively apolitical focus on white heterosexual bourgeois romance. The inclusion of this kind of dangling political commentary in a film that focuses on white characters without a strong demonstration of how these forces shape the way *they* live, is of unclear value.

Significantly, Angot's novel auto-fictionalises her relationship with two black men. Denis and Angot chose to make the triangle completely white in the film, adding the character of the mixed-race son, perhaps as a nod to Clovis's actual children or perhaps as a way of keeping the reality of racial difference alive in the story. It is perhaps surprising that Denis would eschew the opportunity to cast black actors in two of the three major roles of the film, given her history of engaging with blackness. Denis has anecdotally related that she and Lindon discussed shooting something early in the pandemic – she had another project in the works with Angot but it was impossible to shoot at the time, and they turned to Angot's recently published novel. This is likely to be the practical reason that we end up with the cast we do – Denis wants to work with actors she knows well during a time of global uncertainty, and Lindon was central to the early stages of the project. That said, the changes in characters' racial identities seem like a missed opportunity to engage with the ways these dynamics may shape Sara/Angot's own relationships, as opposed to reflecting on the relationships her lovers have had in the past with *other* white women (as in *Voilà*). In addition to race, in the novel, class shapes the relationship dynamics, but does so less clearly in the film. Jean doesn't have a credit card, but has a comfortable background and a place to go to if the relationship fails, with his mother in Vitry. Alex – Jean's equivalent in the novel – is from Martinique. He is underemployed and financially dependent on the narrator. Thus, his threats to leave or to go back home carry almost no weight, as he can't afford a plane ticket, a fact the narrator and the François character (Vincent) remark on several times. The interpersonal dynamics in the film, then, are quite different. Again, a detailed comparison of novel and film isn't necessarily useful, but in this case it highlights some missed opportunities for more complexity in the screenplay, as well as emphasising the ways that to date, Denis's explorations of female desire have remained quite white. The film's lack of any connection between the larger world that we glimpse at Sara's job and her relationship are unfortunate. Of course, this may be the point: perhaps the film is highlighting the relative privilege of the white couple in contrast with the reality of the 'outside world'. The only other narrative detours occur in relation to Jean's mother and son. Here, perhaps, is a way of connecting the political discussions that occur at Sara's job, with the characters' lives.

While Sara and Jean have been together nine years, Sara's relationship with his son Marcus is non-existent, represented as if they are polite acquaintances, and any interest she takes in him is because he is part of Jean's life only. One may infer that their relationship is one of the reasons that Jean seems so alienated from his son. This appears to be supported by the footage that runs after the initial closing credits. Now that Jean has left Sara, we see him and Marcus scouting together at a rugby match. Marcus seems lighter and happier in this sequence and receives more close-ups than he has in the entire film, as if he can now be centred in the frame/Jean's life in a way that was impossible while Jean was with Sara. Marcus is central to one of the film's most uncomfortable moments, unique to the film adaptation, which notably goes unmentioned in most reviews of the film. Jean drives to the suburbs to talk to his son about his future. He paces back and forth as he lectures Marcus about his options and tells him that his race need not hold him back. When Jean asks Marcus who has it the hardest in France, Marcus answers 'Arabs and Blacks'. Jean proceeds to explain to him that his race is not his identity, that it doesn't determine who he is or the choices he makes, and that he doesn't have to perform the script that dominant society gives him. It is unclear if this hearkens back to Lilian Thuram's discussion of race earlier in the film – i.e. Jean is encouraging Marcus to not be fixed in a racial identity, and not to let the dominant racist construct control his self-image. It is not so much the content of the speech here that is profoundly uncomfortable, but the sight of a white man pedantically lecturing his child about race, when we have seen almost no evidence that he plays a meaningful role in Marcus's life. Perhaps if Jean was not white and had experienced what it is like to be black in France (he seems to think his experiences are translatable), or if Jean had any consistent role as a mentor figure or emotional presence in his son's life, this speech wouldn't feel so inappropriate. One of the few reviews that mentions this scene seems to give Denis the benefit of the doubt, writing

> When he [Jean] blusters at Marcus . . . spewing out incoherent thoughts on racism and on downward mobility, we're aware of just how poor a place he's in to dole out advice. The movie's sophistication comes from its sharp observations of its characters' weaknesses, even as they deny those flaws in themselves and call them out in everyone around them. (Willmore 2022)

In fact, the film's perspective on Jean at this moment is unclear, and we are not given any indication as to how we are meant to read the scene. Of all the characters, Jean is positioned as the moral centre of the film – ironically he is the only one who has served time in prison.[21]

Finally, it seems likely that the insular nature of Angot's writing (it is autofictional; she writes multiple books drawing from the same people or events in her life; presumably, her readers look for the connections between her writing and her personal life), creates a potentially esoteric self-referential world. Thus, any attempt to adapt and truncate one of her narratives, removing context and altering characters, produces some degree of narrative difficulty. Some of the alterations to the source material are what make the film work less well than the novel in terms of coherence. By way of illustration, in the film, Sara attends the opening of the rugby scouting agency and is invited to go into a room to see François – it would be their first reunion. She is awkward about going to this room and it occupies a bit of screen time until she finally heads in and meets him. François returns from Romania later in the film to hold a press event that he wants Sara to attend. These two moments feel unintuitive but make perfect sense in the novel. Since both Angot's partners are musicians, in fact the 'room' is a VIP area she is invited to after her ex's concert, and when he returns from Romania, it is at another one of his concerts that he requests her presence. These invitations feel much more organic and make more sense – a musician with whom her husband is working, whom she dated before him, invites her to his concerts and it is at these events that feelings are cultivated and jealousies emerge. A press conference for your lover's business partner doesn't work quite the same way, nor does having to go to a room to meet that person seem a logical narrative device, when one would likely run into them anyway at their own event. In some ways the changes to the script muddle or make situations more confusing beyond the elliptical nature of Denis's storytelling. And it is unclear if wanting to cast Lindon and Colin is the reason that these changes were made (perhaps they are more convincing as rugby scouts than as musicians). Again, I raise these points because *Un Tournant de la vie* is rooted in a world of repeating characters and extratextual knowledge – its adaptation does not offer as complex, potentially political or relatable a representation of female desire in part because of the source material itself and in part because of the changes made in its filmic reworking.

CONCLUSION

Avec amour et acharnement, then, returns us to the consistent features of the films discussed here: interested in female desire, they focus on white characters, and perhaps in the process miss something of the central interest that Denis's earliest work had. This is still evident in films like *35 rhums* and *White Material*, which foreground non-white stories without thematising race as an issue, *or* explore the relationship between whiteness and colonial spaces and bodies. Looking back at *Vendredi soir*, the continuities with Denis's previous sensuous non-verbal style are clear, despite her experimentation with new cinematic devices. This style was further bolstered through the choice of source material in Bernheim's writing. Denis's collaborations with Angot have been much more rooted in dialogue, less so in the kinds of soundscapes, smells and textures that have come to be regarded as characteristic of her work. This, again, is arguably shaped by the style and content of Angot's writing. Denis is nothing if not a surprising director, and it remains to be seen if and how she might continue to explore female desire in her work.

NOTES

1. Judging from the source material, *Stars at Noon* (2022) will also focus on a white heterosexual couple (in Central America). The novel is an untraditional love story, told from the perspective of the female protagonist. Even *White Material* (2009), a film that is not about romance or sexual desire, is centred around a female protagonist, diverging from much of Denis's earlier work.
2. See, for example, Susan Hayward (2002).
3. I am wary of making too many generalisations about her work, since Denis is always a surprising director, and even within the last fifteen years has made films that don't fit easily into some of the trends I'm identifying here.
4. See Beugnet (2004, 184).
5. After her death, Ozon adapted Bernheim's novel *Tout s'est bien passé* (2021), which tells the story of her father's assisted death in Switzerland.
6. 'Quand j'ai commencé à écrire, mon influence a été le cinéma. Les romans, c'est ma façon de faire des films.'
7. 'silences et aux non-dits' (Bernheim 2017).
8. 'L'absence de commentaires, de "psychologie" et de fioritures, le refus d'expliquer, de justifier ou de condamner.'
9. 'Elle rejeta la tête en arrière et respira l'air froid. Malgré les gaz d'échappement, il lui semblait encore percevoir l'odeur de cet homme.'

10. 'Il la rapporterait sûrement chez lui. It la donnerait a la femme avec laquelle il vivait at elle essaierait devant lui. Elle était sans doute très grande et très mince, la jupe serait trop large et trop courte. Il regarderait ses longues jambes et puis il s'approchait d'elle.'
11. As Devereux Herbeck identifies in '*The Smiling Madame Beudet* (1922) Gets a Facelift' (Devereux Herbeck 2011), Amy Taubin noted the many commonalities between these films in her 2003 *Film Comment* review of *Vendredi soir*.
12. See Devereux Herbeck (2011), for example.
13. See Edwards (2018).
14. 'Claire Denis on *Let the Sunshine In*' (2019). *Criterion Channel*. https://www.criterionchannel.com/videos/claire-denis-on-let-the-sunshine-in.
15. There is perhaps a second contender for a 'sex scene' in a sequence with Isabelle and her ex-husband in bed, but the physical intimacy is so short-lived, and the encounter focused on dialogue, that it reinforces my point here.
16. Incidentally, this also reminds one of Barthes's discussion of 'Rumours' in *The Lover's Discourse* (see discussion below).
17. For example, Brody (2018), Pinkerton (2018); Slaymaker (2018).
18. In one interview Denis refers to inquiries from Barthes's estate about the source material, which perhaps has encouraged her denial of any relationship between text and film. See Sophie Monks Kaufman, n.d.
19. 'Claire Denis on *Let the Sunshine In*' (2019).
20. At the outset of the novel, the author's daughter also lives with them.
21. This seems to be a pattern with Lindon's casting in Denis's films, he is a stable, grounded, often ethical presence in her work, whereas Colin has played fairly smarmy characters in his last couple of Denis films.

CITATIONS

Angot, Christine. 2018. *Un Tournant de la Vie*. Flammarion.
Archer, Neil. 2008. 'Sex, the City and the Cinematic: The Possibilities of Female Spectatorship in Claire Denis's *Vendredi soir*.' *French Forum* 33. 1/2: 245–60.
Assa, Sonia (2007) 'Et ce fut tout: *Vendredi soir* d'Emmanuèle Bernheim.' *Women in French Studies* 15: 53–66.
Barthes, Roland. 1977. *A Lover's Discourse*. Translated by Richard Howard. New York: Hill and Wang.
Bernheim, Emmanuèle. 1998. *Vendredi soir*. Paris: Gallimard.
Bernheim, Emmanuèle. 2017. 'Mort de la scénariste, passionnée de cinéma.' *Ouest-France* 5 November. https://www.ouest-france.fr/culture/livres/deces-de-la-romanciere-et-scenariste-emmanuele-bernheim-4983790, accessed 17 August 2022.
Beugnet. Martine. 2004. *Claire Denis*. Manchester: Manchester University Press.
Brody, Richard. 2018. 'The Exquisite Talk of Claire Denis's *Let the Sunshine In*.' *New Yorker*, 2 May. https://www.newyorker.com/culture/richard-brody/the-exquisite-talk-of-claire-deniss-let-the-sunshine-in, accessed 17 August 2022.
Ceuterick, Maud. 2020. *Affirmative Aesthetics and Wilful Women: Gender, Space, and Mobility in Contemporary Cinema*. New York: Palgrave Macmillan.
Devereux Herbeck, Mariah. 2011. '*The Smiling Madame Beudet* (1922) Gets a Facelift: Claire Denis's Modern Portrayal of Female Desire in *Friday Night* (2002).' *French Forum* 36, 2: 239–56. DOI: 10.1353/FRF.2011.0022.

Edwards, Natalie. 2018. 'Autofiction and the Law: Legal Scandals in Contemporary French Literature.' *Contemporary French and Francophone Studies* 22, 1: 6–15.

Hayward, Susan. 2002. 'Claire Denis's 'Post-colonial' Films and Desiring Bodies.' *L'Esprit Créatur*, 42, 3: 39–49.

Hole, Kristin Lené. 2016. *Towards a Feminist Cinematic Ethics: Claire Denis, Emmanuel Levinas, and Jean-Luc Nancy*. Edinburgh: Edinburgh University Press.

Kaufman, Sophie Monks. n.d., 'Claire Denis on how Etta James inspired *Let the Sunshine In*.' *Little White Lies*. https://lwlies.com/interviews/claire-denis-let-the-sunshine-in/, accessed 17 August 2022.

Mayne, Judith. 2005. *Claire Denis*. Urbana and Chicago: Illinois University Press.

Pinkerton, Nick. 2018. 'Let the Sunshine In.' *ReverseShot*, 24 April. http://reverseshot.org/archive/entry/2365/let_sunshine_in, accessed 17 August 2022.

Romney, Jonathan. 2005. 'Between Dream and Reality.' *Sight and Sound* 15, 9: 41–2.

Slaymaker, James. 2018. 'We Won't Grow Old Together: Claire Denis's *Let the Sunshine In*.' *Kinoscope*, 27 April. https://read.kinoscope.org/2018/04/27/wont-grow-old-together-claire-denis-let-sunshine/, accessed 17 August 2022.

Taubin, Amy. 2003. 'Some Enchanted Evening.' *Film Comment* 39, 3: 22–24. http://www.jstor.org/stable/43455956.

Willmore, Allison. 2022. 'Claire Denis's Brutal *Both Sides of the Blade* Cuts through Grown-up Delusions.' *Vulture*, 9 July. https://www.vulture.com/2022/07/movie-review-claire-denis-both-sides-of-the-blade.html, accessed 17 August 2022.

Yoonsoo Kim, Kristen. 2018. '"Let the Sunshine In": Director Claire Denis Doesn't Think Dating is Exhausting.' *GQ*, 27 April. https://www.gq.com/story/claire-denis-let-the-sunshine-interview, accessed 17 August 2022.

CHAPTER 9

In the Cracks: Claire Denis's Cinematic Choreographies

Danica van de Velde

A man in a nightclub leans casually against a mirrored wall as he takes a drag on a cigarette. Tracing the outline of the dance floor, he loops into a double pirouette before crouching on one bended knee. Dressed in a black shirt, black dress pants and black and white brogues, he is a lone figure reflected in the diamond cut mirrors of the club, with the darkness lit by miniature pink strobe lights. The film has taken the viewer to this place before, but not like this. Previously, the nightclub has been filled with the swaying of lustful bodies of men and women. Emptied of other patrons, the nightclub is now the man's stage. Gently grasping the beat with his fingers, he allows the music to move though his body in abrupt, disconnected gestures before he launches into an entropic dance frenzy. As he catapults his body in contorted shapes to the pulsing tempo of Corona's 1990s worldwide dance hit 'The Rhythm of the Night', the extreme release of the dance sequence mirrors the song's references to having 'nothing left . . . to yearn' and 'no reason to repent'. In a study of contrasts, the scene immediately preceding this moment is a quiet meditation on solitude. The very same man makes his single bed with exacting precision, stepping back to ensure that no creases remain in the covering blanket, and then lies down, holding a gun in his right hand. The slight hesitation at the beginning of his dance scene parallels this moment of pause as he lies nursing the gun, and the violent exaltation of his choreography is a symbolic visualisation of the pulling of the trigger: 'Goodbye and good riddance, Frenchie. Don't ever come back.'

This elegiac performance by Denis Lavant as Galoup in the denouement of French auteur Claire Denis's fifth feature film, *Beau travail* (1999), has rightfully reserved a place as one of the most striking endings in cinema. As a tormented and bodily confession of the action that has preceded it – specifically

Galoup's shameful discharge from the French Foreign Legion (FFL) after his jealous bullying of a young legionnaire, Gilles Sentain (Grégoire Colin), results in Sentain going missing in the Djiboutian desert – this scene, and *Beau travail* as a whole, has attracted substantial scholarly attention, particularly in reference to movement and corporeality (del Río 2003; Hayward 2001; Lippe 2000). Although these themes are important in a reading of *Beau travail* – as well as numerous works in Denis's eclectic oeuvre spanning feature films, short works, documentaries and music videos – it is Denis's cinematic construction of an oneiric psychological space in the dance sequence that warrants detailed critical analysis. Unlike the rest of *Beau travail*, which is structured through the voiceover recollections in Galoup's diary, his dance sequence is not a memory, but an imaginative projection that opens up a narrative interstice untethered from the film's mnemonic trajectory.

As a moment poised on the threshold of life and death, Galoup's dance scene exemplifies Denis's elliptical style of storytelling whereby her films eschew conventional approaches to narrative continuity and closure in favour of the construction of emotional landscapes. This interest in working to collapse the distinctions between interior and exterior space – as well as material reality, memory and dream – is captured in Martine Beugnet's characterisation of Denis's work as 'a cinema of the senses' (Beugnet 2004). Although the senses, particularly sight, sound and touch, are central to Denis's films, it is the manner in which she connects sensuality to spatiality that is peculiar to her filmic sensibility. Fashioning what contemporary artist Doug Aitkin enigmatically calls 'ambient landscapes that are a little disjointed' (Aitkin 2006, 96), Denis's cinema is not merely concerned with capitalising on the medium's capacity to visualise fantasy and recollection; it also uses film to navigate these emotive spaces.

Significantly, Denis's traversal of terrains of emotion is not confined to her fiction works; it is also present in her documentaries. For *Vers Mathilde* (2005) – her documentary on Mathilde Monnier, the choreographer and stage director at the Choreography Centre in Montpellier – Denis declined Monnier's offer to film one of her completed projects in favour of intimately charting Monnier's creative process (Walker Art Center 2006). Significantly, *Vers Mathilde* bears scant resemblance to traditional examples of the documentary genre. For example, there is little in the way of background information, subtitles are not employed to introduce speaking subjects or provide context to the on-screen action and, at first glance, there appears to be no clear narrative structuring the film beyond the presence of Monnier. Rather, Denis is concerned with what she describes as 'the movement of Mathilde's thoughts' (Denis n.d., 'vers mathilde'), and it is this interior journey that provides the thread of the documentary.

At times, the unfolding orientation of Mathilde's thought process intriguingly manifests as a strange echo of Galoup's dance in *Beau travail*, in which

Monnier's choreographic practice has a spatial dimension that she claims is concerned with 'resistance and abandon'. In one work-in-progress sequence, set to the P. J. Harvey song 'The Whores Hustle and the Hustlers Whore', Monnier, much like Galoup, starts slowly by feeling the music and testing the limits of her body to push up against invisible obstacles. Eventually launching into ferocious headbanging that then regresses into smaller controlled actions, the unpredictable motion of Monnier's body gestures less towards fluid dance steps and, instead, becomes a complex negotiation of space that emphasises physical intervention and, at its most extreme, invasion. Indeed, Monnier articulates her approach to dance through a metaphor of spatial conquest: 'Whenever you make an incursion into a space, that space is altered. I like this idea of leaving a scratch because that space is altered by that scratch after. It's like a piece of paper that has a mark on it and is no longer blank. There's something dirtying it.' As *Vers Mathilde* progresses, the film camera, wielded interchangeably by Hélène Louvart and long-time collaborator Agnès Godard, captures Monnier's muscular frame in varying rehearsal scenarios as she attempts to carve and pierce the space surrounding her body. Monnier is, by her own admission, searching for 'cracks' within which she can 'invent things'.

Although Denis does not explicitly align her filmic work with that of her subject in *Towards Mathilde*, there are clear parallels. Denis has referred to the 'expandable structure' of a film as one 'where space is invaded by the actors' (Ancian 2002). Moreover, she has often employed choreography as a framework for discussing the relationship between the filmmaker, the actors and the film camera: 'I see it more like choreography [. . .] Directing and acting exist in an organic relation similar to a dance between director and actors' (Mayne 2005, 59). As both the final scene in *Beau travail* and the entirety of *Vers Mathilde* indicate, the act of dancing is an important motif in Denis's cinema and one that is repeatedly revealed across her body of work – from the adolescent swagger of a boy dancing in his bedroom in her short film *US Go Home* (1994) to a slow dance of passage and separation of a father and daughter in *35 rhums* (*35 rhums*, 2008) and the romantic waltz of strangers set to Etta Jones's 'At Last' in *Let the Sunshine In* (*Un beau soleil intérieur*, 2017).

Even Juliette Binoche's masturbatory movements in the 'fuck box' on the spaceship that is the claustrophobic setting of *High Life* (2018) transpire as an erotic *pas de deux* between Binoche and the film camera. However, it is important to emphasise that Denis's reliance on choreography as a metaphor for her cinema not only testifies to an already well-documented interest in bodies (Maule 2008, 221–8), but also, more evocatively, links back to the relationship between space and emotion in her work. To this end, in her precis of *Vers Mathilde*, Denis emphasises the importance of the body and dance, but is ultimately concerned with the *mise en scene* (Denis n.d., 'vers mathilde'). In other words, it is the landscape or setting that she seeks to investigate and the body provides the means by which this exploration is mobilised. This line of thought is not intended to undermine or detract from extant readings of Denis's films that place the body at the forefront; rather it provides an alternative method of examining how the 'dance between director and actors' combined with the cinematography, works to choreograph landscapes of memory and trauma, as well as dreams and nightmares.

While I have emphasised a sustained interest in the creation of emotional topographies across Denis's oeuvre, this chapter will interrogate this idea with reference to three feature films: *Beau travail*, *L'intrus* (2004) and *Les salauds* (2013). Although the films are bound together by the reoccurring performances of Grégoire Colin and Michel Subor, as well as Denis's repeated collaboration with Jean-Pol Fargeau in the creation of their screenplays, the divergence of their narratives crucially allows for the uncovering of repeated thematic and visual patterns in Denis's cinema, particularly with Godard at the helm of the cinematography for all three films. Embedding exile and haunting into their cinematographic textures, this cinematic trio sheds light on the way Denis employs the representation of place to problematise notions of identity and belonging. With detours to consider aspects of Denis's work beyond the fictive silver screen, including her documentaries *Vers Mathilde* and *Man No Run* (1989), I will seek to uncover the dialogue between the different genres within which she works. By critically examining the relationship between cinematography and the creation of spatial intervals, this chapter will ultimately seek to examine Denis's unique visual language which, much like Monnier's 'cracks', inhabits transgressive interstices.

TOWARDS BELONGING: VISUALISING FOREIGNNESS

One of Monnier's performance rehearsals fleetingly featured in *Vers Mathilde* is for *Allitérations* (2002), a work inspired by a text written by contemporary theorist Jean-Luc Nancy, who also makes an appearance in the piece. Fluctuating, in Monnier's words, 'between conference and spectacle' (Monnier n.d., 'allitérations'), the rehearsals for *Allitérations* combine Nancy's philosophical narration with a jarring, alien soundscape created by composer erikm. These aural cues take place alongside the choreographed struggles of four dancers as they attempt to squeeze their bodies between the gaps in structures wrapped in perforated latex. Although the meaning and intent of *Allitérations* remain vague in *Towards Mathilde*, the statement on Monnier's website highlights how the piece continues her fascination with creating work within unexpected crevices, whereby Nancy, erikm and the dancers collectively attempt to 'work on the interstices and gaps that occur when one goes from listening to a text, a music, a sound to the perception of a movement' (ibid.).

For his part, Nancy recites a number of excerpts, one of which relates to the charged space that exists between a dancer and an observer through a lens of otherness:

> Another . . . if it's another, it's another body. I don't join it, it keeps its distance. I don't observe it, it's not an object. I don't imitate it, it's not an image. It passes through it, it mobilises it or shakes it. It gives it its pace. The observation of a male dancer or a female one has more than once illustrated what was once known as empathy or 'intropathy': the reproduction of the other within oneself, the sensation, the echo of the other person.

While Nancy's narration gestures towards a form of somatic identification between the observer and the dancer, Nancy's initially tentative regard of the dancer also resonates in Godard and Louvart's grainy 8 mm and 16 mm camerawork. Generating a sense of strangeness in the documentary's imagery, Godard and Louvart often film the performers' bodies in such tight close-ups that it is difficult to discern who or what is inhabiting the frame. Their camerawork traces the dancers' bodies, constructing ambiguous images that oscillate between gentle caresses and interrogative provocations that continually deny a cohesive view of the performance. During the rehearsals for *Allitérations*, the film camera captures the dancers' laborious engagement with the restrictive architecture of their props, but whether the dancers – and by extension the camera – wish to remain inside or outside these structures is unclear. This lack of visual assimilation not only parallels the remoteness and unfamiliarity in Nancy's observations of a dancer ('I don't join it, it keeps its distance') and Monnier's focus on 'interstices and gaps', but also reinforces a visual strategy in Denis's cinema that precariously teeters between intimacy and withdrawal. The viewer is thus held in a position in which they are both inside and outside the action.

In frustrating the viewer's desire for combined proximity and legibility in *Towards Mathilde*, Godard and Louvart's fragmented images link back to a broader concern in Denis's work that contemplates place and belonging. Reflecting on the significance of these themes in her cinema, Denis commented in a discussion with fellow filmmaker Atom Egoyan:

> I always want to be inside and often I feel outside. And I think it's something that cinema can convey better than literature. Cinema has its own power. And for me that power has to do with exile. I know exile is a very powerful word. It means something very strong and very dramatic. But exile is sometimes in very tiny details . . . Maybe it's because the audience is also in this position. Outside the world of the film and yet so close (Egoyan 2004, 76).

The desire to be 'inside' is also alluded to in Denis's short film *Towards Nancy* (*Vers Nancy*, 2002), which forms a part of the collaborative project *Ten Minutes Older: The Cello*. Philosopher Nancy makes yet another appearance in the constellation that makes up Denis's cinematic universe, with *Towards Nancy* enacting a conversation between him and a student (Ana Samardzija) during a train journey to an unknown destination. Nancy questions the student's preference to not be perceived as a foreigner in France, which leads to her response: 'Yes, I wanted to gain admittance, be here, not be seen as different and not disturb the established order.' Arguing that the acceptance of difference can paradoxically lead to its erasure and that the conception of foreignness is necessary for the formation of identity, Nancy claims that the arrival of a foreigner is made out to be an 'intrusion' and is therefore marked by 'disorder, . . . turmoil and . . . threat'. The presence of an unknown man (Alex Descas) who appears to be listening to the conversation from somewhere in the train manifests as the intrusion in *Towards Nancy*. However, any threat that his intrusion foreshadows is ultimately benign as he enters Nancy and the student's train compartment at the end of the film, simply asking, 'When do we get there?'

Towards Nancy draws on the theories espoused in Nancy's autobiographical account of the aftermath of his cardiac transplant, titled *The Intruder* (*L'intrus*, 2000), in which he imagines the transplantation of an alien heart into his body through a lens of 'nations and borders, of exiles and foreigners' (Morrey 2009, 127). However, Denis's eighth film, *L'intrus*, deals more explicitly with the encroachment of borders and acts of transgression at the literal and metaphorical heart of Nancy's text. Regarded by Nancy as an 'adoption' (Lampropoulos 2014, 167), as opposed to an adaptation, Denis's *L'intrus* shares with Monnier's choreography an attentiveness to spatial incursion and border crossing. As Denis discussed in her introduction to a screening of *L'intrus* at Metrograph in New York:

> He [Nancy] wrote something called *The Intruder*, about his heart transplant. He compared the intrusion in his body to the intrusion across a border. And he said, in a way, you cannot intrude without a certain violence. If it's soft, it's not an intrusion. Intrusion has to be brutal. Otherwise, it's not an intrusion anymore. And for the people who want to cross the border, it's also brutal. . . . It mixed this feeling of having in his chest the heart of someone he doesn't know, and the people trespassing the borders (Denis n.d., 'Claire Denis Introduces *L'intrus*').

However, in Denis's 'adoption', this allegory of intrusion is not confined to the crossing of bodily and geographical margins, but is woven into the structure and the textures of the film itself, with Denis claiming that 'each scene is an intrusion scene' (European Graduate School Video Lectures 2007).

She and Godard secure this pervasive feeling of invasion by rendering the central character, Louis Trebor (played by Subor), in Denis's own words, as 'the flesh and heart of the film . . . to convey a sense that [each image] was generated by his mind' (Smith 2005). In capturing this disorientating mobility between interior and exterior space, the act of viewing *L'intrus* is also prefigured as a form of intrusion whereby the viewer is privy to Trebor's internal thoughts, dreams and anxieties. The cinematic violation of Trebor's mindscape is foregrounded in the film's prologue in which a young Russian woman (Katia Golubeva) appears from the darkness, lights a cigarette and informs the viewer in voiceover, 'Your worst enemies are hiding inside, in the shadow, hiding in your heart'. Rather than securing Denis's wish to be inside, as discussed in her conversation with Egoyan, the intrusion into Trebor's mindscape comes at a cost that renders the distinction between reality and fantasy within the film's diegesis almost inscrutable.

Following a journey of self-determination that collapses into restless nomadism, *L'intrus* begins with Trebor's life of solitude in the Jura Mountains on the threshold of France and Switzerland where he lives in a wooden shack with his two dogs and maintains scant contact with his son, Sidney (Colin). Hit with the reality of a failing heart, he abandons his home, his dogs and his pharmacist girlfriend (Bambou) and crosses into Geneva, where he obtains the funds to pay for a black-market heart transplant. This 'emergency solution', which he orders via cryptic computer messaging in Russian text, is not depicted in the film; however, the scars of the surgical intervention are evident on Trebor's chest when he is filmed in a hotel room in South Korea being attended to by a blind healer. He subsequently makes a deal to purchase a large ship in the port city of Busan, which he claims to be a gift for his son. It is not until, yet again, the film shifts its geographical focus to Tahiti that it becomes clear that the ship is not intended to be for Sidney, but for a lost son located in French Polynesia. When his son refuses to meet with him, the Māori community, headed by his old friend Henri (Henri Tetainanuarii), attempt to enlist a replacement as Trebor's heart troubles continue and he is admitted to hospital. Rejecting his replacement son, Toni (Jean-Marc Teriipaia), the film ends with Trebor miraculously leaving hospital and setting sail on his boat.

This simplified rendering of the plot, while attentive to the linear chronology of Trebor's travels, does not do justice to the complexity of the film's intersection of irreconcilable timelines and visions. As *L'intrus* progresses, Trebor's journey is interspliced with violent, hallucinatory visions of him being dragged, with his feet bound, through the snow by the Russian woman on horseback, a discarded heart bleeding into the snow next to an unidentified corpse and Sidney's dead body, bearing scars identical to those inscribed in Trebor's chest following his heart surgery (Figure 9.1). In her analysis of *L'intrus*, Beugnet argues that Denis's 'filmmaking agenda' is one of 'cinema

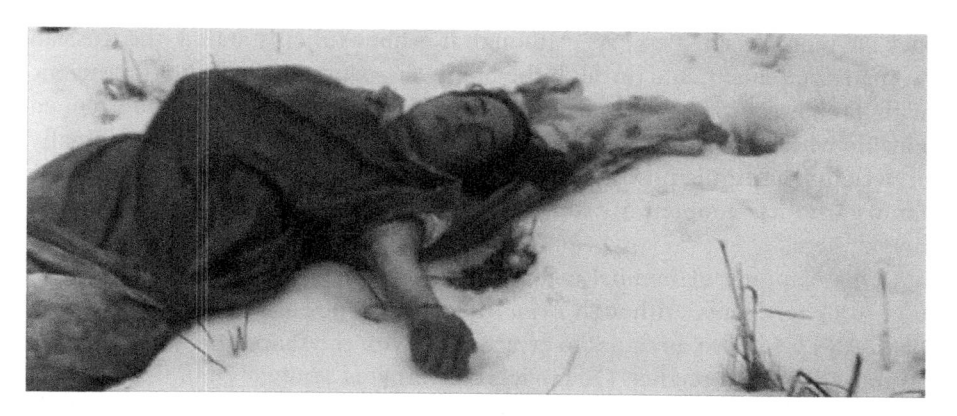

Figure 9.1 Trebor's horrific visions in *L'intrus* (2004).

envisaged as a practice of foreignness' (Beugnet 2008, 46) and that 'to try to elucidate the destiny of *L'intrus*'s main character is to ignore the impossibility of disentangling the real from the fantasized' (ibid., 40). Although foreignness is interwoven into the textures of the film's dream sequences, it is more clearly explicated in Trebor's interactions as he moves across the globe. The early scenes of him sunbathing naked and riding his bicycle through the Jura portray Trebor as an extension of the setting – what Laura McMahon describes as a 'textured symphony of skin, surfaces and landscapes' (McMahon 2008, 34). In this space, his belonging is not questioned, however, when he sits alone in an eatery in Busan, he is observed curiously by three Korean men:

Man 1: See that, a foreigner? He's all alone.
Man 2: Because he's far from home.

As two of the men depart, one remains, pours Trebor a glass of soju and joins him at his table. After using an empty soju bottle as a microphone to serenade Trebor with the lines from a Korean military song, the man moves on to his 'favourite song', a short, crooning rendition of 'Are You Lonesome Tonight', which Trebor instantly recognises as an Elvis Presley hit.

This scene crucially provides one of the few instances in which intrusion is met with a sense of reciprocation. When the Korean man directs the question in Presley's song to Trebor, he acknowledges the universality of foreignness and attempts to erase some of the difference between them. The double bind of this acceptance, which is emphasised in *Towards Nancy*, is made clear when the reciprocity of this moment is undercut as Trebor and the Korean man walk through the streets looking for a taxi and are trailed by the Russian woman. When Trebor turns around to confront her and says, 'Stop hounding me. I have a sick heart. Go away!', he is met with the reply, 'Your heart's not sick anymore. It's just empty.' Although it is not explicitly stated, the Russian woman's statement cuts through the family crisis upon which the film pivots, with Trebor refusing to love his real son, Sidney, in favour of an undeveloped kinship with a son in Tahiti he has never met. Indeed, when Trebor eventually arrives in Tahiti, his position is conveyed to him frankly by a man from the family who has adopted his son: 'I have nothing against you. But you don't belong here.'

This mapping of familial exile onto the settings of her films is a consistent trope for Denis. Although *Beau travail* developed as a result of a proposal from ARTE for five directors to create films with the shared theme of 'being a stranger, being a foreigner' (NanovicND 2012), it is, strangely, not the scenes of the FFL in Djibouti that are rendered foreign, but the scenes of Galoup's exile in Marseille. The presence of the Legion is occasionally met with the locals' somewhat bemused collective gaze, but the truly foreign act that remains irreconcilable and leads to Galoup's suicide is his ejection from what Julia Borossa refers to as the 'family romance' (Borossa 2004, 93) of the Legion. Similarly, in Paris-set *Les salauds*, Denis tasked long-term musical collaborator Stuart Staples of the Tindersticks with aurally tainting the film's vision of the French capital with a sense of the unknown.

Charting the return of a sailor named Marco Silvestri (Vincent Lindon), who arrives in Paris in the wake of his brother-in-law's suicide, the impending bankruptcy of his family's shoe business and the hospitalisation of his sexually abused niece, *Les salauds* removes Marco from the inviolability of his constructed family on the sea to the hostile terrain of the Paris inhabited by his biological family. As Staples commented in an interview,

> When they're at sea, their life is simple . . . As soon as they step on dry land, their life becomes complicated and anything can happen. As soon as [Marco] stepped on land, he was in an alien world, and I wanted to create an alien world around him. That became electronic music because that was alien to me (Rizov 2016, 44–5).

The resulting aural imagining of Paris in *Les salauds* is distinct from Denis's previous films set in the city, such as *Trouble Every Day* (2001), *Vendredi soir* (2002) and *35 rhums*, which also feature music composed by Staples. Inflected with foreign sounds from synthesisers and electronic drums, the sonic landscape of *Les salauds* parallels Marco's estrangement from his previous surroundings. When he departs his ship, with Egyptian singer Hani Shaker's 'Show Me the Reasons of Gladness' softly playing in the background, Shaker's song fades and is ominously replaced by Staples's instrumental piece 'Marco', which soundtracks Marco's arrival on dry land and inhospitable territory.

UNSETTLED GEOGRAPHIES

Les salauds opens with a shot of heavy nocturnal rain that renders everything within the frame indecipherable before cutting to a view inside an empty apartment where a man slowly puts on a tie and a suit jacket. The scene then transitions to a street view lit by the flashing lights of an ambulance, where paramedics place a cloth over a body. The camera then cuts to another dimly lit street where a disoriented girl is filmed from behind, clothed in nothing but a pair of stiletto sandals. Although these opening moments foreshadow the plot of the film, the sequencing is arguably less concerned with securely locating the viewer within the film's narrative than instilling a feeling of unease. Exemplifying Mia Carter's assertion that Denis's 'films have become increasingly silent; the viewer must learn to read the politics of space and place in order to understand fully what he or she is witnessing' (Carter 2006, 69), the opening moments offer very little in the way of clear exposition and, instead, rely on the viewer to acquire some sense of meaning from the developing atmosphere. However, a reading of 'the politics of space and place' clearly cannot be achieved in a concrete, architectural sense. Much like the memory structure of *Beau travail* and the dream sequences in *L'intrus*, the film carves out an internal space, with the fragmented opening sequence adopting the viewpoint of Marco, who is attempting to arrange isolated pieces of evidence to uncover his family's demise.

The viewer will deduce later in the film that the setting for *Les salauds* is Paris, based predominantly on the Haussmann architecture of the apartment that Marco rents. However, the framing of the city does not lend to the construction of an instantly recognisable cartography. Indeed, an accurate representation of the landscape and topographical markers is not important in Denis's films, with the films' settings functioning more as outward manifestations of the characters' interior states. This is also encapsulated in Denis's use of sound in *L'intrus* when she requested that the sound exist within the film not with the purpose of 'describing the landscape but describing a vision of place' (Smith 2005). Just as the Paris in *Les salauds* is filtered through the myopic and distressed vision of Marco, Denis's films, whether they are set in France, Djibouti, South Korea or French Polynesia, are seemingly unhinged from their locations. This is not to suggest that they are not sensuously and attentively filmed by Godard; rather, the lack of reliance on distinguishable iconography is key in emphasising the state of transitional crisis of Denis's characters, which Judith Mayne has evocatively defined as 'vagabondage' (Mayne 2005, 30).

Denis, as a self-confessed 'dreamy person' (G. Smith 2006, 29) whose identity has been shaped by her peripatetic upbringing between West Africa and France, is particularly attuned to the significance of place and geography and brings to her imagining of filmic space a feeling of restless movement and estrangement – as she stated in an interview with *Film Comment*, 'I have never been totally in real life, I think. I have never felt familiar anywhere' (ibid.). From Galoup's state of limbo on the cusp of death in *Beau travail* to Trebor's uncertain fate in *L'intrus*, her films' characters are continually confronted with the impossibility of settling or finding a home and are, instead, relegated to the margins of the films' narratives, suspended between reality and fantasy. Denis's placement of her subjects on symbolic thresholds is also poetically realised in her music video for the Sonic Youth track 'Jams Run Free' (2006), in which she assembles a jumbled series of images that oscillate between shots of Kim Gordon singing, dancing and running through the streets of Paris and shots that appropriate Gordon's point of view. As the music video progresses, the movements of the handheld camera quickly unravel the cohesive stability of the visuals, with light, colour and shape dissolving into abstraction. Damon Smith regards the visual effect as situating Gordon 'in a liminal state between titillation and anxiety' (Smith 2009).

Through the embedding of liminality into the visual textures of the music video, 'Jams Run Free' bears an auteurial lineage to Denis's feature films and evidences a consistent approach to effacing topographical actuality with an affective terrain. Gordon's Paris is not the same as the one captured by Godard in *Les salauds*; however, it is framed with an analogous rootlessness whereby the camera traces recognisable features of Paris's scenography of mansard roofs as well as a fleeting glimpse of the Eiffel Tower. However, Gordon is never fully integrated into the setting; she is desperately hunting for a place to be. Denis's first documentary feature, *Man No Run* (1989), in which she accompanies Cameroonian five-piece bikutsi band, Les Têtes Brulées, on the French leg of their world tour, is equally concerned with the emotional impact of place on her subjects. Significantly, *Man No Run* does not, as is often customary in a music documentary, focus on the band's origins and rise to fame; rather, much of the film is dedicated to understanding Les Têtes Brulées' experience of touring from a viewpoint of homesickness.

Throughout *Man No Run*, Denis captures the band's electrifying live performances and behind-the-scenes moments of sound checks, travelling between cities and the intricate preparation required for the band members to metamorphosise into their visual identity via costuming and body paint. These scenes are also complemented by moments of intense introspection. Indeed, one scene of the documentary follows the band members as they take a sightseeing tour of a mountainous region of France. Upon reaching the peak of the mountain, a band member comments off camera, 'You no longer see where you come from'. This feeling of being out of place later culminates in a moment of frustration and quiet despair when bassist Martin Maah confides to the camera that he wants to go home and that France tells him 'nothing worthwhile'.

The intimacy of Denis's engagement with the band is foregrounded in the opening moments of the documentary when the band members introduce themselves and their faces are framed in tight close-ups that focus only on their eyes and exclude their mouths. Each introduction appears more like an interior monologue than the usual talking-head style interviews appropriated to provide verisimilitude to the documentary genre. As with her feature films, Denis is not interested in ascribing authenticity to anything other than her subjects' interior states – a documentarian approach that is also employed in *Vers Mathilde* and runs counter to Bill Nichols's contention that 'Because documentaries address *the* world rather than *a* world imagined by the film-maker, they differ from the various genres of fiction' (Nichols 2017, xi). Although *Man No Run* is not a fictionalised account of Les Têtes Brulées' tour of France, it shares with Denis's feature films a reliance on complicating narrative cohesion through structural ellipses. Accordingly, the band's homesickness is replicated in the documentary's editing, which moves from city to city without ever making the band's location clear. Indeed, the final two-minute shot of *Man No Run* is framed through the window of a travelling tour bus as it takes in an endless horizon. Anticipating the landscape shots that Denis and Godard will later employ in *L'intrus*, it is uncertain whether the band is getting closer to or further away from home, and as the documentary fades to a quote by anthropologist Philippe Laburthe-Tolra, the band is suspended in perpetual motion.

In *L'intrus*, the viewer is absorbed by similar landscape shots that capture the imposing denseness of the forests in the Jura, the vastness of the Sea of Japan off the coast of Busan and the inexhaustible expanse of the South Pacific Ocean surrounding Tahiti; however, these shots neither locate the viewer nor foreground the film's various settings. Instead, they appear as pillow shots that underscore Denis's comment that *L'intrus* is 'like a boat drifting on the water' (Smith 2005). Although the pillow shot, as formalised by Noël Burch with reference to the cinema of Yasujirō Ozu, functions as a poetic intermediary to present a 'de-centering effect when the camera focuses for a moment, often a long one, on some inanimate aspect of Man's environment' (Burch 1979, 161), through Godard's lens the pillow shot is an image of haunting ambiguity that could be a memory, a dream or a 'real' fragment in the film's diegesis. Within the context of Ozu's films, Burch claims that:

> while these shots never contribute to the progress of the narrative proper, they often refer to a character or a set, presenting or re-presenting it out of narrative context. The *space* from which these references are made is invariably presented as outside the diegesis, as a pictorial space on another plane of 'reality' (ibid.).

Conversely, the pillow shots in *L'intrus*, although initially appearing ancillary to the main action, do not simply gesture towards another reality, but impinge on the film's diegesis. For example, Toni, Trebor's replacement son, is seen surfing in the ocean in a scene that occurs before he is properly introduced in the narrative when he approaches Henri to visit Trebor in hospital and take on the role of his son. As the scene of Toni surfing is not contextualised, its presence extends beyond the role of a pillow shot and becomes an uncanny fragment that is hauntingly stitched into the film.

UNCANNY OCCURRENCES

Vers Mathilde concludes with Monnier's solo performance of *8mn*, a piece in which she employs dance and movement to open up an interrogative space between the real and the unreal. This is achieved via a film projected onto the surface of the stage that features Monnier performing steps that vaguely resemble her movements in the live performance. Initially filmed in split screen, the documentary captures two Monniers dancing next to each another; however, they are disconnected and out of sync, following which the movements of one appear as a ghostly echo of the other (Figure 9.2). When the camera cuts back to a view of only one Monnier, a visual tension is underscored by the disjointed choreography of her body, her projection on the stage floor and her shadow, which is also performing its own dance on the periphery.

On a simplistic level, the performance further showcases Monnier's innovative approach to choreography, but from a more evocative angle, it also aligns with Denis's predilection to playing with almost imperceptible visual repetitions.

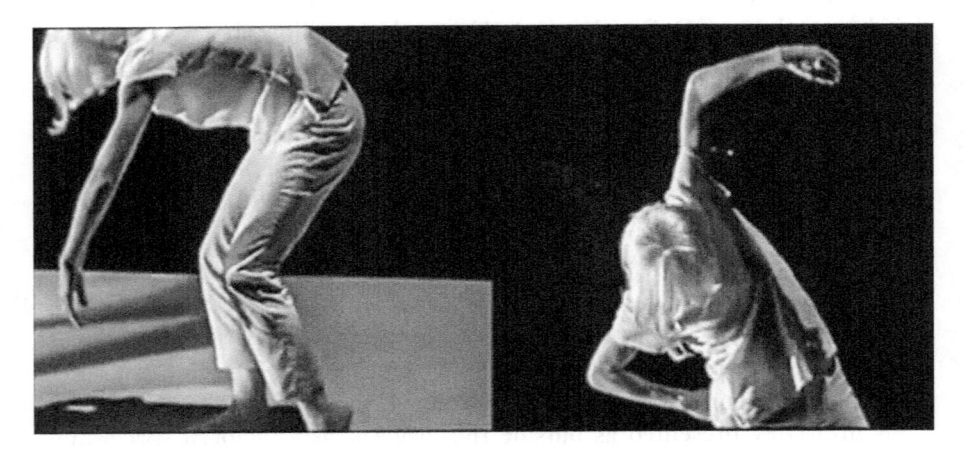

Figure 9.2   The ghostly echoing of Mathilde Monnier in *Vers Mathilde* (2005).

This chapter opened with Galoup's farewell dance in *Beau travail*, which, on a first viewing, appears to be the only time we see him out of uniform in Djibouti and dressed totally in black. However, this vision of Galoup has already graced the screen in a much earlier scene in which he watches the legionnaires taking turns to carry one another on their shoulders as they walk through Djibouti's deserted back streets. Dressed in the same outfit and smoking a cigarette, he watches his fellow legionnaires but, strikingly, he is not captured in the same frame. His voiceover states, 'In triumph, they carried one of their own', underscoring in the scene not only his isolation from the group, but also his impending suspension from the Legion. Only twenty-four minutes into the film, Galoup has already assumed the spectral presence that he will embody in the film's dying moments. *Beau travail* is not necessarily a ghost story, but it is haunted by Galoup's unassimilable memories.

Although each feature film I have discussed in this chapter contains its own locus of haunting – from Galoup's retrospective voiceover that overshadows the action in *Beau travail* to the Russian woman in *L'intrus* who stalks Trebor across the globe and to whom Denis refers as his 'Angel of Doom' (Smith 2005) – it is the image in *Les salauds* of the naked girl walking the streets of Paris that exemplifies the manner in which Denis employs uncanny repetitive images to destabilise her film narratives. Not content to leave the viewer with the initial image of the girl who is Marco's niece Justine (Lola Creton), the scene is played a second time in the first third of the film. This time the camera moves closer, with an extended close-up of Justine's dazed face, before cutting to her lying in a hospital bed. It is not until Justine later escapes from the hospital that the full extent of her injuries is revealed when the scene pierces the linear chronology of the film again. This third and final apparition revisits the same dark and empty street; however, the camera pans from Justine's face, past her bare breasts to her vagina, where the sticky flow of blood trails down her thighs.

By repeating the scene, Denis frames the image of Justine's trauma as a perverse establishing shot. Rather than employing an establishing shot as a means of 'securely mapping the viewer in space' (Bruno 2002, 271), Denis confounds expectations of linear narrative continuity with an image that is not merely a flashback, but a recurrent and inescapable vision of abuse. In refusing to structurally move past this scene, the repetition of Justine's nocturnal traipsing through Paris replicates the sensation of haunting that Avery F. Gordon describes as being 'when things are not in their assigned places . . . when disturbed feelings cannot be put away' (Gordon 2008, xvi). Gordon's definition of haunting is also an apt metaphor for the complex feelings elicited by viewing Denis's films. Indeed, the power of Denis's cinematic imagery stems from her intricate choreography of space and emotion, as well as her keen ability to align the viewer's affective responses to her characters' personal journeys. Irrespective of the genre or medium in which she works, Denis's films drift through emotional recesses and displaced voids, accumulating the residues of her characters' memories and dreams. Crucially, in charting this territory, Denis is not concerned with guiding the viewer to discern the difference between the exterior spaces and interior realms that unfold on the screen; rather, she invites the viewer to dwell within the cracks.

CITATIONS

Aitkin, Doug. 2006. *Broken Screen: 26 Conversations with Doug Aitkin – Expanding the Image, Breaking the Narrative*. New York: Distributed Art Publishers.

Ancian, Aimé. 2002. 'Claire Denis: An Interview.' *Senses of Cinema* 23, https://www.sensesofcinema.com/2002/spotlight-claire-denis/denis_interview/, accessed 12 December 2021.

Beugnet, Martine. 2004. *Claire Denis*. Manchester: Manchester University Press.

Beugnet, Martine. 2008. 'The Practice of Strangeness: *L'Intrus* – Claire Denis (2004) and Jean-Luc Nancy.' *Film-Philosophy* 12, 1: 31–48.

Borossa, Julia. 2004. 'Love of the Solider: Citizenship, Belonging and Exclusion in *Beau Travail*.' *Journal of European Studies* 35, 1/2: 92–105.

Bruno, Giuliana. 2002. *Atlas of Emotion: Journeys in Art, Architecture, and Film*. London and New York: Verso.

Burch, Noël. 1979. *To the Distant Observer: Form and Meaning in Japanese Cinema*. Berkley: University of California Press.

Carter, Mia. 2006. 'Acknowledged Absences: Claire Denis's Cinema of Longing.' *Studies in European Cinema* 3, 1: 67–81.

del Río, Elena. 2003. 'Body Transformations in the Films of Claire Denis: From Ritual to Play.' *Studies in French Cinema* 3, 3: 185–97.

Denis, Claire (n.d.), 'Claire Denis Introduces L'intrus.' *Metrograph*, https://metrograph.com/claire-denis-introduces-lintrus/, accessed 3 October 2021.

Denis, Claire (n.d.), 'vers mathilde.' Mathilde Monnier, http://mathildemonnier.com/en/creations//vers_mathilde, accessed 22 October 2021.

Egoyan, Atom. 2004. *Subtitles: On the Foreignness of Film*. Cambridge, MA: MIT Press.

European Graduate School Video Lectures. 2007. 'Claire Denis and Jean-Luc Nancy. L'Intrus. The Intruder 2007 1/3.' YouTube, https://www.youtube.com/watch?v=CoTGowlhABk, accessed 1 April 2022.

Gordon, Avery F. 2008. *Ghostly Matters: Haunting and the Sociological Imagination*. Minneapolis: University of Minnesota Press.

Hayward, Susan. 2001. 'Claire Denis's Films and the Post-colonial Body – with special reference to *Beau Travail* (1999).' *Studies in French Cinema* 1, 3: 159–65.

Lampropoulos, Apostolos. 2014. 'Between Two Transplants, An Adoption.' *Contemporary French and Francophone Studies* 18, 2: 167–74.

Lippe, Richard. 2000. 'Claire Denis and Masculinity: *Beau Travail*.' *Cineaction* 51: 63–5.

Maule, Rosanna. 2008. *Beyond Auteurism: New Directions in Authorial Film Practises in France, Italy and Spain Since the 1980s*. Bristol: Intellect.

Mayne, Judith. 2005. *Claire Denis*. Urbana: University of Illinois Press.

McMahon, Laura. 2008. 'The Withdrawal of Touch: Denis, Nancy and *L'Intrus*.' *Studies in French Cinema* 8, 1: 29–39.

Monnier, Mathilde (n.d.), 'allitérations.' Mathilde Monnier, http://mathildemonnier.com/en/creations//alliterations, accessed 22 October 2021.

Morrey, Douglas. 2009. 'Listening and Touching, Looking and Thinking: The Dialogue in Philosophy and Film Between Jean-Luc Nancy and Claire Denis.' in *European Film Theory*, ed. Temenuga Trifonova: 122–33. New York: Routledge.

NanovicND. 2012. 'BEAU TRAVAIL – Introduction by Director Claire Denis.' YouTube, https://www.youtube.com/watch?v=jc-eoMD8tkU, accessed 15 November 2021.

Nichols, Bill. 2017. *Introduction to Documentary*, 3rd edn, Bloomington: Indiana University Press.

Rizov, Vadim. 2016. 'More than Words: Music in the Films of Claire Denis.' *Fireflies* 3: 42–6.

Smith, Damon. 2005. 'L'Intrus: An Interview with Claire Denis.' *Senses of Cinema* 35, https://www.sensesofcinema.com/2005/conversations-with-filmmakers/claire_denis_interview/, accessed 18 December 2021.

Smith, Damon. 2009. 'The music videos of Claire Denis: "Incinerate" and "Jams Run Free".' *Reverse Shot*, http://www.reverseshot.org/archive/entry/111/music_videos_claire_denis_%E2%80%9Cincinerate%E2%80%9D_and_%E2%80%9Cjams_run_free%E2%80%9D, accessed 2 February 2022.

Smith, Gavin. 2006. 'Off the Map.' *Film Comment* 42, 1: 26–30.

Walker Art Center. 2006. 'Vers Mathilde (Vers Mathilde).' Walker, https://walkerart.org/calendar/2006/towards-mathilde-vers-mathilde, accessed 14 January 2022.

CHAPTER 10

Stars and Acting in Claire Denis's Films since 2010

Douglas Morrey

INTRODUCTION

Claire Denis has always adopted an elliptical or fragmentary approach to narrative filmmaking. In the words of Emma Wilson, 'her films have consistently retained ambiguities of narrative that transpire only on the margins of the viewer's consciousness' (Wilson 2019, 18). In her pioneering analysis of Denis's work, Martine Beugnet concluded that hers was 'a filmmaking that privileges the visual and the rhythmic . . . over scripted dialogue and plot' (Beugnet 2004, 14). As such, Ian Murphy contends that Denis's cinema is 'closer to music than the language of narrative cinema. This in turn facilitates a deeper engagement with the memories, perceptions and intuitions that make up the viewer's inner life' (Murphy 2012, p. 1 of 5). One way in which Denis's cinema operates through this process of suggestion or inference is by creating intertextual echoes between films. This is facilitated by the director's regular use of a troupe of actors – Grégoire Colin, Alex Descas, Nicolas Duvauchelle, Florence Loiret-Caille, Michel Subor, etc. – such that their roles in one film inevitably bleed disconcertingly into another. As Beugnet remarks, it is anyway the case that Denis's non-linear plots and fragmented sequences generate 'a "porous" kind of time, where the present is constantly inhabited by the past', 'the tales told in her feature films appear haunted by the ghost of another, buried story' (2004, 25). In Denis's later work, as her reputation on the global festival circuit has grown, she has increasingly worked with major stars enjoying an international profile. In this way, the spectral narratives or ghostly characters that haunt the director's recent films are drawn more from the well-known filmographies of her stars and indeed Denis often deliberately exploits star personas as a kind of shorthand enabling the creation of a tone in her work. This article examines four recent films by Denis and her deployment of the star image of four high-profile performers – Isabelle Huppert, Vincent Lindon, Robert Pattinson and Juliette Binoche – in order to determine how her access to celebrity actors has enabled the director to maintain and develop her distinctive, enigmatic style.

WHITE MATERIAL

White Material (premiered at film festivals in autumn 2009; on general release in spring 2010) is in many ways a representative movie of Denis's mature career: an unsympathetic gaze trained upon European (neo-)colonialists in Africa (as in *Chocolat*, 1988 or *Beau travail*, 2000), the elliptical, chronologically looped narrative takes in war, murder and madness without ever adopting an unequivocal ethical stance with regard to the events depicted. The film's star, Isabelle Huppert, was at the origin of the project, having approached Denis with the suggestion of adapting Doris Lessing's novel *The Grass Is Singing* (1950) (Hayon 2020, 166). While Denis decided against this specific project, *White Material* clearly bears the authorial stamp of Huppert's established star persona. Huppert's Maria Vial directs operations on her ex-husband's coffee plantation and insists on continuing production even as a civil war breaks out in the unnamed African country. Her inexplicable stubbornness comes to define her character as her manic devotion to the coffee crop causes Maria to lose everything: her family, her home and her humanity. This single-mindedness to the point of autism recalls other Huppert roles from the same period, notably Ann Hidden from *Villa Amalia* (Benoît Jacquot, 2009) who, upon discovering her husband's infidelity, abandons every single aspect of her former life and career with 'a momentum that comes from the depths of her being, that nothing can explain, and nothing can stop' (Joudet 2018, 173).[1]

In particular, Maria Vial appears to care little about her grown son, Manuel (Nicolas Duvauchelle). When he is confronted, humiliated – and possibly sexually assaulted – by child soldiers, Maria seems more concerned about the plantation, inspecting the holes in her fence in preference to the wounds on her child. More precisely, her attitude might be described as one of impotent regret, appalled by what her son has become. Criticising his lazy habits, she says, 'Listlessness is the most repugnant quality in a man. It's abject.'[2] Maria Vial recalls countless other unfit or unhappy mothers in Huppert's filmography: the murderous stepmother of *Merci pour le chocolat* (Claude Chabrol, 2000), the incestuous mother of *Ma mère* (Christophe Honoré, 2004), the abandoning mother of *Nue propriétée* (Joachim Lafosse, 2007). Above all, Maria forms a diptych of roles with Huppert's colonial mother in Rithy Panh's Duras adaptation *The Sea Wall* (*Un barrage contre le Pacifique*, 2008). There, the mother laments her children's ingratitude even as she encourages her daughter to prostitute herself with a wealthy local businessman in order to save her own plantation. For Kaya Davies Hayon, *The Sea Wall* is a problematic postcolonial text because it centres its narrative so determinedly around the plight of the white woman that the exploitation of local workers is largely overlooked (Hayon 2020, 160). *White Material*, on the other hand, deploys Huppert's unsettling persona precisely in order to imply all that is most corrupt and morally bankrupt about the colonial project.

For all the ambivalence that Maria Vial shows toward her son, for instance, there are intriguing parallels between them, beyond the obvious physical resemblance of their extreme blondness. At one stage, Manuel, having apparently lost all sense of proportion or personal safety following his assault, rides recklessly up to the child soldiers on a motorcycle, hailing them with a broad grin. It is the same motorbike – and perhaps something of the same delirious abandon – with which we saw Maria cavorting at the beginning of the film. She is the mother and on the plantation, as she herself tells her workers, 'I'm the one in charge'. Yet there is something oddly childlike about Maria in her wilfulness and her apparent inability to measure the gravity of her situation. The figure of the child-woman is familiar from Huppert's filmography ever since her earliest roles such as *Les Valseuses* (Bertrand Blier 1974) or *Violette Nozière* (Claude Chabrol 1978) where, despite her evident youthfulness, she appeared sophisticated beyond her years. Her characters' seeming open-mindedness in matters of sexuality often conceals a degree of psychological damage that implies a fixation in childhood and renders problematic their supposed erotic agency: they are, as Murielle Joudet puts it, 'now the initiator, now the initiated' (Joudet 2018, 191).[3] This is the case in some of Huppert's most famous mature roles, such as *The Piano Teacher* (Michael Haneke 2001) or *Elle* (Paul Verhoeven 2016), but more discreetly, too, in *White Material*: a tiny (five foot two) pale woman in pretty girlish dresses, overwhelmed by an oppressive landscape[4] and yet it is suggested via a scene that may be flashback or dream sequence, seemingly enjoying a sensuous, drug-enhanced relationship with the local mayor. A display of complete and permanent control despite somehow appearing utterly helpless, this 'programmed awkwardness', as Pedro Guimarães calls it, has come 'to contaminate all of Huppert's characters in regard to the actor's dual performance style' (2020, 41). By portraying women whose behaviour typically occurs in response to some deeply entrenched trauma, even though those women as a rule have little to no conscious access to the nature or extent of that underlying impetus, Huppert can give the impression, as Guimarães puts it, of being 'both inside and outside her characters at all times' (2020, 42).

Huppert's costumes in *White Material* add to this sense of her as an ambiguous child-woman. She is, as Marzia Caporale notes, 'the one who literally and figuratively wears the pants in the house', dressing in practical brown trousers and shirts for her work on the plantation (2013, 250). Yet Maria always puts on very feminine dresses in order to go and present the public face of the plantation to the local community. In pale pinks and pale yellows, these dresses are, as Caporale puts it, 'symbol[s] of femininity and purity par excellence' (2013, 253). Somehow, however, in keeping with the duality of Huppert's persona, these costumes succeed in being at once sexual and demurely frumpy. It is evidently so hot in the region that she wears nothing beneath these dresses to allow the air to circulate around her limbs; but their modest, classical cut, with high necklines and hems below the knee, rather evoke the colonial mistress who is wary of exciting the locals. The spectator's eye is particularly drawn to these costumes since they provide one of the keys to ordering the disjointed narrative, the yellow dress belonging to a relatively harmonious time before the outbreak of war while the pink marks the time of trauma and tragedy. The dresses then become freighted with additional symbolic weight when the Vial property is ransacked in the chaotic fighting such that Maria comes face to face with a barely adult woman who threatens her with a gun while sporting her own forcibly reappropriated yellow frock.

As Darren Waldron has argued, in Huppert's iconic mature roles, 'hers is a facial display that, while allowing proximity, imposes separation' (Waldron 2020, 35). The camera frequently lingers on the actor's face in close-up, but she typically withholds easily legible markers of emotion. How, for instance, should we interpret Maria's murder of her father-in-law at the end of the film? Is it, as Kaya Davies Hayon proposes, 'an unanticipated expression of anger against the colonial system he represents' (Hayon 2020, 166), this 'embodiment of an imperialistic order' receiving summary justice for the exploitative regime he had installed? (Caporale 2013, 261). Or is she simply a mother driven insane upon apprehending the violent death of her son? Was her sanity perilously balanced all along, as the proximity between her and her erratic son might suggest? The film will not answer these questions, instead doubling down on Huppert's famously inscrutable face by repeatedly filming her from behind with a regularity that becomes a veritable visual motif.[5] The stubbornness with which the camera often avoids Maria's face underlines her solitude and her awkwardness with communication. At times, the camera feels almost anthropomorphised, as though – in common with everyone else, workers and family alike – it were reluctant to follow Maria in her blatantly self-destructive enterprise.

At the same time, however, the dorsal filming serves to emphasise Huppert's hair and thereby to stress her distinctive strawberry blonde colouring and its incongruity under the blazing central African sun. Hair, and particularly blond

Figure 10.1 Maria (Isabelle Huppert) from behind. *White Material* (2009).

hair, becomes an important symbol in the film of the inappropriateness of the colonial family in this landscape, and of the vulnerability that underlies their economic power. As a prelude to his assault, Manuel has a lock of his blond hair unceremoniously cut from his head and it is curiously sniffed by his child assailant. In the aftermath of the attack, he angrily shaves his head before stuffing a handful of his own hair into the protesting mouth of his father's African concubine. In the oneiric, intoxicated scene that Maria shares with the mayor, he tells her that 'extreme blondness attracts misfortune – it is something to be vandalised. Blue eyes are disturbing.'[6] The line reads almost like an unveiling of the hidden logic – the magical thinking – that underlies Isabelle Huppert's entire career in film, a logic given terrifying reality by Claire Denis's implacable narrative detachment and by screenwriter Marie Ndiaye's persistent recourse to uncanny heuristics.

LES SALAUDS

Les salauds (2013) reunites Denis with Vincent Lindon, who had previously appeared in *Vendredi soir* (2002). As in the earlier film, where he plays a mysterious stranger with whom the protagonist enjoys a one-night stand after giving him a ride during a transport strike, in *Les salauds*, on which he had an associate producer credit, Lindon plays an inscrutable but magnetically attractive man in middle age. Much of Lindon's enigma stems from his tight-lipped performances: taciturn and enunciating poorly, he mumbles most of his dialogue from the gravelly throat of a long-term smoker. In interview, he has admitted that he speaks less and less in his film roles, relying on gesture to convey character (Rouyer and Tobin 2009, 25). As in other roles such as the ex-convicts of *Quelques heures de printemps* (Stéphane Brizé 2012) or *Mea Culpa* (Fred Cavayé 2014), Lindon's Marco in *Les salauds* has deliberately cut himself off from others, including his family; a ship's captain, he notes bluntly, 'That's what sailing is for' ('Ça sert à ça, la marine'). Like the ex-cop of *Mea Culpa*, convicted of a causing fatal drink-driving incident, Marco has chosen to leave his family rather than confront the painful emotional terrain of guilt and shame associated, in *Les salauds*, with his relatives' rampant capitalism and their links to the dubious super-rich figure of Edouard Laporte (Michel Subor). He returns, reluctantly, only after his old friend and brother-in-law, Jacques (Laurent Grévill), takes his own life. As Joan Dupont has commented, Lindon's 'finest moments come when playing men who seem to be tied in invisible knots' (2016, 34). Even more than in other roles, however, Lindon's Marco combines mystery and menace with sexual magnetism since his character mixes austerity with glamour. Raphaëlle (Chiara Mastroianni), the woman drawn to him, observes that he lives in an empty apartment and pawns his wristwatch, even as he drives a vintage Alfa Romeo sportscar and wears €400 shirts. The shirts will become important currency in the developing attraction between the two: Marco drops one from his balcony to deliver cigarettes to Raphaëlle and she spreads it languorously on her bed and lies down beside it. The return of the laundered shirt provides a pretext to renew contact and subsequently allows Marco to impose himself upon his neighbour with a performance of macho dominance – 'You didn't even iron it!' – that initiates their first sexual encounter.

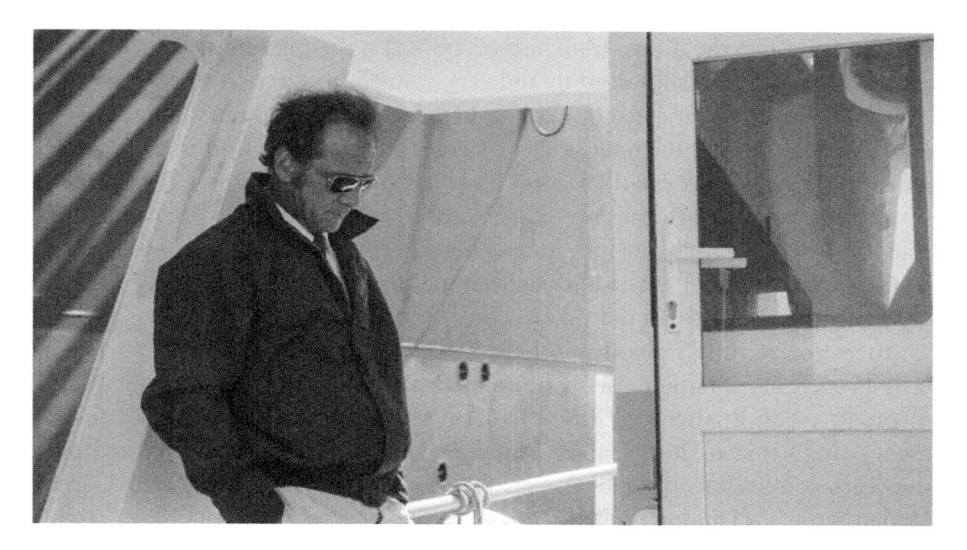

Figure 10.2 Marco, sailor (Vincent Lindon). *Les Salauds* (2013).

The ambiguity of this encounter – their first sex scene is rough and wordless – is significant since *Les salauds* revolves around a revenge plot: not only has Marco's brother-in-law killed himself, but his niece is hospitalised following a sexual trauma; Raphaëlle is the young wife of Laporte, whom Marco suspects of playing a role in these tragedies. It is thus initially unclear whether Marco's approaches to Raphaëlle stem from real attraction or from a Machiavellian plot (a fantasy insert, juxtaposed between shots of Marco smoking alone in bed, implies that he would consider targeting Raphaëlle's own child as a form of primitive justice). Lindon, in other words, plays a vigilante in *Les salauds*, as he does in other films of the period. The ex-cop of *Mea Culpa* takes matters into his own hands in order to protect his ex-wife and child after the latter witnesses a crime. In *Pour elle* (*Anything for Her*, Fred Cavayé, 2008), Lindon's character single-handedly plans and executes a jailbreak for his wife, who has been wrongfully convicted of murder. Lindon's solid but unshowy persona suggests that he is on the side of right even if he must break the law in order to achieve his ultimately laudable ends. In *Les salauds*, the sympathetic-if-flawed Marco is counterposed to the presumed villain Laporte, played by Denis regular Michel Subor. Laporte's menace derives from intertexts – as Rosalind Galt notes, his character eerily evokes the shadowy figure played by Subor in Denis's *L'intrus* (2004); from the dark pigmentation around the actor's eyes, emphasised by the moody lighting in the apartment where he stares meaningfully at Marco; and from his implied sexual threat, underlined when his first on-screen interaction with Raphaëlle is an injunction to 'jerk me off' (2015, 277–8). But, as Galt astutely notes, Laporte is only 'a congealed form of the film's distributed hostile visuality' and a Manichean division of the dramatis personae into good and evil is quite untenable here (2015, 282). Unlike in Lindon's other revenge plots – or in comparable action narratives of the period like the *Taken* franchise (2008–14) – the pursuit of justice fails in *Les salauds*: Marco is shot dead by the very woman he is trying to rescue, while his niece returns to her abusers and kills herself along with them (deliberately or not, we can't be sure: the oneiric scene suggests that all involved in the fatal car crash are heavily intoxicated). Denis's film self-consciously adopts the tropes of film noir – numerous scenes are set at night, the first sequence opens in heavy rain, the Silvestri family business makes high-heeled women's shoes, in a gesture to the iconography of the traditional femme fatale – but it takes the narrative pessimism of the genre to radical extremes.

In its unremittingly gloomy outlook, *Les salauds* at times resembles a particularly French instantiation of noir filmmaking: the so-called 'poetic-realist' cycle of the 1930s. In this sense, Vincent Lindon can be seen as embodying a similar archetype to that of Jean Gabin. Many French actors have been posited over the years as inheritors of Gabin's signature style – Jean-Paul Belmondo, Gérard Depardieu – but Lindon perhaps comes closest, even without matching Gabin's near-universal popularity. With its narrative role for boats, its murky incest plot and its tragic denouement, *Les salauds* particularly evokes Marcel Carné's diptych of Gabin vehicles *Le quai des brumes* (*Port of Shadows*, 1938) and *Le jour se lève* (*Daybreak*, 1939). Lindon resembles the poetic-realist Gabin in his strategic use of props and costume: the actor admits that characterisation in cinema is largely a matter of 'the right clothes, the right car and the right haircut' (Rouyer and Tobin 2009, 26). Where Gabin's cloth cap and bicycle emphasised his humble origins, Marco's apartment with a mattress on the floor, a packet of new shirts, a carton of cigarettes and a laptop suggests the character's lack of attachments and his single-mindedness of purpose. Ginette Vincendeau, following Richard Dyer's classic assessment of the ideological function of film stars, saw Gabin as reconciling, through his body and his naturalistic performance, tensions within the competing demands placed on masculinity (2000, 69). We could see Lindon's character as achieving a similar feat: as a tanker captain, he is a worker yet has a natural authority (see the deference with which a subordinate sailor interrupts his breakfast of coffee and cigarettes); he is capable but kind (see how, with minimal fuss or comment, he repairs the bicycle of Raphaëlle's son); he is restrained to the point of aloofness yet has violent outbursts of anger, particularly against his sister. Lindon, who admits to being a voracious consumer of classic films, acknowledges that he has seen 'all of Gabin's black and white movies' and that he loves the French cinema of 'Duvivier, Renoir, Becker, Grangier' (Dupont 2016, 38–9). Dupont, while noting the undeniable class difference (Lindon comes from a family of wealthy Parisian intellectuals), sees something of Gabin's career trajectory in the ageing Lindon: 'too haunted to be the suave lady-killer and too classy to be the loser' (2016, 34). Needless to say, despite all the facile parallels drawn following the rise of populist movements during the last decade, the 2010s were not the 1930s and any comparison between two bodies of work from these eras can ultimately only be superficial, taking little real account of the considerable economic and aesthetic differences between the film industries of their times. For Galt, the contemporary moment, and by extension Denis's cinema, is marked by an economic regime 'that forecloses completely on the possibility of working-class belonging or revolutionary subjectivity', which remain horizons of possibility in Gabin's classic roles (2015, 281). But, as Vincendeau (1985) famously demonstrated, the sense of working-class community in these films was typically enacted in a nostalgic mode, as (always?) already belonging to the past. To dismiss these interwar films as betraying a romanticism unknown to the cynically disabused Denis would be to do a disservice to Carné, Prévert, Gabin et al. Gabin's characters may indeed believe in a romantic ideal, but the women he covets are far from the ingenues he imagines, while the incest plot in *Le jour se lève* is finally just as sordid and unresolved as in *Les salauds* (was Valentin [Jules Berry] the lover or the father of Françoise [Jacqueline Laurent], or neither or both? Neither we nor François [Gabin] will ever know for certain). It is instructive, then, to note the influence of a canonical, mainstream French cinema over a filmmaker more typically arranged in the lineage of lone mavericks like Robert Bresson or her international mentors Wim Wenders and Jim Jarmusch.

HIGH LIFE

Robert Pattinson arrives in the universe of Claire Denis necessarily unable to escape his indelible association with the *Twilight* franchise (2008–12). Even though he has carefully curated, like his co-star Kristen Stewart, a selection of edgy roles with auteur directors, Pattinson will doubtless for many years be indissociable from the teen heartthrob of the high-school vampire movies. As Edward Cullen, the 'vegetarian' vampire, Pattinson was typecast as the basically good or honourable young man who endeavours to do the right thing even as he is tormented by violent instincts and rendered darkly fascinating to his peers by his mysterious and presumably traumatic past. As though in an effort to erase the clean-cut image (however partially ironic it may be) associated with *Twilight*, Pattinson has embraced a series of roles that allow him, literally and metaphorically, to get his hands dirty. Where *Good Time* (Safdie and Safdie 2017), for instance, saw him sport dirty hoodies, a stubbly beard and inexpertly dyed blond hair, in *High Life* (2018), the thick, dark hair that was part of Edward Cullen's visual appeal is mostly shaved off and the actor is dressed in unflattering dungarees and baggy T-shirts that grow more faded and tattered as the film advances, implying their incessant use over several years.

Figure 10.3   Monte (Robert Pattinson). *High Life* (2018).

The early scenes of *High Life* show Pattinson's character Monte caring, alone on a spaceship, for a child – Willow – who is almost toddling. In keeping with the actor's persona, he is tender and patient – teaching the child to walk or sewing an arm back on to her doll – yet there are also hints of darker elements to his personality. We learn through flashbacks that he is a convicted murderer, and it is intimated that his relationship with his own father was hardly affectionate: 'If my old man could see me now', Monte muses aloud, before parroting him: '"You break the laws of nature, you'll pay for it. You little son of a bitch!"' There is a garden on the spaceship to grow food for the passengers, and the scenes of Monte and Willow picking vegetables, filmed with Denis's typically sensuous attention to detail (extreme close-ups of artificially generated moisture on ripening pumpkins and peppers), creates a properly Edenic image. But, as Nick Pinkerton observes, the garden of Eden evokes not just freedom (here, limited to the space of the ship) and abundance (necessarily precarious in deep space), but also the spectre of incest, 'the necessarily inbred origins of a human race that starts from a single couple' (Pinkerton 2019, 26). *High Life* thus forms an intriguing pair with *The Lighthouse* (Eggers, 2019): two films in which Pattinson's character is effectively stranded alone with one other person, tormented by memories of his violent past and managing a mostly unspoken sexual tension.

Prior to Monte and Willow's isolation, we learn, sexual tension and sexual abuse had been the constant background to life on their spaceship. Dr Dibs (Juliette Binoche), a seemingly deranged scientist (she claims to be 'totally devoted to reproduction', despite having killed her own children back on Earth), pursues mostly ill-fated experiments in artificial insemination on her fellow inmates in what is effectively a prison ship. Dibs's expertise, her age (most of the other passengers are barely out of their twenties) and her control of behaviour-defining medications give her a natural authority on the ship, one bolstered by a perverse hierarchy of evil: 'You're a bunch of common criminals, petty thugs', Dibs tells her fellows as she strides around the corridors. 'My crime was the only one worthy of the name.' Monte is the only male crew member who refuses to provide sperm samples having, as he puts it, 'chosen abstinence over indulgence'. The fatal attraction of the unavailable develops between them until Dibs helps herself to Monte's semen by mounting him after drugging the whole crew into a deep sleep before inseminating Boyse (Mia Goth). This surreptitious and technologically assisted rape is pointed up in the film by the extreme violence of the sequence in which another young man (Ewan Mitchell) attempts to rape the restrained Boyse, in the process punching both her and a female witness in the face, before being beaten to a pulp by Monte and stabbed through the eye with a glass shard by one of the women.

The violence, both primal and technological, of sexuality is figured in the film's 'fuck box', a dark room furnished with a prosthesis-equipped chair to facilitate enhanced masturbation. Although all the crew except Monte are said to use the fuck box, only Dibs is shown inside, in a performance of extraordinary courage and abandon for an actress of Binoche's age (fifty-four upon the film's release) and prominence. The camera sways and twirls as Dibs gyrates on the machine, a shot of her long black hair tumbling down her back recalling variously Goya's *Witches' Sabbath* (for Wilson 2019, 22) or the 'tenebrous darkness' of Caravaggio (for Pinkerton 2019, 28). Dibs's combing, stroking and playing with this thigh-length hair becomes a veritable motif in the film. There is, as Wilson suggests, something animal-like about it, yet at the same time, the sheer improbability of maintaining such a lustrous mane after years in deep space further confirms the unequal distribution of the spoils of science on board the ship (2019, 22).

The awkward cohabitation of nature and technology is a deep structuring principle of the science fiction genre, just as it is of the Western, two American genres par excellence. No doubt Claire Denis's outsider eye, together with her exposure to the structuralist film theory that has had a lasting influence over French film criticism, made her the more acutely aware of this central dichotomy. As mentioned, *High Life* opens with misleadingly lush shots of the ship's garden, a commonplace in films depicting long-haul space travel, from classics like *Silent Running* (Trumbull 1972) to more recent examples such as *Passengers* (Tyldum 2016). The accompanying sound of a baby's cries reinforces this natural imagery only to be undercut by the subsequent slow pans around sterile, empty corridors. The tense relationship between nature and technology is further highlighted by the necessity for the crew to log a mission report every twenty-four hours in order to ensure the continued operation of the ship's life-support systems, even though it is repeatedly suggested that no one on Earth will ever receive these transmissions. As members of the party die or are killed, their comrades remove identifying chips from beneath the skin of their fingers in order to falsify these reports. The whole process bespeaks humanity's perverse hijacking of nature and its resources, equally evident in the suicide mission that underlies the entire enterprise: an almost certainly futile attempt to 'capture a black hole's rotating energy' in order to provide humans with unlimited resources.

Denis has described *High Life* as more of a prison movie than science fiction, the production design deliberately eschewing NASA white in favour of dull beige (Pinkerton 2019, 28). As such, the film's palette and tone are curiously reminiscent of *Alien³* (Fincher, 1992), set on a prison planet – the mining colony Fiorina 161 – rather than a spaceship, yet designed in the same mixture of dirty beige, grey and brown. In Fincher's film, the arrival of a woman (Sigourney Weaver) and, with her, an alien, figures the return of the repressed, the disruptive appearance of sexuality into this monkish community of repentant convicts who have found religion. Sexuality never disappeared from the universe of *High Life*, but it is awkwardly contained within the fuck box and

Dibs's test tubes; what returns, rather, in this airless environment is the unexpected promise of life itself, of hope and of tenderness. Images of Earth, when they appear as flashbacks in the early part of the film, are not much more colourful than the prison ship, yet their focus on rain and mud appears impossibly exotic in the context of the sterilised spacecraft. The images from Earth have a different grain to the rest of the cinematography and underline the film's distance from Denis's work heretofore: as Pinkerton points out, *High Life* is 'unique among Denis's films in taking place almost entirely in a constructed environment', whereas all the others are shot on location (2019, 28). The grain of the earth(l)y images generates a nostalgia for the sense of place that has been so central to Denis's filmography and yet the film implies beyond doubt that no return home is possible. Wilson reports that British novelist Zadie Smith was originally intended as co-screenwriter on *High Life* until she and Denis clashed over a mooted return to Earth: '"What the fuck do you mean, going home?" Denis said she asked Smith. "There's no one alive there anymore"' (Wilson 2019, 18).

UN BEAU SOLEIL INTÉRIEUR

If we have chosen to take the last two films out of chronological sequence, it is because *Un beau soleil intérieur* (*Let the Sunshine In*, 2017) is exceptional in the director's oeuvre in being a comedy albeit, as Wilson suggests, a comedy marked by 'existential darkness' (2019, 23). As the analysis of the preceding three films has demonstrated, Denis's filmography is singularly sombre in its outlook, regularly returning to themes of exploitation, incest and murder without ever offering the spectator the comfort of a self-righteous moralising point of view. Likewise, *Sunshine* avoids openly judging its protagonist Isabelle (Binoche) or her partners on their search for romantic and sexual fulfilment in middle age, but its more frivolous plot (for once no truly criminal activity is depicted) facilitates the development of a wryly humorous, at times even gently farcical tone. As such, the film marked an important milestone in the career of Juliette Binoche who, after a career almost exclusively devoted to auteur cinema and worthy international co-productions, had begun to demonstrate the ability to laugh at her somewhat solemn persona in the romantic comedy *Telle mère, telle fille* (*Baby Bump(s)*, 2017) or her 2017 guest appearance on the Netflix hit series *Dix pour cent* (*Call My Agent!*).

Analysing Binoche's persona after the first two decades of her career, Vincendeau noted that she appeared 'altogether more cerebral, more anguished and more fragile' than other French women who have achieved international recognition on screen, typically for their powerful sex appeal (2000, 242). Vincendeau notes, for instance, that Binoche is often cast as a visual artist (most famously, perhaps, in *Les amants du Pont-Neuf* [1991], but more recently, for instance, in *Camille Claudel 1915* [2013]), a move that draws on the performer's extratextual interest in painting and 'connotes sensitivity and reinforces her identification as an art cinema actress by stressing her empathy with the world of the films and their directors' (2000, 249). In *Sunshine*, too, Binoche plays a painter, and one brief shot shows her beginning a large canvas on the floor of the studio space that occupies the ground floor of her Parisian house, a spatial luxury that implies her considerable wealth. Indeed, most of Isabelle's interlocuters and suitors in the film are drawn from this affluent cultural milieu – gallery owners, actors, etc., plus one international banker – and one episode turns around her friends' dismay when she goes out with a working-class provincial ('What do you talk about?', they wonder incredulously).

Given Vincendeau's stress on Binoche's unattainable cerebral quality, her contrast to the earthy sexuality of French actresses like Bardot, Bonnaire or Dalle, it is striking that *Sunshine* opens with Isabelle naked and in mid-coitus. This is in keeping, however, with other Binoche roles of the period – not only the 'fuck box' scene from *High Life* described above but also *Cosmopolis* (2012), where she is first seen writhing on Robert Pattinson's lap. It is as though Binoche's intellectual credibility, earned over decades of high-brow roles, has enabled her to display her body without risking objectification: in *Clouds of Sils-Maria* (2014), too, Binoche strips naked to run into a mountain lake, and in *Camille Claudel 1915* she has her clothes removed in only her second scene.

As the opening scene implies, *Un beau soleil intérieur* takes a frank look at middle-aged sex and desire. In the assessment of Emma Wilson, Isabelle 'has every reason to be happy. But she wants to be fucked' (2019, 25). Isabelle has four sexual partners, plus two or three additional suitors, in an indeterminate timeframe that presumably covers several months. The film is disarmingly honest about the way in which sex in middle age is haunted by each partner's sexual history: 'Did your last boyfriend come more quickly?', asks Vincent (Xavier Beauvois) aggressively, while Isabelle is turned off by an unfamiliar gesture that her ex-husband has picked up in the bedroom. In keeping with sex-positive traditions of French feminism (for instance, Badinter 2010), Binoche's character is here defined by her ongoing sex life and never by her motherhood – her daughter is glimpsed in only a single shot. As Erika Balsom comments: 'Denis allows her protagonist an emotional and practical freedom, never punishing her for her exploratory openness, instead affirming it while registering its toll' (2018).

While reviews of *Sunshine*, particularly those written by women, routinely stressed Binoche's 'radiance', the men of the film are strikingly unappealing. Vincent, the banker, is a boorish bully; the actor (Nicholas Duvauchelle) is an indecisive drunk; Mathieu (Philippe Katerine), a hopeful neighbour, is bizarrely dressed and doesn't listen to her; Sylvain (Paul Blain), the ageing seducer who cruises the provincial nightclub with his leather jacket, is a French cliché. As Isabelle's friend Fabien (Bruno Podalydès) comments about the latter: 'I understand why he's fallen in love with you, just not the reverse.' The film seems to make a deliberate joke out of the way that romantic comedy will often enable immature or irresponsible men to couple with stunningly attractive and accomplished women. As Emma Wilson comments: 'Binoche is a goddess. That even she, as Isabelle, is faced with so much erotic disappointment makes the film the more sardonic in its despairing recognition of the misogyny and ageist triviality women face' (Wilson 2019, 25).

Balsom refuses to accept the film as a romcom: 'There is no meet-cute, no implicit moralizing, no happy ending. Indeed, Denis's every move seems tailored to diverge from how the perennial problem of forming the heterosexual couple is typically represented' (2018, n.p.). This suggests a somewhat narrow conception of romantic comedy that fails to recognise the extent to which 'postmodern' iterations of the genre have themselves moved away from the 'happily-ever-after' implications of the concluding marriage ceremony in recognition of the diversification of models of domestic and sexual contentment in contemporary society (Harrod 2015, 34). Still, the ambiguous ending of *Sunshine* is in keeping with Denis's deliberate frustrating of spectatorial pleasure in narrative resolution. On a moonlit walk, Isabelle takes the hand of her gallery-owner friend Marc (Alex Descas) and the two admit that they have secretly admired each other for a while. But in the context of the preceding seventy minutes or so, this scene fails to convince: it is too quick, too short and too little prepared after a sequence of failures to be taken seriously as a romantic epiphany. Indeed, Marc refuses to go home with Isabelle, announcing instead that he is about to leave on holiday with his children for a month. Instead, the film's real closing sequence features a cameo from Gérard Depardieu, comically improbable as a fortune teller, who soothes Isabelle's romantic woes by promising the arrival of 'a bigger man, with more charisma, more dimension', in other words: himself.

The Depardieu scene is typical of the unstable tone of *Un beau soleil intérieur*: the episode, despite being given privileged placement at the very end of the film, is entirely unannounced and precariously balanced between the maudlin and the hilarious – at certain moments, Binoche looks as though she could either burst into tears *or* burst out laughing. Denis's film seems to work to make explicit the bittersweet tone of romantic comedy: the genre, even as it serves up moments of joy, hope and tenderness, necessarily deals frequently in the terrain of loneliness and disappointment, and *Sunshine* works to keep these possibilities always in the balance – the undecidable temptation to laugh or cry is in fact almost constant in the film. This is seen, for instance, in the film's costumes. Although locations and wardrobe are, for the most part, entirely plausible for the milieu depicted, there is something rather jarring about Binoche's

Figure 10.4   Incongruous outfits: Isabelle (Juliette Binoche) in *Un beau soleil intérieur* (2017).

outfits at times. She wears a pair of thigh-length high-heeled boots in more than one scene and at one point does her shopping in an ill-assorted ensemble of a leather mini-skirt with stilettos, and a bright red jumper. A big green scarf is wrapped around her neck but the sweater's plunging neckline exposes her chest on this rainy (autumn?) day. For anyone familiar with the conservative nature of Parisian women's fashion – designed to defend against both the climatological elements and the male gaze – such sartorial choices, especially in Isabelle's bourgeois class, are comically unlikely even as they point, poignantly, to her increasing sexual desperation.

The unprepossessing nature of Isabelle's lovers, mentioned above, is also a source of wary comedy. Vincent's bullying tendencies are so overt as to be laughable – he berates an unfortunate young waiter with lines like, 'I said a *small* Perrier!' – while also placing her in real danger of emotional abuse. 'Crying is for servants', he tells her when she asks him to leave, 'and for monkeys, sometimes.' Likewise, the actor's alcoholism is confined to the *mise en scène* in a gently mocking way but is nonetheless unnerving: he sinks three beers during one short conversation with Isabelle, at one point winking at an off-screen server as he finishes one glass before picking up another full one, without even looking, from below the bottom of the frame. In a similar way, the dialogue, written by Denis with novelist Christine Angot, is comical in a way that makes us cringe. Resisting the slick repartee of much romantic comedy, *Sunshine* focuses instead on inarticulacy and awkwardness, particularly in Isabelle's exchanges with the actor. 'I feel like all you want is for me to get out of your car', she tells him three times before ending up in bed with him. Isabelle's hesitancy and deference is the focus of much humour, as in the scene where she tries to confront a gallery owner (Josiane Balasko) over her alleged affair with Isabelle's ex-husband – 'It's very awkward, I'm sorry, it's very, very awkward . . .' she begins – or when she profusely thanks Vincent's chauffeur for driving her home: 'Sir, thank you so, so, so much', but it's also clear that this lack of confidence or assertiveness around her own dignity and entitlement plays into the disarray of her romantic life. In short, *Un beau soleil intérieur* achieves the delicate feat of drawing its humour from its own realism: it is brutally honest about the self-defeating strategies that people deploy to combat their loneliness, which makes it funny, but it declines to leaven that realism with the glimmer of a happy ending such that, at length, a melancholy mood comes to pervade the film.

CONCLUSION

In her work with stars in the 2010s, Claire Denis has tended to choose performers who have grown famous for their taciturn, enigmatic persona. Juliette Binoche is a possible exception here, and hence well suited to *Un beau soleil intérieur*, probably the 'lightest' and most verbose of all Denis's films; but even Binoche's face often appears as an inscrutable mask: 'its beauty and luminosity attract the camera like a magnet, but its smoothness refracts the gaze of the spectator' (Vincendeau 2000, 249). These are stars whose performance style, and whose intertextual persona, often imply behaviours motivated by buried past trauma and, as such, they suit the haunted landscapes and half-spoken stories of Denis's cinematic universe. These stars have facilitated, through their filmographic associations, Denis's ongoing exploration of film genres, comparable at this point, in its breadth, audacity and aesthetic achievement, only to the catalogue of Stanley Kubrick. At the same time, these experiments with stardom and genre serve further to muddy the waters of Denis's already complex and uncompromising gender politics. It would be possible to offer hopeful feminist readings of all of these films: *White Material* represents one woman's act of revenge against a patriarchal, imperialist order; *Les salauds* condemns a world 'in which sexual violence provides the very foundation of social relations' (Galt 2015, 276); *High Life* celebrates a mature woman's powerful sexuality and implies a kind of redemptive immaculate conception; *Un beau soleil intérieur* is a sex-positive portrait of a middle-aged woman's pursuit of pleasure in a society of double standards. Yet it rapidly becomes difficult to sustain these positive readings in the face of the textual evidence: *White Material*'s Maria Vial is more manly than the men around her, an exploitative boss placing profit before lives; far from exposing the sordid sex ring at the heart of *Les salauds*, Marco is killed by the woman he is trying to rescue while his niece chooses a suicidal return to the arms of her abusers; *High Life* demonstrates only that sexual coercion, abuse and incest are apparently endemic to humanity, immediately tainting the experiment of a new community away from Earth; and *Sunshine* offers the somewhat depressing spectacle of self-defeating behaviours from a woman who, despite her beauty and privilege, apparently lacks any real self-respect. In short, Denis's cinema ably demonstrates the patriarchal oppression of women but never shies away from representing women's thorough-going collusion with that insidious power. Hence for all the brilliance and magnetism of its stars, the singular airlessness of this extraordinary and bleakly compelling body of work.

NOTES

1. 'un élan qui vient du fond de l'être, que rien n'explique et que rien ne vient arrêter.' (Joudet 2018, 173).
2. 'L'avachissement, c'est ce qu'il y a de plus répugnant chez un homme. C'est abject.'
3. 'Tantôt initiatrice, tantôt initié' (Joudet 2018, 191).
4. Andrew Asibong notes that Maria is 'on the one hand too tiny to be able to move with ease across the gigantic, blocked-off terrain, on the other hand too big, too unwieldy, too white to pass through its nooks and crannies unnoticed' (2011, 160).
5. Shots of Huppert moving away from the camera were also a recurring motif in *Villa Amalia* where her character became defined almost exclusively by her flight, her inextricable desire to leave.
6. L'extrême blondeur attire une forme de malheur – c'est quelque chose qu'on doit saccager. Les yeux bleus sont gênants.'

CITATIONS

Asibong, Andrew. 2011. 'Claire Denis's Flickering Spaces of Hospitality.' *Esprit créateur* 51, 1: 154–67.
Badinter, Élisabeth. 2010. *Le Conflit: La femme et la mère*. Paris: Flammarion.
Balsom, Erika. 2018. 'Bad Boyfriends.' *Art Forum*, 23 April. https://www.artforum.com/film/erika-balsom-on-claire-denis-s-let-the-sunshine-in-2017-75001.
Beugnet, Martine. 2004. *Claire Denis*. Manchester: Manchester University Press.
Caporale, Marzia. 2013. 'The Aesthetic of the Unspoken: Representing Female Silence in Claire Denis's Film *White Material*.' In *The Unspeakable: Representations of Trauma in Francophone Literature and Art*, edited by Névine El Nossery and Amy L. Hubbell, 249–63. Newcastle upon Tyne: Cambridge Scholars Press.
Dupont, Joan. 'The Secret Sharer.' *Film Comment* 52, 2 (March–April): 34–9.
Galt, Rosalind. 2015. 'Claire Denis's Capitalist *Bastards*.' *Studies in French Cinema* 15, 3: 275–93.
Guimarães, Pedro. 2020. 'The Calculated *Maladresse*: Isabelle Huppert's Dual Performance Style.' In *Isabelle Huppert: Stardom, Performance, Authorship*, edited by Darren Waldron, 41–58. New York: Bloomsbury.

Harrod, Mary. 2015. *From France with Love: Gender and Identity in French Romantic Comedy*. London: I. B. Tauris.

Hayon, Kaya Davies. 2020. 'Embodying the White (Colonial) Woman: Isabelle Huppert's Roles in Postcolonial Film.' In *Isabelle Huppert: Stardom, Performance, Authorship*, edited by Darren Waldron, 157–76. New York: Bloomsbury.

Joudet, Murielle. 2018. *Isabelle Huppert: La vie ne nous regarde pas*. Paris: Capricci.

Murphy, Ian. 2012. 'Feeling and Form in the Films of Claire Denis.' *Jump Cut* 54. https://www.ejumpcut.org/archive/jc54.2012/IanMurphyDenis/index.html.

Pinkerton, Nick. 2019. 'The Point of No Return.' *Film Comment* 55, 2 (March–April): 24–9.

Rouyer, Philippe and Tobin, Yann. 2009. 'Entretien avec Vincent Lindon: Les contraintes, ça m'aide.' *Positif* 577 (March): 25–9.

Vincendeau, Ginette. 1985. 'Community, Nostalgia and the Spectacle of Masculinity.' *Screen* 26, 6: 18–39.

Vincendeau, Ginette. 2000. *Stars and Stardom in French Cinema*. London: Continuum.

Waldron, Darren. 2020. 'Intimate Distance: The Face of Isabelle Huppert.' In *Isabelle Huppert, Stardom, Performance, Authorship*, edited by Darren Waldron, 21–40. New York: Bloomsbury.

Wilson, Emma. 2019. 'Love Me Tender: New Films from Claire Denis.' *Film Quarterly* 72, 4: 18–28.

CHAPTER 11

Life Imitates Art: The Intimacy of Family in the Work of Claire Denis and Yasujiro Ozu

Kate Taylor-Jones

D enis once commented:

> Late Spring is very personal for me, very close to that relationship between my mother and my grandfather. I took my mother once to an Ozu retrospective to see Late Spring, and she thought it was beautiful – she said, 'I didn't know you could make a film with such a simple story'. So, I made up my mind. I wanted to make that film for her. (Claire Denis 2009, n.p.)

In this oft-quoted statement, Denis expresses her desire to pay recognition to Japanese director Ozu Yasujiro with her 2008 film *35 rhums*. With this acknowledgement, Denis joined the ranks of other global directors such as Hirokazu Koreeda, Hou Hsiao-hsien, Wim Wenders, Wes Anderson and Alain Gomis who have utilised Ozu as both a source of inspiration and a site of reference and homage. Discussions of Ozu have often focused on his aesthetics, and as I have argued elsewhere (2018), a comparative study of cinematic aesthetics potentially allows us to draw a clear creative lineage between Ozu's style, both visual and thematic, and the work of Claire Denis. This chapter will develop these links further and will locate Denis as part of the global screen legacy of a director who, rather than being a historical figure in Japanese cinema, plays a vibrant and enduring part of global cinema narratives and visions. In this chapter I wish to explore some parallel developments between Denis and Ozu in terms of both theme and approach with specific reference to the ideas of family.

This chapter has three key aims: first, to highlight the ways in which putting such directors into conversation is both productive and useful; second, I will explore how Denis's affective engagement with the idea of family can find resonance with Ozu's intimate portraits and, finally; how the space of global capitalism is written across their works as a reflection of the socio-political moments that surrounded their individual careers. These parallel developments and approaches are found across a wide variety of their films and despite the clear differences in culture, language, space and history, a concurrent exploration of their works allows a further nuanced understanding of both directors.

COMPARATIVE MOMENTS

Denis is clearly an important figure in French cinematic development as this collection and many other works of scholarship illustrate. Throughout her career she has been the subject of a diverse range of criticism and scholarship for her work as vicariously part of wider debates on contemporary French cinema (Powrie 1999), postcolonial legacies (Hayward 2001), questions of the body (Del Río 2003) and women auteurs (Beugnet 2004), to name but a few of the key interpretative lenses through which her work has been explored. Ozu, likewise, is another director of global stature whose work has been examined extensively using a wide variety of methodologies and approaches (see Yoshimoto 2013). His films first entered English language scholarship via Paul Schrader (1972) and then later studies by scholars such as Richie (1974), Desser (1985), Boardwell (1988) and Thompson and Bordwell (1976). These studies often situated Ozu's work inside a very specific vision of Japanese cinema and his own unique authorial style. However, more contemporary scholars such as Geist (1983), DiPaolo and Stein (2015), Miyao (2021), Yoshimoto (2013) and Joo (2017) have sought to deepen and widen the approach taken to both his works and his position in global cinema. In Japan, writers such as Hasumi Shigehiko (1983, 1997), Tado Sato (1977, 1982) and Yoshida Kiju (2003) have promoted Ozu's work and his career. Hasumi is partially notable for his reading of Ozu as transnational and, as Aaron Gerow remarks in his study on Hasumi's linkage and discussion of Ozu and Hou, 'celebrates the cinematic crossing of national boundaries, in part so as to critique, national and cultural explanations, for their reductive categorizations' (Gerow 2018, 53). In a similar vein, Wada-Marciano (2018), Brown (2017), Sendra and Green (2021) and many others have focused on exploring the relationship between Ozu and filmmakers as diverse as Joanna Hogg, Alain Gomis, Hou Hsai-Hsein and Wim Wenders (with whom Denis worked before her debut, *Chocolat*).

This productive approach to placing Ozu in conversion with other filmmakers has resonance for comparative film studies because as Paul Willemen notes, they 'find a way of overcoming the limits that any intellectual paradigm suffers from by virtue of, necessarily, being elaborated within a specific geo-historical field' (2005, 99). The question about such a comparative approach, as Willemen sees it, is 'how do cinemas emerging from within different socio-historical formations negotiate the encounter between capitalist modernisation and whatever mode of social-economic regulation and (re)production preceded that encounter?' (2005, 99). He concludes in a later study that 'Such a reading has to proceed with forensic care, paying attention to the ways in which, in different geo-cultural regions, films orchestrate their modes of address, the relations between the indexical, iconic and symbolic dimensions of substances and forms of content' (2010, 362). My own background as a scholar means that such a call moves me – originally raised in Belgium and trained in French cinema during my earlier career, I would later move into East Asian Studies. Both the linguistic and cultural ebbs and flows of this process leave me minded of both my privileges (white, Western) and my disadvantages (female, disabled) as an interlocutor participating in such an activity. I am therefore very conscious of Mitsuhiro Yoshimoto's timely reminder that 'comparative film studies would not automatically function as a critically productive engagement with the dominant scholarship on cinema', and that one must be sensitive to both the language and mode of film scholarship (2013).

Despite these concerns, these two directors allow us to posit a comparative and productive analysis of these individuals and their contexts in a sustained way. Yingjin Zhang writes of 'the multiple directionality with which film studies simultaneously looks outwards (transnationalism, globalisation), inwards (cultural traditions and aesthetic conventions), backwards (history and memory), and sideways' (2006, 31). This approach has deep resonance with any exploration of Ozu and Denis – a desire to look at both the specifics of their work and their histories alongside a wider sense of the global screen worlds and their interplay.

While time and space divides them, Denis and Ozu, were, and are, notable, for maintaining a group of frequent collaborators both in front of and behind the camera and it is from a process of collaboration that their works emerge. Writer Kogo Noda worked (and by all accounts drank heavily) with Ozu on twenty-seven of his scripts, including thirteen of his sixteen post-war features including *Tōkyō Monogatari / Tokyo Story* (1953), *Banshun / Late Spring* (1949), *Ochazuke no Aji / Green Tea over Rice* (1952) and *Tōkyō Boshoku/Tokyo Twilight* (1957). Other regular collaborators included cinematographer Yūharu Atsuta, who brought his technical ability to ensure that Ozu's unique vision was presented as he desired (see Sakamura and Hasumi 1998). Agnès Godard likewise has brought her talented cinematography to bear on sixteen films with Denis. The writer Jean-Pol Fargeau has worked with Denis on over ten films and as for music, the Tindersticks are notable for bringing their melancholic tones to a range of Denis's feature films. Both directors often utilise(ed) the same actors in their works (see Douglas Morrey's chapter in this collection for a discussion of Denis and performers). For Ozu, Chishū Ryū (fifty-two films out of Ozu's fifty-four productions), Setsuko Hara (six films), and Haruko Sugimura (thirteen films) were important collaborators on the screen and for Denis, on-screen collaborators include Alex Descas (eight films), Gregoire Colin (seven films), Michel Subor, Alice Houri, Juliette Binoche and Isaac de Bankolé (three films each). While the number of films they have made differ radically, they are both consistent in utilising a clear 'family' of actors or workers on their films.

These material similarities of close collaboration are suggestive of similar experiences of making film. Yet this is perhaps where the two directors in many ways divide markedly in terms of their material production experiences. Ozu spent his entire career working inside the very hierarchical Japanese studio system with limited international attention during his lifetime, while Denis has worked in independent film with numerous awards and recognition to her name but an uneven global response to her films (see Galt 2014). Ozu started his career in silent cinema in Imperial Japan and served time in the army. He would die in 1963 after making fifty-four films. Denis in comparison was born into the French colonial milieux and made her first feature film in 1988 and continues to work to the present day. Ozu never married and spent his life living with his mother until her death, and his work was rarely shown overseas until the 1960s. Denis, in comparison, has worked globally to make her films, and she and her films are a regular presence at international film festivals. These are directors working in different eras with different historical legacies to respond to and yet their work is not alien from each other. Via an examination of their works, we can see numerous resonances in their exploration of family and both the external and internal pressures that family units face as a result of the historical and cultural moments in which they exist.

FAMILY AFFAIRS AND THE MODERN MOMENT

Willemen (2005) states that a productive entry point into the problems of comparative cinema studies is by way of an analysis of a text's mode of address. As Elizabeth Ellsworth comments, attention to mode of address, as multifaceted as it can be, enables a focus on how all products allow us to 'make visible and problematic' the processes by which products 'invite their users to take up particular positions within knowledge, power and desire' (1997, 2). Here, I want to explore how ideas around images and conceptions of the family are the dominant structure through which we can read the films.

The key role of family can be seen in all the very short summaries of the films this chapter is exploring. In *35 rhums* and *Late Spring*, a widowed man and his daughter have a close and happy relationship which, by the film's end, has been disrupted by the daughter's marriage and eventual departure from the family home. In *Tokyo Story*, the elderly couple are unable to adapt to the new fast-paced modern lives of their children. *Tokyo Twilight* follows a family into the trauma of a failed marriage, a mother's abandonment, abortion and eventually a tragic death. *Nénette et Boni* (1996) focuses on an unwanted teenage pregnancy while *Les salauds* (2013) shows a family's brutal decline after the father's suicide, the daughter's rape and the return of Marco, the uncle, determined to uncover the truth.

While the plots of all these films are both tragic in places, melodramatic in others, joyful in some small moments, the focal point remains an exploration of the space and place of family as both potential sites for succour and support as well as trauma and abuse. The family is certainly not static and is defined by the endless struggle to find, and then keep a position, space or role in an ever-changing environment. In many ways, the linchpin is the obvious comparison of *Late Spring* and *35 rhums*. The plots are almost the same although Denis's film has a distinctly more positive outlook than Ozu's. Denis's film follows Josephine and Lionel, a father and daughter who live together happily while maintaining friendships with work colleagues and neighbours. Josephine will eventually marry Noé, their upstairs neighbour, and Lionel is left drinking the mysterious 35 shots of rum before returning to their empty apartment. *Late Spring* also focuses on a father and daughter but for this duo, societal pressures mean that the father feels he must ensure his daughter marries despite her reluctance and eventually manages to get her to agree to an arranged marriage by pretending to her that he is considering remarrying himself (and thus she would no longer have a place in his house). For the fathers in both *Late Spring* and *35 rhums*, the movement and changes that are taking place in their small worlds see them struggle to find a space for themselves as their respective daughters move towards a new future. The re-inscribing of the self into a space that has changed beyond recognition is a struggle that Denis's films such as *Beau travail*, *Chocolate* and *White Material*s clearly oscillate around but Ozu's characters frequently face in the post-war moment as well.

Yoshida's exploration of Ozu's work is interesting here; he defines it as his 'anti-cinema', a form that rejects the 'new and dramatic' to offer instead the contemplation of life in all its myriad and often mundane forms, inviting 'contemplation of non-narrative, non-human agency' (Davis 2009, n.p.). This sense of multiple strands of time operating inside the same cinematic space is echoed in the work of Daisuke Miyao, who summarises the approach that has been taken to *Tokyo Story* where we see two temporalities of duration coexisting, both linear (the elderly couple and their movement across Tokyo) and a frozen space exemplified by their daughter-in-law Noriko, who remains endlessly widowed and reflective of her lost husband and the past of Japan. He notes that

'The layers of the two temporalities of Tokyo Story are visualised in mise-en-scène and are vocalized in dialogue' (2021, 62). What we see in these images is a conflict between what Joo calls 'the reality of everyday' and 'a retrospective tendency' (2017, 183–4). This has real resonance with the work of Denis in many of her films, from the empty movements across the sand in *Beau travail* (1999) to the disengaged spaces of *White Material* (2009) and *L'intrus* (2004).

With *35 rhums*, the balance between two modes of temporality is framed around the film's engagement with movement. Like with Joo's reading of *Tokyo Story*, we have the 'reality of the everyday', where we see father and daughter follow their routines (work, university, concerts) but we also have a reflective or frozen space that both Lionel and his daughter are entrapped in until she makes the decision to leave via her marriage to Noé. Neither appears able to move beyond their home or each other – Josephine seems to reject romantic overtures and Lionel has clearly not managed to forge a relationship beyond Josephine, despite their neighbour and friend Gabrielle's attempts. When they go to Germany to visit her deceased mother's grave, her grandmother reminisces about her dead daughter and her fear of swimming. As Lionel gazes at the image of his dead wife with a new-born Josephine in a sling on her chest the weight of his grief for his vanishing family is palpable. In *Late Spring*, Noriko's slow and painful realisation of this moment of change occurs as she and her father watch a Noe theatre performance and he performs the lie of his potential remarriage via a silent nod to the proposed women. This emotionally charged moment means that Noriko will agree to her own marriage despite her lack of desire. In a scene with no words, the effectiveness and visual display of a family disintegration is presented as Noriko reflects on her options.

For Lionel, this moment of reflection comes in the café when he realises that Noé and Josephine are more than just friends. As they dance, we see him at the bar watching their courtship with clear sadness. On the way back from Germany, Lionel and Josephine stop at the beach to camp for the night in the frozen wasteland. For Lionel, the meaning in his life comes from the moments where time is suspended, where the everyday actions of life can stop and allow him to remain in stasis with his beloved daughter. On the day of the wedding he denies Gabrielle's attempts to help Josephine get ready and he grasps at the last few moments of solitude with his departing daughter.

It is telling that his fantasy sequence is about him and Josephine riding a horse along the very train tracks he drives, taking them both into a new space that is outside any normative or real experience. He notes to his depressed former colleague René (Juliet Mars Toussaint) that on the dark and endless train track he keeps dark thoughts away by his dreams of his daughter. Movement away from, and then back to the family unit, is a frequent site of tragedy in both Denis and Ozu's work. Ozu's films often depict images of trains, and as Donald Richie notes, his films often end at, or near, train stations. For Richie, trains in Ozu's film represent nostalgia: 'The mournful sound of a train in the distance, the idea of all those people being carried away to begin life anew elsewhere, the longing or nostalgia for travel – all these are still emotionally potent for the Japanese.' Here we have the train offering a sense of possibility, a space where something could happen, and yet all too often in Ozu's film the train is left as a hollow broken promise. 'Life anew' is marked with sorrow as the train and the station space fail to present new chances or stories. The train travels of Shūkichi and Tomi in *Tokyo Story* lead to their sense of isolation from their children and grandchildren, and it is on the train to Osaka that Tomi's final illness becomes apparent. The trains that allow people to travel and explore modern Japan also grant their three children the ability to quickly abandon their father shortly after their mother's funeral. *Tokyo Twilight* sees Akiko killed at a train crossing, and her sister Takako refuses to go to the train station to bid a final farewell to their estranged mother. Their mother departs for her new life in Hokkaido with the relationships with her remaining daughter left in a frozen limbo, unable to move forward and unable to find a suitable conclusion. Takako will tell her father she is returning to her abusive husband simply to try to avoid her son, experiencing her own fate as a child from a broken home; yet this return is not a joyful reunion, rather a depressing vision of Takako's own limited choices. In *Les salauds*, Marco (Vincent Lindon), summarises that that is how he saw the navy – as a method to cut his ties with his dysfunctional family. Yet he returns from the ship to try to help his niece and sister-in-law, only for his movement to become more and more constrained. His finances force him to sell his car, and he ends up navigating Paris by bus.

For Lionel, the train meanders around his life as he runs the circular RER routes around Paris bringing workers into the city from the surrounding suburbs. The tragic fate of René is a bleak warning about how Lionel's own life might be if he did not have Josephine. René has spent his working life moving around the Paris rail network but rather than start a new life anew when he retires, he loses his routine and reason for living and will die on the train tracks. The film's narrative makes this link clear, since Josephine enters Noé's apartment in a rage after she sees the for-sale signs in a scene that we never see, but we can conclude that they decide to marry at this point, and in the very next scene we then move to the train lines as Lionel, with René sitting beside him.

Shaviro's reading of Bresson (another director who, like Ozu, was classed by Schrader as transcendental) notes that far from aiming for spiritual emptiness, film works like those of Bresson allow for the 'the radical incompossibility of worldly and spiritual existence', where 'everything is thrown back upon the everyday and upon the body' (1994, 249), now raised 'to the utmost level of carnal intensity' (1994, 251). Ozu is a director who is mired in the everyday, and this focus on the body has clear resonance with Denis. While Ozu's films are not filled with the 'carnal intensity' of the images rendered in Denis's work, prostitution, abortion, a wide range of domestic abuse and gripping images of poverty and depressions are found throughout his films. The family story in the worlds of both directors is told via both the bodies of the characters and the items that surround them.

For Martine Beugnet, contemporary French cinema 'betray[s] a characteristic sensibility to and awareness of cinema's sensuous impact and transgressive nature' (2008, 174). For Beugnet this aesthetic of sensation, a cinema of the senses, offers a new challenge to the audience to explore the very materiality of the film medium. Martin articulates Denis's works as 'of the body' and yet as Ian Murphy has noted, Denis's films deploy 'still or "empty" frames in which the human figure is frequently edged off the screen', privileging 'depopulated spaces, inanimate objects, and natural or industrial environments' (2012). For Laura McMahon, this emptying out of the cinematic frame of the human is not a rejection of the body, but rather we see films that are 'profoundly shaped by an intermingling of body and landscape, human and non-human, the geopolitical and the geological. In resonance with the insights of Deleuze and Nancy, both films attend to times that stretch before and beyond the anthropocentric' (2014).

The idea of an innocent item as a site of vicariously meditation or meaning is key to both directors' representation of the obliqueness of the concept of family. We see the vase in Ozu transformed into a rice cooker that can be utilised, for want of a better word, as a floating cypher that is open to a multiplicity of readings. The vase in *Late Spring* is vicariously dependent on the scholar, a transcendental moment in a specific directorial decision (Schrader), a reflection of the Japanese post-war moment, a disruption in the intense emotional narrative (Thompson and Bordwell 1976) or simply a reflection of the director's love of pottery (Yamada 2002), Hasui writes eloquently how a simple neck scarf can reveal the dissolution of the family in Ozu's work. As Akiko goes to see the mother who abandoned her as a child, 'she tilts her head slightly and removes the neckerchief in a single quick motion. This chilly gesture suggests strongly that she is rejecting her mother' (Hasumi 2004).

For Lionel, the double rice cookers are both a symbol of his and Josephine's symbiosis but also, by the film's end, clear evidence of their growth apart. The rhetoric around this can be seen in the numerous articles that ask the question 'when is a rice cooker more than a rice cooker'. Scholarship has ranged from reading this cooker as both a moment of time-image (Troy 2020) or joyful resignation to the new situation (Vecchio 2014). In *Nénette et Boni*, Boni fixates on bread dough, first as part of his obsession with the local baker's wife but then later as he begins to feel tenderness for Nénette's (unborn) child. In *Bastards*, the horrific appearance of the bloodied corncob that Justine was raped with appears first when her uncle visits the site where she was abused (although he is unaware of this fact at the time). The cob is left on the floor of the barn covered in what looks like red paint and we only make the connection when the end of the film shows her father looming over her armed with the cob and we remember her bloodied thighs as she is found walking in the streets of Paris.

FAMILY AS THE SITE OF EXCHANGE

The sites and locations of these exchanges and individual stories are telling. The modern city space plays a vibrant and important role in all the films: from Tomi and Shūkichi's sightseeing tours around Tokyo, the RER for Lionel, Justine found wandering the streets Paris covered in blood and Boni's endless attempts to navigate both his local area (via his obsession with the baker's wife), and the hospital setting where Nénette eventually gives birth. The Tokyo of *Tokyo Twilight* is so contaminated that the characters are forced to wear masks, and we see the enforcement of anti-prostitution laws and even the sight of men arrested for stealing women's underwear. The modern family must move between the private space of home and the public open spaces that surround them. The work of Laura Marks, channelling the terms or ideas of Deleuze, defines these sites as 'any-space-wherever'; in short, the space between. While this has clear resonance with Auge's idea of non-place, perhaps we can draw a distinction between the two with the minor but nevertheless important focus on creativity. Augé certainly has a more dystopian vision of the proliferation of 'non-places' as the site of neglect of productivity but for Deleuze, this lack of identity might also offer infinite possibility for connection (Deleuze 1986, 109). As Marks continues, 'These are sites where one can rediscover or remake oneself, often in isolation' (2000, 27). Deleuze may have described the any-space-wherever in the post-Second World War landscape as 'deserted but inhabited, disused warehouses, waste ground, cities in the course of demolition or reconstruction [. . .] but he continues that this is '(where) a new race of characters was stirring, kind of mutant' (quoted in Marks 2000, 27).

Modernity and post-war economic development in Japan were mired by two conflicting narratives, the embarrassment of defeat in the Pacific War moment, and the other modern option offered by the USA during and after the allied occupation. For France, in the 1980s onwards as Denis started her career, the post-dirigiste moment,[1] heralding a new shift in the French state and the national economies was underway. In this new post-dirigiste state, the capitalist market economy rules and those who fail to thrive in such a situation are left behind, as many of Denis's films testify. Martin O'Shaughnessy, Phil Powrie and Rosalind Galt, among others, have explored French national cinema in the context of neoliberalism, with Galt in particular citing Denis as a director whose films 'render visible the neoliberal structures of race, sexuality and colonial power as a mode of resistance of dominant modes of representing the world and they ask us to look otherwise at the networks and circuits of French cinematic globalism' (2014, 107). For Galt, *Les saludes* is a key example of this, but we can also see it in *Vendredi soir*'s exploration of the Paris Cityscape during a public transport strike, *Trouble Every Day*'s vision of murderous sexualities between transnational couples and *J'ai pas sommail*'s network of disenfranchised individuals struggling to find a space in the French state. *Tokyo Twilight* was made at the later stage of Ozu's career and visualised the collapse of the family across the generations. The daughter's husband drinks too much, has anger issues and, as a result, abuses her and the child. When the father suggests he intervene she comments that there is no point – nothing will change. Later the father notes that perhaps he made a wrong choice in strongly encouraging her to marry the person she did over the man she preferred. While one daughter flees her marriage the other child, Akiko, is living out the ideal modern life with a boyfriend, Western clothing and trips to bars, mahjong parlours, noodle shops and late night cafés. However, for Akiko, this ends in an unwanted pregnancy and a boyfriend who abandons her on learning this. Denis's *Nénette et Boni* also features a teenage pregnancy. Nénette arrives unwanted and uninvited at her older brother's house and only later informs him of her pregnancy. While he is intent on rejecting her and keeps insisting she leave, the announcement of her pregnancy seems to spark a new sense of connection with Boni and, after her abortion fails and she is forced to bear the child, he goes against her wishes and kidnaps the new-born at gunpoint and the film ends with him cradling the baby as Nénette sits impassively on an outside swing. Her opinions and thoughts are hidden from view.

Neither director wishes to bear witness as judge and jury to their characters. While both Nénette and Akiko are pregnant out of wedlock, the films do not seek to critique these young women for their choices. Rather we are presented with the structures that surround them leading to the restriction of their own choices. Both women face the dilemma of abortion when the respective fathers fail to support them. For Nénette, she takes the drastic, and ultimately unsuccessful, option of attempting to self-abort at seven months while Akiko cannot face the spectre of unwed motherhood and opts for a costly termination.

The never-seen father of Nénette (it is implied that her own father may be involved) and the uncaring response of Akiko's boyfriend makes it clear that the films are not offering judgement on the women, rather on a system that leaves them stranded in their moment of need. *Tokyo Twilight* focuses on the rather dismal bar venue of Etoile, where countless men and women seem to be in the middle of relationship disputes. Akiko is trapped there by a predatory male visitor who refuses to let her leave the bar and who turns out to be a plain clothes police officer who arrests her for no apparent reason other than 'staying out late'. While the actions of the man seem to support some sense of a moral code that young women should agree to, the lack of care and support for

Akiko is seen as the responsibility of the absent mother, and of the father and sister who are unaware of her actions (and her pregnancy). Like Justine, Akiko roams the cityscape. She frequents bars, dark alleys, gaming parlours and the riverside searching for her missing lover. Justine is seen wandering the streets, naked, bloody and unable to tell anyone what has happened to her. By the end of the film we learn that she was taken to the barn where she was raped by her own father as part of a transaction between them and manipulative financier Laporte (Michel Subor). Her mother, we learn, was aware of this abuse but chooses to keep the events secret from everyone and pressures her daughter to do the same. As Galt comments, 'Denis deploys both the weight and the fragility of filmed bodies to figure the less visible wounds of global politics' (Galt 2015, 275). Akiko is the victim of a post-war milieu that sees women caught between the old traditional bonds of marriage and family and the possibilities of a new modern state that all too often proves hollow and empty. Akiko survives her abortion but is then hit by a train when she runs away from her disloyal boyfriend. Although she manages to make it to the hospital and have a last conversation with her family, we learn that she later dies of her injuries.

The family is shown via not only the internal machinations but also the physical location of the actions. For Akiko, her narrative is mediated via the city space of Tokyo and there are clear resonances with the tragedy of Justine – albeit less horrific. Justine is abused by her own father and left physically and mentally damaged wandering the Paris streets and the remote countryside surrounding the city. She cannot cope with the intensity of her feelings and in a surreal night-time drive sequence she crashes the car with two of her abusers killing all three

Figure 11.1   Akiko in *Tokyo Twilight*: the girl as a lost figure on the margins of society.

Figure 11.2 Justine in *Les saludes*: the girl as a lost figure on the margins of society.

of them. For Galt, the 'scene seems to promise intimacy and outlaw energy, but in fact signal only Justine's desperation and the impossibility, for her, of this apparatus leading anywhere but death' (2015, 286). As we see her mangled body removed from the car wreck we realise that it is not just Justine who is unable to escape this cycle, as her death removed from Marco any chance of saving Justine and redeeming the family. Marco returns to try to protect his niece and solve his brother's death but his investigations into Laporte and his attempts to become closer to the truth, including starting a relationship with Laporte's mistress Raphaëlle, will end in his own death. In the moment of confrontation, Raphaëlle chooses to protect Laporte, and stabs Marco despite the ill-treatment she has received at the hands of Laporte. As Galt notes, 'there is no way out is precisely the point: familial bonds are no more than the most intimately effective form of exploitation' (2015, 288). Justine and Marco are both ensnared in their dysfunctional and abusive family unit and are unable to escape.

The Sugiyama family in *Tokyo Twilight* are significantly less extreme than the family of Justine and Marco and yet they too operate as a bond that offers neither succour nor safety. As Takako sadly notes with relation to Akiko, 'she grew up without a mother's love. That's why she is lonely.' The films are not unsympathetic to the female characters, but it becomes clear that the modern state is not moving or changing fast enough to allow these women any real sense of choice or ability to move into the public sphere without the restraints of both familial pressures and societal gender constraints.

CONCLUSION AND REFLECTING THE SOCIAL MOMENT

Janet Bergstrom presents Denis's work in terms of a 'mise-en-scène of fragmentation' (Bergstrom 2003, 71), in which narrative gaps are often left open as a point of form. Vecchio aptly describes Denis's work as 'the presentation of details rather than the digestion of a finished story simply waiting to end' (2014, xiv); if you compare this with Donald Richie's description of Ozu's films as spiral narratives, stories that do not close the circle completely, but often begin 'a new if similar film in the final minutes' (Richie 1974, 161), you can see some clear resonances. For both directors, their films are marked by the rendering of oblique and unknowable symbols and imprecise endings. We are left with endless gaps, schisms and open wounds. In this way, the family in the works of Denis and Ozu are no longer the private, regulatory bodies of modern capitalist envisioning. It is inside the family unit that the renegotiation of public and private, individual and collective ideas of space and place, gender and sexuality are all undertaken in often upsetting and unresolved ways.

I will end not on the films themselves but rather two of the leading actors. In an interview, Claire Denis herself made the link between Descas and the actors of Ozu: 'I told him, "I have the feeling I'm going to work often with you, because there is something in you that is so calm, that . . . helps me to create a character with you." . . . Like Chishū Ryū was' (quoted in R. Davis 2009).

This sense of working with an actor to create one's characters and to develop a long sustainable relationship was seen in Ryū's and Ozu's long-standing collaboration. Born in France to parents from the West Indies, Alex Descas has moved from young man *J'ai pas sommeil/Can't Sleep* (1994) and *S'en fout la mort* (1990)) to husband in *Trouble Every Day*, to father in *35 rhums*. When he is not a family member in a film, he often administers care in a wide variety of ways as a doctor in both *Nénette et Boni* and *Les salauds* and a priest in *L'intrus*. He provides a nuanced, calm and fluid performance of what being French means in the cinematic works of Denis. In an interview with *Film Quarterly*, Denis stated:

> my main desire was to make it simple and solid . . . calm, since all the characters are black, and I wanted to make it very clear that they do not live like clandestines. They have real lives, they are settled, they are French. (Bíró 2009, 38)

Denis's desire to present a vision of people in a settled, stable, integrated community engaging and operating in their everyday life is important. In an interview, Descas has spoken openly about his trials as a black actor in the French film industry and praised Denis and her working practices:

> She does all this in a very beautiful way because she first films people, not their skin color or their origin. But this should be the rule and not the exception. We live in a diverse society, we should be able to find evidence of such a gaze in our cinema. (Mandelbaum 2009, translation my own)[2]

As Richie notes via his work with actors such as Ryū Chishū and Hara Setsuko, 'Ozu offered a "process of remembering, recording and inscribing what it means to be a citizen of Japan"'. Ryū, like Ozu lived and fought through the war period, they operated in the post-war Japan of grinding poverty and American occupation to then thrive in the post-occupation modern milieu. What people often forget is that the 1950s and 1960s were decades of tremendous social and cultural upheaval in Japan, from the Anpo and Miike coal-mining protests and riots to political assassinations and crises (on both the far right and the far left), together with a radical rise in social living standards, consumerism and development. Japan in this period was a complex and ever-changing environment where the family became the site of many of the changes that the society was undergoing. Although radically different, France post-1980 saw dramatic institutional, structural, financial, political and cultural changes and this movement and tension are reflected throughout Denis's works. What the works of Denis and Ozu offer the audience is a nuanced reflection of how the family is caught in the crosshairs of national development. In their films, the boundaries between father and daughter, brothers and sisters and the enduring legacies of complex pasts and the fear of unknown futures are rendered on screen.

NOTES

1. A term that focused and developed the state control of economic and social matters.
2. 'Elle fait tout cela de manière très belle parce qu'elle filme d'abord les êtres, non leur couleur de peau ou leur origine. Mais ce devrait être la règle et non l'exception. Nous vivons dans une société multiple, on devrait pouvoir retrouver l'évidence d'un tel regard dans notre cinéma.'

CITATIONS

Bergstrom, Janet. 2003. 'Opacity in the Films of Claire Denis's in *French Civilisation and its Discontents: Nationalism, Colonialism, Race*, edited by Tyler Stovall and Georges Van Den Abbeele, 69–101. Lanham, MD: Lexington Books.

Beugnet, Martine. 2004. *Claire Denis*. Manchester, NH: Manchester University Press.
Beugnet, Martine. 2008. *Cinema and Sensation: French Film and the Art of Transgression*. Edinburgh: Edinburgh University Press.
Bíró, Yvette. 2009. 'A subtle story: 35 Shots of Rum.' *Film Quarterly* 63, 2: 38–43.
Bordwell, David. 1988. *Ozu and the Poetics of Cinema*. Princeton, NJ: Princeton University Press.
Brown, William. 2017. 'Spares or Slow: Ozu and Joanna Hogg.' In *Reorienting Ozu: A Master and His Influence*, edited by J. Choi, 269–84. Oxford: Oxford University Press.
Davis, Robert. 2009. 'Interview: Claire Denis on 35 Shots of Rum.' *Daily Plastic*, March http://www.dailyplastic.com/tag/35-shots-of-rum/.
Deleuze, Gilles. 1986. *Cinema One: The Movement Image*, Translated by Hugh Tomlinson and Barbara Habberjam. Minneapolis: University of Minnesota Press.
Del Río, Elena. 2003. 'Rethinking feminist film theory: Counter-narcissistic performance in Sally Potter's Thriller.' *Quarterly Review of Film and Video* 21, no. 1: 11–24.
DiPaolo, Marc and Wayne Stein (eds). 2015. *International: Essays on the Global Influences of a Japanese Auteur*. London and New York: Bloomsbury Publishing.
Ellsworth, Elizabeth. 1997. *Teaching Positions: Difference, Pedagogy, and the Power of Address*. United Kingdom: Teachers College Press.
Galt, Rosalind. 2014. 'Claire Denis and the World Cinema of Refusal.' *SubStance* 43, 1: 96–108. http://www.jstor.org/stable/24540741.
Galt, Rosalind. 2015. 'Claire Denis's Capitalist Bastards.' *Studies in French Cinema* 15, 3: 275–93.
Geist, Kathe. 1983. 'West Looks East: The Influence of Yasujiro Ozu on Wim Wenders and Peter Handke.' *Art Journal* 43, 3: 234–9.
Gerow, Aaron. 2018. 'Ozu to Asia via Hasumi.' In *Reorienting Ozu: A Master and His Influence*, edited by J. Choi, 45–58. Oxford: Oxford University Press.
Hasumi, Shigehiko. 1997. 'Sunny Skies.' In *Ozu's Tokyo Story*, edited by David Desser and translated by Kathy Shigeta, 118–129. Cambridge: Cambridge University Press.
Hasumi, Shigehiko. 2004. 'Ozu's Angry Women.' *Rouge*. Accessed 1 March 2023. http://rouge.com.au/4/ozu_women.html.
Hasumi, Shigehiko. *Kantoku Ozu Yasujiro: Zoho ketteiban* [Director Ozu Yasujiro: expanded and definitive edition]. Tokyo: Chikuma shobo, 1983. Reprint, 1992.
Hayward, Susan. 2001. 'Claire Denis's Films and the Post-colonial Body – with special reference to Beau travail (1999).' *Studies in French Cinema* 1, 3: 159–65.
Joo, Woojeong. 2017. *The Cinema of Ozu Yasujiro: Histories of the Everyday*. Edinburgh: Edinburgh University Press.
Mandelbaum, J. 2009. 'Claire filme d'abord les êtres, non le couleur de leur peau: entretien avec Alex Descas.' *Le Monde*, 18 February: 21.
Marks, Laura. 2000. *The Skin of the Film: Intercultural Cinema, Embodiment, and the Senses*. Durham and London: Duke University Press.
McMahon, Laura. 2014. 'Beyond the human body: Claire Denis's ecologies.' *Alphaville: Journal of Film and Screen Media* 7: 94–111.
Miyao, Daisuke. 2021. 'The melodrama of Ozu: Tokyo Story and its time.' *Journal of Japanese and Korean Cinema* 13, 1: 58–79.
Murphy, Ian. 2012. 'Feeling and Form in the Films of Claire Denis.' *Jump Cut* 54. Accessed 17 March 2023. http://www.ejumpcut.org/archive/jc54.2012/IanMurphyDenis/text.html.
Nayman, Adam. 2009. 'Claire Denis Interview', *Reverse Shot: Museum of the Moving Image*, 26 June. Accessed 17 March 2023. https://reverseshot.org/interviews/entry/395/claire-denis.
Powrie, Phil. 1999. 'Heritage, History and "New Realism": French Cinema in the 1990s'. In *French Cinema in the 1990s: Continuity and Difference*, edited by Phil Powrie. Oxford: Oxford University Press.

Richie, Donald. 1974. *Ozu: His Life and Films*, Berkeley: University of California Press.
Sakamura, Ken, and S. Hasumi. 1998. 'From Behind the Camera: A New Look at the World of Director Yasujiro Ozu'. Tokyo: Tokyo University Digital Museum.
Sato, Tadao. 1977. 'From the Art of Yasujiro Ozu.' *Wide Angle* 1, 4: 44–48.
Sato, Tadao. 1982. *Currents in Japanese Cinema*. Translated by Gregory Barrett. Tokyo: Kodansha.
Schrader, Paul. 1972. *Transcendental Style in Film: Ozu, Bresson, Dreyer*. Berkeley: University of California Press.
Shaviro, Steven. 1994. *The Cinematic Body*. Minneapolis: University of Minnesota.
Taylor-Jones, K. 2018. 'Rhythm, texture, moods: Ozu Yasujiro, Claire Denis and a vision of a postcolonial aesthetic.' In *Reorienting Ozu: A Master and His Influence*, edited by J. Choi. Oxford: Oxford University Press, pp. 215–32.
Thompson, Kristin, and David Bordwell. 1976. 'Space and Narrative in the Films of Ozu.' *Screen* 17, 2: 41–73.
Troy, Eddy. 2020. 'Intersubjectivity and the cinematic thing: diasporic Being-with in Claire Denis's 35 Rhums.' *Studies in European Cinema*, Online, ahead of print, 1–16. Accessed 1 March 2023. https://www.tandfonline.com/doi/abs/10.1080/17411548.2020.1848095?journalCode=rseu20.
Vecchio, Marjorie, ed. 2014. *The Films of Claire Denis: Intimacy on the Border*. London: I. B. Tauris.
Wada-Marciano, Mitsuyo. 2018. 'A Dialogue with "Memory" in Hou Hsiao-hsien's Café Lumière (2003).' In *Reorienting Ozu: A Master and His Influence*, edited by J. Choi, 59–76. Oxford: Oxford University Press.
Willemen, Paul. 2005. 'For a comparative film studies.' *Inter-Asia Cultural Studies* 6, 1: 98–112.
Yamada Sakae. 2002. 'Ozu eiga no kimono to kodogu/Props and Kimono in the Films of Ozu.' *Cinema Dong Dong* 1: 16–18.
Yoshida, Kiju. 2003. *Ozu's Anti- Cinema*. Translated by Daisuke Miyao and Kyoko Hirano. Ann Arbor: University of Michigan Press.
Yoshimoto, Mitsuhiro. 2013. 'A future of comparative film studies.' *Inter-Asia Cultural Studies* 14, 1: 54–61.
Zhang, Yingjin. 2006. 'Comparative film studies, transnational film studies: interdisciplinarity crossmediality, and transcultural visuality in Chinese cinema.' *Journal of Chinese Cinema* 1, 1: 27–40.

CHAPTER 12

'The Stranger and the Surprise': Hospitality, Community and Coming to Our Senses in *Vendredi soir*

Jacob Hovind

'Good evening. Can I get in?' 'Yes, of course.' So goes the opening exchange between strangers Loure and Jean in Claire Denis's beguiling, sensually charged portrait of one long enchanted night's brief encounter in *Vendridi soir* (2003). Neither of them have surnames or occupations, backstories or even psychologies beyond all that's discernible in the film's unfolding present, and yet by the night's end they'll come to have meaning for one another in a way requiring none of those conventional markers of identity or recognisably shared social terrain. Two people who were apart who decide to spend even just one evening together, one asking the other to be let inside and the other immediately offering her hospitality; while the film's actual narrative doesn't amount to much more than the heady bliss of a one-night stand, Denis turns this threadbare set-up into a casually magical evocation of what we can call both a politics and an ethics, a way of being with others made possible by a certain way of choosing to be in the world.

Locked in a dense snarl of Paris traffic due to a transit worker's strike, en route to somewhere she doesn't much seem to feel like going (in more ways than one), Laure's battered little Volvo might feel like one atomising monad stuck between so many others. But on a night like this, Denis's film finds, Laure might learn instead something about the porousness of certain borders, all the ways in which the world can be let inside as opposed to remaining so seemingly fixed, so far apart, on the outside. Her sudden welcoming of Jean's stranger, a man who arrives in front of her face with no context but his request for a ride, might even become something like the fundamental gesture of what amounts to a Denisian ethical system, one whose aim is always to get closer to the world as it is rather than to remain on the outside of a world only as it's assumed to be. In *Vendridi soir*, perhaps her most superficially apolitical film and her most thrillingly alive and sensuous, Denis suggests that every ethics ultimately begins as a welcoming, one that first occurs in the realm of the senses. On the way toward other social orders and communities, toward less tyrannically fixed ways of being together, ones that might be prepared to welcome the stranger within themselves, one must first be prepared to let the world inside, with all its own quotidian strangenesses and surprises.[1]

The ethical import of Denis's cinema has found its fullest exploration by Kristin Lené Hole, in *Towards a Feminist Cinematic Ethics* (2016). Building on the thought of both Emmanuel Levinas and Denis's frequent collaborator Jean-Luc Nancy, Hole suggests that, as with each philosopher's thought, Denis's ethical vision is always 'interruptive' in the way its unfolding shatters any illusions her characters may have of their isolation or discrete apartness from otherness (2016, 12). Rather than a normative ethical agenda that might offer some prescriptive 'moral of the story', Denis's films invite their viewers into a more open-ended and less straightforwardly defined 'ethical awareness', a way of being with other people 'that stems from a particular understanding of our own subjectivity and inter-relationality' (2016, 6). Like the Levinasian encounter with the trace of the always transcendent Other via the encounter with the face, or as with Nancy's conception of Being as always 'Being-with', the ethics that emerges from Denis's work, as Hole argues, 'comes to center on a bodily encounter with otherness, which reveals our original relationality – in other words, our sense of self-sufficiency and discreteness is interrupted in every way by our relatedness to others and to the world' (2016, 12).[2]

And the way in which Hole stresses the corporeality of Denis's ethics – that the encounter with Otherness happens first in the realm of the senses as a touch or a glance – suggests that Denis's ethical subject is always primarily a body among other bodies, and that the way toward being with others lies primarily in the body's realm before it can ever find conceptualisation in the mind as a worldview, or in the social sphere as a political reality. As Hole writes of the ethical commitment inherent in Nancy's thought on 'being-with', his '"originary ethics" requires a disposition towards the world that is attentive to the sense that we *are*; that refuses the comforts of myth and identity in favour of creative newness, flux and exposure to the unmasterable world' (2016, 47, emphasis Hole's). An 'interruptive ethics of sense' that is ultimately simply a heightened feeling of being alive, in this shared world, both sensible to and prepared to welcome its phenomena and its others; remaining exposed with neither the claims to ownership nor the ideological obfuscation suggested by 'masterability' (ibid.) Thus the world is not to be preconceived as one thing or another according to any pre-existing framework (moral, political, legal). Approaching the world instead from the position of 'flux and exposure', I want to suggest, can be understood as a stance of perpetual openness; open toward the world's sensual possibilities, and also to the otherness of the people sharing the world with us. And once open to those more immediate entities, the world might even be transformable by means of an openness toward other, grander possibilities as well, other ways of being together, other kinds of human relations, other kinds of shared human community.

Being rooted in bodily experience, whatever ethical vision emerges from Denis's films remains intimately intertwined with her films' sensuality, or sensibility. Ever since the dense corporeality of *Chocolat* (1988), a film whose colonising and colonised bodies exist in some shared space comprised of equal parts fellow feeling, erotic longing and spectre of violent parasitism, Denis has carved out her own singular métier in contemporary cinema as perhaps the greatest filmmaker of the bodily life of the senses. And it is no accident that *Vendridi soir* might just be among her most sensually vivid films, one whose vision of the enchantment of the sensible life, I want to show, hides a potent ethics right in plain sight. If her films feature very little actual sex – not even one whose narrative amounts to not much more than a prelude to a one-night-stand – they nevertheless overwhelm with sensuality in the way they privilege, inspire and evoke the fundamental pleasures of sensory experience. Her cinema of the senses consistently explores both the ordinary thrills and the thrilling risks of simply being in the world as a sensory being, on that wavelength where one is both intimately in tune with the body itself and released from its isolating confines in being as receptive as possible toward all that surrounds it.

One need only think of Shane's ravenous hungers in *Trouble Every Day* (2002), ones that of course prove disastrous and self-destructive but can also erupt from the mere touch of a hotel bedspread, as he tenderly ponders the imprint left by a chambermaid's body, overwhelmed by the lingering scent of her presence. Or the way Galoup's crisis in *Beau travail* (1999) might be best described as an optical awakening to vision as an aesthetic experience; undone by the cruel, confusing, maddening sting of suddenly and really seeing what has been there all along right in front of his face, but understanding neither why he's seeing it or what it's making him feel. If he finds himself ultimately fixated on the handsome young recruit Sentain, that might just be one way of trying to control his awakening to the pleasurable possibilities of visual sensation, surrounded by all these masculine bodies meant to be nothing more than beautiful, perfect machines, yet never having really pondered what their beauty truly is and means. Scents, sights and touches in Denis's cinema can frequently overwhelm, they might even destroy one; and yet for all the ways in which the life of the senses might threaten some of her characters' assumptions about their selves' stabilities and cravings, it also has the capacity to give much more than anyone might have expected. Welcoming the world in, rather than shutting it out, might just be the first essential step on the way toward entering the ethical life. Laure's encounter with Jean in *Vendridi soir*, I ultimately argue, doesn't simply have to be a sensual poetics;

it must also be a sensible politics, a communion that also becomes the beginning of a community.

Martine Beugnet has indeed argued that Denis has crafted a 'cinema of the senses', one 'that relies, first and foremost, on the sensuous apprehension of the real, on a vivid and tactile combination of sounds and images that expands cinema's primarily visual power of evocation' (2004, 132). And it's this stress on the life of *all* the senses, not simply cinema's typical foregrounding of vision, that characterises both the formal strategies of Denis's films and the very textures of their worlds. Moreover, I'd add, Denis is as interested in awakening both her viewers' senses and her characters' senses as she is in pondering the possibilities of what comes next. If the life of the senses isn't simply privileged as an end to itself, then the question becomes, to what else might her characters be awakened when they enter into such heightened sensibility? This awakening, as suggested above, always comes with a risk, but a necessary one. Indeed, following from the logic established by Laure's own act of unquestioning hospitality in *Vendridi soir*, there's a way in which she's rendered herself wholly powerless against Jean's brooding, ruggedly handsome stranger; in getting into her cramped little car, he brings not just his own private subjective world with him, but all its potentially attendant dangers and threats; he might just as well take her life as arrive at his destination, they might end up in a hotel room in the throes of passion, or in darker places re-treading some of the same tortured cravings that Denis explored in *Trouble Every Day*'s poetics of corporeal dread.

It's worthwhile here to consider perhaps the most overt sensualist in all of Denis's cinema, the way Boni's almost polymorphously perverse teenager in *Nénette et Boni* (1996) can find some soul-stirring delight in nearly everything there is to touch, taste, smell or hear. Even his raging hormonal life, directed as it is toward the neighbourhood boulangère, seems but a youthfully misguided misplacement of his deeply felt sensory overload. When he has one especially graphic assaultive fantasy, its visions of ownership and debasement are soon transformed into abstract pulses of light, and he eventually collapses into a swoon, not from any cheaply earned libidinal satisfaction, but from the sheer overwhelming intensity of his new American-style coffee maker's intoxicating gurglings as they fill the film's soundscape. A young man who can fall in something like love with a sound – or with a touch, whether the soft fur of his pet rabbit or the luscious texture of pizza dough – might just come to stand as a key figure in Denis's cinema of the senses, one who, unlike Shane and Galoup after him, doesn't find himself destroyed by all this sensory intrusion, but rather uses the fundamental fact of his corporeal openness to find other ways of being open. 'Is it the wind that gets you so jittery?' his neighbour jokingly asks him during one especially agitated morning, though the answer is surely a resounding yes; its touch on his skin, some heightened kind of quotidian intoxication, the sheer rush of getting to be alive. 'What's the grand prize?', he asks the object of his obsessive adoration, Valeria Bruni-Tedeschi's neighbourhood boulangère, after she invites him to take part in the bakery's raffle game. 'It's right in front of your face!' she answers with a beaming smile; referring, of course, to the gift basket on the counter, but also simply to the world as it is, and maybe even the world as it could be.

And as Beugnet has powerfully argued, Boni's way of remaining always open to, always potentially intoxicated by, all that's right in front his face is but the same impulse that allows him to envision other political realities as well. Sharing with his sister a disappeared mother and a criminally ineffectual father (one, the film at least hints at, who may even have incestuously abused Nénette), Boni ultimately sees their broken family tree not as a cause for despair or resentment, but as simply an opportunity to imagine other kinds of family life. 'The erasure of the father figure', Beugnet writes, 'is coextensive with Boni's attempt at reconstructing a unit', one free from 'the spent system of values' that the traditional patriarchal father may have represented (2004, 162–3). While Nénette desperately tries to abort her unwanted child with mustard baths, unprepared to welcome it into a world without the anchor of the conventional family unit, Boni knows that the breakdown of the old is just an opportunity to make something wholly new in its place; he patiently sets up a nursery while his sister holds on to ideas that long ago stopped making sense, preparing to invent a new kind of family for messier and perhaps even more interesting human realities. Remaining sensually open to the world as it is, Denis suggests, makes Boni uniquely equipped to be politically open to worlds that could be.

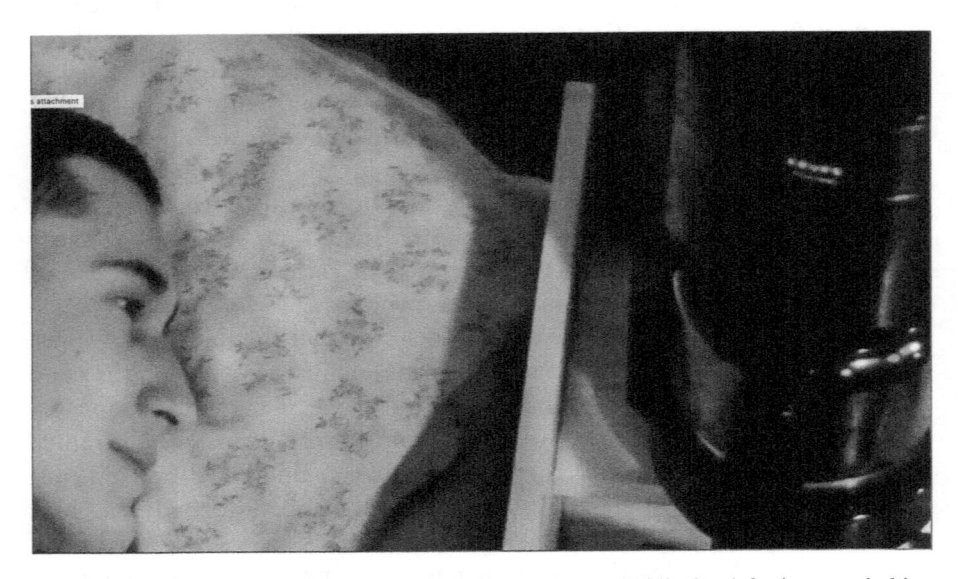

Figure 12.1 Boni's hyperactive sensory life finding an almost libidinal satisfaction even in his new coffee maker.

And what Boni's sensibility allows him to imagine can happen to families might, in *Vendridi soir*, also be possible for cities and communities as well, as the later film remains similarly driven by the tensions between the social realities of the world that Laure has been given and the one that might emerge from the opening of the life of the senses. Before her act of welcoming Jean's stranger, Denis has already delicately considered many of the ways in which modern urban living invites us to be alone, to remain shut up in the borders we let enclose us. In the film's opening ten minutes, a poetic and melancholy kind of nocturnal city symphony as Paris descends into twilight and this one magical Friday night begins, Agnès Godard (Denis's frequent collaborator as cinematographer) sends her camera floating up above the city's streetscape, pondering the buildings' myriad windows as so many gleaming, welcoming harbours from the night's cold; all these people living their unseen lives behind their curtains, each in their own private little rooms, safe but apart, untouching and untouchable.

Once Laure sets off on her eventually aborted quest through the city streets to join friends for dinner, on this last night before moving into her (never-seen) boyfriend François's apartment, all the cars clogging the streets initially seem but roving versions of those practically hermetically sealed chambers. But driving, Laure soon finds, is after all a much more public way of being alone together, as here at least no curtains hide drivers and pedestrians from one another, every wall contains its own perpetual possibility of being opened; all these fellow drivers and passengers stuck in the same frustrating situation, each of them alone with their vaguely sad visages, but performing that aloneness on some kind of shared stage. Writing on *Vendridi soir* as a distinctively feminine vision of new pleasures and possibilities engendered by its way of looking, seeing the world from the vantage point of participatory spectatorship rather than something of the detached ownership of the Levinasian 'I' untouched by the Other, Neil Archer even reads something liberatory into this idea of the traffic jam, so many lonely steel boxes all trapped, but trapped in the streets together. Rather than 'the cataclysm of an individualist and consumerist society', he argues that Denis has turned the phenomenon into the site of 'the possibility of new experiences of (inter-)subjectivity' (2008, 246). Forced to drive at such slow speeds, mostly doing little more than inching forward in fits and starts (a delicate interplay of movement and acquiescence that Godard films in one uncannily beautiful sequence, her camera trained solely on the cars' headlights and front tires, with a kind of balletic delicacy), the drivers and their passengers find themselves literally forbidden from hurtling blindly through urban modernity. All these other people in the streets who would otherwise be reduced to passing phantasms become undeniably real, as drivers are forced instead to pay attention – if they choose – to everything around them that driving has usually trained us not to pay much attention to. 'The restricting of speed', he writes, 'acts as a kind of discipline which ultimately reacquaints perception with the habitual(ised) spaces of everyday life' (2008, 251).³ Seeing with neither goal nor purpose, nor even a certain destination in mind, but simply passing through the world as it is, taking it all in, welcoming it even; a way of discovering what the boulangère knew in *Nénette et Boni*, that the grand prize isn't where you think you're trying to go, but it's already here, 'right in front of your face!'

As Laure participates in this new kind of communal dance of the aleatory, one in which whatever idea each driver may have had of 'getting there' is transformed into 'being here', one man suddenly emerges from the crowd of passers-by in the streets, a reminder that even the carless are part of the dance as well. First glimpsed simply as a darkly clad torso and a hand determinedly beating on her window as he's asking to be let in to her car, he appears to Laure as the shock of an intruder, having notably interrupted her as she was using her heating vents to dry her hair; a bit of time-saving that's also something like bringing the apartment's hermetic privacy out into the open, too alone, too little aware of the shared public sphere she's sent herself into. Quickly locking her door to maintain her privacy against this unwelcome intrusion, Laure spots the man's face again a few minutes later, as he drifts by in the passenger seat of another car, one whose driver was more willing to let the outside in. As he passes, the man gives Laure a glare that might be annoyed and accusatory if it weren't so almost bemused; as if he's trying to convey to her something of the fact that there's nothing to be so frightened of after all, especially on a night like this, when the accident of the transit strike practically demands we try to be with one another differently, that we might turn our atomising machines into their own kind of community. The spaces that seem to make us feel most alone are, after all, quite shareable, only if we choose to let them be.

His unspoken lesson is one urged quite plainly by the voice on the radio programme that Laure intermittently sets her dial to, as a woman gently urges her listeners to find a way to let compassion replace mistrust; when the city unexpectedly finds itself in crisis, what might be cause for annoyance can actually become its own kind of opportunity. 'The city is choking, everyone is exhausted' she reminds her audience. 'At times like this, we need to be charitable toward others. Try carpooling! If you see cold and weary people hitching a ride, take them part of the way with your car. Try it! I did once, it was fun!' A veritable call to political solidarity masquerading as a gentle reminder of charity, the newscaster's advice amounts, in context, to a profoundly ethical challenge, one whose ramifications extend far beyond this night's particular traffic jam. Indeed, after picking up Jean, Laure tunes the dial back to the same programme, with the voice now reminding her listeners that, tonight, 'there's no hope in sight:' 'Paris is at a standstill, and you're stuck for the evening, tonight, and tomorrow. If you've been invited to dinner, it's going to get cold.' Hospitality itself, as previously understood, seems to be at some kind of crisis point; plans made under sunnier circumstances now proving impossible, dinners awaiting their guests all over the city left to grow cold. So rather than give up on hospitality entirely, perhaps we can imagine new kinds instead to replace the old models that are no longer usable. Instead of simply reshuffling plans into the future with the same old guests, ones so familiar that they're hardly even guests in any way but the most loosely defined term, we might even find a way to make room for new guests, ones brought in from outsides that we haven't yet had to imagine.

And questions of hospitality in the broader sense seem indeed to have been on Denis's mind during the filming of *Vendridi soir*, as the same year saw the release of *Ten Minutes Older: The Cello*, one of two paired omnibus films conceived to reflect on the theme of time after the turn of the millennium.[4] Premiering, like *Vendridi soir*, at the Venice Film Festival in 2002, *Ten Minutes Older: The Cello* features contributions from the likes of Bernardo Bertolucci, Jean-Luc Godard and Jiří Menzel, with Denis's own twelve-minute segment ('Vers Nancy'), devoted to the thought of Jean-Luc Nancy, especially *L'intrus*, his 2000 essay that she would go on to adapt to feature length the following year. Set in a train carriage as it hurtles through the French countryside, the film features Nancy in dialogue with a young immigrant student, presumably of Balkan descent, as they discuss the nature of borders, national identity and intrusion. The film opens in mid-conversation, with Nancy questioning the student's unseen claim that she had come to France as a foreigner with the wish to be 'imperceptible'. 'Yes', she explains in halting French, 'I wanted to gain admittance, be here, not be the established order'. Knowing that throwing herself into the realm of visibility – readable as guest, as outsider – by the state and the status quo could quickly lead to rejection and deportation, she chose instead the cloak of invisibility by means of assimilation as a kind of way of remaining outside the law while still within that law's realms; adapting herself to the status quo rather than existing so clearly apart from it.

In response to her politics of subterfuge, the conversation turns to Nancy's own poetics of intrusion, one that recognises 'the need to welcome the foreigner', and 'to normalize, to standardize this welcome'. Explaining that his thought on the matter is directed toward those whom the student identifies as 'the host', Nancy questions a welcome that 'must lead to assimilation for foreigners and immigrants' ('along with the American concept of "the melting pot"'). Indeed, such a welcome can only be a kind of poisoned gift, one that pretends to celebrate what is usually erroneously called 'diversity', only so long as otherness acquiesces to the sameness of the status quo. Difference is welcome here, but only if you cease to be too different, goes the running logic of the typical liberal bromides of multiculturalism. But, he goes on, when increasingly diverse societies no longer even have a shared centre of expected assimilation (only ones that are ideologically enforced, rather than grounded in actual fact), we need instead new models of welcoming and living with difference, ones where what's heterogenous can enter into 'the homogeneous zone, and hope, at the same time, to retain what we call an identity'. This identity, while not adapting itself to the demands of assimilation and integration (and thus obliterating itself in the process via that process of imperceptibility), should also 'not necessarily be seen as intrusive in this homogeneity'. A hospitality, a welcoming, can provide harbour for otherness while still inviting the other to maintain its own otherness; a homogeneity can make a space for what is heterogenous, an outside that's able to live on the inside.

To return to the imagery of the radio announcer's plea in *Vendridi soir*, it's as if Nancy is suggesting that, in this age of unprecedented human flow and displacement, when people by the millions are on the move more than ever before and only moving farther and more quickly, the old dinner plans have to be cancelled. The cosy domestic productions of some liberal fantasy of a culturally and linguistically homogeneous society (not to mention the reactionary ideals of ethnonationalism) have to be allowed to grow cold while we respond to the accidents and upheavals of the actual present in order to make new, more viable plans instead. 'The city is choking', she'd reminded her listeners, 'everyone is exhausted'. And what holds true for Paris during a transit strike might just be a microcosmic vision of a certain state of the global condition in the twenty-first century. As unprecedented heatwaves and floods shatter records all over the world, as Arctic ice loss rapidly grows and sea levels rise and whole communities experience sudden and total destruction, as wildfires ravage vast swaths of land, as the already ongoing refugee crisis becomes ever more linked to these cataclysmic natural disasters, as nativist and nationalist tribalisms emerge in response to both increased human migration and the exacerbation of social iniquities driven by the (still) ongoing Covid-19 pandemic, all as the globe hurtles to 2 degrees Celsius of warming; it seems that those in the Global North especially, those raised on the dreams of that self-same homogeneity discussed by Nancy, need to scrap their dinner plans and come up with workable alternatives.

'If you see cold and weary people hitching a ride, take them part of the way with your car', is the radio announcer's suggestion, and it seems Denis and Nancy both hope her plea reaches as wide an audience as possible. It's a plea that Laure, at least, suddenly decides to embrace, with all its attendant possibilities, both its risks and its potentials for pleasure. Jean may emerge out of the night from the start as a figure simmering with the potential of sexual interest (indeed, as he appears, Denis cuts to another female driver as she primps herself, presumably in anticipation of his arrival), but he's also fundamentally simply a neighbour, an other from the outside, one of these 'cold and weary people' who need to be welcomed on the inside.

'Whenever there's intrusion', Nancy explains in the short film, 'there's disorder, there's turmoil, and there's threat.' That threat may entail a necessary vulnerability, an exposedness, but better that than the 'stone-like' identity that refuses the possibility of intrusion and change at all. 'That sounds like a call to me', the student finally muses after Nancy's reflections, demonstrating that what had seemed like a philosophising monologue is but one part of a conversation, ideas that would mean very little unless there's always an interlocutor prepared to receive them and to then do something with them. 'It seems to say', she says of that call, '"Come. Come, foreigner, but when I least expect it. Surprise me!"' Nancy agrees with her interpretation, though adding the slight emendation that a true surprise can't be asked of the stranger, can be neither planned nor expected. As he writes in 'Being Singular Plural', in language echoing Levinas's own ideas regarding the vulnerable exposedness of the self in the face of Otherness, 'the essence of Being is the shock of the instant. Each time, "Being" is always an instance of Being (a lash, blow, beating, shock, knock, an encounter, an access')' (2000, 33). If Being is truly always inexorably comprised of its attendant 'with', then Being maintains itself as the perpetual openness toward the unexpected intrusion, marked by the exposure that 'with' always inherently entails.[5] A true way of maintaining welcomeness to the intruder, the foreigner and the stranger, then, might amount to a condition of perpetual openness; neither inviting nor challenging the stranger to come, but simply being prepared, all the time, for whenever it is that they do end up arriving.

And within Denis's own cinema, Laure, like Boni before her, becomes readable as a model of how we can come to live with the fact of intrusion, how we might live with openness as a perpetual condition. Inspired as she is by the radio host's challenge to open her doors, Laure learns what it means to welcome the stranger and the surprise into herself and her access to the world, without having to settle into the false comforts of easily held assumptions about what's allowed in and what's kept out. Neil Archer, in his sensitive exploration of how *Vendridi soir* invites such radically new possibilities for being in the world (as spectator, as participant), curiously raises the questions of the film's ethical vision only vis-à-vis Laure and Jean's encounter as an adulterous 'betrayal' (2008, 257) of the unseen François. Pointing out how little interest the film seems to have in Laure's ethics regarding her romantic partner, Archer argues that this is only because 'these ethics need to be considered within the film's exploration of Laure not so much as a "real" being, but as the identificatory figure through which the play of feminine cinematic pleasure, experienced as a parenthesis in social reality, can take place' (2008, 256). Any potential ethical weight of her potential betrayal (though we ultimately know very little about her relationship with François, practically nothing) becomes itself unnecessary to contemplate if her Friday night is readable only as 'a personal fantasy' (ibid.). I'd argue, on the other hand, that there's no reason to imagine that Laure and Jean's experience isn't terribly real, and that whatever ethical misstep occurs in relation to off-screen romantic ties, the ethical power of what unfolds on-screen is where Denis's real interest lies. François is, after all, largely reduced to a key chain on which he has handwritten 'Chez nous', glimpsed as Laure was packing up her apartment at the film's beginning, a message that might be read equally as a tender love note and a potentially suffocating reminder of everything she's about to lose. And aside from such fixed ties and all their impositions of moral limits and experiential borders, on this night at least, Laure remains interested only in the unanticipated, the unnamed, the unplanned; choosing to embrace the latter with her own kind of ethical intensity while the former waits to be dealt with in the morning.

Two key moments shortly before Jean's sudden intrusion, before his emergence from anonymity and strangeness into facticity and proximity, provide some hint as to just how and why Denis suggests that Laure's so prepared to heed the radio announcer's call. After her first failure of welcoming, and before she's realised that the dinner plans she has with friends will have to be cancelled, she gets out of her car to telephone her fiancé François, into whose apartment she's moving the following day. While no real anxiety about that impending move has been clearly articulated, a certain sense of something at least like ambivalence had been telegraphed in the film's opening sequence, as Laure finished packing up the apartment that she alone had called home. As she busies herself making last-minute decisions about the few remaining items, she picks up and tries on a silky red skirt with a seductively high slit up its side. Pondering in the mirror how it still looks on her, her hands caressing the fabric's texture as she determines what it does to her legs, to her hips, she quietly whispers to herself 'Shall I keep it?' After a hushed answer in the affirmative, she collapses on her unmade bed, a deep sigh as she gazes around this space that was up until this point so intimately hers and now will be someone else's. 'I'll keep you', she tenderly tells the skirt, before taking it off and gently folding it up to be placed in a box.

A seemingly throwaway moment, but one littered with all the indecision, and second-guessing and uncertainty and existential exhaustion that seem to be plaguing Laure on the eve of this enormous change. And back in the traffic jam's present, as she leaves a message for François, she stumbles while trying to convey her excitement about moving into what she at first calls 'your place': 'Our place, I mean. I have to get used to that.' Her own private apartment now packed up in boxes, in various states of abandonment or transition and not yet settled into the realm of her and François's 'our', Laure is as if cast adrift for one night; a way of being with neither socially conferred identity nor even a private place to call home, suddenly cast adrift in the world as it is, that world of Nancy's brought into existence by so many singularly plural beings together.[6]

Shortly afterwards, immediately after that previously mentioned balletic sequence of headlights and bumpers as all these drivers and passengers participate on the world's stage with one another, and just two shots before Jean's sudden arrival out of the dark, Godard's camera slowly pans over a neon sign in a shop window, a giant pair of neon blue eyeglasses. While presumably from Laure's point of view, as her boredom and exhaustion behind the wheel leave her with little to do but ponder the world around her, the shot is strikingly without context or motivation; like Nancy's stranger, it's an almost shocking intrusion into what had been a delicate nocturne built of so many faces and car parts, bodies and shells. The eyeglasses playfully become both premonition and wake-up call, something like a statement of purpose for Laure as her night's right on the verge of an enormous and enormously unanticipated change: don't just let all this world around you inertly be, but actually look at it. Pay attention, and in doing so, find a way to let it all in.

It's surely not too large a leap to suggest that the appearance of the eyeglasses and their command to pay attention, just as much as the radio announcer's call to hospitality, help prepare Laure for Jean's arrival. As Laure welcomes him into her car without question, their relationship from the start becomes one navigated in the realm of the bodily senses. With none of the usual comforts and proprieties of getting-to-know-you chitchat, he soon relaxes the passenger seat to make himself comfortable, as Laure takes his presence in via an unhurried collection of sense impressions. Pondering the look of his relaxed face as he rests with his eyes closed, taking in the way he rubs his neck with his hand, as if wondering what such a touch might feel like; later, she even in makes a point of deeply inhaling his exhaled cigarette smoke. As with the Levinasian

Figure 12.2 Laure's secret smile as she inhales the stranger's cigarette smoke pervading her car's newly opened space.

encounter with the Other, or Nancy's arrival of the stranger within the realm of homogeneity, there's no need to ask questions, to make the intruding face conform to this pre-established identity or that one, but simply the command that he be welcomed as he is, as a corporeal being first and foremost. 'The nudity of the face', Levinas writes in 'The Trace of the Other', 'is a destitution without any cultural ornament, an absolution – a detaching in the very midst of production' (1969, 352). Without identity, with no knowledge of his backstory, or even his destination ('I didn't hear where you want to go', Laure offers. 'Leave me where you want'), Jean simply is, the arrival of his own access to the world into Laure's; and his intrusion into her car, into her night, into her life, becomes the coming into being of a shared world between them.

Discussing her writing process of *Nénette et Boni*, Claire Denis described to an interviewer how she tried to do so that, in imagining and bringing to life the film's place and its people, its world's textures and its various sounds and feelings, she was becoming 'impregnated with fragments of the world' (quoted in Beugnet 2004, 148). Filmmaking as openness and receptivity, welcoming the world, any of its accidental or aleatory fragments, to the point of then being able to give birth in turn to the world from the site of the self that's welcomed it in; a perfectly Nancyean model of what he describes as singular selves as 'access' points to the world, the latter of which is brought into existence by the comingling of so many of the former with one another. And indeed, this act of creation, of bringing the world into existence by sharing our mutual entry points into it with those of others, is for Nancy ultimately an act of curiosity: 'We are interested in the sense of being intrigued by the ever-renewed alterity of the origin, and, if I may so, in the sense of having an affair with it' (2000, 20). While Denis describes this act, on her own level of creation, as an act of impregnation, Nancy's rhetoric of the affair is of course perhaps more appropriate to Laure's experience.

Her hospitality, both at the level of the senses and at the level of community, having learned the paired lessons of those neon eyeglasses and the radio announcer, amounts to a way of being in love with the world. It's the kind of love that Levinas knew lies at the ground of the ethical attitude, that nonnormative 'ethical awareness' described by Hole in her account of Denis's own ethical worldview. Rather than being in the world as a matter of utility or propriety, enjoyment becomes, for Levinas, the primary means by which one meaningfully inhabits the world, and feels at home enough to be prepared for the arrival of otherness: 'We live from "good soup", air, light, spectacles, work, ideas, sleep, etc.', he writes in *Totality and Infinity* (1969, 110). And such 'enjoyment' becomes 'the ultimate consciousness of all the contents that fill my life – it embraces them' (1969, 111). Without such nourishment and enjoyment, one would remain trapped in the logic of ownership and utility, never capable of welcoming otherness because always only able to turn otherness into more of the same. But when well-nourished by the life of the senses, on the other hand, one exists in a state of satiety, a contentedness that doesn't need anything more than what's already given it sustenance and pleasure, and so otherness can arrive as something disruptive and transformative rather than another thing to be incorporated. The world – a man's touch, a traffic jam's impromptu kind of community, an invitation to look a bit more carefully – can even be marvelled at, rather than simply taken as more of the same.

Such a state, Levinas writes, 'is the *love of life*, a pre-established harmony with what is yet to come to us' (1969, 145, emphasis Levinas's). Like that train hurtling toward some uncertain future, but perhaps a more hospitable and happily heterogenous one, in 'Vers Nancy', Levinas's love of life finds enjoyment in what is a precondition to welcoming anything on the horizon that might be possible. Such a train's ideal kind of passenger might be Laure herself on this singular night of transition, with no home in the sense of private property to really call her own, but simply relishing all the delights of being at home in the world as such. And as her night with Jean does indeed end up unfolding as a blissful (and blissfully temporary) erotics, it's also the most intimate kind of model of a globally significant ethics that haunts Denis's entire oeuvre, one so concerned as it is with all the ways bodies exist with other bodies. From the life of the senses to the touch of a stranger to a kind of community on its way to becoming, being prepared simply to look, to welcome, to remain open, to be alive, to be with.

NOTES

1. Describing Denis's relationship with the idea of being 'political' filmmaker, Judith Mayne points out that Denis 'resists the notion of any kind of "political" message in her work', quoting the filmmaker as having told an interviewer that 'films are always political, whether we want them to be or not' (2005, 30). Even an erotics, for Denis, is always also a politics.
2. On the 'originary' nature of this relationality, see, for instance, Jean-Luc Nancy's *Being Singular Plural*, where he finds coexistence at the very ground of Being's being in the world, the latter of which only emerges from so many mutually constitutive singularities always being brought into existence via their plurality: 'if Being is being-with, then it is, in its being-with, the "with" that constitutes Being; the with is not simply an addition' (2000, 30). For Levinas, similarly, while being as and in the constricted ipseity of the 'I' allows one to feel 'at home with myself in the world' (1969, 33), the resulting interiority, with neither openness nor precarity, becomes only a way of refusing or ceasing to 'participate' in the world, whereby participation would mean 'to have an unfold one's own being without at any point losing contact with the other' (1969, 61). While one can enjoy the world by simply seizing ownership of it as an 'I', 'a meaningful world is a world in which there is the Other through whom the world of my enjoyment becomes a theme having a signification' (1969, 209). For both thinkers, then, the stance of openness becomes a way of making a world that is more than there, but that, as a shared project and

commitment, as something more than a merely onanistic projection or plaything, becomes meaningful and imbued with significance.
3. See also Judith Mayne's extended reading, in *Claire Denis*, of *Vendridi soir* as an awakening to presence and possibility: 'The space of her car becomes an enclosure, a protection, against the potential anxiety of changing one's way of life; yet it is also a very new kind of space, one that allows Laure to navigate the public sphere of Paris in a radically different way' (2005, 119).
4. *Ten Minutes Older: The Trumpet*, with contributions from filmmakers such as Aki Kaurismäki and Spike Lee, as well as Wim Wenders and Jim Jarmusch, two figures Denis had notably worked with as assistant director early in her career, had premiered earlier in the year at the Cannes Film Festival. The project was conceived by the producer Nicolas McClintock as a reflection on time at the turn of the millennium.
5. Here we may also think of Jacques Derrida's conceptions of radical hospitality as a way of welcoming the guest such that even conventional notions of guest and host are entirely dismantled in the very same gesture: 'Unconditional hospitality implies that you don't ask the other, the newcomer, the guest to give anything back, or even to identify himself or herself. Even if the other deprives you of your mastery or your home, you have to accept this. It is terrible to accept this, but that is the condition of unconditional hospitality: that you give up the mastery of your space, your home, your nation. It is unbearable. If, however, there is pure hospitality, it should be pushed to this extreme' (1998, 71).
6. See also Elizabeth Newton's 'The Phenomenology of Desire', as an account of Laure's night as one of phenomenological reduction, a heightening of the senses in the present made possible by a bracketing 'of her habituated modes of existence' (2008, 27).

CITATIONS

Archer, Neil. 2008. 'Sex, the City and the Cinematic: The Possibilities of Female Spectatorship in Claire Denis's Vendridi soir.' *French Forum* 33, 1–2 (Winter/Spring): 245–60.
Beugnet, Martine. 2004. *Claire Denis*. Manchester: Manchester University Press.
Derrida, Jacques. 1998. 'Hospitality, Justice, and Responsibility: A Conversation with Jacques Derrida.' In *Questioning Ethics: Contemporary Debates in Philosophy*, edited by Richard Kearney and Mark Dooley. London: Routledge.
Hole, Kristin Lené. 2016. *Towards a Feminist Cinematic Ethics: Claire Denis, Emmanuel Levinas and Jean-Luc Nancy*. Edinburgh: Edinburgh University Press.
Levinas, Emmanuel. 1969. *Totality and Infinity: An Essay on Interiority*. Trans. Alphonso Lingis. Pittsburgh: Duquesne University Press.
Mayne, Judith. 2005. *Claire Denis*. Urbana, IL: University of Illinois Press.
Nancy, Jean-Luc. 2000. *Being Singular Plural*. Trans. Robert D. Richardson and Anne E. O'Byrne. Stanford: Stanford University Press.
Newton, Elizabeth. 2008. 'The Phenomenology of Desire: Claire Denis's *Vendridi soir* (2002).' *Studies in French Cinema* 8, 1: 17–28.

CHAPTER 13

Claire Denis's *Beaux Familles*

Daniel Dufournaud

For all its unsettling scenes, Claire Denis's *High Life* (2018) begins and ends in tender places. It opens with Monte (Robert Pattinson) whispering 'Willow', his infant daughter's name, over the radio in order to calm her down while he fixes their spaceship, and it closes with Monte and a teenaged Willow (Jessie Ross) holding hands as they hurtle towards a black hole and possibly their death. As her name implies, Willow figures the force of nature's stubborn growth amid inauspicious circumstances. Conceived onboard the ship carrying death row inmates from Earth, she owes her life to the fanatical obsessiveness of the ship's doctor, Dibs (Juliette Binoche). Yet Willow's growth and maturation imbue the film with a redeeming energy. She softens Monte by the end of the film – a remarkable achievement given the violence and cruelty in the flashback scenes that preoccupy much of the film. *High Life* can be profitably read as an allegory for the exploitation of the human body and nature by science, an allegory that has the bond between father and daughter symbolise the power of human relationships to transcend cold, compassionless forms of reason.

If *High Life*'s outer-space setting and English-language dialogue make it unlike any other film in Denis's oeuvre, the attention it devotes to Willow and Monte's relationship exhibits Denis's abiding interest in kinship, one spanning her entire career, which is now in its fifth decade after the release of *Both Sides of the Blade* (2022) and *Stars at Noon* (2022). Denis's aesthetic itinerancy can make this through-line difficult to perceive. Her adaptability has taken her from Africa to Europe, yielding earnest portraits of former French colonies as well as films that belong to such genres as horror, science fiction and romantic comedy. Yet Denis grounds her generically dissimilar films in a stable series of themes and motifs. Her recurrent focus on sexuality and the body has attracted a great deal of critical attention, but no less central to her work are the social bonds that constitute a family, as well as the political and economic sources of family dysfunction. Denis's films often coalesce around a family, or a series of families – be they families bound by blood ties or symbolic families in which kith provides the basis for intimacy.

No account of Denis's work is complete, then, without a thorough exposition of the figure of the family in her films. Although there is precedent for bringing critical attention to bear on the family in Denis's corpus, critics have only pursued this line of thinking to a limited extent, and Denis's steady output over the years further limits the scope of their work. Judith Mayne points out that 'virtually all of Denis's films demonstrate a preoccupation with kinship, with family ties and, more often, with what takes the place of family ties' (2005, xii). However, Mayne expands only on the sibling relationships at the core of *US Go Home* (1994) and *Nénette et Boni* (1996), and she penned her comment at a time when Denis had yet to make *35 rhums* (2008), *White Material* (2009), and *Bastards* (2013), three films in which the sustenance or disintegration of the family is a principal focus. Mia Carter echoes Mayne in contending that the 'families in Denis [*sic*] metropolitan films can be interpreted as symbolic representations of the democratic state' (2006, 71). Carter, though, subordinates this point to an examination of 'scopic authority' in Denis's work (71) – authority, Carter argues, that undermines the gazing subject's power-laden relation to the object of the gaze and instead fosters sympathy between filmgoers and characters. With the benefit of more Denis films to put in conversation, Catherine Wheatley 'attempts to provide a corrective to the marginalisation of family within the writing that surrounds Denis's films' (2014, 64). Yet Wheatley's inquiry ultimately leads her away from the political and economic dimensions of the worlds that Denis recreates on-screen; Wheatley concludes that an 'examination of family and kinship allows us to zoom in from a wide-angle vision of large-scale politics to the close-up intimacy of personal relationships' (74).

By contrast, this chapter argues that the private family functions in Denis's films as a site in which impersonal political and economic forces unfold on intimate terrain. In some of Denis's films, these forces are sources of dysfunction within the family, and in others, they find symbolic expression in the relational dynamics between family members. In both cases, the figure of the family does not, *pace* Wheatley, allow viewers to 'zoom in' from supra-individual issues, as though it embodied the private sphere insulated from the public sphere, so much as it suggests that the boundary between private and public is, at best, porous and, at worst, non-existent.

Denis's treatment of the family as an institution shaped and/or unsettled by large-scale forces captures the core idea of philosopher Jean-Luc Nancy's work – the idea that nothing exists without touching something else, without coexisting with alterity. Nancy and Denis are frequent interlocutors, not only in interview format but also as mutual sources of inspiration.[1] Denis's *L'intrus* (2004) bears the same title as one of Nancy's essays. In the film, Denis weaves a story about a father's estrangement from his sons into an examination of multiple forms of intrusion and strangeness, from illegal border crossings to the father's heart transplant enabled by a market of unethically sourced organs. Similarly, in his essay Nancy takes his own experience of receiving a heart transplant as an opportunity to consider the paradoxical strangeness at the heart of identity. Nancy concludes that 'the truth of the subject is its exteriority and excessivity: its infinite exposition. [. . .] The *intrus* is no other than me, my self; none other than man himself' (2002, 13). The medical intervention that prolonged Nancy's life enacts the idea that one's identity takes shape according to a principle of intrusion; the self is no less an opening onto otherness than a closure.

This idea aligns with Nancy's political philosophy. In *Being Singular Plural*, Nancy contends:

> Nothing exists that is 'pure', that does not come into contact with the other, [. . .] because touch alone exposes the limits at which identities or ipseities can *distinguish themselves* from one another, with one another, between one another, from among one another. (2000, 156)

Nancy inverts the Heideggerian schema that privileges the individual experience of 'being' (*Dasein*) over the social experience of 'being-with' (*Mitsein*). Because touching is a connection that implies both separation and proximity, amplifying rather than muting difference, it carries symbolic heft in Nancy's work. As Anne O'Byrne explains, whereas most political philosophy and psychoanalytic theory lay stress on separation, be it the separation of the private from the public sphere or the separation from the maternal body that establishes selfhood, Nancy emphasises touching as the condition of both community and particularisation across the entire spectrum of human sociality, from caressing to intercultural exchange (O'Byrne 2002, 171). For Nancy, one becomes singular only through contact with others.[2]

While critics have pointed out the resonance between Nancy's philosophy and Denis's films, no one has emphasised the figure of the family in Denis's films as a site in which this overlap finds dramatic expression.[3] For Nancy, attempts to disavow the foundational predicament of being-with, the inextinguishable strangeness touching the familiar, can lead to violence in the service of an abstract notion of oneness or purity (such as nativists defending themselves and their nations against foreign elements), and in many of Denis's films, the family is a social arena where the illusion of oneness or purity, as well as the concomitant force of propriety and enforced loyalty, can likewise occasion harsh disavowals of alterity. Denis treats the family as a social enclosure always opening onto difference – a site implicated in bodies touching, private and public touching, coloniser and colonised touching, and desire and cultural

233

taboo touching. As these couplings suggest, touching rarely occurs without power imbalances reframing the strangeness at the heart of identity as an abject threat. Denis's families often exhibit the consequences that arise when inequality or discrimination mediates contact between family members or between the family and the outside world.

The present chapter fleshes out this argument by examining six of Denis's films. Instead of following Denis's recommendation that her first three feature films be viewed as a 'trilogy' (Reid 1996), the following sections divide her films according to setting, which carries special organising power due to its association with different political dispensations and social realities. To that end, the next section investigates her films set outside France: *Chocolat* (1989), *White Material* (2009), and *Beau travail* (1999). The third section turns to her films set in France: *J'ai pas sommeil* (1994), *35 rhums* (2008) and *Bastards* (2013). Given that *Nénette et Boni* arguably deals more explicitly with family dynamics than any other Denis film, its absence from this list may seem a glaring exclusion. Yet the point of this chapter to illuminate the less obvious places in Denis's corpus where her abiding focus on families holds significant political, and thus meta-familial, weight. As this essay reveals, interrogating the vicissitudes of family life in most, if not all, of Denis's films gets at the heart of these films' political messages.

FAMILY IN *CHOCOLAT*, *WHITE MATERIAL* AND *BEAU TRAVAIL*

The three films examined in this section feature either a literal or symbolic family comprised of Europeans living and working in French colonial or postcolonial outposts. Setting gives each film a great deal of political weight, reminding viewers of the barbarism of the French colonial regime. With her languorous shots and minimalist dialogue, Denis uses the figure of the family to ground each film's ideological concerns in dramas of everyday life. While the figure of the family tends to embody the force of rootedness and tradition, Denis's families mirror, extend or metonymically encapsulate the abstract tensions and crises that constitute the political terrain of each film. The central families in these three films are shot through with feelings of alienation and repressed desire, and their efforts to sustain order hurtle them towards dysfunction, disclosing the oppressiveness lying beneath veneers of propriety.

Chocolat, Denis's most autobiographical film, captures this instability. Although the main narrative of the film unfolds as one long flashback from the perspective of France Dalens (Mireille Perrier), the induction scene signals the film's exploration of thematic antinomies. France, whose very name bespeaks a combination of privilege and alienation, has returned to Cameroon, where she grew up while her father served as a colonial administrator in the 1950s. The opening shot frames a Black father and his son cavorting in the ocean before a long pan reveals France watching them play. The formal flourish aligns Denis's directorial eye with France's gaze, thereby foregrounding the family as the film's main object of cinematic inquiry.

In coupling the intimacy of kinship with the wistful gaze of the outsider, the opening shot frames the family as a locus where the familiar and the strange meet. Affirming this point is the image that prompts France's recollections; moments after staring at the father–son duo, she accepts a ride into town from the older man, and she sits in the back watching the boy blithely enjoying his father's company. In France's memory, this image finds its double in a moment shared not between her and her father but between her and Protée (Isaach de Bankolé), the Dalens' Cameroonian servant and France's constant companion. Conversely, the overlap between the family and the outsider finds confirmation in the final scene of the film: the father giving France a ride reveals that he is not a native Cameroonian but an African American who decided to return to his ancestral homeland and now feels a sense of unbelonging.

Denis, then, establishes a distinction between innocence and experience, associating the untroubled experience of family life with childhood and the weight of sacrifice and disappointment with adulthood. In France's memory, Protée spends more time with her than her parents; he is arguably a bigger part of her domestic life than her father, Marc (François Cluzet), and her mother, Aimée (Giulia Boschi). On trips into town, France (Cécile Ducasse) and Protée sit in the back of the truck together, as if they are equals within the hierarchised colonial society. He also takes her for walks around the family farm, watches her eat and teaches her words from his indigenous language. Illustrating Nancy's point that communication distinguishes subjects as much as it connects them on equal footing, France displays a genuine openness to the native Cameroonians employed by the Dalens. This form of sociability unmediated by stereotype leads Adam Muller to argue that France serves as an 'embodiment [. . .] of a cosmopolitan ideal', a figure of moral purity who treats others with respect and dignity, no matter their skin tone or cultural practices (2006, 741).

Yet the circumstances of France and Protée's relationship underscore her unique position within her powerful family. Marc and Aimée, inured to the inequality created by French colonialism, leverage their authority to outsource the daily responsibility of caring for France to Protée. France's age-related naiveté renders her incapable of perceiving the social barriers dividing Europeans from Africans. She cannot fully grasp the social hierarchy that frames her relationship with Protée, to say nothing of the colonial history of exploitation and dispossession.

Furthermore, part of what allows France to embody a morally upright position is her prepubescent freedom from the throes of sexual desire. The political situation in Cameroon has generated feelings of suspicion and hatred on both ends of the Africa–Europe divide, and this tension inflects how the characters pursue their desires. France is too young to question the strength of her parents' marriage; she is incapable therefore of understanding the temptations that threaten to pull her family apart. Unlike France and Protée, who frequently communicate, Marc and Aimée only exhibit a *pro forma* togetherness. They share few moments of genuine tenderness. In one scene, an inebriated Marc sings for one of his servants, and his reluctance to name his wife as his better half suggests a loveless marriage. Later, a visitor to the family's farm intimates that he and Marc have shared a moment of sexual intimacy – a potentially threatening revelation, given Marc's professional commitment to sustaining heteropatriarchal norms.

Aimée struggles with a similar tension between the standards of propriety and the pull of desire. She labours to maintain order on the farm while Marc is away and embodies the figure of the dutiful wife when he returns. Through her growing dissatisfaction, she comes to fetishise Protée. In one shot near the end of the film, Protée enters Aimée's room, and in the corner of the frame, she sits with her knees pressed to her chest. She reaches out to touch him, as if to establish a connection with him that has nothing to do with their respective social positions (Figure 13.1). Yet Protée responds in anger, aggressively forcing Aimée to her feet, as though restoring her to a standing position would compel her to realise that they cannot engage in any form of passionate, politically uncontaminated intimacy. This exchange embarrasses Aimée, causing her, subsequently, to wield her power and have Protée removed from the house, a selfish act that separates France from her closest friend on the farm.

Figure 13.1   Aimée touches Protée's leg.

Muller contends that Aimée's 'attempt to seduce Protée is presented to us as an act of self-abasement, her subsequent abjection following his refusal signifying, among other things, her failure to accept him as similarly human' (2006, 745). Yet these 'other things' are crucial to understanding how Denis leverages the figure of the family to dramatise the social dysfunction generated by colonialism. Aimée's attraction to Protée is born of a complex set of circumstances; while partly a form of dehumanising objectification, it also issues from a more fundamental drive to escape her perennial disappointment as the wife of an absentee husband. If she seeks in the romanticised otherness of Protée an end to her suffering, then her behaviour is bound up with the pressure she feels as a member of a family with a great deal of power in colonial Cameroon. In *Chocolat*, then, the family functions as a site in which the social tensions associated with French colonialism find ostensibly non-political expression.

White Material is a natural companion piece to *Chocolat*, given that it centres on a French family living in an unnamed African country amid a violent revolution. Like *Chocolat*, *White Material* shuttles between present and past. The opening series of shots frame the family home plundered and burning. The film then jumps back in time, revealing Maria Vial (Isabelle Huppert) alone on a dirt road, a worried look on her face. Maria is the obdurate administrator of a coffee plantation that she refuses to abandon, even though the threat of violence is closing in on her and her family. Through this opening juxtaposition – a domestic space in ruins with an improvident matriarch committed to remaining on her plantation – Denis locates political crisis in the family.

As the film unfolds, scenes depicting a murderous rebel army, mostly composed of uniformless child soldiers, are intercut with scenes capturing the frayed relationships within Maria's family. This narrative trajectory gives viewers cause to read the lies, silences and failures of communication within the Vial family as symptoms of the precarious political situation in which settler–native coexistence no longer seems possible. When Maria finds a severed goat's head at the fringes of the plantation, a warning from the rebels, she buries it, as if by instinct, instead of sharing the news with her ex-husband, André (Christopher Lambert). And as Maria struggles to hire new workers to replace those fleeing the plantation, André is in town negotiating a deal to sell the land to a politician in exchange for safe passage to the border. Compounding André's deceitful, if ultimately clear-eyed, behaviour is the fact that his father, Henri (Michel Subor), intimated to Maria that he would make her the official proprietor of the plantation. This scheming, leaving Maria powerless over the land she fights desperately to keep, sets the stage for the final scene of the film, in which Maria kills Henri after discovering the burned corpse of her son, Manuel (Nicolas Duvauchelle).

Manuel's demise is the film's most dramatic case study of the relationship between political conflict and the breakdown of communication within the family. Denis presents Manuel as a languid teenager with a boyish desire for belonging. He first appears in the film as Maria's indolent son whom she implores to get out of bed, her entreaties seeming to have no effect on him. If, according to Nancy, communication is the condition of individual distinction, then Manuel's silent, passive behaviour at the beginning of the film indicates self-estrangement. The communicational impasse between mother and son is partly attributable to the alienation Manuel feels as an outsider within his home country. Inextricably tied to France by virtue of his family and skin tone but born in the unnamed African country, Manuel can only attain a fleeting sense of belonging by turning on his family, descending into madness and joining the rebel army in a fit of anarchist glee.[4]

Manuel's crazed self-expression constitutes a kind of nihilistic death drive, suggesting that the family is for him a source of unhappiness and repression. In the scene marking his radical transformation, Manuel evokes the spirit of one of cinema's classic misfits, Robert De Niro's Travis Bickle from *Taxi Driver* (or perhaps Vincent Cassel's Vinz from *La haine*), and shaves his head in the bathroom before terrorising the family's maid. He then becomes an agent of chaos, helping the child soldiers raid his family's plantation. The very army that poses a threat to his family's safety is the only outlet for Manuel's need to belong. A brief shot revealing the dead body of André conveys the consequences of Manuel's transformation most forcefully. In the figure of Maria's unhinged son, Denis presents a frighteningly surreal exhibit of the pathologies induced in the human representatives of French imperialism.

Ironically, Maria's struggle to save her home serves as a foil to Manuel's betrayal while at the same time highlighting the untenable position of the Vial family. Stuck in town as her family compound goes to pieces, she implores strangers for a ride 'home', a display of desperation that ends with her embracing a Black woman and crying into this stranger's shoulder (Figure 13.2). The woman's sympathy is striking for its contrast with both the coldness characterising the relationships in the Vial family and the Manichean racial strife that has engulfed a nation attempting to purge itself of French influence. As everything Maria associates with the idea of home, her family, her business and her country is coming apart at the seams, the embrace between the two women enacts the foundational openness that Nancy has in mind when he contends that 'coexistence [. . .] forms the essence and the structure of the world' (2000, 44). With Maria no longer grounded to a stable form of existence, such interpersonal contact represents nothing more – and nothing less – than raw human compassion. The women do not constitute a symbolic family; unlike the Vials, they are neither allied against a common enemy nor do they benefit from a common source of inequality. Rather, they are paradoxically joined by the fact that they share nothing.

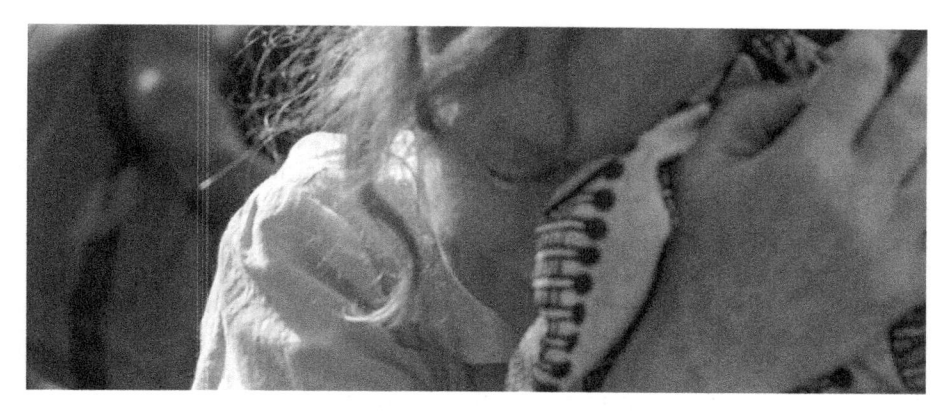

Figure 13.2   Maria embraces a stranger.

This form of touching widens the film's thematic purview to include an ethical concern over the European family that benefits from imperialist structures abroad. What ultimately makes the embrace between the women possible is the revolution imperilling the political and economic structures of the unnamed country, the structures sustaining the Vial family's hegemony. The film suggests that within a highly unequal social order, both economically and racially stratified, the privileged family is incapable of avowing their fundamental co-implication with others. Since the Vials' connection to the country is principally economic and thus exploitative, any tender contact between members of the family seems less an expression of a community of singular individuals than a sign of oneness against the excluded have-nots. Furthermore, the Vials cannot reach out to the native community without serving their financial interests, without their goodwill becoming the source of 'white material'.

Family dynamics are more muted in *Beau travail*, Denis's loose adaptation of Herman Melville's *Billy Budd*, than in the other films because it revolves around a symbolic all-male family of French legionnaires stationed in Djibouti. Denis adopts the same analeptic formal strategy in this film that she does in others. Galoup (Denis Levant) lives a solitary life in Marseille as he recalls the events leading up to his discharge from the army. The combination of flashback and Galoup's voiceover intensifies the highly subjective and interiorised drama of the film, which, as Denis has explained, involves the series of emotions associated with 'being a foreigner to one's own life' (Romney 2000). The conflict of the film revolves around the jealousy and resentment that Galoup feels towards a recent recruit, Gilles Sentain (Colin Grégoire), who quickly becomes the eroticised favourite of Commandant Bruno Forestier (Michel Subor).

Galoup's mounting anger is part of the social dynamics amongst the soldiers that are repeatedly given a familial cast. Sentain tells Forestier that he has no family, a revelation that gives us cause to read the soldiers as a kind of surrogate family. More tellingly, Forestier calls his subordinates 'sons', and Galoup refers to his colleagues as a 'family.' The idea of a metaphorical family of soldiers does not only encode injunctions against same-sex desire; when this idea comes from Galoup's and Forestier's mouths, it gives them cover, so to speak, allowing them to disavow this desire where they most feel it. Like she does in *Chocolat* and *White Material,* Denis uses the figure of the family in *Beau travail* to stage a clash between carnal urges and the force of propriety. This tension explains why Galoup's treatment of Sentain is a kind of reaction formation whereby impulsive attraction becomes hatred and intolerance.

Critics have read *Beau travail* as an allegory of Biblical narratives associated with the figure of the family. In a short piece, Nancy evokes the Christian Trinity – Father, Son and Holy Spirit – in arguing that Sentain is a Jesus-like figure in a secular world, a saviour who disrupts the social order of the legionnaires: '[H]e who loses a saviour belongs to an impeccable order [. . .] symbolised here by the Legion [. . .] which is made up of a body of observances closed upon itself, referring only to itself' (2004, 15–16). Ironically, although Nancy suggests that the Legion makes no room for the androcentric family of Christian belief, his description of this militaristic community calls to mind the conventional formulation of the family as a social unit demarcated from the sociality of the public sphere and bound by a series of intimate exchanges and rituals. It is this notion of the family that Wheatley has in mind when she contends that the film conjures up 'the tale of Cain and Abel': the struggle for the 'affections of the father figure' culminates with 'a fratricidal act' attempted by the embittered Galoup, displaced as he is in the eyes of Forestier by the newcomer Sentain (2014, 69).

But in locating the dramatic tension of the film in the gulf between the Legion's insularity and Sentain's salvific aura, Nancy paves the way for a reading of the film that associates its figuration of the family with ethico-political concerns. For Nancy, the Legion's refusal to countenance outsiders is reflected in the formal aspects of the film, namely, the collection of shots that seem less concerned with moving the story forward than with lingering on muscular male bodies. Like the 'impeccable order' of the Legion, this 'ostentation of the image' is an 'autonomous, exclusive order, representing for itself the immanence of its own transcendence, appropriating it in its self-image. It is none other than fascism as fascination of auto-sacrality and of auto-figuration' (2004, 16, 17). Sentain, in other words, imbues both the Legion and the cinematic frame with moral weight that neither can support, and Galoup's homoerotic jealousy is equally unsustainable because it begs to be viewed in the light of a moral structure, one that troubles the Legion's irreproachable hierarchy. His narration proffers a story of victimhood and iniquity that belies the order of the Legion, as well as the film's formal fascination with the body. With his use of such words as 'fascism' and 'sacrality', Nancy intimates that aesthetic and social orders repress their foundational connection to alterity by enforcing visions of how people ought to act and how they ought to organise themselves.

Accordingly, the homoerotic triangle that forms within the bounds of homosocial experience cannot be disentangled from the militaristic dimensions of the narrative. Nancy is no doubt correct in pointing out that Denis deploys spare dialogue and open displays of the male body to impart an impressionistic veneer to the film, but she also cuts to the impassive presence and uncomprehending gazes of the natives to underscore that the athletic European bodies that preoccupy her frames are a feast for the eyes only for a certain observer; for others, these sights are strange impositions and perhaps even exhibitions of colonial residue in post-independence Djibouti. And when the soldiers enjoy their debaucherous nights in town, their crisp uniforms stand out against the backdrop of the locals' casual attire. This collision of distinctive cultures highlights the enforced sociality amongst the symbolic family of soldiers, a family bound less by choice than by circumstance. The narrowness of their world charges Galoup's pettiness with heightened intensity. By the same token, Forestier's affections seem less the whims of a lecherous man than significant social capital.

Thomas Elsaesser, after elaborating on the political dimensions of *Beau travail* in his Nancy-inflected reading, concludes that Galoup constitutes a kind of abject figure whose dismissal from the Legion opens up space for a different vision of community, one in which people are bound by their differences rather than their adherence to rigid codes of conduct or their support for abstract ideas of national togetherness (2012, 721–3). We might add to this interpretation that Galoup views his dismissal from the Legion as an exclusion from a symbolic family. No longer embedded within this tight-knit social unit, he punctuates the film with an uninhibited, campy, queer dance in a nightclub. This prologue is a stark departure from the opening scene in which the soldiers train. Galoup seems, finally, to enjoy himself.

FAMILY IN *J'AI PAS SOMMEIL*, *35 RHUMS* AND *BASTARDS*

When Denis sets her sights on the figure of the family within France, the political thrust of her work shifts, of course, from the violence of French colonialism and imperialism to the failures of French society. This shift yields portraits of the family in which less stress is placed on symbolism than on the socioeconomic and cultural problems besetting the family. This is not to say that Denis's portraits of the family are reducible to a binary of symbolism and realism; it is simply a matter of emphasis. In her France-set films, efforts to maintain family togetherness encounter such cultural problems as widespread xenophobia and consequent feelings of unbelonging felt by minoritarian groups, as well such socioeconomic difficulties as class inequality and the predations of capital. These issues are sources of either dysfunction or tension within the family, and the aggregate result is an ambivalent picture of family as a site of tenuous security and of potential trauma no less than love and affection.

This ambivalence is nowhere more prominent than in *J'ai pas sommeil* (1994). The film begins with two white patrolmen laughing as they surveil Paris from a helicopter. This image of contemporary panopticism, evoking Michel de Certeau's distinction between the 'planned and readable city' viewed from above and the contingent and unknowable city of everyday urban existence (1988, 93), generates a sense of pervasive distrust that finds confirmation in the rest of the film as the police frequently stop people deemed 'suspicious' and radio pundits discuss the fear of strangers compounded by a recent spate of murders. Meanwhile, the film plots the trajectories and intersections of three families: Martinican brothers Théo (Alex Descas), a struggling violinist who hates life in France, and Camille (Richard Courcet), an HIV-positive drag performer in a tempestuous relationship with a white man (Vincent Dupont), who doubles as his accomplice in killing and robbing old-aged women; parents Théo and Mona (Béatrice Dalle), who fight for control of their infant son after Théo unilaterally decides that the family will remake their life in Martinique; and extended family Daiga (Yekaterina Golubeva), who drives from Lithuania to France in hopes of becoming a model, and her aunt Mina (Irina Grjebina), who introduces Daiga to a group of Lithuanians living in poverty.

In setting the portrait of two contemptible brothers against a backdrop of social and economic inequality, Denis challenges viewers to accommodate opposing moral sentiments. On the one hand, the brothers' behaviour is, in Théo's case, imperious and, in Camille's case, odious. (Camille is based on real-life serial killer Thierry Paulin.) Théo's demand that his family move to Martinique smacks of toxic masculinity. The threat of violence looms over his refusal to consider Mona's point of view, creating an atmosphere of secrecy within the family, one that leads to Mona taking their son away without telling Théo. And when the police finally detain Camille, he looks remorseless, his impassiveness suggesting indifference.

On the other hand, Denis leavens her portrayal of each brother's ugly behaviour with attention to the precariousness of minoritarian groups in Paris. The film presents a picture of France in which individuals who deviate from social norms – immigrants, people of colour and queer people – face stigma. Part of Nancy's project in *Being Singular Plural* is to underscore that nationalistic forms of unity rest on exclusivity and thereby abandon the fundamental predicament of 'being-with', one in which 'a "we" [. . .] is the condition for the possibility of each "I"' in all its singularity (2000, 65). In a social world predicated on an aggressive disavowal of that condition, Théo feels an understandable sense of unbelonging. Even though he displays a stubborn refusal to build a life for himself in France, the inauspicious social circumstances demand a measure of sympathy for him and his desire to return to Martinique. And before Camille is revealed to be a serial killer, he provides a window into the underground cross-dressing and gay-male community of Paris. In one scene, Camille performs in drag for an audience of male clubbers; their rapt gazes indicate that he is something of a star in this queer milieu. Camille's HIV diagnosis only contributes to the feeling created by this dance scene that the gay community is largely secretive and exposed to uncommon levels of insecurity.

Nikolai Lübecker contends that the film 'dedramatizes' violence: it displaces the sensationalism of its source material with 'moments where individuals co-exist without taking part in necessary conflictual relations' (2007, 31). Lübecker has in mind the enigmatic relationship between Camille and Daiga, one that culminates with the two briefly touching hands in a bar. Denis herself lends credibility to this reading (Reid 1996). She has spoken about the influence that Frantz Fanon's writings had on her early work, and the fleeting intimacy between Camille and Daiga recalls the final chapter of *Black Skin, White Masks*, where Fanon wonders whether 'a genuine communication can be born' between white and Black people (2008, 206). Prefiguring Nancy's emphasis on touching, Fanon concludes with a rhetorical question: 'Why not simply try to touch the other, feel the other, discover each other?' (206).[5]

That said, in de-dramatising violence, the film shifts its treatment of conflict into a milder key that strikes a dramatic note within the context of the family. The moment of contact between Daiga and Camille arrives at the end of a film in which romantic partners and brothers are incapable of offering each other respite from the cruel contingencies of the world. In addition to his peremptory seizure of power within his family, Théo is alienated from Camille, who makes an abortive attempt to share his HIV diagnosis. Their failure of communication leads to a moment in the metro where Théo, misidentifying the cause of his brother's sadness, gives Camille money before the two are separated by the doors of the train, a metaphor for their emotional estrangement. Thus, the film eschews spectacle and sensationalism in order to examine the sources of family dysfunction and the concomitant failure of the family to provide a space of support within a society that unevenly distributes hardship.

The opposite occurs in *35 rhums* (2008), Denis's loose remake of Yasujirō Ozu's *Late Spring* (1949). Instead of a family strained by a dearth of understanding, father, Lionel (Alex Descas), and daughter, Joséphine (Mati Diop), understand each other too well, a relationship putatively strengthened by the tragedy of Joséphine's mother dying at a young age. They happily coexist in the same apartment where their relationship flourishes under the weight of humble circumstance. Even though the site of their nightly repast is the cramped kitchen, their silence while eating does not suggest dissatisfaction but rather evinces their untroubled intimacy, which, according to Wheatley, 'has quasi-erotic undertones' (2014, 71).

By the force of contrast, Joséphine and Lionel's closeness highlights the insularity of their neighbours, who yearn for the security of a family – Noé (Grégoire Colin) and Gabrielle (Nicole Dogué) – and of Lionel's colleague, René (Julieth Mars), whose retirement amplifies his loneliness and thereby sets the stage for his death by suicide. Yet the film never establishes the distinction between the happy family and the lonely outsiders as a firm dichotomy. Joséphine, desiring romantic partnership, loves Noé, who lives in the penthouse he inherited from his late parents. But Joséphine and Noé only express their affection for each other in fits and starts owing to her co-dependent relationship with Lionel. Denis captures the awkwardness of this situation with a restaurant scene in which Joséphine and Noé slow dance in front of Lionel before she pulls away. Meanwhile, as Joséphine's trajectory takes her further away from Lionel, Gabrielle longs to fill the maternal and wifely role in the family, even though no amount of wishful thinking can create space for her among Lionel and Joséphine.

Gabrielle's and Joséphine's desires create literal and symbolic tension between entering and leaving the family that never assumes melodramatic shape, despite Denis's own assertion that the film is 'a sort of tragedy, in a family sense' (Hughes 2009). Instead, as James S. Williams puts it, the film proffers a 'warm and tender, almost mellow portrait of working-class family life' (2009, 44). Lionel shows his care for Joséphine by picking her up after work and by travelling with her to Germany to see her maternal aunt. Their scenes together are suffused with a calmness that blunts the emotionality of their moments of contention. Moreover, the film casts a positive light upon filial duty. Encountering no patriarchal rule against indulging her affection for Noé, Joséphine evinces nothing but solicitous feelings for her father. An endearing example of this daughterly respect occurs when she hides her newly purchased rice cooker upon learning that Lionel has also bought one for the apartment. Denis's decision to end the film with Lionel opening Joséphine's rice cooker after she marries Noé brings the narrative full circle while also symbolically embracing the necessity of parents stepping aside in order to allow new relationships to preoccupy their children's lives (Figure 13.3).

With most of the central characters living in the same apartment building in a Paris *banlieue*, the film has a decidedly narrow scope. But the political thrust of the film lies in this ostensible myopia. As Williams explains, although 'race is not really an issue' in *35 rhums*, 'the simple fact of portraying freely and without a pre-set agenda the quotidian reality of one of France's many immigrant communities is rare in itself for a French film' (2009, 47).[6] Drawing on Heidegger and Nancy to build on this observation, Eddy Troy examines the

Figure 13.3 Lionel unpacks Joséphine's rice cooker.

agency of non-human objects in the film, particularly their capacity to mediate social relations (2020). In René and Gabrielle, however, the film contains just as many examples of isolation as it does of connection, and it is only the heteronormative institution of marriage that saves Noé from an atomistic existence. What the film enjoins audiences to contemplate, then, is the power of the family, a rather conventional family no less, to soften the difficulties of diasporic and working-class life. 'Being is together', writes Nancy, 'and it is not a togetherness' (2000, 60) – an assertion that can be read as a caution against interpreting the end of the film as happy. Familial *togetherness* has widened through marriage, to be sure, but the conclusion is bittersweet. For Denis has limned another picture of France in which family unity seems to provide the only succour against an abiding sense of existential meaninglessness.

Although *35 rhums* contains a scene in which Joséphine and her classmates discuss the IMF's use of debt to control third-world countries, it is in *Bastards* that Denis dramatises the effects of debt on the family. The principal character is Marco (Vincent Lindon), a divorced father of two whose relationship with his ex-wife has devolved into arguments about child support. A naval captain, Marco abandons his post after his brother-in-law, Jacques (Laurent Grévill), dies by suicide and his niece, Justine (Lola Créton), becomes the victim of a brutal sexual assault. His sister, Sandra (Julie Bataille), blames Edouard Laporte (Michel Subor), a wealthy financier, for her husband's death and her daughter's assault. Marco soon begins an affair with Laporte's wife, Raphaëlle (Chiara Mastroianni), and then learns that Laporte is the creditor keeping his family's shoe factory solvent, the business run by his sister and deceased brother-in-law. He discovers, finally, that not only did Sandra and Jacques offer their niece to Laporte as a form of debt repayment but Jacques himself participated in her rape. Two questions remain: whether Jacques engaged wilfully in incest or against his will to satisfy Laporte's deviant sexual appetite, as well as whether Justine harboured a quasi-Oedipal desire for her father. Denis makes a customary move by leaving the answers ambiguous.

Like *J'ai pas sommeil*, *Bastards* stages the intersections of three families; but unlike that film's effort to de-dramatise violence, it labours to hyper-dramatise the violence of debt within a contemporary capitalist dispensation. Even though achieving security by borrowing (e.g. obtaining mortgages, tuition loans, credit card spending) has become an increasingly common paradox for individuals, indebtedness, Maurizio Lazzarato explains, 'is an economic relation which, in order to exist, implies the molding and control of subjectivity' (2012, 33). To accept credit is not only to become indebted but to enter a constitutively unfree relationship and thereby account for one's future self along the lines laid out by the creditor.[7] Distilled to its purest form, this economic relationship is between the empowered and the disempowered. Denis's film assumes allegorical shape in transforming this relationship into a narrative that buffets viewers with its literal treatment of sexual depravity and taboo.

Interpretive work is thus misguided in attempting to dispel the ambiguities of desire in *Bastards*. When critical pressure is applied to the function of debt, attention shifts from what the characters do or do not want to how inequities shape their pursuit of self-fulfilment. The motif of technologically mediated images – press photos of Laporte as well as the incriminating photos of Jacques – conveys this point along different lines; indeed, the film concludes with a close-up of a camera before cutting to grainy pornographic footage of Jacques and Justine together in bed, as if Denis were forcing viewers to contemplate the power the filmmaker holds over them.

Similarly, because credit channels one's future in a more or less prescribed path, it promises and compromises agency at once. Indeed, when Justine walks listlessly through the streets of Paris after her sexual assault, she wears nothing but high heels, the product churned out by her family's factory and thus a symbol of Laporte's power over them. The relationship between creditor and debtor is anathema to Nancy's metaphor of the 'stage' of co-presence where no one has control over another (2000, 65). Such horizontal relationality is felt through its absence from Denis's film; instead, debt and its consequences mediate human contact, which as a result bears no resemblance to the touching at the heart of Nancy's philosophy.

Accordingly, in *Bastards*, debt is the principal source of family dysfunction. Unlike Lionel and Joséphine's relationship in *35 rhums*, economic precariousness underpins the stilted and awkward parent–child relationships in this film, fostering, in Sandra's family, the complete breakdown of intimacy.

As Christina Álvarez López puts it, 'the failure of [Sandra and Justine's] affective relationship is accentuated by the fact that the two actors share not one single scene in the whole film' (2019). Marco's feeling of duty to Sandra suggests the power of sibling bonds, but his commitment, first to avenge and second to uncover the truth about Justine's sexual assault, leads him to neglect his own daughters. His febrile pursuit of evidence finds him desperately cashing out his life insurance policy, an improvident decision compounded by his ultimate death. Ironically, he tells Sandra that he is glad he divorced, because the unsavoury business with Laporte will not taint his daughters' lives. Yet there is every indication that financial insecurity awaits his ex-wife and daughters.

Although no family reaches the end of the film unscathed, the only one with an opportunity for a semblance of happiness is that of Laporte, Raphaëlle and their son. When Laporte learns that Raphaëlle has had an affair with Marco, he takes their son away. Yet in the penultimate scene, Raphaëlle shoots and kills Marco when he fights Laporte. Perhaps she wants nothing more than to save Laporte, but their loveless marriage and his power to keep her apart from her son suggest that she views killing Marco as a form of penance: her best chance to remain a fixture in her son's life. In contrast to the other parent–child relationships in *Bastards*, Raphaëlle generates the impression that one's child is worth fighting for. Like the other characters, however, she remains subject to the whims of her wealthy husband, the creditor.

CONCLUSION

If such critics as Robin Wood (1998) and Stanley Cavell (1981) have taught us anything, it is that intimacy between people can function as a means by which filmmakers signal the need for alternative, radical modes of existence. To that end, Denis does not allow her cinematic families to naturalise the behavioural norms associated with this institution: patriarchal dominance, female submissiveness and sexual normativity. She places too much emphasis on inequality to make her families seem like building blocks of the liberal-capitalist order. Rather, Denis gives the antiracist, anticolonial and anti-capitalist dimensions of her films a greater sense of urgency by grounding them in the figure of the dysfunctional or oppressive family. Even in *35 rhums*, the images of precarity that run through the film suggest that the family is a tenuous safety net keeping marginalised people from insufferable existences.

Although Denis has spoken lovingly about her parents, her depictions of family life in her films throw into relief her comments about her reluctance to start a family of her own:

> Maybe from early on I realized that the idea of family – living with a man to have kids with him – wasn't out of the question in my head, and to have a man I loved wasn't out of the question, but my preference was toward a sort of nomadism. [. . .] And to create a family requires that you come home and be a somewhat stable person. I did not know how to do this. I am either passionate or depressed. For me to accept to have kids I would have had to meet someone so balanced that they were capable of being balanced for two, however I could not take on that responsibility. (Nancy 2014, 56)

Her verbiage is telling. For 'nomadism' is arguably what the families at the heart of her Africa-set films deny in order to enforce their visions of order and propriety. The absence of 'balance' and 'stability', moreover, drives much of the family drama in her France-set films. She seems to recognise intuitively that a conventional family would threaten what she appears to value most in Nancy's philosophy – namely, the idea of community bound by difference, of touching as an idiom for the strangeness that does not threaten so much as constitute the familiar.

Accordingly we might locate a sense of familial *being-with* in Denis's working life. Her fascination with the family seems to have just as much to do with her choice of collaborators as with her aesthetic decisions. Viewing multiple Denis films generates the impression that she has formed family-like bonds with her collaborators. The list of people who have worked on more than one Denis film includes members of the Tindersticks; screenwriter Jean-Pol Fargeau; cinematographer Agnès Godard; editor Nelly Quettier; and actors Isaach de Bankolé, Alex Descas, Michel Subor, Juliette Binoche, Vincent Lindon, Nicolas Duvauchelle, Yekaterina Golubeva, Béatrice Dalle, Mati Diop and Grégoire Colin.

As Quettier opines in an interview, 'I think she [Denis] would be incapable of filming someone she didn't love' (Johnson 2014b, 14). And as Descas says:

> this friendship we [Denis and Descas] share is very strong – when you love people it's not just friendship. When you really love someone, you might call it a friendship because you don't live together or you don't sleep together, but in some ways Claire and I have brought many things into being together. (Johnson 2014a, 33)

Although they do not use the word 'family' – and perhaps, in this case, to name is to contaminate – both Quettier and Descas intimate that Denis's sets tend to be family affairs.

NOTES

1. For a better understanding of their ideological and philosophical overlap, see Denis's candid interview with Nancy (Nancy 2014).
2. Perhaps unsurprisingly, Alex Descas, one of Denis's frequent collaborators, draws on the grammar of contact in describing his approach to acting: 'The only thing that exists is sensation and touch, even if you aren't really touching a person. People touch you and you touch them in your own way, that's how it works' (Johnson 2014a, 30).
3. It is difficult to account for all the critical work making the connection between Denis and Nancy; an incomplete list includes Beugnet 2008; Baross 2015; Elsaesser 2012; Hole 2016; Troy 2020.
4. As Denis explains, one element apart from the figure of the family that links her films is the experience of 'being a foreigner': 'it's common for people who are born abroad [that] they don't know so well where they belong' (Romney 2000).
5. Much of Fanon's writing, in *Black Skin, White Masks*, rests on the argument that Black people are de-individualised and objectified in white-supremacist society, and in an interview, Denis echoes Fanon's effort to overturn this situation: 'In my films, black people are never objects. They are subjects who actively choose what they want' (Reid 1996).
6. As Denis herself explains when asked about her decision to make the film about a Black family, 'I wanted it to not be a concept but to realize they were *French*, that they were *there*. There was nothing else to see. In France, whenever you see dark-skinned people, it's always violent. [. . .] I think the real thing is that there is a community that is French and also has black skin, that is integrated but also rejected' (Hughes 2009).
7. As Miranda Joseph avers, the extension of credit-fueled growth from industry to quotidian life belongs to a broader '*dialectics* of abstraction and particularization through which capitalism operates' (2014, 15). That is, debt is not merely a feature of some abstract system of finance but also actively produces certain kinds of subjects, helping to inscribe divisions within the social body. This system interpellates certain groups of people as exploitable and/or creditworthy.

CITATIONS

Baross, Zsuzsa. 2015. *Encounters: Gérard Titus-Carmel, Jean-Luc Nancy, Claire Denis*. Sussex: Sussex Academic Press.
Beugnet, Martine. 2008. 'The Practice of Strangeness: *L'intrus* – Claire Denis (2004) and Jean-Lucy Nancy' (2000). *Film-Philosophy* 12, 1: 31–48.
Carter, Mia. 2006. 'Acknowledged Absences: Claire Denis's Cinema of Longing.' *Studies in European Cinema* 3, 1: 67–81.
Cavell, Stanley. 1981. *Pursuits of Happiness: The Hollywood Comedy of Remarriage*. Cambridge: Harvard University Press.
De Certeau, Michel. 1988. *The Practice of Everyday Life*. Translated by Steven Rendall. Berkeley: University of California Press.
Denis, Claire, dir. 1988. *Chocolat*. Orion Classics.
Denis, Claire, dir. 1994. *J'ai pas sommeil*. Wellspring.
Denis, Claire, dir. 1999. *Beau travail*. Pyramide Distribution.
Denis, Claire, dir. 2004. *L'intrus*. Mongrel Media.

Denis, Claire, dir. 2008. *35 rhums*. Mongrel Media.
Denis, Claire, dir. 2009. *White Material*. Wild Bunch.
Denis, Claire, dir. 2013. *Bastards*. Wild Bunch.
Denis, Claire, dir. 2018. *High Life*. A24.
Elsaesser, Thomas. 2012. 'European Cinema and the Postheroic Narrative: Jean-Luc Nancy, Claire Denis, and *Beau travail*.' *New Literary History* 43, 4: 703–25.
Fanon, Frantz. 2008. *Black Skin, White Masks*. Translated by Richard Philcox. New York: Grove Press.
Hole, Kristin Lené. 2016. *Towards a Feminist Cinematic Ethics: Claire Denis, Emmanuel Levinas and Jean-Luc Nancy*. Edinburgh: Edinburgh University Press.
Hughes, Darren. 2009. 'Dancing Reveals So Much: An Interview with Claire Denis.' *Senses of Cinema*, April 2009. https://www.sensesofcinema.com/2009/conversations-on-film/claire-denis-interview/.
Johnson, Kirsten. 2014a. 'Interview with Alex Descas.' In *The Films of Claire Denis: Intimacy on the Border*, edited by Marjorie Vecchio, 25–39. London: I. B. Tauris.
Johnson, Kirsten. 2014b. 'Interview with Nelly Quettier.' In *The Films of Claire Denis: Intimacy on the Border*, edited by Marjorie Vecchio, 13–24. London: I. B. Tauris.
Joseph, Miranda. 2014. *Debt to Society: Accounting for Life under Capitalism*. Minneapolis: Minnesota University Press.
Lazzarato, Maurizio. 2012. *The Making of Indebted Man*. Translated by Joshua David Jordan. Los Angeles: Semiotext(e).
López, Christina Álvarez. 2019. 'Put Your Love in Me: Close-Up on Claire Denis's "Bastards".' *Mubi*, 15 April. https://mubi.com/notebook/posts/put-your-love-in-me-close-up-on-claire-denis-s-bastards.
Lübecker, Nikolai. 2007. 'The Dedramatization of Violence in Claire Denis's *I Can't Sleep*.' *Paragraph* 30, 2: 17–33.
Mayne, Judith. 2005. *Claire Denis*. Urbana: University of Illinois Press.
Muller, Adam. 2006. 'Notes Toward a Theory of Nostalgia: Childhood and the Evocation of the Past in Two European "Heritage" Films.' *New Literary History* 37, 4: 739–60.
Nancy, Jean-Luc. 2000. *Being Singular Plural*. Translated by Robert D. Richardson and Anne E. O'Byrne. Stanford: Stanford University Press.
Nancy, Jean-Luc. 2002. 'L'intrus.' Translated by Susan Hanson. *CR: The New Centennial Review* 2, 3: 1–14.
Nancy, Jean-Luc. 2004. 'A-religion.' *Journal of European Studies* 34, 1–2: 14–8.
Nancy, Jean-Luc. 2014. 'Interview with Claire Denis.' Translated by Nathalie Le Galloudec. In *The Films of Claire Denis: Intimacy on the Border*, edited by Marjorie Vecchio, 41–59. London: I. B. Tauris.
O'Byrne, Anne E. 2002. 'The Politics of Intrusion.' *CR: The New Centennial Review* 2, 3: 169–87.
Reid, Mark A. 1996. 'Claire Denis Interview: Colonial Observations.' *Jump Cut: A review of Contemporary Media*. https://www.ejumpcut.org/archive/onlinessays/JC40folder/ClaireDenisInt.html.
Romney, Jonathan. 2000. 'Claire Denis Interviewed by Jonathan Romney.' *The Guardian*, 28 June 2000. https://www.theguardian.com/film/interview/interviewpages/0,6737,338784,00.html.
Troy, Eddy. 2020. 'Intersubjectivity and the Cinematic Thing: Diasporic Being-with in Claire Denis's *35 rhums*.' *Studies in European Cinema*. DOI: 10.1080/17411548.2020.1848095.

Wheatley, Catherine. 2014. 'La Famille Denis.' In *The Films of Claire Denis: Intimacy on the Border*, edited by Marjorie Vecchio, 63–77. London: I. B. Tauris.
Williams, James S. 2009. 'Romancing the Father in Claire Denis's *35 Shots of Rum*.' *Film Quarterly* 63, 2: 44–50.
Wood, Robin. 1998. *Sexual Politics and Narrative Film: Hollywood and Beyond*. New York: Columbia University Press.

Index

Akerman, Chantal, 6
Angot, Christine, 10, 148, 152–8, 160, 163, 196
Avec amour et acharnement, 10, 147, 148, 153, 154, 158, 163

Barthes, Roland, 8, 55, 156, 157
Bankolé, Isaach de, 121, 248
Bernheim, Emanuèle, 10, 55, 148–50, 155, 163
Beugnet, Martine, 1, 9, 68, 88–90, 124, 140, 172, 182, 207, 219–20, 228
beau soleil intérieur, Un, 50, 55, 109, 123, 132, 135–6, 144, 147–8, 153–63
Beau travail, 3, 5, 7, 8, 21, 22, 24, 29, 34, 37, 39, 43–5, 48, 50, 51, 54, 55, 59, 66, 73, 77, 80, 84, 93, 110, 123, 140, 141, 144, 147, 166–9, 175, 179, 183, 218, 239–41
   Galoup, 22–5, 34, 39–43, 48, 50–2, 54, 59–63, 67–75, 79–80, 93–5, 141, 166, 168, 179, 219, 239–41
   Forrestier, Bruno, 5, 59, 67–8, 153, 239
   Sentain, Gilles, 24, 28–9, 34, 39–42, 51–2, 59–62, 67, 70, 72, 93, 141, 167, 218, 239
Binoche, Juliet, 3, 6, 77, 87, 121, 136, 148, 168, 183, 193–5, 197, 203, 248

biography, 2, 29, 36, 65, 74, 140, 171, 234, 248
blood, 4, 71, 89, 106–7, 115–16, 131, 134, 137, 179, 207, 210, 232

cannibal(ism), 101, 107, 109, 110, 115, 134
carceral, 77, 144
Carroll, Noël, 134
Chocolat, 1, 3, 7, 20–2, 25, 27, 32, 34, 36, 110, 121–3, 126, 128, 131, 138, 140, 144, 147, 183, 218, 234, 237, 240
   France (character), 22, 26, 129–30, 138, 140, 234–8
   Protée, 26, 129–30, 138, 235–7
cinematography, 10, 29, 36, 54, 65, 89, 121, 150, 155, 159, 169, 193, 221
Colin, Grégoire, 3, 20, 73, 93, 121, 162, 169, 182, 203
colonialism, 20, 53, 74, 110, 111, 121, 123, 129, 138, 235, 237, 241

Dalle, Béatrice, 3, 121, 134, 194, 248
dance(ing/ers), 22, 28, 39, 42, 54, 60–3, 67, 77, 93, 166–79, 205, 222, 243
Descas, Alex, 3, 37, 121, 182, 203, 212, 213, 248
Djibouti, 21, 39–42, 50, 60, 62, 65–7, 75, 78, 81, 93, 141, 174, 179, 239

INDEX

Fanon, Frantz, 133, 243
Fargeau, Jean-Pol, 3, 10, 121, 148, 154, 169, 202, 248

Gallo, Vincent, 121
Galt, Rosalind, 6, 33, 71, 188, 208–11
Godard, Agnès, 9, 10, 20, 29, 121, 154, 168–70, 172, 175–7, 202, 221, 248
Godard, Jean-Luc, 5, 36, 223

Heidegger, Martin, 8, 51–4, 56, 61–2, 233, 244
High Life, 5, 8, 21, 29, 35, 66, 76, 78, 80, 83, 84, 86, 103–17, 121, 126, 135, 137, 168, 190, 191–3, 197–8, 231
  Boyse, 77, 80, 83, 101, 107, 113–14, 191
  Dibs, Dr, 6, 77, 80, 86–8, 101, 105–8, 113–15, 137–8, 191, 231
  Monte, 12, 29, 76–80, 86, 101, 104, 107, 113–16, 121, 137–9, 191–2, 231
  Willow, 77–80, 86, 101, 114, 116, 121, 137, 191, 231
Huppert, Isabelle, 3, 11, 183–6

Jarmusch, Jim, 1, 5, 36, 190

Lavant, Denis, 166
Lindon, Vincent, 11, 57, 160, 162, 183, 186, 188–9, 248
L'Intrus, 4, 8, 32, 70, 75, 78, 84, 89, 109, 141, 147, 171–73, 175, 179, 188
Louvart, Hélène, 29, 168, 170

Marx, Karl, 35, 39, 43
Mayne, Judith, 2–6, 20, 32, 66, 74, 78, 148, 152, 175, 232
Melville, Herman, 55, 63, 66, 141, 239
Melville, Jean-Pierre, 5
milk, 83, 106–8
Monnier, Mathilde, 3, 29, 167–9, 178

Nancy, Jean-Luc, 72, 74, 90, 169–71, 173, 207, 217, 224, 228–9, 231–2, 238, 240–1, 244–5, 248
Nénette et Boni, 20–2, 24–5, 27, 29, 37, 73, 84, 95, 97, 124, 131, 140, 144, 204, 207–9, 212, 219–20, 222, 228, 232, 234
New Wave (*Nouvelle Vague*), 36, 85

Ozu, Yasujirō, 6, 176, 200–13

Paris, 1, 21, 33, 43, 50, 54, 55, 57, 65, 102, 136, 140, 174–6, 206, 208, 216, 202, 224, 242–6
Piaget, Jean, 122, 124–5, 127, 143
postcolonial, 9, 14, 77, 80, 111, 114, 121–123, 138, 147, 184, 201, 234
post-human, 85

Ramsay, Lynne, 34–48
rape, 102, 108, 136, 138, 191, 204
realism, 32, 36, 38, 43, 46, 105, 197, 241

35 rhums, 3, 21, 28, 32–48, 56, 66, 74, 123, 147, 163, 168, 174, 200, 203–5, 212, 232, 243, 245–7
Joséphine (character), 34, 43, 142, 204–6, 243–5
Lionel (character), 21, 28, 34, 43–5, 47, 142, 204–7, 243–6

Salauds, Les, 1, 4, 11, 15, 21, 29, 32, 123, 135, 144, 169, 174–6, 179, 186–9, 197, 204, 206, 212
scar(ing), 92, 95, 107, 142, 172
semen, 106, 115, 191
Subor, Michel, 5, 27, 29, 169, 188, 203, 248

Tindersticks, 87, 120, 174, 202, 248
Trouble Every Day, 4, 6, 15, 21, 24, 100–15, 123, 130–6, 143, 148, 150, 155, 174, 212, 218

Vecchio, Marjorie, 2, 207, 212
Vendredi soir, 50–63, 142, 147–63, 174, 186, 216–29
  Laure, 50–9, 149–53, 216, 218–19, 221–3, 224–8
  Jean, 50–1, 52, 56–9, 61, 149, 150–1, 152, 154, 216, 219, 221, 224, 225–8, 229

Wenders, Wim, 1, 5, 36, 190, 200
White Material, 1, 21, 27, 34, 66, 74, 110, 131, 142, 143, 163, 183–5, 205, 234, 237–40
Vial, Maria, 6, 8, 27, 61, 74–6, 79, 183–6, 197, 237, 238–40
  André, 74, 237–8